Phonetics and Speech Science

Phonetics is a fundamental building block not just in linguistics but also in fields such as communication disorders. However, introductions to phonetics can often assume a background in linguistics, whilst at the same time overlooking the clinical and scientific aspects of the field. This textbook fills this gap by providing a comprehensive yet accessible overview of phonetics that delves into the fundamental science underlying the production of speech. Written with beginners in mind, it focuses on the anatomy and physiology of speech, while at the same time explaining the very basics of phonetics, such as the phonemes of English, the International Phonetic Alphabet, and phonetic transcription systems. It presents the sounds of speech as elements of linguistic structure and as the result of complex biological mechanics. It explains complicated terminology in a clear, easy-to-understand way, and provides examples from a range of languages, from disorders of speech, and from language learning.

Ian R. A. MacKay is retired Professor of linguistics at the University of Ottawa. He has taught phonetics and speech science for 45 years to students of linguistics, speech–language pathology, and audiology.

D1710661

Phonetics and Speech Science

Ian R. A. MacKay

University of Ottawa

Shaftesbury Road, Cambridge CB2 8EA, United Kingdom

One Liberty Plaza, 20th Floor, New York, NY 10006, USA

477 Williamstown Road, Port Melbourne, VIC 3207, Australia

314–321, 3rd Floor, Plot 3, Splendor Forum, Jasola District Centre,
New Delhi – 110025, India

103 Penang Road, #05–06/07, Visioncrest Commercial, Singapore 238467

Cambridge University Press is part of Cambridge University Press & Assessment, a department of the University of Cambridge.

We share the University's mission to contribute to society through the pursuit of education, learning and research at the highest international levels of excellence.

www.cambridge.org
Information on this title: www.cambridge.org/highereducation/isbn/9781108427869
DOI: 10.1017/9781108604642

First published 2023

Printed in the United Kingdom by TJ Books Limited, Padstow, Cornwall 2023

A catalogue record for this publication is available from the British Library.

A Cataloging-in-Publication data record for this book is available from the Library of Congress.

ISBN 978-1-108-42786-9 Hardback
ISBN 978-1-108-45203-8 Paperback

Additional resources for this publication at www.cambridge.org/MacKay

With few exceptions, illustrations were created by Pascale Cherry.

For JoDo, with thanks for everything

Brief Contents

Contents

Figures

Tables

Acknowledgments

Any author of a textbook such as this must recognize the many people who have assisted in its writing and production. I wish, in particular, to thank Senior Commissioning Editor Helen Barton of Cambridge University Press for her support in accepting and assisting the creation of the book. Her ongoing patience and backing of the project have been instrumental in its writing. I likewise wish to thank Editorial Assistant, Isabel Collins, for assistance along the way.

Family is unavoidably affected when one writes a book; I owe a great deal for the unreserved support and patience I have been accorded.

A number of individuals have helped in myriad ways. Natalia Fullana, Ph.D., of the University of Barcelona (Universitat de Barcelona) read early chapters and made many helpful suggestions. Tom Goldman, Ph.D., provided helpful feedback on portions of the final chapter related to hearing.

It would be impossible to fully express the depth of my gratitude to the illustrator, Pascale Cherry, for her wonderful drawings. Pascale showed great dedication to the project, and she shows such talent for creating clear drawings, whether anatomical or graphical, that are informative and easily interpretable.

Nicola Chapman headed the production team at Cambridge University Press, and I am most grateful to her for performing this complex task with great professionalism and flexibility. Leigh Muller was copy-editor, and I am most grateful to her for her excellent suggestions for improvements, and for catching mistakes.

I would like to thank a number of anonymous individuals. One group of three reviewed the prospectus and read sample chapters. I am grateful for their encouragement. Later, the nearly completed manuscript was read in full by two individuals who submitted detailed commentary. I wish to thank them for their positive comments, as well as for their many helpful suggestions and criticisms, all of which were carefully considered, and most of which were incorporated.

Of course, any academic owes so much to the great number of scholars who built the knowledge base of the discipline. I want to thank them as well as my own professors and colleagues.

A university teacher gains from the wisdom – and struggles – of one's students. Teaching phonetics for many years has influenced how many of the subjects within the book are presented, based on what made the best sense to my students. Several classes of mine used early versions of some of these chapters as their assigned reading, and their feedback was invaluable in improving those chapters.

1 Phonetics and Language

1.1 Phonetics

What happens when we talk? How do we make the sounds of spoken language? What does the human talker do to make those sounds? What physical laws link the actions of the talker to the specific noises that come out of our mouth and nose?

Of course, making sounds is not the only thing that happens when we talk. There is the process of ideation, thinking of what we want to say. There is the process of converting what we want to say into the units of language (words, sentences, and so on). There is the process of how we select the sounds we intend to say, based on these linguistic units. In this book, we will concentrate on the aspects mentioned in the first paragraph above, the domain of study called *phonetics.*

1.1.1 Phonetics and language

The production of the sounds of speech does not exist in a vacuum. It is a phenomenon that is part of the overall structure of *language* (linguistic structure). The "design" of human language influences how phonetic systems can be structured, as do the physical shape of our vocal tract, its musculature, and the nature of our neurological system.

As we will see in Section 1.3, much of the vocabulary in this field of study consists of ordinary words, but with specialized senses attached to them. Let's examine the word *language.*

A familiar way this word is used designates verbal communication systems. English is a language, Spanish is a language, Russian is a language. These three are languages, among 7,000 or so others. We've emphasized the -s on the end of the word *languages* to draw attention to the fact that, in this sense, the word *language* has a plural form; languages (in this sense) can be counted.

But there is a second important sense of the word *language*, one that we used in the first paragraph of this section. In that (second) sense, *language is what is common to all of the languages (first sense) in the world. It is what is common to the cognitive functioning of all individuals on earth who can speak a language (first sense). Language*, in this sense, is a somewhat abstract concept; it is the essence of what is necessary for languages (first sense) to exist at all, and to exist in the minds of human beings. When used in this sense, the word *language* has no plural.

One of the reasons why this might seem confusing is because in English we use the same word for both concepts. To summarize:

	The term ...	... refers to
Sense 1	language, languages	Individually, English, Spanish, Quechua, Inuktitut, Russian, Swedish and some 7,000 other individual systems
Sense 2	language (in the abstract, no plural form)	The abstract concept of what is common to all languages and what is in the mind of all humans who speak a language (sense 1), no matter which language that might be

Individual languages differ in the complexity and nature of their phonetic systems. In some ways, among the languages of the world, English is quite ordinary phonetically, but in some ways its characteristics are typical of only a small number of the world's languages. Therefore, in learning about the phonetics of English, some of what you learn is of very general applicability, but other aspects are typical of English and a handful of other languages. In Section 1.4.1 we will discuss language further.

1.2   Use of typography, symbols, and punctuation

Since phonetics is an aspect of language, a book about phonetics brings up the problem of *metalanguage*: language used to talk about language. In such a circumstance, it is easy to become confused as to which elements of the writing are simply the *medium of communication* with the reader, and which elements in the writing are language being used as the *topic* that is being discussed. Ambiguities can result, so we use a number of typographical conventions to help make the discussion clear. The symbols and typographical elements below are used in their usual way, but also have special uses to deal with the potential confusion.

The symbols introduced in the following subsections are summarized in Table 1.1.

1.2.1   Angle brackets < >

Angle brackets enclose the normal spelling of a word or individual letters or groups of letters, where the focus is on the letters of the ordinary *latin alphabet* (see Sidebar 1.1). Example:

The letter <u> in the word *use* represents a sound that is not strictly a vowel.

1.2.2   Single quotation marks ' '

Single quotation marks enclose a meaning (not the spelling of the word, not its sound, but its meaning).

> The word *wind* meaning 'twist around' contains a nasalized diphthong.

1.2.3   Double quotation marks " "

Double quotation marks enclose the way a word is said, its pronunciation, but expressed in normal spelling, not in the *International Phonetic Alphabet (IPA)*. Double quotation marks may enclose a word written in its normal spelling, or the sound of a word may be written in a way consistent with English spelling.

SIDEBAR 1.1 Latin alphabet

The *latin alphabet* (also called the *roman alphabet*) is the ordinary alphabet that we use to write English, and which is used to write most European languages and many others.

So, when we write *latin alphabet*, this refers to ordinary spelling in the ordinary alphabet used for English, *not* to the phonetic alphabet.

This book favors the term *latin alphabet* rather than *roman alphabet* for reasons explained in Chapter 2.

> The word *one* is pronounced "wun." The word *lead* can be pronounced like the word "led."

1.2.4   Italics

Italics are used in the conventional way found in material written on other topics. They emphasize or identify a word as a word, as well as drawing attention to a word or writing foreign words.

> The word *valet* is pronounced with a final /t/ in British English.

1.2.5   Bold italics

Bold italics are used when introducing new terminology. They may also be repeated when reusing a technical term from a previous chapter or any time the word has not been used for many pages, as a reminder that it is a matter of technical vocabulary. Note that technical vocabulary is associated with a precise and specific meaning, even if the word in question is also an ordinary word with a more general sense.

> The term *voice* is used to designate the sound made by the vibrating vocal folds.

NOTE: If a new technical term is used in a chapter and it shows only in italics, not bold italics, that means that it is not important to commit that term to memory at this point in the book.

1.2.6   Slash marks or virgules / /

Slash marks (traditionally called **virgules**) enclose a less detailed or broader phonetic transcription in the *International Phonetic Alphabet* (IPA). This may also be called a *phonemic transcription.*

/ækt/

1.2.7   Square brackets [ ]

Square brackets enclose detailed or *narrow phonetic transcription* in the IPA.

[æk̃t]

1.2.8   Summary of special uses of symbols and typography

Table 1.1 Use of special marks in the text

Feature	Example	Uses
Angle brackets	<use>	Spelling of a letter as a letter of the alphabet, not a phonetic symbol
Single quotes	' '	Meaning
Double quotes	" "	The pronunciation of the word, but written in normal orthography
Italics	*pitch*	Word as a word, not as a pronunciation or a meaning. Also, the conventional usage of emphasis and foreign words.
Bold italics	*Consonant*	Introduction or reintroduction of a technical term
Slash marks or virgules	/ækt/	To enclose broad phonetic, or phonemic, transcription in the IPA
Square brackets	[æk̃t]	To enclose fine phonetic transcription in the IPA

All of these symbols are also used in the conventional way.

1.3   Notes on terminology

1.3.1   Talkers and hearers

In a course of phonetics, both the professor and the textbook often need to refer to a person who is talking, and to refer to a person who is hearing what another person is saying. In this field, we use special terms for these people in order to maintain neutrality and not to make implications that would be misleading.

1.3.1.1   Talker
It is more usual to call a person who is talking a *speaker*, but we normally avoid that word in technical writing because it has a range of other meanings. A *speaker* can be a person giving a formal talk or address to an audience; even if there is no formal audience, the *speaker* in a group is the person holding the floor; and *speaker* can refer to an electronic device. In this field, we often wish to refer to the person doing the talking, but in none of these senses; we call that person a **talker**. There is one exception to this usage, as follows.

1.3.1.2   Hearer
In everyday language, we often refer to the *listener* if a different person is doing the talking. However, the word *listener* implies a purpose, a deliberate action. But oftentimes we hear speech without trying to; sometimes we hear one thing when in fact we are listening (or trying to listen) to something different.

   Therefore, in technical terminology, we refer to the person hearing speech (whatever the reason) as the **hearer.**

1.3.1.3   Speaker
We usually say that someone *speaks English* or *speaks Swedish*, in the sense that they are *capable* of doing so. When we say that person is *talking English* or *talking Swedish*, we typically are referring to *what they are doing*, not to their *abilities*. And we always say that a person is *an English-speaker* or *a German-speaker*, never *an English talker* or *a German talker*. Because of how odd it would sound to use *talk* or *talker* in this context, we will normally write **speak** and **speaker** when associated with the idea of *ability* in a particular language.

1.3.2   Terminology – general principles
Each field of human endeavor comes with its own specialized vocabulary. While jargon can be criticized, there is very good reason, in a scientific discipline, to have a technical vocabulary to identify things and concepts of high relevance and importance in the field. The reason is to keep these different things distinct, reducing the possibility of confusion among them, and ensuring that a term brings to mind a single, specific concept, and not an imprecise or fuzzy one.

   In good scientific terminology, technical terms refer to a single concept. It is important to learn the association between the term and the specific concept, and to keep the definition in our mind as precise as we can.

   Something that makes the technical terminology in phonetics more challenging than in some other fields is the fact that many of the technical terms are also ordinary words that have ordinary, everyday meanings. Words like *consonant, vowel, pitch, tone,* and *voice* all have very specific technical meanings that are – at least to some degree – in conflict with the everyday meanings of these words. So when words whose meaning you think you know are introduced as technical terms, it is important to *unlearn* the usual meaning and to reserve only the technical meaning for them when dealing with the subject matter of the book.

If a technical term has multiple meanings, it has, in effect, no meaning at all. If, for example, the word *accent* is used in a technical context, its meaning is highly ambiguous. Is it a matter of a foreign accent? A regional accent? A mark over a letter in spelling? *Accent* in the sense of stress or accentuation? Focus? In the face of such ambiguity, the term has not communicated anything precise, but rather may have communicated the wrong meaning – and, worse, each person in the conversation may think they know what is meant, but have different meanings in mind. In everyday conversation, we cope reasonably well with ambiguity, and the level of misunderstanding is usually kept manageable, largely due to conversations focusing on topics that are known to all participants. However, if in this book the term *consonant* is used, and the reader thinks the author means one of a group of letters of the latin alphabet, but the writer means a particular type of speech sound, then the message is misunderstood. The distinction is a very important one for the understanding of even the most basic notion of phonetics. For instance, the first sound of the word *use* can be classed phonetically as a consonant despite the fact that, in writing, the first letter is <u>.

If a chemistry professor uses the term *paradichlorobenzene* or a physics professor refers to *strontium-90*, students will realize immediately that they are encountering terms with special meanings related to those fields. They won't think of the everyday meaning of those words, because those words do not have any everyday meaning. But in language studies, including phonetics, when the professor or textbook uses the term *consonant* or *voice* or *stress*, students may not realize that these are technical terms with very specific meanings different from the everyday meanings of those words, and this may lead to misunderstanding fundamental issues in the field.

The upshot of this is that the vocabulary is important. Develop the habit of paying attention to words that are used as technical vocabulary; don't rely on thinking you know what the word means, but learn the specific technical meaning and bring that to mind as you read and listen to lectures and discussions.

Vocabulary lists are provided for most chapters, and these can be used as a very effective means of review and self-testing. The technical terms refer to concepts of importance. Testing yourself by writing explanations of each of the terms in a list of vocabulary is an excellent means to ensure that you're aware of the concepts of the topic.

1.4   Human language

The study of phonetics involves an examination of the sound system of language. We will turn our attention now to a few aspects of language so as to place this study in context.

1.4.1   Natural human language (NHL[1])

Language is an example of a word that is a technical term in this field but whose meaning differs from the way it is used in everyday conversation. In this section, we will clarify what is meant by the word, and, by extension, what defines the domain of phonetics as studied here. The material here builds on Section 1.1.1.

When language specialists use the word *language*, they are referring to **natural human language**. By contrast, in everyday use, *language* also refers to other things, such as computer languages or invented (constructed) languages such as Klingon. *Natural human language* refers to language that has evolved naturally and is spoken by a group of people we call a **speech community**. The language is the native language of at least a good portion of the speech community. One characteristic of such a language is change through time; despite the efforts of some grammarians, natural language is always in flux, not stable and unchanging.

It is popular for fans of the TV show and movie series *Star Trek* to learn the Klingon "language." We've put *language* in quotation marks because Klingon is not a natural human language. It is entirely artificial, invented by people, and the high quality of this invention (in terms of adhering to design features of natural human language) does not make it an NHL. Even though devotees "speak" it to one another at conventions, that group of speakers does not constitute a natural speech community. Klingon is nobody's native language, nor anybody's only language.

In the same way, "dead" languages such as Latin and Attic Greek are not now NHLs. Latin (somewhat different from the "classical" form) was once an NHL, as it was the everyday language of Romans and people throughout the Roman Empire. But today it is not; there is no community of native speakers, so Latin is now a fixed, unchanging entity. Hebrew was once a thriving everyday

---

[1] NHL is not an official abbreviation and you won't see it elsewhere in this book or in other sources. It is used here to avoid repeating the full phrase *natural human language* over and over again in this section.

NHL, but it then ceased to be a daily vernacular. For about 1,700 years, it was used almost excusively for religious observances. Then it was revived as the language of Israel, and now has a large community of native speakers.

The reason that the concept of NHL is important is that natural human languages are not static, unchanging things like an insect preserved in amber. The dynamics of use of an NHL by a speech community creates a great deal of variation and change through time. This is true at all levels of language structure, but our interest here is in the sounds of the language. The phonetic details of natural human languages are quite complex when viewed at the fine level.

1.4.2   Speech

Human beings communicate with one another primarily by speech, and speech brings human beings closer together than one might imagine. Speech sounds travel through the air at the rate of about 340 meters per second, whereas impulses travel along nerve pathways in the body at a rate of less than 60 meters per second. The time it takes for a word spoken by someone close to the hearer to be heard and understood by a hearer may be shorter than the time it takes for a neural message to travel from the toe to the brain. In this sense, speech brings people closer to the minds of others than they are to parts of their own bodies!

For most of the time that humans have been on this earth, writing has been unknown. Only in very recent times have large populations been able to read and write. In many countries today, there are relatively few literate people; even in industrialized countries with universal education, illiteracy is rampant. (There is more on the difference between written and spoken language in Section 13.2.)

Talking just comes naturally to us, and our thoughts are expressed more easily in speech than in writing. Not only is speech a more natural way of expressing thoughts than writing, it is also the chief means by which most of us secure information from others. This truth may be obscured – particularly for students, academics, and professionals – by the fact that we tend to obtain information of a scholarly or learned nature from written sources, and these sources somehow seem more "important" than casual daily conversation or videos or podcasts. But it remains true that nearly everyone receives more information from hearing words than from reading words. Video clips shown in many forums are a common source of information, while, mixed with visual images, the narration is often the element that contains the greatest information.

Speech is often easier to understand than the written word, and speech and writing may complement one another. In taking courses, you listen to lectures and read your textbooks. The lectures serve in part to help you to understand the texts. It is a common experience to discover that, after you have heard an author speak on a topic, his books or articles are easier to read.

To take another example, persons with physical anomalies and disabilities – whether by birth, accident, illness, or aging – tend to socialize in ordinary ways with the population at large, but the profoundly hearing impaired do so to a much reduced degree, if at all.

Not only is speech extremely important to us culturally, it is what sets us apart from our fellow creatures on this planet. Biological species are often named for a distinctive characteristic. One prehistoric human species is called *Homo erectus*, stressing the erect walking posture that separated them from other primates. Modern humans are classified as *Homo sapiens*, 'thinking (hu)man,' but it has been suggested that a better name might be *Homo loquens*, 'talking (hu)man,' stressing our linguistic faculty.[2]

1.4.3 Diglossia

We are a culture that places a lot of importance on the written word. The written word can adhere to more formal rules than personal writing (emails, texts, tweets), in sources such as textbooks, manuals, magazines, and so on.

As a result, when the professor gives an example from popular speech, there may be a temptation to "translate" the example to its more formal pronunciation. For example, in parts of the United States, the word *winter* may be pronounced "winner," and this example could be used when explaining certain phonetic processes (cf. Chapter 10). Students hearing the example might tend to "correct" it in their minds to the more formal pronunciation, and, if they do, the point of the example may be lost.

Diglossia is the situation where people in a language community are exposed to (at least) two different forms of the language. The two may be only slightly different, or they may be considerably different. An example of a strong form of diglossia is found in the part of Switzerland where Swiss German is spoken. Swiss German is very different from German, to the extent that it is largely (though by no means completely) incomprehensible to speakers of German in Germany and Austria. However, there is no standard writing system for Swiss German. Newspapers and other documents in the "German" part of Switzerland are written in standard High German. School children learn to read and write standard German, while they speak Swiss German at home.

---

[2] Pulgram (1970, p. 310) states: "Clearly man's faculty of speech too is a function of the superior cerebral equipment that evolution has bestowed upon him. Homo loquens is therefore no less suitable a name for the species than is Homo sapiens." One book on language (Fry, 1971) goes by the title *Homo Loquens*.

Diglossia is not particularly strong in most parts of the English-speaking world. However, there remains a significant difference between the pronunciation of many words in everyday speech and their formal "correct" pronunciation.

In our study of phonetics, we are interested in the sounds ordinary talkers make when they say things out loud. There will be a certain degree of emphasis on the way ordinary people say words and phrases and a de-emphasis of formal, deliberate pronunciations of words.

To return to the point begun above, this book and your phonetics professor may bring up examples of pronunciations that are different from how a dictionary says the word "should" be pronounced, and different from how *you* pronounce the word or phrase in question. These examples are not to be rejected, but rather should be taken as examples of natural language use.

1.4.4   Citation form and weak form

A particular case of how language is pronounced in the context of connected speech[3] – one that is important to understand – is the difference between the **citation form** and the **weak form** of words.

The **citation form** of a word is the pronunciation typically shown in dictionaries, or the answer to the question "How do you pronounce ...?" The weak form is how the word is pronounced in connected speech where there is no particular emphasis on that word.

Let us take the example word *to*. Imagine that a non-native speaker of English pointed to a written occurrence of that word and asked how it is pronounced, you would likely reply pronouncing it like *two* or *too* (i.e., /tu/ in IPA). This is the *citation form* of the word.

Now think about saying this sentence in reply to someone asking what you're doing: "I'm going to the store." The word *to* in that sentence is not pronounced like *too*; indeed, very little of the word may be uttered at all, perhaps just a partial articulation of the initial t-sound. This is a *weak form* of the word *to*.

Note that there are multiple weak forms. The word *to* is sometimes pronounced with a weak, short (so-called *reduced*) vowel: /tə/; sometimes with the t-sound fully articulated, but without a vowel (especially if the next word starts with a vowel, as in "I'm going to Alabama"). Sometimes, the entire word disappears in context. So *citation form* to *weak form* is a continuum, not simply two points, and the weak form of some common words involves virtually no phonetic realization of the word at all.

---

[3] The expression *connected speech* refers to normal conversational speech, not individual words pronounced in isolation.

1.4.5 Register

Another feature of spoken language that can affect pronunciation is what is called *register*. In simple terms, register is the degree of formality of speech, and it is largely determined by social constraints. For example, one might say *walkin'* and *talkin'* and *goin'* with one's friends, but might tend toward saying *walking* and *talking* and *going* in a more formal situation such as applying for a job.

The thing to note about register is that it is socially governed. An interesting result of this in the phonetics classroom is that one expects a slightly more formal (higher register) of speech in a university classroom than outside the class. Therefore, there is a tendency to reject some of the examples of informal speech.

1.4.6 Hyperspeech and hypospeech

As we will see in greater detail in Chapter 10, a number of features of the articulation of speech sounds by the typical talker vary according to communicative needs. We could loosely characterize these features as involving the precision and effort devoted to the task of articulating sounds. Depending on a range of factors, such as background noise, individual talkers will make greater (*hyper*) or lesser (*hypo*) effort as they produce speech sounds, giving another reason for variation in them.

These variations interact with, but are a separate phenomenon from, register. Register is governed socially, whereas the **hyperspeech–hypospeech** continuum refers primarily to communicative function (e.g., speaking in a noisy environment).

1.4.7 Dialect

Another kind of variation in language that affects pronunciation (as well as other features of language) is *dialect*. The term refers to variant forms of a language that are defined largely by region or by social group. The term can be used in a broader or a narrower sense. For instance, it makes sense to speak of the American dialect of English, as opposed to English spoken elsewhere in the world. But of course, English is spoken differently in different regions of the United States, and so one can identify different speech patterns in different regions of the country, and different speech patterns in distinct social groups, and these too would correctly be called dialects.

Here is another example of having to "unlearn" the everyday meanings of words. The word *dialect* is often used in daily speech to identify a language that one considers to be inferior or unimportant. I have heard individuals refer to one or another language indigenous to the Americas as a "dialect." No, these are *languages*. (Some indigenous languages in the Americas have many speakers spread over a large geographical area, and have a range of dialects, just as English has a range of dialects. It may therefore be correct to identify different dialects of a given indigenous language, while the language in the broader sense is a *language*, not a *dialect*.)

You may speak a different dialect of English from the one that is most often identified in the examples cited in the book, or indeed from that of your instructor. This leads us to the following concept.

1.4.8   Use of key words and example words

In the sections from 1.4.3 to 1.4.7, we've looked at ways in which there can be variation in language. These include *dialect* and *register*; the normal functioning of *diglossia* likely means that how you believe you pronounce many words (closer to the citation form) is different from how you really do pronounce those words in casual speech (closer to the weak form). All of these ways can involve differences in pronunciation, although many can involve other aspects of language such as vocabulary or grammatical structure.

Textbooks of phonetics often provide **key words** or example words, usually written in their standard spelling, which are used to illustrate given sounds or phenomena. On occasion, in this book, these will be accompanied by a notation about region or about how formal or informal (strong or weak) the pronunciation is.

The difficulty with this approach is that readers are likely to substitute their own pronunciation for the one that is intended – if writer and reader have important pronunciation differences – and thus the key word serves to mislead rather than guide the reader/learner.

Using one's knowledge of the intended dialect ("General American"), guidance by the professor, and online resources, this can be turned into a relatively small problem. But the reader should keep firmly in mind that the key words may not represent *their* usual pronunciation, and they must make the necessary adjustments to know what pronunciation the key word actually represents.

1.5   Using the book

As noted above, the book provides key word examples that need to be understood to refer to the pronunciation of those words in a particular variety of English. As noted also, the book provides examples of casual register and weak forms for which it is necessary to think of the pronunciation of the word in rapid casual speech, and not "convert" it to a formal citation form.

In addition, the book directs the reader to introspect, to pay attention to their own speech movements and their own anatomical structures. This is an aid to understanding and to learning; involving more senses than simply reading the text gives one's memory and understanding additional mental "hooks" to which to attach and integrate the information.

This brings up an additional caution. Some aspects of phonetics are very subtle, and talkers who are not native speakers of English, even ones who speak English fluently and with little accent, may not make exactly the same speech gestures as native speakers. Keep this in mind when introspecting.

Additionally, there are subtle differences among dialects, not just the ones that are obvious to the ear. If you are a native speaker of a variety of English other than the one being described here, then when you introspect, you may reveal facts different from those in the text.

1.6   Phonetics and phonology

The reader may take a course in *phonology* as well as phonetics, or may be exposed to phonology in another course. Given that both phonetics and phonology study the sounds of language, the student may be distressed or confused by differences between the approaches taken to seemingly the "same" material by the two different disciplines. Sometimes the two approaches may appear to the student to be not only different, but actually contradictory. Further confusing the matter is the fact that material addressed in both disciplines used to be collectively called *phonetics*.

Many different theoretical approaches to phonology have been advanced during the last few decades, and material called *phonology* in one source may be very different from similarly labeled material in another source. Relatively recent work under the heading *laboratory phonology* includes methodologies that previously were the exclusive domain of experimental phonetics.

The purpose in this short section is to introduce the reader to these concepts in a way that helps the reader avoid confusion later. The treatment is deliberately light on detail.

1.6.1   Difference versus contrast

At the most basic level, phonetics is focused on *differences* among speech sounds, whereas phonology is focused on *contrasts* among sounds. What does this mean? Consider the English words *pan* and *tan*. The difference between these 2 words is to be found in the initial sound of each (see Sidebar 1.2).

The 2 words *pan* and *tan* are distinct words, and any speaker of a major dialect of English would hear them as different, would identify each correctly when hearing them, and would produce them with the different sounds. Therefore, we can conclude that the p-sound [p] and the t-sound [t] (see Sidebar 1.2) are *contrastive* in English. That is, in English, words can be distinguished or contrasted by the difference between these 2 sounds.

SIDEBAR 1.2 Sound versus letter

You may be inclined to say "the initial letter" of a word, rather than "the initial sound." But in this book on phonetics, it is the *sound* difference that counts. Even if there were no writing system at all for English (therefore no letters <p> and <t>), or a Chinese-style writing system in which sounds are (in large measure) not directly recorded, these 2 words would still differ in their first sound. *That's our focus: the form that comes out of our mouths when we talk, not the form that's written on the page or screen.*

This may seem obvious, but there could be languages in which that is not the case.

Additionally, this fact tells us that there are **minimal pairs** based on these sounds. That is, there are pairs of words, such as *pan* and *tan*, that are the same (phonetically) except for this one difference, that between [p] and [t].

1.6.2 Example 1: *pot, spot,* and *stop!*

Now consider these English words, and the sounds that are emphasized in bold: *pot, spot,* and *stop!*[4] The sounds that are emphasized in each word, which you would identify as a p-sound in each, are in fact phonetically different from one another. While we will look in greater detail at the different types of p-sound in Chapter 5, for the moment we can make the following observations:

Word	Comment
pot	Hold your hand flat in front of your mouth, half an inch or a centimeter from your lips, and pronounce the word out loud several times. You will feel a puff of air accompanying the p-sound. While you may not notice it, the puff of air creates a sound in itself.[a]
spot	Repeat the same experiment. You will not feel a puff of air when the p-sound is produced. The sound of the puff is missing, though native speakers of English are unlikely to notice whether it is present or absent.
stop!	In this case, say the word as if you're saying the word as an order. Many talkers (especially in North America) will hold the p-sound closed – that is, the lips will stay together – rather than *releasing* it, or opening the lips again. This same phenomenon can occur without the word being spoken as an order, but, for it to occur, *stop* must be the last word in the utterance.

[a] If you are not a native speaker of a major dialect of English, the facts in this demonstration may be different. The results shown apply to speakers of major dialects of English, and the pronunciation described for the third word may be more characteristic of North American English than English spoken elsewhere.

[4] The exclamation mark with the word *stop* is intended to show that the word *stop* is spoken sharply as an order and that no words follow.

So we have three kinds of p-sound in English. Phonetically, they are *different* from one another. However, they are not **contrastive** in English. It is not possible to find a pair of words, one of which has the p-sound of *pot* and the other has the p-sound of *spot*, but otherwise the two words sound the same. There are no such minimal pairs in English.

There could be a minimal pair in a language other than English. In fact, many languages make a contrast between these two kinds of p-sound. It is a property specifically of English, and not a universal phonetic truth, that English (like many languages) does not distinguish between these sounds.

One goal of phonetics is to *describe the details* of speech sounds. Swapping the p-sounds in each of the words *pot* and *spot* would result in the words sounding as if they were being spoken with a bit of an accent. So the *details* of the production of individual sounds are important to study, especially if one is dealing professionally with accents, disorders of speech, getting the pronunciation of a foreign language just right, or describing a language's sound system in detail.

So, in one sense, the p-sounds of English *pot*, *spot*, and *stop!* are the "same" sound: English speakers without special training would say that they are the same sound, and these sounds never contrast with one another. This conclusion, that they are the same, means they are the "same" sound in a superficial **phonological** assessment. The emphasis is on the characteristics of the particular *language*.

In another sense, the p-sounds of these 3 English words are *different* sounds: the movements of the speech production mechanism are to some degree different in each case, the sound (the acoustic output) of each is different, and speakers of some languages can consistently distinguish the first 2 of them. This emphasis on the differences is a particularly *phonetic* approach. The emphasis points more toward the *speech patterns* in the particular language.

1.6.3   Example 2: *leap* and *full*

Consider the sounds that are emphasized in bold in these two English words: *leap* and *full*. These two l-sounds are different from one another (and that has nothing to do with the second one being spelled with a double <ll>; our focus is sounds, not spelling).

Everyday speakers of English with no particular training in phonetics or phonology would say that these two sounds are "the same." They are both l-sounds. However, phonetically, these two sounds are different in important ways. They do not sound the same, even if speakers of English pay no attention to the difference.

To hear the difference, say each of the words but prolong the l-sound in each word: "l-l-l-l-leap" and "full-l-l-l-l-l." If you pay attention, you should be able to hear the difference. You should also be able to feel the different configuration of your tongue when you prolong the sounds.

As in the previous example, these differences involve subtleties of the pronunciation of English. If you are not a native speaker of English, even if you speak fluently, you might not make the same gestures as a native speaker. It is also possible that native speakers of some varieties (dialects) of English may not produce these sounds in the way that they are produced in General American.

In English, these two l-sounds are phonologically the "same" sound if we consider only the simple question: do these two l-sounds contrast in English? That is, can we find minimal pairs, pairs of words in English whose only difference is that between these two l-sounds? The answer to that question is No. These two sounds *do not contrast* in English; the difference between them is *not contrastive*.

However, there is an important phonetic difference between these two sounds. If a learner of English uses the wrong l-sound, native speakers will hear that as a foreign accent. This is part of the reason why we will examine these two sounds in the appropriate section of a later chapter: the two are phonetically different.

When sounds differ phonetically, it is possible (but not obligatory) for a language to use that difference to contrast words. The two sounds exist in English, but English does not base any contrast on this difference. Like English, Russian has both sounds, but, unlike English, Russian contrasts the two sounds. Use the wrong l-sound in Russian and you may well have said a completely different word. Russian /stol/[5] (with an l-sound like "leap") means 'so,' but Russian /stoł/ (with the l-sound of "full") means 'table.'

In general, students new to phonetics are more accepting of studying the differences between sounds that are contrastive in their native language than the differences between sounds that are not contrastive. This section has demonstrated that such differences do exist, and that the correct sound is necessary for natural-sounding speech and for understanding the processes of speech, whether normal or disordered.

1.7   Same phonetic variable, different significance

As we examine a range of phonetic phenomena, and particularly as we look at phonetic phenomena in languages other than English, or in dialects other than General American, we need to keep in mind that, in acoustic or articulatory

---

[5] These Russian words are written in the International Phonetic Alphabet (IPA). The Russian sounds are not identical to the English ones, but are similar enough for the purpose of this illustration of principle.

terms, a phonetic phenomenon may be similar or the same in two languages, but the *significance* of that phenomenon may be very different in the two languages. It is important to avoid confusing these two different concepts.

Turning to a phonetic example, let us compare two ways that the word *No* might be said in a conversation: "No!" (a sharply negative, annoyed reply to a request) and "No?" (questioning the negative answer received, particularly with a pitch of the voice that falls, then rises, a tone that might be considered whiny). As a speaker of English, you would recognize that the word *no* has the same dictionary meaning in both cases, and you would interpret the very different intonation in the two cases as affecting the overall interpretation of what the individual said (though the word *no* still means 'no' in both instances). In the first case, what was said would mean "No, and I really mean no!"; and in the second case, it would mean, "Do you really mean 'no'? – please reconsider your decision." In both cases, there would be a strongly emotional content added to the simple dictionary meaning of the word *no*.

But if you were a speaker of Mandarin, and the word spoken was *ma* rather than *no*, you would recognize the word *ma* with the tone of "No!" as meaning 'scold,' and the word spoken in the questioning tone as meaning 'horse.' You would not detect any particular emotion in the way the words were said; you would think they were said with neutral emotion. You would not interpret one as a strong statement and the other as a question, you would just hear someone say 'scold' in a neutral way and then say 'horse' in a neutral way.

The point is that the same phonetic adjustment (in this case, the duration of the articulation and the pitch of the voice) has a different function within the grammar of each language. In English, these differences add a level of emotion and imply a broader interpretation of the single word (as outlined above). In Mandarin, these differences mark the two words *ma* as being different in meaning.[6]

Both kinds of analysis are pertinent: (1) what is happening phonetically; and (2) what role such a change plays within the grammar of that particular language.

SIDEBAR 1.3 Utterance

We use the term *utterance* to mean something someone said – that is, something linguistic (or an attempt at something linguistic). A cry of pain, for example, is not an utterance, but, like an utterance, it is a vocalization.

We use the term *utterance* to avoid characterizing the thing said as a word or a sentence, which might be a distraction. For example, if we want to concentrate on the sounds in an utterance, we don't want to be distracted by whether it is a "real" word or whether it is slang, or a mistake, or whether it is a "full" or "proper" sentence, because that does not matter in this context.

---

[6] There is more about tones in Mandarin in Section 11.13.

1.8   Kinds of information in speech

When a person talks, information is relayed. (Whether that information is relayed *to* another person depends on whether another person is there to receive the information and able to hear it and decode it.) Note that exactly what information is relayed depends upon a number of things, and, as you'll see in this section, some kinds of information do not require that the talker and hearer even speak the same language.

As we examine these information types, our purpose is to anticipate the discussion of phonetics and the various parts of the speech signal we'll be examining throughout the book.

Table 1.2 Traunmüller's information sources in speech (Traunmüller, 1994)	
Phonetic quality	Linguistic, conventional, specific to humans
Affective quality	Paralinguistic, communicative, not specific to humans
Personal quality	Extralinguistic, informative (symptomatic) about the speaker, not about his message
Transmittal quality	Perspectival, informative about the speaker's location only

Traunmüller (1994) examined the types of information in speech, and his analysis will serve us well in thinking about the information contained in speech.

1.8.1   Phonetic quality

The phonetic quality[7] refers to that part of the speech signal (that is, the sounds of speech) that directly carries linguistic information. At this point in your studies, you may feel that such information is about which particular consonant or which particular vowel is being produced (and acoustically transmitted) at any given moment. And yes, that is certainly a very large part of it, but as we shall see at various places throughout this book, there are other phonetic variables – such as the quality of the voice, the pitch of the voice, and others – that carry linguistic information.

Table 1.2 from Traunmüller states that the **phonetic quality** of vocalization is unique to humans. That means that, while other species may have vocalizations that communicate meaning of some sort (aggression, capitulation, warning, etc.), as far as we know at present, animal vocalizations do not consist of phonetic building-blocks (units of sound) that can

---

[7] Traunmüller's term *phonetic quality* would better be called *phonological quality*; his usage reflects the fact that the term *phonetic* has historically been used to cover both phonetic and phonological phenomena.

be recombined into different meaningful units in the way a t-sound [t], an a-sound [æ] and a k-sound [k] can be combined and recombined into the words *tack, cat, tact,* and *act*.[8] (See Sidebar 1.4.)

Traunmüller states in Table 1.2 that the phonetic quality is linguistic in nature. That is, it is a matter of the structural units that make up language, and that are decoded by the hearer through the complex of rules for decoding utterances (see Sidebar 1.3) in a language; being able to do this is part and parcel of the knowledge of a person who speaks a given language. The units of sound that characterize a language such as English are defined by the grammar of English.

Traunmüller makes the important point that the phonetic information in speech is of a variable nature. A given phonetic unit – say, a p-sound – is different systematically at different places in a word or utterance (pot, spot, stop! contain sys-

> ### SIDEBAR 1.4 Hierarchy of units
>
> Words are made up of individual speech sounds that combine in various ways.
>
> An important part of linguistic structure is that there are units at various levels of the grammar that can be combined into higher-level units that themselves can be combined into yet higher-level units.
>
> Words (and some other units of language beyond our purpose here) are made up of phonetic or phonological units (Traunmüller's phonetic quality of vocalizations).
>
> These words can then be combined in different ways to make up phrases (parts of sentences), which can then be combined into sentences.

tematically different kinds of p-sound, as noted above) and is systematically different among different individuals; there is also some, relatively small, random variation. Therefore, the phonetic information contained in speech is not a matter of matching a precise template; our mental speech decoder must be robust enough to accept variation, and even accept variation that allows one phonetic unit to be the same as a different phonetic unit yet lead to distinct interpretations.

So, the phonetic quality in Traunmüller's terminology refers to the elements of language structure that are encoded into speech. Often, when thinking about spoken language, that is the only aspect that we think about.

1.8.2   Affective quality

In the terminology of psychology, **affect** is what is more commonly known as *emotion* or *feeling*. Speech contains information about the affective (emotional) state of the talker, or the emotional attitude of the talker about the subject being talked about or their attitude toward the intended hearer.

---

[8] Just prior to the publication of this book, there has appeared some evidence of recombination of sound units in the vocalizations of some intelligent non-human species, such as some primates and some aquatic mammals.

It is interesting to note that the sound of an utterance, and therefore of the individual speech sounds, differs considerably as a result of the affect (emotion) of the talker. Our decoding of the linguistic message (i.e., the meaning of the utterance) must therefore be robust and adaptable enough to decode the phonetic content consistently, despite sound changes created by differences in affect.

Traunmüller says that the affective quality of speech is *paralinguistic*. That is, it is somewhat linguistic (in the sense of communicating a degree of meaning), but not truly or formally linguistic (in terms of language structure). The notion is that the affective quality of speech can lead to a change in the linguistic message or meaning received. For example, imagine two different people reacting to an invitation to accompany another person who is going out to walk the dog. Both people respond to the invitation "Would you like to come with me?" by saying, "I'd love to." But the two people have opposite attitudes toward walking the dog; one loves to do it (or loves any excuse to go for a walk) and the other hates to do it (or hates going for walks, period). While a skilled person might be able to hide their affect when talking, most of us will betray our feelings. So the first person says, "I'd love to" with enthusiasm, the second with heavy sarcasm.

Those different affects slightly change the sounds that are emitted from the talkers' mouths (as compared to how they would sound if they felt entirely neutral, or if they were simply asked to repeat the sentence "I'd love to"). The message the dog-walker will hear is positive in one instance and negative in the other. Thus, the meaning of the message differs in the two cases, and meaning is a linguistic (language) domain. Nonetheless, the strictly linguistic content of the two utterances is the same, encoded in the words "I'd love to." However, the interpretation of the utterance as spoken by each invitee would be different, and so there is a quasi-linguistic element. Thus, the term *paralinguistic* is used.

Traunmüller says that the affective quality of vocalization is not specific to humans. Of course, some elements of affect and how that affect modifies vocalization are specific to humans, but Traunmüller means that, in other species, affect modifies vocalization. Some fundamental emotions are apparently shared with many other mammals – emotions such as fear and aggressiveness. Many owners of dogs can determine whether a bark they hear from another room is a happy bark or an angry/aggressive bark. Similarly, dogs are very adept at reading human emotion from speech; they are accurately reading the *affective quality* of speech. Indeed, some of the modifications in how vocalizations are produced in different emotions are shared across at least some mammalian species. For instance, a dog's "angry" bark has heightened air pressure and increased amplitude, just as angry speech has in humans.

Some aspects of the affective quality of speech may be transmitted to a hearer who does not speak the same language as the talker. However, there are many aspects of speech that are part of the linguistic code of the talker's language or matters of social convention where that language is spoken (e.g., rate of speech, loudness of speech, and rapid pitch changes) that can be misinterpreted as affect. Indeed, attempting to judge affect of a talker of a language we do not understand is very fraught; it is easy to think that speakers of certain languages are angry, for example, when in fact they are not. So, while it is often unfair and inaccurate to make such judgments, the fact is that (correctly or incorrectly) we can receive affective aspects of speech even when we do not share a common language with the talker, though we interpret them in a way consistent with our native language.

1.8.3 Personal quality

In Traunmüller's words, "The term *personal quality* refers to all *extralinguistic* information about the speaker's person and state." By extralinguistic, it is meant that the elements of personal quality do not have anything to do with the linguistic content of the message, not the specific speech sounds made, not the words, not the meaning.

Personal quality is about the talker's "person and state." That is, it is about the following factors, insofar as those factors make audible differences to the sound of their speech: age, sex or gender, state of health, comfort, long-term psychological state (beyond the short-term affective state, captured in the previous quality), and the environmental situation of the talker (e.g., a certain level of environmental noise will lead the talker to speak more loudly, deliberately, and slowly – known as the *Lombard effect* [Lane, 1971]).

If the hearer speaks a different language from the talker, considerable information about the personal quality can still be determined. Nonetheless, some aspects of the speech of the talker can reveal certain personal qualities only to a fellow speaker of the language – for instance, a kind of breathy or creaky voice can be part of the phonetic quality in one language, whereas it can signal respiratory or laryngeal problems in speakers of any language.

1.8.4 Transmittal quality

The *transmittal quality* concerns the route by which the talker's voice gets to the hearer; it tells the hearer about the relative position of talker and hearer. Is the talker to the right or to the left? Higher, lower, on the same level? Close or distant? Is the voice live, or recorded? Is the voice passing through a telephone connection, or is it live?

1.8.5   Information in speech

As we discuss various aspects of speech sounds and speech production throughout this book, keep in mind these different kinds of information that speech contains.

Just a note about terminology: in Traunmüller's usage, *phonetic* means *linguistic in nature* – that is, what is phonetic in speech is the communication of the linguistic code. More usually, we use the term *phonological* in this sense. Generally, the term *phonetic* is used more generally for all aspects (linguistic or not linguistic) of the production of speech and the speech itself. The distinction between the phonetic and phonological level of analysis was described in Section 1.6.

We will most commonly use the more general meaning of the word *phonetic*, which includes both linguistic and non-linguistic aspects of the sounds, but the discussion of information types in speech should bring us to ask ourselves this question throughout: is this about transmitting the linguistic message, is it about the way emotion affects speech and the resulting message, is it about how I differ physically and mentally from the next person, or does it merely locate me in space relative to the hearer?

1.9   A single speech sound

We would agree that a word like "cat" contains 3 individual sounds, corresponding to the 3 letters of its spelling. The word "ship" also contains 3 individual sounds; the first 2 letters of its spelling represent a single sound. English spelling being what it is, the correspondence between letters and sounds can be a very poor one. The word "though" contains 2 individual sounds, the first represented by the combination <th> and the rest of the letters representing, together, a single vowel sound.

We need a word to refer to a single individual speech sound, and there are several in use (though their meanings differ to some degree):

- a speech sound
- a phone
- a segment
- a phoneme

Speech sound, *phone*, and *segment* are commonly used to reference a single unit of spoken language, a single speech sound. They are largely interchangeable.

The term *phoneme* is often imprecisely used with the same meaning. However, the term should be reserved for a speech sound that has been determined to be a contrastive unit in the language, in the sense we saw in

Section 1.6. Following an example in that section, the l-sounds of "leap" and "full" are two different *phones*, but in English they together form one single *phoneme*. In Russian, these two *phones* belong to two different *phonemes*. There is an important difference in meaning between *phone* or *segment*, on the one hand, and *phoneme* on the other.

A single phone might also be called:

- a consonant
- a vowel

However, it must be kept in mind that, in phonetics, the words **consonant** and **vowel** *do not refer* to kinds of letters in the spelling of English. They refer to different kinds of phones, based on phonetic, not orthographic (spelling), reasons.

- The first sound of the word "use" is not a vowel; that sound is normally categorized with consonants.
- The last sound of the word "though" is a vowel.

For the most part, the letters used in spelling English correspond roughly to what we call them every day: the letters we call *consonants* usually represent consonant sounds, and the letters we call *vowels* usually represent vowel sounds, but there are exceptions, as noted above. But the meaning of the words *consonant* and *vowel* in reference to speech sounds is very strict: it is never determined by which letters represent them, but by how the sounds are created (the topics of Chapters 5 and 6).

1.10   Cautions

1.10.1   English and phonetic universals

A primary focus of this book is the English language, and more particularly the English language as spoken in North America, and in the United States in particular. This may lead to a misunderstanding of the scope of the information provided.

Another focus is on general or universal principles of phonetics that apply across the board to human language. This information helps us understand many of the "why's" about phonetics, and allows the reader to understand the underlying processes. Readers of this book may be interested in languages other than English, non-native accents in English, communication disorders, teaching English as a second language, and so on. The universal principles of phonetics help us understand these things in ways that a simple description of the sounds of one geographical variant of English will not do.

SIDEBAR 1.5 Morphophonemic alternation

Also called *morphophonological alternation*.

The words *magic* and *magician* illustrate a feature that is common in English (and in many other languages). The element *magic* is the same in both *magic* and *magician* – the same *morpheme* in linguistic terminology. But 3 of the 5 phones are pronounced differently in the 2 words; the biggest difference is in the sound represented by the letter <c> in them.

Similar alternation occurs in many words. Look at the <t> in pairs of words such as *connect – connection, invent – invention, right – righteous*; the <c> in *reduce – reduction, produce – production*; the <s> in *tense – tension*; and so on.

In English, the spelling often uses the same letter for different sounds, as in these examples. A strictly phonemic writing system would result in the root *invent* being spelled differently in the word *invention*. This may or may not be a bad thing, but English writing could not have it both ways: different forms of the same word being spelled with the same letters (so that they are similar visually) and sounds being reliably represented consistently with a single letter for each sound. A language such as Spanish has this problem to a much lesser extent than English, so it is not an issue in the spelling of Spanish.

A potential source of misunderstanding is to confuse what is said about English with what is said about phonetics in general, or to confuse what is said about the variety of English being described with what is true of all major varieties of English.

Every effort is made to ensure that the distinction is clear. However, you may wish to ask your professor if you are unsure or to review the section you are reading in order to clarify the distinction.

1.10.2   Phonetic(s) doesn't mean …

You will sometimes hear people say, "English is not a phonetic language." But of course, spoken languages, including English, are *always* phonetic, in the sense that they consist of articulated speech sounds.

What people generally mean by the idea of English not being "phonetic" is that the English writing system does a poor job of representing the sounds of the spoken language. That is a different matter, and is not what *phonetic* means in the context of the material presented in this book. Additionally, a writing system is not a language, and a language can exist exclusive of there being any conventional way of writing it.

While one of the skills learned by students of phonetics is to write using a special international alphabet, phonetics exists in the absence of writing. Languages that have no writing sys-

---

⁹ Sign languages of the Deaf are considered to be natural human language though they do not consist of sounds, but rather gestures. Physical and linguistic aspects of those gestures can be studied and, by metaphor, be called the "phonetics" of gestural language. See, e.g., Wilcox (1992).

tem at all are still "phonetic" in the sense that they consist of articulated speech sounds that can be studied and measured and classified in the absence of writing.[9]

Indeed, it can be argued that "phonetic" spelling in English would be a terrible system. If spelled "phonetically," the words *magic* and *magician* would have only two letters in common (and tens of thousands of other groups of related English words would lose their visual resemblance to one another). It is not clear that losing the visual resemblance of the words *magic* and *magician* would represent an improvement in English writing (though the question is open to debate). See Sidebar 1.5.

Many languages (such as Spanish and Finnish) have phonemic or near-phonemic writing systems, and this type of writing works well for many languages. In such a system, if applied to English, the two kinds of l-sound in English words "leap" and "full" would be represented by the same symbol. In a *phonetic* writing system, the two l-sounds would be written differently; that would add complexity to the spelling of English without adding any clarity for everyday use. But even a phonemic writing system would introduce new issues into English writing, as shown by the "magic – magician" example above.

1.11   Vocabulary

affect

citation form

consonant

contrast, contrastive

dialect

difference

diglossia

extralinguistic

hearer

hyperspeech

hypospeech

International Phonetic Alphabet (IPA)

key word

language

latin alphabet

metalanguage

minimal pair

morpheme

morphophonemic alternation

morphophonological alternation

natural human language

paralinguistic

phone

phoneme

phonetics

phonology

quality:
- phonetic
- affective
- personal
- transmittal

register
roman alphabet
segment
speaker
speech
speech community
speech sound
talker

transcription:
- phonemic, broad
- phonetic, narrow

transmittal quality
utterance
virgule
vowel
weak form

2 Phonetic Transcription

2.1 Phonetic transcription: history and principles

2.1.1 The International Phonetic Association

Interest in the teaching of second languages, and in particular the sounds of second languages, led to the founding in Paris in 1886 of what was then called Dhi Fonètik Tîcerz' Asóciécon (The Phonetic Teachers' Association), made up of language teachers from England and France. In 1889, the name was changed to L'Association phonétique des professeurs de langues vivantes (The phonetic association of teachers of living languages), with an official journal titled *Le Maître phonétique* (The Phonetic[s] Teacher). The association gained its current name, the *International Phonetic Association*, in 1897. The journal became *Journal of the International Phonetic Association* in 1971.

One of the initial goals of the Association was to create and promote a phonetic alphabet to be used internationally for writing the sounds of languages. At the beginning, the alphabet was to be used for language teaching, though its uses have multiplied since then. (Other goals were to teach principles of phonetics to be used in second-language teaching, as well as techniques in teaching pronunciation to second-language learners.)

2.1.2 The International Phonetic Alphabet

The International Phonetic Alphabet (IPA) was based in part on the *Romic Alphabet* proposed by the nineteenth-century English phonetician Henry Sweet.[1] The developers of the IPA wanted their new alphabet to be based on a number of principles, as indicated in the following sections.

> **SIDEBAR 2.1 Henry Sweet**
>
> Henry Sweet was in part the model for the character Henry Higgins in George Bernard Shaw's *Pygmalion*, later the musical, then the film, *My Fair Lady* (1964). Sweet was a very influential English phonetician.

2.1.2.1 One sound, one symbol

The most basic requirement of a phonetic alphabet is that there be a one-to-one correspondence between spoken sounds and symbols (letters) on the page. While

---

[1] The organization and content of the material throughout this section was influenced by the website of Kevin Russell, University of Manitoba Linguistics Department.

this may seem obvious, it is a principle that is broken by a large proportion of the spelling systems of "alphabetic" languages around the world.[2] Specifically, this principle means the following:

1. The sound that a letter represents does not depend on the language being represented. While the letter <j> represents different sounds in the orthography of English, Spanish, and French, the phonetic symbol [j] represents a given sound irrespective of the particular language.

2. A given sound is always represented by the same symbol. While the same English sound is represented in different ways in normal English spelling, as shown in the following words, in the IPA a given sound is represented only one way: *fine, phone, tough*. The sounds shown in bold in each of these words are all represented by [f] in the IPA.

3. A given sound is to be represented by a single letter, not by a sequence of letters. In each of these English words, a single sound is represented by at least two letters: *shine, this, thought, thought, phone, rhythm, write*, etc. In the IPA, if there are two letters, they represent two different sounds. (Sometimes the IPA symbol requires an accent mark – properly called a *diacritic* – to represent a particular single sound, however.)

4. A given symbol of the IPA must represent only a single sound, not a sequence of sounds. In the normal orthography of English, the letter <x> of the word *six* represents a sequence of two sounds. That is not permitted in the IPA; the sounds represented by the <x> of *six* would be written [ks] in IPA.

SIDEBAR 2.2 Visible speech

Alexander Melville Bell, the father of Alexander Graham Bell, developed an alphabetic system that he called *Visible Speech*. One of its chief characteristics was that it attempted to illustrate the positions of the speech articulators when producing the sound in question. However, its unfamiliarity and perceived difficulty inhibited its widespread adoption.

2.1.2.2 As much as possible, use letters of the latin[3] alphabet

In the nineteenth century and previously, a number of systems had been proposed for representing the sounds of language in a consistent way. A

---

[2] This is true of languages such as English or French, whose orthographies are known to be highly inconsistent, as well as languages such as Spanish that have much more regular orthography, sometimes claimed to be "phonetic," though it is not. Note the use of <b> and <v> in Spanish, as well as the use of <j> and <x>. Additionally, the letters <c> and <g> in Spanish represent different sounds depending on the letter that follows.

[3] The regular alphabet used in English and many other languages is often called the *latin alphabet* or the *roman alphabet*. We will favor the use of the term *latin alphabet*. The reason is that, as we shall see in this chapter, a distinction is made between two styles of

common characteristic of these systems – including shorthand – was that they used an entirely novel set of letters or characters. This made them harder to learn and discouraged their adoption because of the psychological barrier of a large number of new and strange-looking symbols.

A founding principle of the IPA was to use the *latin alphabet* as its basis. This made the task of learning the IPA less daunting, and that contributed to its successful adoption.

There are hundreds of speech sounds in the world's languages, much much more than the 26 letters of the most common version of the latin alphabet. The IPA attempts to solve this problem of an inadequate number of different letters in the latin alphabet while maintaining the familiar look of the letters through a number of techniques, as follows:

1. The sounds of many of the letters of the IPA are immediately familiar: /p b m t d n g k/ all broadly represent the expected sounds.
2. The vowel symbols may seem to be less immediately familiar to a speaker of English, as compared to the consonant symbols in point (1) above, but they are familiar to speakers of many languages. It is, in this instance, the spelling of the English language that is out of sync with common international usage (see Sidebar 2.3).
3. Most commonly, *lower-case* ("small") letters are used, not capital letters, though there are exceptions, as noted below.

After the 26 letters of the latin alphabet are used, extra letters will be needed. The IPA uses one of the following techniques, in order to reduce the unfamiliarity of the letters:

4. ... take latin letters and reverse them or turn them upside down: [ə ɔ ɹ ʁ ɯ ɔ ʌ ɟ ʍ].[4]

> ## SIDEBAR 2.3 Vowel "symbols" or "letters"?
>
> Why have we written "vowel symbols"? Why not just "vowels"? In phonetics, a *vowel* is a kind of speech sound; it is not a kind of letter. If, in the context of phonetic science, a person says or writes "vowel" or "consonant," it should refer exclusively to a kind of sound, and not to a letter of the alphabet.
>
> Mostly, letters English speakers call *consonants* represent consonant sounds, and the same applies for vowels. However, there are instances where this is not true of English spelling. For example, the first sound of the word *Europe* is a consonant, and the last sound of the word *though* is a vowel, so it is correct (phonetically) to say, "*Europe* starts with a consonant and *though* ends with a vowel."

letters: *roman* and *italic.* There is risk of confusion between roman style of letter and the roman alphabet. While we will avoid the term here, *roman alphabet* is a correct name for the ordinary alphabet we use in English.

[4] We will encounter many of these sounds in Chapters 5 and 6. Note that [ʍ] is an upside down <w>, not an <m>.

5. ... use both lower- and upper-case letters, though the upper-case letters should be small, the same height as vowel letters: [g ɢ r ʀ y ʏ i ɪ].

6. ... add an additional stroke: a longer tail, a curlicue, or other flourish: [ŋ ɲ ɳ ɓ ç ɬ ɗ]. In some instances, a similar curlicue is added to a class of sounds that all share a certain characteristic, so the curlicue itself represents a particular phonetic fact, therefore reducing the load on the memory when learning the IPA (see Sidebar 2.4).

7. ... use letters that are found in versions of the latin alphabet used by languages other than English: [æ œ ø ç ð].

8. ... borrow letters from the Greek alphabet: [β θ χ].[5]

9. ... borrow from archaic alphabets, such as one letter used in Old English: [ʒ]

10. ... make a distinction between a more *roman* style and a more *italic* style of letter (more on these styles in Section 2.3.4). Compare these letters: [u ʊ], [a ɑ], and [v ʋ]. In some cases, the serifs (Section 2.3.5) become important for distinguishing the shapes.

11. ... entirely new symbols may be created, but keep this to a minimum: [ʃ ⊙ ʕ ɢ]

2.1.2.3　Big differences versus small differences

Another principle of the IPA is to use different letters where there are major differences between the sounds, but to use diacritics (accent marks) to show smaller differences. Base letters of the IPA are often used in combination with diacritics or with the curlicues mentioned above to make important distinctions. (Some diacritics in the IPA are placed under the letter in question, not above, while others are in the familiar location above the letter.) Here are a few examples – at this point in your reading, these are meant simply to illustrate the principle; all will be discussed in later chapters:

---

[5] [β] is a Greek letter, and while it is used in the spelling of German, it is not listed under (7) because its sound in German is unrelated – it represents an s-sound, not a b-like sound made with the lips – and therefore did not influence its use in the IPA. The German letter comes from an archaic way of writing the sequence <sz> in cursive (handwriting).

[o] [õ] The first is a normal (oral) vowel; the second is the same vowel, but nasalized.

[t] [t̪] The first is a t-sound made as it is in English; the second is a t-sound made more as it is in French and Spanish, with the tip of the tongue touching the back of the upper front teeth (incisors).

[m] [m̥] The first is a normal m-sound, made with vibrating vocal folds; the second is the same sound made without vocal fold vibration (called *voiced* and *voiceless* respectively).

[a] [a̤] The first is a normal a-sound made with ordinary voicing; the second is the same sound made with *breathy voicing* (also called *murmur*).

In sum, most of the letters of the IPA, and the most common ones used in the transcription of English, look like regular letters of the latin alphabet, or are not too different from familiar letters. Paying attention to how the less familiar ones were designed can help in remembering them.

2.1.3   Use of the IPA in the English-speaking world

Unfortunately, the IPA has not caught on as universally as would be useful, especially in the English-speaking world. English-language dictionaries (in book form and, disappointingly, now online) and textbooks of foreign (and especially ancient) languages tend to use myriad different symbols for spoken sounds – often completely idiosyncratic and mutually contradictory – thus leaving ambiguous and unclear what could easily be written clearly. At the time of writing (2023), the English edition of Wikipedia is unusual among online reference materials in English in providing pronunciation guides written in IPA under a great number of entries. This usage in the popular online reference source is important for the spread of the IPA, and important in promoting a single, consistent written guide to pronunciation.

2.2   Why are there differences among experts' transcriptions?

Something that is frustrating to students taking phonetics or using phonetic transcriptions is that even the people who claim expertise in the area differ in how they may transcribe the same word or phrase. The reaction of the learner may be to question whether the experts know what they are doing.

There are a number of legitimate reasons for differences in transcriptions. Understanding the reasons for differences should make it easier for you to understand why 2 of your professors transcribe a word differently, and to understand what the instructor of the course you are taking requires you to do.

2.2.1   Convenience

It is sometimes convenient to substitute incorrect symbols – that is, symbols not properly part of the IPA, or part of the IPA but for a different sound – and thus such usages are often found even in scholarly materials. The most common example in English-speaking areas is the use of the symbol [r] for the North American English (NAE) r-sound, whose IPA symbol is [ɹ], an upside-down <r>. In the IPA, the symbol [r] represents a sound that does not occur in NAE (but which occurs in some varieties of English spoken, for example, in England and Scotland). Therefore, why use a symbol that is awkward to write, and not use a symbol that is easy to write, when a substitution can be easily made?

Given current technology, it is easy to use the correct symbol, and that is preferable; excuses hanging over from the days of typewriters are no longer convincing. However, the topic of the next section may explain why you still may see such non-conforming usages.

2.2.2   Tradition

Some of the sort of substitution of symbols mentioned above are a holdover from before the time when IPA became relatively easy to write in text-edited documents. This refers to both the time when text was created with a typewriter and the first 25 years or so of text-editors and computer fonts, when it remained tricky to use the IPA with digital systems.

The example of [r] versus [ɹ] above, and the use of [D] for the flap [ɾ] (Section 5.12), and others, are part of these traditions. Some have become established to the point that, even though it has become straightforward to use IPA in text-edited documents, these traditions linger on.

2.2.3   First language (L1) or native dialect (D1)

The transcriber is likely to be influenced by their native language, or their native dialect in that language, as well as by their familiarity with the language that is being transcribed. With speakers of 2 different dialects of the same language, there is likely to be a pull toward the sound of the native dialect of each speaker, even when transcribing the pronunciation of another individual.

In this context, it is worth quoting the phonetician Björn Lindblom (1990, p. 408) extensively:

> That conclusion [which relates to the influence of mental processing constraints on the perception of speech sounds] is sometimes vividly illustrated in introductory classes on auditory analysis and phonetic transcription. When students know a language and are thoroughly familiar with the transcription conventions they show a high degree of interperson[al] agreement. The

segments and their phonetic values are by and large "heard correctly" (= according to the conventions taught). However, as soon as the speech sample comes from an unknown language subjects tend to differ more widely both with respect to segmentation and quality judgements. Interestingly, the transcription errors generally make good sense from a physical-acoustic viewpoint and in terms of phonetic similarity.

A similar situation arises when the trained phonetician compares his own transcriptions with spectrograms. Although he knows the language and has considerable experience from listening analytically, he is nevertheless continually surprised by the spectrographic patterns that typically show omissions and contextual modifications in excess of his expectations.

What is going on here? It seems that, if we know a certain language, we cannot help imposing that knowledge on the signal. Physically ambiguous information is disambiguated and incomplete stimulus information is restored. It appears as if the signal-complementary processes modulate the input and shape the percept in a most tangible way. And the process is highly automatic.

2.2.3.1   Categorical perception

Babies and small children can produce a much wider range of speech sounds than can typical adults. As we mature and acquire our native language, our brain establishes "categories" for each of the distinctive sounds of our particular language. These categories differ for different languages. Looking at the examples from Section 1.6, speakers of English group different kinds of p-sounds into a single category, and they group the different l-sounds into a single category.

These mental categories affect how we perceive speech sounds. Without special training, we tend to perceive different sounds in each category as the "same." This affects what we believe we hear; it is truly a matter of how individuals perceive sounds.

One of the goals of training in phonetics is to be able to transcend the categories left by our native language and hear differences *within* categories. But this requires constant effort and is not always successful.

Categorical perception is also called *categorial* perception. There is more on categorical perception in Section 13.4.7.

2.2.4   Phonetic versus phonological

As we saw in Chapter 1, the sound system of a language exists at two different levels. The first of these is the *phonological level*, which relates to the abstract mental representation of the sounds of the language. It is at this level that the p-sound of *pot*, *spot*, and *stop* is the "same" sound – and that accords with the intuition of speakers of English who have not studied phonetics or phonology. The second of these is the *phonetic level*;

at this level, all three p-sounds are different, and can be represented in the IPA with different combinations of symbols. These differences (which may be obvious to speakers of other languages in which they are different phonemes) are much less obvious to speakers of English, which is why a course in phonetics is required in order to bring these and other differences to students' attention.

Therefore, one of the reasons for differences among different individuals' transcriptions may be found in the fact that one transcriber is making a *broad* or *phonemic* (i.e., phonological) transcription, while the other is making a *narrow* or *phonetic* transcription. Both types of transcription are entirely legitimate, as long as the person interpreting the transcription knows which is intended. In principle, a phonetic transcription is placed between square brackets [kʰætʼ] and a phonemic transcription between slash marks or virgules /kæt/. However, this is not so much a binary distinction as a continuum from phonetic to phonological, and there may be reason to treat different parts of the same transcription differently.

On a given occasion, for a variety of reasons, a person may transcribe some parts of a word or expression broadly, but other parts narrowly – while a different person might make a different choice, even though both are correct. Reasons for doing this are discussed in the following section.

2.2.5   Focus

When speech is transcribed phonetically, this is done for a purpose. The purpose will determine the degree of detail in the transcription. For example, if the transcriber is looking in particular at how a certain class of sounds is pronounced – for instance, *plosive* consonants such as the various p-sounds mentioned in the previous section (cf. Section 5.7) – in the speech of a particular talker or a particular language, then the plosives are likely to be transcribed in great detail, whereas other phonetic elements in the same words are transcribed broadly.

Where 2 individuals differ in their transcriptions of the same word or phrase, it may be a matter of the degree to which they are focusing on specific phonetic elements, rather than a disagreement on how to correctly transcribe those sounds.

2.2.6   Vowels vary in three ways

Phones – speech sounds – are, indeed, *sounds*. They are made up of specific acoustic characteristics, as will be examined in some detail in Chapter 12. For our purposes here, it is necessary to point out that vowels vary by a number of different frequency (sound) characteristics, of which

3 are the most important. These are called F1, F2, and F3.[6] The three can vary independently. So here is a hypothetical example: two transcribers have transcribed a particular foreign vowel in 2 different ways; each claims that their own transcription is closer to correct. It is possible that F1 of the disputed vowel is more like Transcriber 1's choice, and F2 of the same disputed vowel is more like Transcriber 2's choice. In that sense, it is possible for both transcribers to be right in one way, while wrong in the other.

The ways in which consonants vary from one another acoustically is somewhat different from vowels for the most part, but none creates a single acoustic characteristic (frequency). Since they vary in several acoustic dimensions, it is possible for 1 unknown consonant to be similar to 2 different consonants, to each in a different acoustic way.

2.2.7 Dialect

Of course, two individuals transcribing the "same" passage may be transcribing different dialects.

2.2.8 Differences in transcriptions

You can see that some differences are entirely legitimate. When you come across differences in transcription, it is useful to take a moment to try to determine the reasons. One reason, of course, may be that one or both are erroneous, but it is also very possible that they represent a different focus, for example.

2.3 A few notions of typography relevant to transcription and the IPA

Typography is a fascinating subject, and one that has far greater depth than the average reader might suspect. A brief exploration of a few notions of typography is useful when discussing aspects of the IPA.

As noted above, the alphabet that is used in English and by other European languages and many other languages around the world is called the *latin alphabet* or *roman alphabet*. It is, with a number of additions, the alphabet that was developed (from other precursor alphabets going back to ancient languages of the Middle East) by the Romans for their language, Latin.

---

[6] F stands for *formant*, so Formant 1, Formant 2, Formant 3. Formants are discussed in detail in Section 12.12.

2.3.1   Font and typeface

A font is a particular design of alphabetic letters, numerals, and symbols such as punctuation. The term refers to a family of designs that will include different sizes as well as bold and italic. The distinction between the words *font* and *typeface* is losing ground as digital technology takes over completely from hot metal type. The terms will be used interchangeably here (see also Sidebar 2.5).

SIDEBAR 2.5 Font means 'melted'

In earlier times, printing was done with fonts that were three-dimensional (only the raised portions took the ink and transferred it to the paper), and were cast out of metal. That is, molten metal was poured into molds to create lines of text (in reverse) that were used to print. The word *font* is related to the English word *foundry* and the French word (used in English) *fondue*. *Fondue* means 'melted'; it is the feminine past participle of the verb *fondre*, meaning 'to melt.' These days, fonts aren't melted metal any more, but are data encoded numerically into bits of information.

2.3.2   Case, majuscule and minuscule, cursive

There are two *cases* of letters: upper case and lower case. Upper-case letters are also called *majuscules*, *capitals*, or, when we were children, "big" letters. Lower-case letters are also called *minuscule* letters, or, when we were children, "small" or "little" letters.

In the *IPA*, the distinction between upper- and lower-case letters is not maintained in the same way as in normal latin letters, though some IPA letters are upper case in shape but not size. For instance, [ɪ] is a letter of the IPA that represents the vowel sound of the word "bit." It is a small upper-case letter <i>. Normally, the upper-case letter is taller than the lower-case – <I i> – but the IPA letter, though upper-case in shape, is the height of other vowel letters: /i o u a ɪ/.

Further, while the IPA uses characters that look like latin upper-case and latin lower-case letters, no case distinction is made (though IPA characters shaped like lower-case latin predominate). Words are not capitalized in the IPA; IPA records the sounds, not the grammatical function of utterances. Of course, many characters ("letters") in the IPA are not letters of the latin alphabet at all, as we saw above under principles of the IPA (Section 2.1.2).

2.3.3   Ascenders and descenders

In most ordinary typefaces, upper-case letters are the full height of the distance between two invisible horizontal lines: <ABCDEFGHIJKLMNOPQRSTUVWXYZ>. There are differences among typefaces, and, particularly with fancy or ornamental typefaces, there may be parts that extend above or below. The letter <J> extends below the lower line in many "ordinary" typefaces, as does the *descender* ("tail") of the <Q>.

By contrast, many lower-case letters are positioned on the lower of those two lines, but their height is only about half the height of upper-case letters: <aceimnorsuvwxz>. Other lower-case letters have either *ascenders* or descenders.

Ascenders are vertical strokes that rise up from the main body of the lower-case letter, typically rising to the height of the upper limit for normal upper-case letters: <bdfhklt>.

Descenders are vertical strokes descending below the lower limit of upper-case letters, and typically going down about as far as the ascenders rise: <gjpqy>.

See Table 2.1.

Table 2.1 Lower-case letters, ascenders and descenders

lower-case letters	a b c d e f g h i j k l m n o p q r s t u v w x y z
neither ascender nor descender	a c e i m n o r s u v w x z
ascenders	b d f h k l t
descenders	g j p q y

Designing typefaces is to a large extent a matter of artistic vision, though for typefaces that are intended for use in large blocks of text, readability (legibility) is a major concern. The upshot of this fact is that there is great variation, and the height of ascenders and length of descenders may vary, and there may be variants of letters having atypical strokes.

2.3.4 Roman and italic

Typefaces in which the ascenders and descenders of lower-case letters and any non-horizontal strokes in upper-case letters are essentially vertical or nearly vertical are called *roman*. When these same strokes lean consistently toward the right (that is, the highest point on a vertical stroke is to the right of its lowest point), the typeface is called *italic*. See Table 2.2 and Sidebar 2.6.

> **SIDEBAR 2.6 Roman *style* and roman *alphabet***
>
> As we've noted elsewhere, the alphabet we use everyday is called the *latin alphabet* or *roman alphabet*. In this section, the word *roman* doesn't refer to the alphabet, but to the style of the letters. *Roman* (style) means vertically upright, whereas *italic* (style) means leaning right.
>
> So, letters of the roman alphabet could be in roman or in italic style.
>
> In general, we have used the term *latin alphabet* rather than *roman alphabet* to avoid this confusion.

Table 2.2 Roman versus italic		
Style	Examples	
roman	typeface	font
italic	*typeface*	*font*

Usually, there are both roman and italic versions of individual typefaces. Typically, when you make text italic with a word processor, the computer simply tilts the roman version of the typeface to create a kind of artificial italic. When designed by a professional typographic designer, italics are not simply tilted versions of the roman letters but are separately designed; while the italics are indeed inclined to the right, various adjustments to the design are required in order that the shape of the individual letters and combinations of letters remains pleasing to the eye and highly legible. A few IPA letters have at least some characteristics of italic, not roman, forms of letters (though not the tilt), for instance [ʋ ʊ].

2.3.5 Serifs

There is a major distinction among typefaces: those with **serifs** and those without serifs. A serif is a short stroke, approximately at right angles to a major stroke in a letter. See Figure 2.1.

The French word *sans* means 'without,' and typefaces that have no serifs are called in English **sans serif**, and sometimes just *sans*. The (in)famous Comic Sans is a sans serif typeface that uses the word *sans* in its name.

Sans serif typefaces are used for continuous text more in Europe than in North America. In Europe, it is not unusual to see long printed documents, even books, printed in a sans serif typeface; however, this is rare in North America. In this book, the headings are sans serif and the main text is in a serif font, a common practice in North America.

A	Sans serif typeface	AaBbCc
B	Serif typeface	AaBbCc
C	Serifs of row B are shown in gray	AaBbCc

Figure 2.1 **Serifs**. The first row shows a sans serif typeface. The second row shows a serif typeface. In the third row, the serifs of the letters in the second row are shown in gray.

In the IPA, some of the letters have serifs and some do not. While the choice between serif and sans serif does not change the value of letters that we use for ordinary writing, in the IPA the presence of serifs can make important distinctions and they may be required. We normally do not add serifs in hand-printed letters, but in the IPA, certain serifs are required so that what we write by hand in IPA will be interpreted correctly. For instance, there is a distinction in the IPA between [u] and [ʊ]. When writing the second of these by hand, it is important to deliberately make the serifs so that this letter is clearly distinguished from [u]. Whether the ordinary [u] is a serif or sans serif design does not really matter: [u] (with serif) is the same IPA character as [u] (sans serif), but [ʊ] cannot be written without the serifs.

Of course, many letters of the IPA may be written with or without serifs, with no change in the sound represented; it simply depends on the font chosen, as with regular latin letters. However, in a few cases, the serifs are essential, and in others they must be avoided. As IPA letters, these two groups of symbols are equivalent: [kʰæt̚] and [kʰæt̚]. But, as noted, serifs are critical for a few IPA letters.

2.3.6 Glyphs

Glyphs are basic symbols that are part of a system of symbols. It might seem from this definition that *glyph* is just another name for a *letter*, at least when alphabetic characters are discussed. In fact, however, the two concepts are different. Some letters have more than one shape: in ordinary writing (not IPA), we can write <a> or <ɑ>, for instance, and we can dot an <i> or make a circle – or even a little heart – instead of the dot. In most contexts, we would read <a> or <ɑ> as the same. However, in the IPA, these two symbols represent very different sounds. These two letter shapes are distinct, and each is a separate glyph.

In our usual writing system, we have decided that the difference between these two glyphs does not matter, and so they are both the "same letter." Most of us would not even notice the difference, as long as the particular glyph used was consistent with the style of the rest of the text. But that does not stop them from being different in an important way.

A particular letter (or character) shape is a glyph. In the latin alphabet, sometimes different glyphs are considered to be the same letter: a and ɑ, e and ɛ, g and ɡ, i and ı (no dot[7]) are the "same" letter, *but they are different glyphs*.

There are two different glyphs that are commonly used for the lower-case version of the letter <G>: they are <g> and <ɡ>. While, in ordinary writing, you can use either glyph of the letter <G>, in the IPA, only the second one is an IPA character: <g> does not occur at all in the IPA.

---

[7] The undotted <ı> is actually a distinct letter of the Turkish alphabet.

The reason this is relevant to our study is this: when ordinary English writing with the latin alphabet accepts different glyphs of a given letter, you are likely to perceive those as "the same." Even seconds after seeing a text, you may be unable to remember which glyph you just saw even though you remember which letter – you remember that it was a <G>, but can't remember if it was <g> or <g>. As a result, you are initially likely not to perceive the subtle differences among IPA characters and are likely to consider some of the shape distinctions unworthy of attention. But the IPA is a different alphabet from the latin alphabet, and the differences among glyphs is often critically important.

2.3.7 Shape and height of letters is important in the IPA

The IPA makes a distinction between [a] and [ɑ]. Likewise, the IPA distinguishes [e] and [ɛ]. Something readers unfamiliar with the phonetic alphabet must learn is to carefully distinguish glyphs or letter shapes that might be considered "the same" in written English, especially when written by hand.

Practice writing the letters of the IPA that you'll need in your studies, paying attention to getting the shapes correct. Additionally, pay attention to the height of the letters and whether they have ascenders or descenders: for example [ɤ] represents a vowel, and is the height of other vowel letters (and, like them, it has no descender), but [ɣ] is a consonant with a descender. Size and placement on the line is the only way to distinguish the two when the characters are written by hand: [a ɤ ɣ g]. (Neither of these new characters represents sounds usually used in English, so you may never use them. But they provide a good example of an important principle.)

2.4   Technical matters related to the IPA

2.4.1 Unicode and IPA glyphs

Currently, most IT systems and email/communication applications encode characters using a system called *Unicode*. In Unicode, each different glyph has a unique code so that characters display the same glyph as originally intended by (and entered by) the writer. Prior to widespread use of Unicode, phonetic characters (letters of the International Phonetic Alphabet) often displayed differently on different computers, leading to confusion and the notion that writing in IPA characters in word-processed documents was completely unreliable. But currently, with Unicode encoding, the character that was intended by the person creating the document or email is the one that displays when the document is viewed by another person or using a different computer – this is true in general, but is subject to the following caveats.

- If the computer that is used to display the text document or email does not have among its installed fonts a font that contains a needed glyph, then an empty box[8] may be displayed instead of the needed glyph. While it can be annoying to see the box instead of the desired character, this is in fact a good thing – the box alerts the reader that they are not seeing what the writer intended. Under older systems, some letter would be shown, but not the correct one, a far more confusing and misleading situation.

- Most current computer operating systems, email apps, and word processors are "Unicode aware" or "Unicode savvy." That is to say, those systems encode text by using Unicode, they preserve the Unicode encoding (which is hidden from the writer and the reader), and they faithfully display the correct Unicode glyphs. However, the changeover to Unicode has been relatively recent and there may be word processors or email systems or apps that fail to respect Unicode standards. In such systems, phonetic characters that appear to be correct when entered may not display correctly when viewed later with another system.

The preceding paragraph concerns text that is saved and/or sent *as text*: a word-processed document or an email. When a document is converted to a PDF (Portable Document Format) on the same computer, the correct phonetic characters should normally be preserved in the PDF if they displayed correctly on the computer that is used to create the PDF.[9]

2.4.2   Install fonts

It may be necessary to install additional Unicode fonts in order to have a full range of phonetic characters available on a given device. The fonts that are typically installed in a computer may not contain the phonetic characters that you will need. Also, there are many pre-Unicode phonetic

---

[8] Or a blank space or a question mark, which is often a white question mark on a black diamond

[9] Note that this must be done on the same device as the one that shows the word-processed document correctly. If that text document is transferred to a different computer, or to an online service, to make the PDF, that may result in errors.

fonts still circulating that will not display correctly if the file is later opened on a different computer. As with other pre-Unicode fonts, these older fonts involve *keyboard mapping*, which is to say that the position of the key on the keyboard determines which characters are encoded, and that encoding is entirely dependent upon having the correct font installed and active on the computer that is displaying the text.

There are some fonts that contain a wide range of phonetic characters; installing one of them can be very useful. *Lucida Sans Unicode* and *Ariel Unicode MS* are a couple of such fonts.

2.4.3   Entering phonetic characters with computers

Finally, there is the issue of how to enter the correct phonetic characters when using a computer to create a text or a message.

- In recent versions of the Macintosh operating system, *Show Character Viewer* under the *Input Source* menu[10] allows you to select and enter any available character; it can be set to display phonetic characters.
- In Windows 11, Start Button → All Apps → Windows Tools → Character Map.
- In Windows 10, Start button → All Apps Windows Accessories → Character Map. In Windows 7, Start button → All programs → Accessories → System Tools → Character Map

In either operating system, holding a key down may result in additional characters being displayed, but it is unlikely that all desired phonetic characters would be available this way, as these systems are oriented toward normal orthography in a range of languages, not to phonetic writing.

At the time of writing, the website www.i2speak.com provides a quick and easy means to enter phonetic characters into text or messages. This may be done from the computer's keyboard; depressing a key reveals a menu of additional characters that are based on the key that was depressed or which visually resemble that letter (sometimes a bit of imagination helps) and one of these characters can be selected with the cursor (or characters may be selected from tables of characters using the cursor). Something to be aware of with i2speak is that copying the entered text (so as to be able to paste it into a document) must be done by pressing the *Copy* button on the i2speak interface. Highlighting the phonetic text in the i2speak display window and copying it may not result in the desired outcome.

---

[10] For this menu to show in the menu bar, it may be necessary to activate the menu item. This can be accomplished in *System Preferences* → *Keyboard* → *Input Sources* → *Show input menu in menu bar*. (The details may change in versions of the OS that are released after this section was written.) Similarly, the steps shown for Windows computers (below) may change with future editions of the operating system.

2.4.4   SAMPA and X-SAMPA

SAMPA stands for the *Speech Assessment Methods Phonetic Alphabet,* a system of phonetic writing developed in the late 1980s in Europe for the purpose of reliably using phonetic script in word-processed documents and emails long before Unicode was widely available. SAMPA used the extended ASCII (7-bit) character set, and thus it could be reliably sent and received correctly by computers restricted to this character set (see Clinical Note 2.1).

In 1995, Professor John C. Wells created the Extended SAMPA or *X-SAMPA,* covering most of the IPA with ASCII characters (see Clinical Note 2.2).

SAMPA or X-SAMPA are needed less than they were in the days before Unicode. However, it remains available and has a documented relationship to IPA characters, so it can be used unambiguously to represent speech sounds. Some computer apps permit inputting of IPA into computer systems based on typing SAMPA characters, a boon for those who are familiar with the system.

SAMPA can still be used in plain text emails to ensure correct transmission of the message. Even persons not familiar with it can use it by looking up a SAMPA table online and informing their correspondent to do the same.

CLINICAL NOTE 2.1 Clinical notes

Throughout the book there are Clinical notes that provide brief commentary on the clinical application of the material. In some instances, these Clinical notes are broadened to include commentary on applications in the fields of language teaching or accent coaching. In that case, the sidebar may be labeled **Clinical/Pedagogical Note**.

CLINICAL NOTE 2.2 Modification of the IPA for clinical purposes

The IPA is maintained by the International Phonetic Association, whose interests largely involve language per se. The IPA is widely used in human communication disorders for, among other things, transcribing disordered speech, something for which the IPA was not conceived. Persons working in this area have developed a number of modifications of the IPA.

X-SAMPA is a version of SAMPA to be used in clinical contexts.

2.5   Vocabulary

ascender

descender

diacritic

glyph

International Phonetic Alphabet
  (IPA)

italic style

latin alphabet

lower case

roman alphabet

roman style

SAMPA

sans serif

serif

typeface

upper case

X-SAMPA

3 | Anatomy and Physiology of Speech

Speech is anatomy made audible.

> NOTE regarding the order of chapters. Chapters 3 and 4 provide background to articulatory phonetics with "Anatomy and Physiology" and "Aerodynamics." Then Chapters 5 and 6 treat "Consonants" and "Vowels" respectively.
>
> If the instructor wishes to initiate practice with phonetic transcription before those topics are covered, they may wish to jump to Chapter 7, which provides a generic overview of the sounds of North American English. In that chapter, technical terms introduced in the intervening chapters are used without explanation, so jumping ahead will require coaching.

3.1 Anatomy and physiology

In a very concrete sense, *speech is anatomy made audible.*[1] That is to say, the sounds we make when we speak are constrained by the interface of physical (acoustic) laws and the physical properties of the so-called "speech organs." If our anatomy were different, we would not be able to make the same sounds as we do now.

This chapter deals with the anatomical structures and some of the physiological processes involved in the production of speech. We will begin by naming major anatomical landmarks; that will give us a vocabulary with which to classify speech sounds by their articulatory positions, which is to say, by the particular anatomical structures or locations involved. We will then examine vocal fold vibration (more detail in Chapter 8), respiration, vocal musculature, and anatomical and some physiological anomalies affecting speech production (in the form of Clinical Notes).

---

[1] This statement is inspired by a similar one made in Nolan (1999).

SIDEBAR 3.1 Orientation

Throughout all discussions of the anatomy, it is assumed that the body is in an upright, standing position. Concepts such as "up" and "down" are to be interpreted in this light. In lateral (side) views, most often the talker's head (and body) will face left, from the perspective of the person viewing the drawing, so you will see a side view or cross-section from the left. Views other than those specified here are used as required.

What is the difference between *anatomy* and *physiology*? Simply stated, *anatomy* is a study of *structures* (bones, muscles, tendons, etc.) – where they are, how they are shaped, and so forth – whereas *physiology* is the study of the *functioning* of those structures. What is generally called *physiological phonetics* includes both anatomical and physiological concepts.

It should be stressed that the overview of speech physiology given here does not cover everything. Students of speech pathology will surely have an entire course devoted to this subject, and students of communication disorders (and many in linguistics) will also study neuroanatomy, and neural functioning in speech and language, topics that are not treated here. Some technical vocabulary is avoided here, but phonetics does insist on some anatomical distinctions that the medical terminology tends to gloss over (particularly involving the hard and soft palate, or *palate* and *velum*).

The study of physiological phonetics is basic to an understanding of both normal and disordered speech. The human repertoire of speech sounds depends fundamentally upon the size and geometry of the vocal tract and the ways that the talker can modify that geometry. The kinds of sounds we make, the kinds of transitions we make between sounds, the combinations of sounds that are possible, and the kinds of sound changes that occur throughout the history of a language all are intimately tied to our vocal apparatus.

The speech sounds humans can make when they talk are determined to a large degree by the precise configuration and size of the vocal tract. While other primates (apes and monkeys) have quite similar vocal tracts to humans, their vocal tracts are not capable of making most of the sounds of human language (and would not be even if these animals possessed the cognitive abilities required for speech).

3.1.1 Body planes
Standard terms are used for different cross-sectional "slices" (planes) through the body, and these terms are used to help orient viewers when they look at an anatomical drawing.

These planes are:

- *coronal* (or frontal)
- *sagittal*, and
- *transverse* (or horizontal or axial).

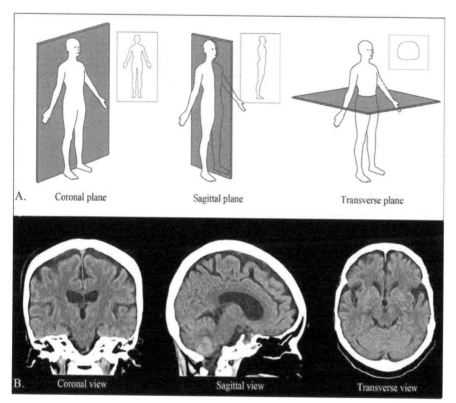

Figure 3.1 Body planes. **A.** The three body planes shown on drawings of the human body
B. The planes are shown as cross-sections of the head

A *midsagittal plane* is a sagittal plane precisely in the middle of the body.
    Figure 3.1 shows these planes on drawings of the human body, and also
these planes when cut through the head.

3.1.2   Overlaid function

It is traditional to say that speech is an *overlaid function.* That is, we have
no unique "speech organs," or anatomical structures not found in other
mammals. Lungs, throat, larynx, tongue, teeth, lips, and brain are all found
in other mammals; these structures all have more primary biological functions than speech, principally respiration and ingestion of nourishment. If
we were to take another mammal, for instance a dog, and compare our own
vocal tract with its, we would find exact analogs for almost every structure, every muscle, even down to the larynx itself. Yet a dog's vocal tract,
and those of other mammals, can produce a very limited range of sounds.
(Samuel Taylor Coleridge said, "Brute animals have the vowel sounds; man
only can utter consonants.")
    So, in one sense, speech has been "overlaid" on these organs through
evolutionary history. Indeed, vocalizations have been "overlaid" onto the
alimentary (food-consuming) and respiratory systems of many animals,

including birds, reptiles, amphibians, and mammals, and the details of vo-
calization-production are largely constant across terrestrial mammals, including humans. But in humans, evolution has resulted in adaptations that
permit a wide variety of sounds to be produced in rapid succession. These
adaptations involve the precise details of the anatomy of the structures, as
well as neurological and cognitive changes.

There has been much discussion in the scientific literature about the nature of the anatomical and physiological changes involved in the transition
from non-speaking human ancestors to modern humans who have speech
and language. To take one example, the human vocal tract has a sharp 90°
bend,[2] and that shape – as well as the shape of the tongue as it is affected
by the bend and the low placement of the human larynx – has important
implications for the kinds and the variety of speech sounds of which humans are capable. So, was the impetus for speech a major factor in the
development of the 90° bend, so the very form of our body was shaped by
speech? Or was the 90° a simple outcome of the change to a bipedal gait
(walking on two legs), and speech exploited changes that had developed
for other reasons?

Another part of the reasoning follows the line that certain characteristics
of our vocal tracts – ones exploited by speech – are maladaptive in other
ways. These include the narrowing of the respiratory tract at the larynx,
and the low placement of the latter, which increases the likelihood of chok-
ing. This line of reasoning suggests that, in human evolution, selection for
speech was a particularly powerful factor. There has also been strong argument against the notion of speech being maladaptive in other ways. See the
references listed under the authors Lieberman, Boë et al., and MacNeilage
for more on this fascinating topic.

3.2   The supraglottal organs

The *glottis* is the name given to the space between the *vocal folds.*[3]
Therefore, the *supraglottal* organs are those *above* (*supra*) the glottis. The
supraglottal organs and the vocal folds are the speech organs mentioned
most often throughout this book. Figure 3.2 gives a schematized cross-
section of the head, with the important articulatory organs identified.

---

[2] The "floor" of the mouth is almost exactly horizontal and the pharynx (throat) is almost
exactly vertical, making a 90° bend between the two. Very few mammals have such a
configuration, not even those primates who are most closely related to humans. Some
animals do, however: for instance, kangaroos.
[3] Commonly called the *vocal cords* or *vocal chords*, terms that are avoided in professional
terminology.

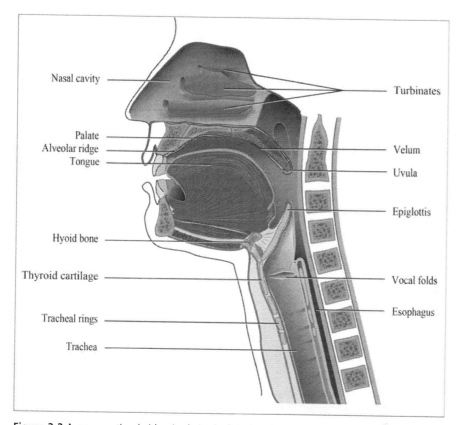

Figure 3.2 A cross-section (midsagittal view) of the head, showing some speech articulators and associated structures

3.2.1   Lips

The *lips* are used to close the oral cavity in the production of some consonants. They may be rounded and extended in the production of certain vowels. The adjective is *labial*; when both lips are involved, we speak of a *bilabial* ('two lips') sound.

3.2.2   Teeth

Sounds involving the **teeth** are referred to as **dental** sounds. The upper teeth are involved in speech production more often than the lower ones. As a place of articulation of speech sounds, it is usually the upper front teeth (the incisors) that are involved. But it is essential to note that the upper side teeth (molars and premolars) are used in speech production, as for

CLINICAL NOTE 3.1 Physical anomalies

In Section 3.2, the various anatomical structures important in speech production are listed and described. Anomalies in these structures, whether due to birth defect, disease, surgery, or injury, can affect speech production to minor or severe degrees. Clinical notes to this effect are not repeated alongside each of the structures. Several common physical anomalies affecting speech production are discussed in later chapters, where relevant to the subject of those chapters.

[t]; the tongue creates a seal along them, although such an articulation is not usually classified as dental.

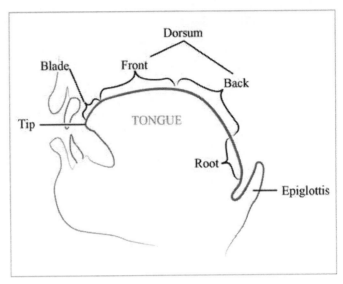

Figure 3.3 Divisions of the tongue surface

3.2.3 Tongue

The *tongue* is the most agile organ of speech, and, for that reason, the word *tongue* means 'language' in many languages. Many gestures of the tongue are used in speech, and the tongue contacts many of the other speech organs. The tongue is divided into five regions: the **tip** or **apex**, the

Table 3.1 Anatomical divisions of the tongue surface used for naming places of articulation		
Name of structure	Term for articulation	Combining form
tongue	lingual	linguo–
tip, apex	apical	apico–
blade	laminal	lamino–
dorsum	dorsal	dorso–
front	Generally, no term is used specifically for the *front* or *back* to the exclusion of the other; i.e., no term describes a *front* articulation that implies that the *back* is not involved. *Dorsal* (dorso–) may be used for both, and sometimes the phonological term **coronal** is used, but this term is not recommended as a phonetic term.	
back		
root	pharyngeal	pharyngo–

blade, the *dorsum* (which is divided into the *front* and the *back*), and the
root; these are indicated in Figure 3.3. The *apex* or *tip* is the very tip of
the tongue. The *blade* is a very short sec-
tion of the tongue surface, the part that
normally lies below the *alveolar ridge* at
rest. The *dorsum* is the large central part
of the surface of the tongue. It is divided
as follows: The *front* (despite its name) is
the middle portion of the oral surface of
the tongue, lying below the *palate* at rest.
The *back* is the rear portion of the oral
tongue surface, lying below the *velum* at
rest. The *root* is that part of the surface
of the tongue that faces into the *pharynx*
or throat cavity. The adjective for *tongue*
is **lingual**, for *tip* is **apical**, for *blade* is
laminal, and for *dorsum* is **dorsal**. Figure
3.3 shows these divisions and Table 3.1
summarizes this information.

3.2.4   Alveolar ridge
The *alveolar ridge*, also called the *gum
ridge*, is the bony ridge directly behind
the upper front teeth. The adjectival
form is *alveolar*. See Figure 3.4.

3.2.5   Palate
The *palate* is the hard, bony part of the
roof of the mouth that extends from the
alveolar ridge to the velum. The adjectival form is *palatal*. See Figure 3.4.

3.2.6   Velum
The *velum* is the soft, muscular rear part
of the roof of the mouth that lacks any
bony framework. It can be raised or lowered by its own musculature. This movement serves a valving function; when
the velum is *raised*, the nasal cavities
are closed off from the rest of the vocal
tract, as they are during oral breathing
or during swallowing. When the velum is

**SIDEBAR 3.2 (Hard) palate
and velum**

Anatomical terminology was originally developed for medical purposes,
not for phonetics. In phonetics, the
distinction between the bony part of
the roof of the mouth and the soft,
muscular part of the roof of the mouth
is a very important one because: (1)
speech sounds made on or near each
of the two places sound very different; and (2) the soft part can move
to create important phonetic distinctions where the hard part cannot
move relative to the skull. Anatomical terminology (for instance, in the
names for muscles) commonly uses
the term *palate* for both parts.

The two can be distinguished with
the terms *hard palate* and *soft palate*.
However, in phonetics, it is common
practice to use the term *palate* (adjective *palatal*) for the bony part and the
term *velum* (adjective *velar*) for the soft
muscular part. That is the terminology
that is used in this book, though occasionally we will use *hard palate* or *soft
palate* for additional clarity.

The term *muscular palate* can be
used for *soft palate* or *velum*, and
this uncommon term has the ad-
vantage of focusing on the central
distinguishing factor of this structure, compared to the (hard) palate.

(The term *velum* comes from the
Latin term *velum palati*, meaning
'veil of the [hard] palate.')

lowered, a passage – the **velopharyngeal port** – between the nasal cavities and the oropharyngeal (upper throat) cavity is open, as it is for nasal breathing; this introduces *nasal resonance* and thus imparts a nasal quality to speech sounds produced with a lowered velum.

Given its great importance in the production of speech, the *velopharyngeal port* is treated in its own section below (Section 3.3), after the present listing of structures.

As with the *alveolar ridge* and *palate*, we use the *velum* as a reference point in describing what position the *tongue* is assuming. If the tongue is arched below the velum, or is touching the velum, we call this a **velar** articulation. On the other hand, when the velum itself moves, performing the valving function just described, we speak of a **velic** movement or articulation. Be sure to distinguish *velar* (referring to the part of the oral cavity below the velum) from *velic* (referring to the velum itself).

Note that the *uvula* attaches to the rear edge of the velum. Do not confuse the small uvula with the velum itself; the latter makes up about two-fifths of the roof of the mouth and stretches from side to side of the oral cavity. The uvula plays a role in the articulation of some sounds in some languages, although English has no **uvular** sounds. See Figure 3.4.

There is more detail about the functioning of the velum in Section 3.3.

3.2.7   Uvula

The **uvula** is a small piece of tissue that droops into the oral and pharyngeal arca from the posterior end of the velum. While the palate and velum cross the oral cavity from side to side, the uvula is centrally located. It has sometimes been described as looking like a small punching bag.

A uvular sound is one that is made with the uvula itself, such as one type of trilled r-sound ([ʀ]), or it is made with the back of the tongue raised close to or touching the uvula.

See Figure 3.5.

3.2.8   Oral cavity

The **oral cavity** (Latin *os/oralis*, 'mouth'/'oral') is a resonating chamber of primary importance to speech, since its size and shape can be modified so greatly. Its internal volume can be changed by modification of the tongue and jaw positions. The oral cavity is visible in Figures 3.6 and 3.7.

3.2.9   Nasal cavities

The **nasal cavities** (Latin *nasus*, 'nose') are cavities within the skull, located behind the nose. They form part of a continuous passageway from the pharynx (throat cavity) to the nostrils. (As we will see, this passageway can be closed or opened.) See Figure 3.6.

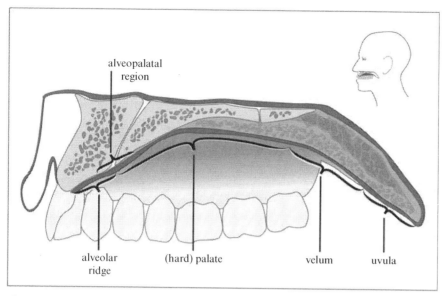

Figure 3.4 The palate and surrounding structures

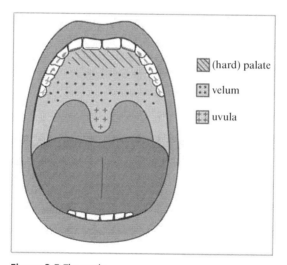

Figure 3.5 The uvula

In phonetics textbooks, the **nasal cavity** is generally shown in lateral (sagittal) cross-section. In such a view, it appears to be a large, open chamber that should have a rich resonance. However, a frontal (coronal) cross section would show that each side of the cavity contains three curled scroll-like membranes called **turbinates**, which swirl the air in the cavities, presumably to increase olfactory (smell) sensitivity and to warm and humidify cold air before it gets to the lungs, as well as filtering out some particles from the air. These structures partially fill the nasal cavity and cut up the remaining space into small passageways. This is of considerable importance phonetically because the nasal cavities, far from being a large, open resonator, in fact form a poor resonator. Notice how muffled nasal consonants sound, and note that they cannot be shouted very effectively.

Velic action (that is, movement of the velum) allows the nasal cavities to be closed or open (or partially open) with respect to the rest of the vocal tract (see also Section 3.3). Opening this passageway allows sound waves to enter the nasal cavities, giving a distinctive nasal quality to the speech sounds thus produced.

3.2.10   Pharynx

The *pharynx* is the cavity above the larynx and behind the oral cavity. In everyday language, we might refer to it as the "throat cavity," or simply the "throat." For precision in making phonetic descriptions, the pharynx can be divided into three parts:

1. the *laryngopharynx*, which is the lowest part of the *pharyngeal* cavity, or pharynx, just above the *larynx*;
2. the *oropharynx*, which is the mid part of the pharyngeal cavity at the very back of the mouth; and
3. the *nasopharynx*, which includes the nasal vestibule (the entrance to the nasal cavities – which is to say, the "entrance" from the pharynx or throat into the back of the nasal cavities).

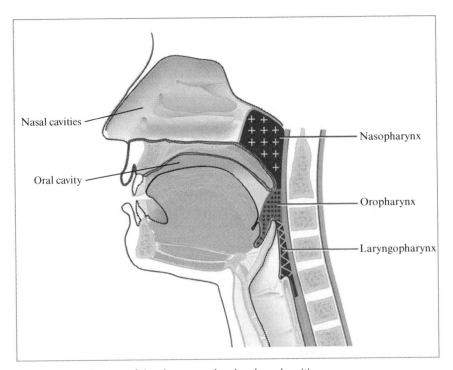

Figure 3.6 The divisions of the pharynx, and oral and nasal cavities

The pharynx is the critical area in which the food passageway and the air passageway cross and are common for a distance. See Figure 3.7. Air is normally inhaled through the nose, enters the back of the pharynx through the velopharyngeal port, and passes through the larynx on its way to the lungs at the *front* of the laryngopharynx. Food enters the *front* of the oropharynx during swallowing and passes through the *back* of the laryngopharynx, where it enters the **esophagus** (Greek. *aesophagos*, 'eating food'), the passage leading to the stomach.

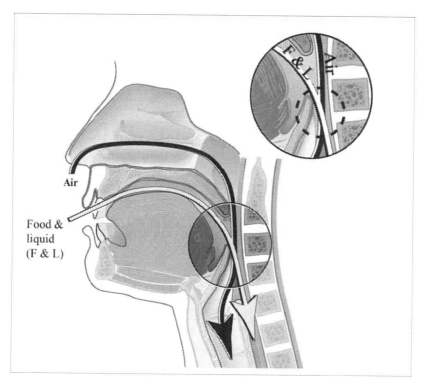

Figure 3.7 The airway crosses the passageway for food and liquid

3.2.11   Trachea

The **trachea** is the air tube that leads from the larynx to where it splits into two **bronchi,** which connect to the **lungs.** It is made up of cartilaginous rings, interconnected with connective tissue; it is generally pictured as looking rather like a vacuum-cleaner hose. We will examine it further in Section 3.5.

3.2.12   Esophagus

The **esophagus** (Figures 3.2 and 3.6) is the tube leading from the lower pharynx to the stomach, permitting food or liquid that is swallowed to pass to the rest of the digestive tract. The esophagus is not used to produce normal speech, but does play a role in speech produced by some individuals (Chapter 9).

3.3   The velopharyngeal passage/port (VPP)

As we have seen above, the nasopharynx is connected to the oropharynx through a passageway that can be opened or shut. This passageway is called the **velopharyngeal port** or **velopharyngeal passage** (abbreviated *VPP*). When the passageway is open, air and sound can flow between the oropharynx and the nasal cavities; when it is closed, the nasal cavities are isolated from the rest of the upper airway. The VPP may also be partially open, which allows a restricted amount of air, and sound of reduced volume, to flow between the areas.

This valving function makes critical phonetic distinctions; many sounds require the passageway to be closed. Various disorders can lead to problems with this valving function, and the consequences for speech can be serious, in some cases rendering speech unintelligible to most hearers (see Clinical Note 3.2).

Most land mammals have this function as well, so the importance of the VPP to speech is recent in human evolution – the VPP function serves important biological needs. The VPP must be closed during swallowing to prevent food from being forced into the nasal passages rather than down the esophagus (and likewise during vomiting). If it is closed during respiration, then air passes through the oral cavity. See Figure 3.8.

CLINICAL NOTE 3.2
Velopharyngeal passage (VPP)

As we will see in subsequent chapters (including Section 8.8), the ability to close the VPP is essential for the production of many consonants. A number of conditions can lead to an inability to close this passageway, and the effects upon the production of intelligible speech can be very great, decreasing the intelligibility of speech to a great degree.

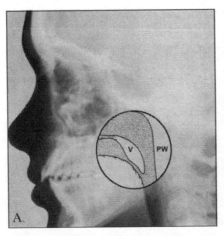
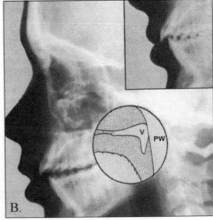

Figure 3.8 Velopharyngeal port, open (A) and closed (B). "V" stands for velum and "PW" for pharyngeal wall. (Images modified from original in order to face left)

The action of the VPP is usually shown in sagittal (lateral) cross-sections, and it is easy to assume that opening and shutting the VPP is simply a matter of raising and lowering the velum. However, the process is more complex than that, and some of these complexities are significant in terms of the production of normal-sounding speech. There are considerable differences among individuals in the exact geometry and contribution of the various gestures, but the following list shows additional aspects of the closing action:

- Notice in Figure 3.8 that not only is the velum raised and lowered, but its shape changes, partly through the action of internal muscles and partly by being pressed against the posterior pharyngeal wall.
- Not seen in a view such as Figure 3.8 is the fact that there is a pair of muscles that can stretch the velum side-to-side, making it wider and creating a more complete air seal of the VPP.
- The walls of the upper pharynx that surround the velum act as a sphincter that closes around or "squeezes" the velum to assure closure.
- Not shown in the individual whose X-ray is displayed in this illustration is the frequent presence of a "bump" of varying size on the posterior pharyngeal wall that also aids in closure of the passage. This structure is called *Passavant's Ridge*.

3.4   The larynx

The *larynx* is a complex cartilaginous structure situated at the upper end of the trachea, below the pharynx. Popularly called the "voice box," it is fundamental for both speech and more basic biological functions. It is so basic to speech because it contains the **vocal folds**, which vibrate, producing a tone necessary for the production of most – and the distinction between many – speech sounds.

In terms of basic biology, the larynx serves several functions. The vocal folds and the *epiglottis* ('on top of the glottis'), internal parts of the larynx, serve to prevent intrusion of food or liquid into the airway during swallowing. If a foreign substance does enter the windpipe, a coughing reflex is triggered that involves the vocal folds. During muscular exertion of the arms and torso, the vocal folds shut tightly, trapping air in the lungs. This keeps the lungs inflated, so that the *thoracic cage* (the rib cage) remains a stable base for the arms to press against while exerting force on other objects. To demonstrate that this is so, try to talk while lifting or pushing something close to your limit of strength, and note how your vocal folds involuntarily close.

The larynx is made up of five cartilages (Figure 3.9). These are the *epiglottis* (which serves relatively little function in speech), the *thyroid* cartilage, the **cricoid cartilage** (which is in effect the topmost cartilage of the trachea), and the two *arytenoid cartilages.*

Locate the larynx in your own neck. The thyroid cartilage faces frontward. Most commonly in men, part of this cartilage (the "Adam's apple") protrudes conspicuously at the front of the neck. Of course, the same cartilage exists in the same place in women and children, but it is generally smaller than in men and the angle formed by its two faces is flatter, so the larynx does not typically protrude as much on the surface as it does in adult men, though there is a great deal of individual variation.

Once you have located the thyroid cartilage, locate the V-shaped notch in the front of it. This is a handy reference point for locating other structures. (Because of the relative size of this cartilage in men and women, and because of differences in the typical distribution of subcutaneous fat, women often have more difficulty than men in locating this notch.) Above the notch, you should be able to palpate (locate by feel) the **hyoid bone**, pictured in Figures 3.9 and 3.2. The hyoid bone, the only bone in the human body not contiguous with any other bone, is attached to the thyroid cartilage by the latter's *superior horns* and by a membrane (descriptively called the *thyrohyoid membrane*) that fills the space between the bone and the cartilage. Below the thyroid cartilage, you should be able to palpate the *tracheal cartilages* and the *cricoid cartilage*, although it may be hard to tell for certain that you have located the latter. Look at Figure 3.9 when feeling for these structures, and try locating them on a friend if you have no success on yourself.

From the phonetician's viewpoint, the laryngeal cartilages are interesting to the extent that they serve to support the *vocal folds*[4] and associated speech muscles (Figure 3.9). The vocal folds are two bands of tissue, made up of muscle and ligament, that serve as a variable valve for air passing into and out of the lungs. The roughly triangular space between the vocal folds is called the *glottis*. When the vocal folds are **adducted** (see Sidebar 3.3) the glottis disappears; like the hole in a doughnut, it is nothing in itself, but is defined by what surrounds it.

The vocal folds attach at the front to the inside of the thyroid cartilage below the V notch. This point of attachment is

SIDEBAR 3.3 Adduction and abduction

To **adduct** the vocal folds is to bring them together, or close them through muscular force. This process is called *adduction.*

To **abduct** the vocal folds is to separate them, or open them through muscular force. This process is called *abduction.*

---

[4] The *vocal folds* are sometimes called the *vocal cords, vocal chords,* or *vocal bands.* These terms suggest, falsely, that they are situated like the strings of a musical instrument. The term *vocal folds* is currently the most usual term.

the apex of the triangular glottis. The rear ends of the vocal folds attach one to each arytenoid cartilage. The arytenoid cartilages sit on the upper edge of the cricoid cartilage; they both slide and pivot, and in doing so they bring the rear ends of the vocal folds together or apart. The vocal folds form the edge of a membrane that stretches from the vocal folds to the cricoid cartilage at the sides and back and to the thyroid cartilage at the front. This so-called **conus elasticus** ('elastic cone') ensures that air can pass only *between* the vocal folds (through the glottis). (See Figure 3.10.)

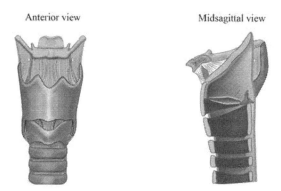

Figure 3.9 The larynx and the laryngeal cartilages

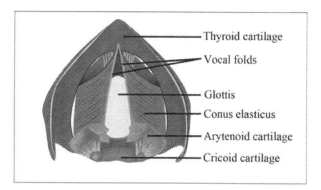

Figure 3.10 The conus elasticus and the vocal folds as seen from above

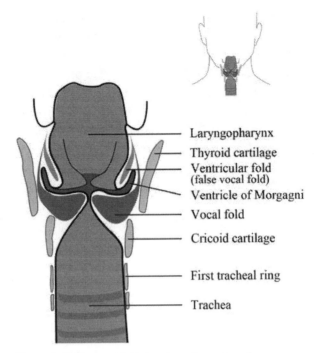

Laryngopharynx
Thyroid cartilage
Ventricular fold
(false vocal fold)
Ventricle of Morgagni
Vocal fold
Cricoid cartilage
First tracheal ring
Trachea

Figure 3.11 The vocal folds in schematic cross-section

The vocal folds are seen in cross section in Figure 3.11. Note that above them is another pair of folds of soft tissue, called the *false vocal folds* or *ventricular folds*. These are separated by a pair of *ventricles* (anatomical terminology for a 'chamber' or 'cavity') called the **ventricles of Morgagni**. These ventricles are shown in a darker color in Figure 3.11, between the ventricular fold and the vocal fold.

3.5 Phonation

The production of many – but not all – speech sounds requires that the vocal folds vibrate. This vibration is known as **phonation** or **voicing**. The vocal folds make other linguistically significant articulations, and these are sometimes lumped together under the term *phonation* as well.

For our purposes here, a quick overview of phonation or voicing will suffice. In Chapter 8, these topics will be examined in considerable detail. Sections 4.7 and 4.8 examine aerodynamic forces in phonation.

The *vocal folds* (**vf, vfs**) vibrate in speech through an aerodynamic process. That means that they don't vibrate through multiple muscle contractions and relaxations. Rather, air flowing over the vocal folds makes them vibrate, rather like a flag flapping in the wind. We understand intuitively that the energy that makes the flag flap does not come from the flag, which is an inanimate object. Rather, the energy is contained in the movement of the air, and that movement (wind) causes the flag to move back and forth in a particular way that we call flapping.

To create the situation where the vfs vibrate, they must take a particular configuration and there must be a particular force of air rising through the trachea. This involves placing the vfs lightly together with a force of air from below that balances, in a very particular way, the forces holding the vocal folds together.

As we will see in Chapter 8, the vfs can be made to vibrate in different ways, called different *modes of vibration.* Think of a breathy or a husky voice quality to get an idea of different modes of vibration. These differences can signal meaning differences in some languages.

Adult female and male voices typically have different rates of vibration. The rate of vibration is called the **frequency,** and the normal frequency of the voice is called the **fundamental frequency** (F_0 – called "F-zero"). Frequency is measured in **hertz (Hz),** which is the number of times per second that a cycle of vibration occurs. Adult males have fundamental frequencies in the range of 85 Hz to 180 Hz. Adult females have fundamental frequencies in the range of 165 Hz to 255 Hz (Baken, 1987; Titze and Martin, 1998).

In speech, phonation is rapidly switched on and off. This is accomplished through minute contractions of muscles internal to the larynx that alternately permit and disable vocal fold vibration.

3.6   Respiration

Phonation and other aspects of speech production depend upon a moving column of air – or static air pressure – produced by the respiratory system; it is to this system that we will now turn our attention. What follows is necessarily a simplified view, but one that will outline the essentials.

The *trachea* (windpipe) descends into the chest cavity from the larynx. It is held open by cartilaginous rings, as already noted. The trachea branches into two primary bronchi, one leading to each lung. The bronchi further subdivide into smaller and smaller tubes until they reach the *alveolar sacs.* These are the small chambers in the lungs where gases are exchanged between the air and blood.[5] For purposes of describing speech physiology, we often consider the lungs to be empty bags or balloons; this can be a useful analogy, but it is important to remember that the vital function of the lungs is carried out in thousands of tiny alveolar sacs having a combined surface

---

[5] Principally, the blood releases carbon dioxide into the air and absorbs oxygen from the air.

area of about 70 square meters (750 square feet). This makes the lungs more like sponges than like empty bags.

Each lung is encased in a membrane called the *visceral pleura*. Another membrane, called the *parietal pleura*, lines the two halves of the *thorax* (chest cavity). These two pleural membranes are in contact, with a very small amount of fluid filling any space between them (the *pleural cavity*). As the space inside the thorax increases through movements of the rib cage or diaphragm, the parietal pleura moves with the thorax. The visceral pleura follows, although it is not directly attached, through the action of air pressure and surface tension and the inflow of air into the lungs to balance atmospheric air pressure with that inside the lungs. Puncturing the pleural lining will allow the lungs to "collapse" since it destroys the linkage between the two pleurae. A "collapsed lung" is a life-threatening condition in which the visceral pleura and parietal pleura are separated by an air space, which means that increasing and decreasing the size of the thorax does not cause the expansion and contraction of the lungs, so air is not drawn in or pushed out.

The thorax is bounded by the *rib cage* and the *diaphragm*. The rib cage comprises the *vertebral column* (popularly, but not very accurately, called the "spine" or "spinal column"), the *ribs*, and the *sternum* (the "breast bone") (Figure 3.12). The ribs are all attached at the vertebral column, and all but the lower two are attached to the sternum (upper sets directly, lower sets indirectly through a common large cartilage, and finally the "floating" ribs). The ribs are joined to the vertebral column and to the sternum so as to permit limited movement. Thus, the sternum can rise and fall (relative to a standing posture) with respect to the vertebral column. This rise and fall has the effect of increasing and decreasing, respectively, the volume or space within the thorax (Figure 3.12).

3.6.1 The muscles of respiration

The *diaphragm* is a muscular wall separating the thoracic cavity from the **abdominal cavity**. It, too, plays a role in respiration, as shown in Figure 3.12, since a downward movement of the diaphragm has the effect of enlarging the space within the thoracic cavity. While popular belief has the diaphragm as *the* muscle of respiration, in fact many muscles besides the diaphragm are involved in breathing.

The muscles of respiration therefore include the diaphragm and the muscles that control the rib cage, which are many in number. The most important of the latter are the *intercostal muscles* (*intercostal* means 'between the ribs') (Figure 3.13).[6] There are essentially two layers of intercostals, with fibers that run at approximate right angles to one another. Descriptively,

---

[6] These are the muscles that make up the meat of spareribs or "ribs."

the outer layer is called the **external intercostals**, and the inner layer the *internal intercostals*. It is only a small oversimplification to say that the external intercostals serve to elevate the sternum for inhalation and that the internal intercostals serve to lower the sternum in exhalation. The mechanism[7] of thoracic breathing is shown in Figure 3.13.

Other muscles can change the thoracic capacity as well. Muscles of the back, neck, and abdomen may play a role in breathing, though there is some controversy as to whether certain muscles whose position may suggest their having a role in respiration do in fact actually play that role. While we will not enumerate them all here, two such groups of *accessory*

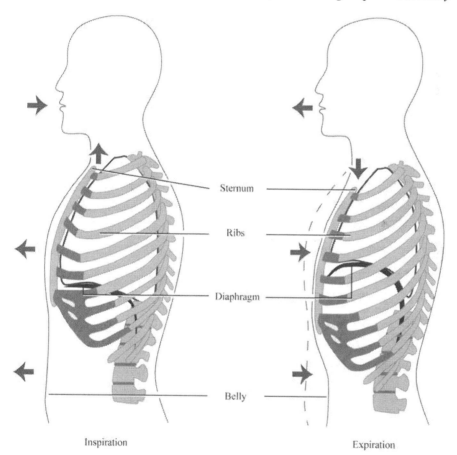

Inspiration   Expiration

Figure 3.12 The thorax in inspiration and expiration. In inspiration, the internal volume of the thorax is increased, and in expiration, its internal volume is decreased. The volume is essentially the space inside the ribs, above the diaphragm and below the collar bones. The internal volume can be increased either by raising of the sternum or by lowering of the diaphragm (which divides the thoracic and abdominal cavities). The internal volume may be decreased by the chest being flattened somewhat, and/or by the abdominal contents pushing up against the lower thoracic area.

---

[7] Mechanism: the process by which something occurs.

respiratory muscles should be mentioned. Certain muscles of the neck, notably the *scalene muscles*, serve to elevate the ribs in inhalation. Certain abdominal muscles serve to pull in the abdomen; abdominal contents thus press against and thereby elevate the diaphragm in exhalation.

3.6.2   The mechanism of respiration

In review, elevating the sternum and/or lowering the diaphragm serves to increase thoracic capacity. Conversely, lowering the sternum or raising the diaphragm serves to decrease thoracic capacity.

However, strictly muscular forces are not the only forces at work in respiration. The elasticity of the tissues involved is also a major factor, as the body tissues, when stretched, tend to *recoil* or return to their resting size, just as a stretched elastic band does. The lungs inflated by inhalation can be likened to a toy balloon or an air mattress. Their walls are stretched when inflated. A release of the neck of a balloon results in a rapid deflation without the application of additional forces; you do not need to squeeze the air out of a balloon. The deflation of the lungs when full to capacity, if all muscles were relaxed, would not be as dramatic as that of a toy balloon, but the effect would be similar in that the lungs would partially deflate.

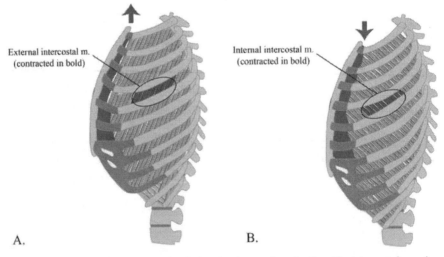

External intercostal m.
(contracted in bold)

Internal intercostal m.
(contracted in bold)

A.

B.

Figure 3.13 The intercostal muscles in inspiration and expiration. The intercostal muscles run between the ribs, essentially in two layers: the internal and external intercostal muscles. The external intercostals have fibers running in the direction of those in the detail in A, i.e., from higher at the spinal (back) end to lower at the sternal (chest) end. The internal intercostals lie beneath at approximately right angles to the externals and have fibers running in the direction of those detailed in B, i.e., high at the sternal end and low at the spinal end. **A. Inspiration.** The external intercostals contract to raise the sternum (detail). **B. Expiration.** The internal intercostals contract to pull the sternum down (detail). In fact, as noted in the text, contraction of the internal intercostals occurs only in maximum expiration. In normal, shallower respiration, it is the external intercostals that act in expiration to slow down the elastic recoil of the lungs.

For both speech and quiet breathing, exhaling by simply relaxing all muscles and to have the air rush out would not be efficient. A force must be applied that will slow down the deflation of the lungs that is brought about by elastic recoil. It is easy to see that the same muscles used to *inflate* the lungs would, if kept contracted, *keep the lungs inflated.* If these muscles were *relaxed slowly*, the lungs would *deflate slowly.* This is in fact what happens. So, in the initial stage of *exhalation*, it is the muscles of *inhalation* that do the work. Indeed, in quiet respiration, the muscles of inhalation (primarily the external intercostals) do all of the work; the expiratory muscles are at rest. On the other hand, in rapid deep breathing, both inspiratory and expiratory muscles are involved.

Another dimension comes into play in speech. The analogy we used of a toy balloon is not useful here, since a balloon more or less *completely* deflates by itself. We will therefore look at an air mattress for comparison. When the plug is first pulled from an inflated air mattress, the air comes out rapidly. The air flow becomes slower and slower, however, and eventually a point of equilibrium is reached at which the air mattress is far from empty of air, but no more air flows out spontaneously. It is then necessary to force the rest of the air out by rolling up the mattress or lying on it.

In a similar way, the fully inflated lungs will deflate spontaneously to a certain volume, the **functional residual capacity**; air pressure and speed of flow out of the lungs will become less and less as this point is neared. When the functional residual capacity is reached, there is still a considerable amount of air in the lungs. Much of this air can be expelled by the action of the expiratory muscles, but there will always remain a small amount of air, the **residual volume**, which cannot be expelled.

In speech, air is drawn into the lungs rather more quickly than in quiet breathing, so as not to interrupt the flow of conversation any more than necessary. Initially speech is produced with the airflow controlled by the **inspiratory** muscles. As the functional residual capacity is reached, **expiratory** muscles may start to play a role in maintaining the necessary air pressure. If one continues to speak after the functional residual capacity is reached, more and more expiratory muscles come into play. In normal conversation, people do not continue talking much beyond the functional residual capacity; rather, they take a fresh lungful of air, usually at a point corresponding to a grammatical or logical break. However, people may continue nonstop when reciting poetry or the lines of a play, singing, arguing emotionally and trying to avoid a pause that would let the opponent break in, or saying a long sentence that has no convenient grammatical break. In regard to this last point, there is evidence that, when talking, we plan our breaths ahead, so that we are rarely caught in the position of having reached the functional residual capacity without an appropriate grammatical break at which to draw air.

The needs of speech modify the respiratory cycle in more than one way. Talking does not require a simple constant subglottal pressure. Rather, the pressure required to maintain phonation at the speech volume we desire varies with syllable structure, stress, emphasis, and other phonetic factors. Therefore, the muscles controlling the air pressure within the lungs are making constant minute adjustments during speech.

3.7   Muscles and muscle names

In preparation for an examination of some important muscles of speech articulation, let us look at some general features of muscles and conventions for naming them.

3.7.1   Terms and conventions

When writing the names of muscles, the word *muscle* should be written (that is, *mylohyoid muscle*, not the *mylohyoid*), but it is common to abbreviate the word "muscle" as *m.* (the period is usually included in the abbreviation). It might not be considered correct to write the name of the muscle without either the word *muscle* or *m.* because the names of some muscles are also the names of other structures.

The ends of muscles are referred to as the **origin** and the **insertion**. The *origin* is the end that is more fixed, which does not move or which moves less than the insertion when the muscle contracts. The *insertion* is the end that moves or that moves a greater distance when the muscle contracts. See Figure 3.14 panel C. There are a number of speech muscles that do not fit neatly into the origin–insertion pattern.

3.7.2   Muscles pull; they don't push

A muscle is capable of exerting a force only by *contracting*, thus by *pulling forcibly in one direction only*. **Muscles do not push.** If a muscle connects points *x* and *y*, it is capable of drawing *x* and *y* closer together or of resisting some other force that would draw *x* and *y* apart – nothing more. Once the muscle in question has drawn *x* and *y* closer together, some other force must draw them apart. Normally this other force is another muscle or group of muscles that serve to pull in the opposite direction (Figure 3.15), although tissue elasticity, aerodynamic forces (in speech), or even gravity may provide the opposing force.

3.7.3   Muscles maintain the same volume whether relaxed or contracted

Imagine a toy balloon filled with water. For our purposes, it is not a round balloon, but one that is longer in one dimension. Now gently press the ends toward the middle. What happens? The balloon gets shorter in the direction you are pressing, but it gets bigger around.

Water cannot be compressed.[8] Therefore, the volume of the water-filled balloon must always stay the same. If one dimension is made smaller, then another dimension or dimensions increase to compensate. The same is true of muscles. Like most body tissues, they contain a large component of water and cannot be compressed. Therefore, when a muscle contracts it becomes shorter but larger in diameter. The example of this that we are most familiar with is when a body-builder shows off their biceps muscles. When the arm is flexed, the biceps muscle becomes shorter, but it bulges outward (i.e., its diameter increases). When the arm is straightened again, the biceps becomes longer and not so big in diameter. (See also Figure 3.15.)

3.7.3.1   Muscles can "push" at the sides
While the primary function of a muscle is to pull its two ends closer together when contracted, as noted in Section 3.7.2, there is an indirect way that muscles can push a little bit at right angles to their fibers. This is because of the fact that the volume of a muscle remains constant, whether the muscle is relaxed or contracted. Since a muscle becomes shorter when contracted, its diameter (thickness) must increase proportionally.

Look at panel C in Figure 3.14. This shows that, as the muscle contracts and its ends move closer together, the center of the muscle bulges, pushing slightly around its sides at approximately 90° (right angles) to the direction of the muscle's fibers. As we will see, this effect of bulging at right angles to the axis of the muscle plays an important role in some speech muscles, most particularly in the way the tongue changes shape. There is no muscle that pulls the tongue wider side-to-side, but pulling the tongue thinner from top to bottom causes its sides to bulge out, making the tongue wider (Section 3.8.4).

3.7.4   Drawings of muscles can help you to infer their action
Muscles are made up of many individual muscle fibers.[9] Muscle fibers have an elongated shape. When they contract, they become shorter and their circumference increases as the muscle tissue "bunches up." The overall muscle

---

[8] In fact, water is very, very slightly compressible. However, compressing water requires enormous pressures to make even the slightest change in volume. In the context of humans talking and using muscles, it is accurate to consider that no compression of water is possible.

[9] There are several hundred thousand muscle fibers in the biceps, for example – a similar number in body builders as in "ordinary" people.

can contract (i.e. shorten and pull) in the direction of the long axis of the individual muscle fibers. Refer back to Figure 3.14.

In typical anatomical drawings, the alignment of muscle fibers is shown by lines or striations; these can be seen in Figure 3.14C and Figure 3.15. The direction of pull is parallel to these lines. When looking at an anatomical drawing such as Figure 3.15, it should be possible for you to examine the orientation of the striation lines and infer the direction in which the muscle can pull.

As noted above, the ends of a muscle are called the *origin* and the *insertion*, depending upon the degree to which each end is fixed or movable. However, particularly with a number of important speech muscles, the reality can be much more complex and less binary. The structure that moves when the muscle that connects them contracts depends on what other forces are acting on the two structures and how movable each of them is.

A.   B.   C.

Figure 3.14 Muscle fibers. Part A shows the typical elongated form of muscle fibers. **Part B** shows the same muscle fibers in contraction. Notice that when the muscle contracts, it does so along the orientation of the muscle fibers. **Part C.** In anatomical drawings, muscles are typically shown with lines or striations along the long axis of the muscle fibers. The muscle is relaxed in panel A of the drawing and contracted in panel B. In panel C, **O** and **I** mark the **origin** end and the **insertion** end, respectively; note that the origin end typically does not move when the muscle is contracted, but the insertion end does. Also note that the sides of the muscle bulge outward on contraction so that the muscle maintains the same overall volume whether contracted or relaxed.

One more thing about the way muscles are depicted in some of the drawings below (especially the ones that show little anatomical detail). We sometimes use pairs of arrows pointing toward one another, as follows

→   ←

These pairs of arrows mean that the muscle contracts, pulling everything along the length of the arrows closer together. An arrow pointing in a single direction means a pull in that direction.

3.7.5   Muscle nomenclature

The names of muscles may appear at first to be long and complicated and impossible to remember. However, the naming conventions for muscles generally follow a few patterns, and understanding these patterns means that muscle names will make sense. Whether you are required to remember muscle names or not, it would be helpful to attempt to see the sense in the names. Things that make sense are much easier to remember, but it also

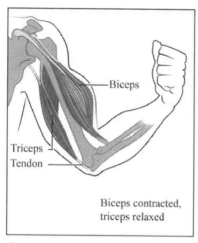
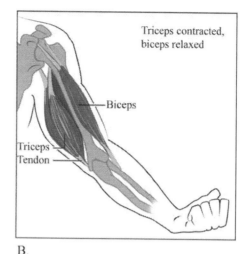

Figure 3.15 Muscles: two important facts
1. Muscles pull, they don't push. To flex the arm, the biceps pulls (A). To straighten the arm, the triceps pulls (B). As a muscle pulls, it becomes shorter, and therefore it bulges. Neither muscle can push. Many skeletal muscles come in pairs (one agonist, one antagonist) such as this. But, as we will see, some speech muscles have a more complex pattern.
2. In anatomical drawings of muscles, striations show the direction of the muscle fibers. This is the direction in which the muscle can shorten, so a glance at an anatomical drawing should provide a strong indication of the direction in which a muscle can generate a force.

helps to understand the overall functioning of the "machine" that generates the sounds of speech. In addition, one of the common naming conventions tells you where the muscle is located (and, conversely, if you know where the muscle is located, you have a good chance of guessing, or at least recognizing, its name). The anatomical names found in the next few sections are shown in drawings later in the chapter.

As a starting point for making sense of the names of muscles, it is a good idea to determine the meaning of terms that may not be obvious, but which are found in a number of muscle names. For instance,

- *gloss, glossus* refer to the tongue;
- *genio-* refers to the chin (typically the inside of the mandible at the chin);
- *palat-, palato-* refer to the palate, but in anatomical terminology, that includes the velum;
- *stylo-* refers to the *styloid process*, a small portion of the skull that protrudes downward below the ear canal;[10] and

---

[10] The styloid process is labeled in Figures 3.17 and 3.22. It can also be seen in Figure 3.24, where its position on the skull is more clearly visible. The styloid process is the sharply pointed small process posterior to the mandible (jaw) and below and slightly anterior to the opening for the ear canal.

- *hyo-* refers to the hyoid bone.
- In anatomical names, *superior* means 'above' or 'at the top,' and *inferior* means 'below' or 'at the bottom.' *Anterior* means the 'front' or 'in front of,' and *posterior* means 'at the back' or 'behind.'

Where a particular Latin term is used in only one or two anatomical terms, it may not be worth remembering it, but sometimes these terms can be decoded in a way that helps with remembering them. See Section 3.7.5.4.

3.7.5.1 Muscles are named for their origin and insertion
Many muscle names are a combination of the name of the origin and that of the insertion, with the origin first, followed by the insertion.

- The *genioglossus muscle* runs between the inside of the chin and the body of the tongue.
- The *palatoglossus muscle* runs between the palate (in this case, at the edge of the bony palate) and the body of the tongue.
- The **sternohyoid muscle** runs between the sternum (breastbone) and the hyoid bone.

3.7.5.2 Muscles are named for their function and/or position
Many muscles have names that describe their function and/or their relative position.

- The *superior pharyngeal constrictor muscle*, the **middle pharyngeal constrictor muscle**, and the **inferior pharyngeal constrictor muscle** are all constrictors of the pharynx that are in different positions along the length of the pharynx; constrictors squeeze the pharynx, making it smaller in diameter.

3.7.5.3 Muscles are named in a way that describes their location and orientation

- The *superior longitudinal tongue muscle* runs lengthwise (longitudinally) along the length of the tongue, near to its upper surface.
- The *transverse tongue muscle* crosses the tongue in the transverse direction, i.e. from side to side.

3.7.5.4 Some word association can help make muscle names more memorable
Few – if any – readers of this book will know much Latin, or even want to know Latin. However, many anatomical names are based on Latin words, and the meaning can sometimes be inferred by knowledge of similar words in English, Spanish, French, or other languages that at least some readers

may have some familiarity with. If the names make sense, they're easier to keep straight.

- The *risorius muscle* pulls up the corners of the mouth into a smile. The *ris-* part of the name suggests forms of the Spanish and French words meaning 'to laugh.' This muscle contracts when you smile or laugh.
- The *buccinator muscle* is located at the corner of the mouth. The *buc-* part of the name suggests the Spanish and French words for mouth (*boca, bouche*).
- The *orbicularis oris muscle* surrounds the mouth, making up much of the body of the lips. The first part of the first word looks a lot like the English word *orbit*, and indeed the *orbicularis oris* "orbits" (circles around) the mouth. And *oris* is another form of the word *oral*, which refers to the mouth.

3.8   A selection of important muscles and gestures in speech articulation

Let us turn our attention now to the muscles of articulation. The complex actions of speech production are made up of individual muscle movements. A look at individual speech muscles will help with understanding how speech articulation functions normally, and how it is affected by various disorders and abnormalities. Once again, remember that this discussion is simplified and that the technical vocabulary used by anatomists has been kept to a minimum; only major muscles are shown.

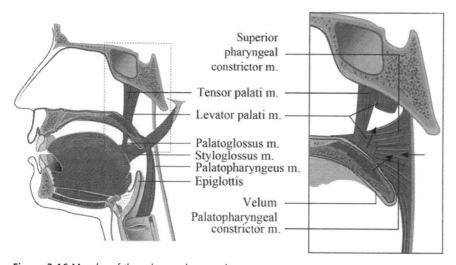

Superior pharyngeal constrictor m.
Tensor palati m.
Levator palati m.
Palatoglossus m.
Styloglossus m.
Palatopharyngeus m.
Epiglottis
Velum
Palatopharyngeal constrictor m.

Figure 3.16 Muscles of the velum and upper pharynx

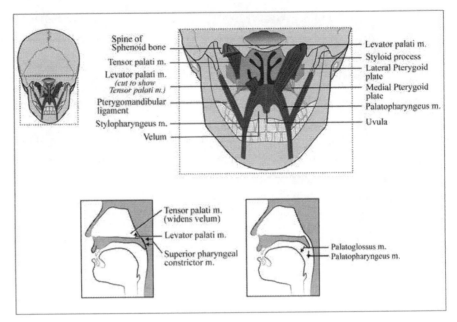

Figure 3.17 Posterior view of muscles of the velum

3.8.1   Muscles of the velum and the velopharyngeal port: nasal versus non-nasal

First, a note on terminology, as a couple of the muscles each has two common forms of their names. The following names on each line are equivalent:

Tensor palati muscle = Tensor veli palatini muscle
Levator palati muscle = Levator veli palatini muscle

We will use the shorter forms, but the longer forms are also in common use.

The *velum* can be used, in combination with other surrounding structures, to open and close the *velopharyngeal port*, as we saw in Sections 3.2.6 and 3.3. How does this function at a muscular level?

Closing the velopharyngeal passage.

As shown in Figures 3.16 and 3.17, the **levator palati muscle** raises the velum. The **tensor palati muscle** stretches the velum wider so that it closes along its edges as well as at the posterior end. The **superior pharyngeal constrictor muscle** and the **palatopharyngeal sphincter muscle** pull the velum closer to the posterior pharyngeal wall. Not shown in the drawings, a muscle in the uvula may contract to change the shape of the back of the velum to enhance closure.

Opening the velopharyngeal passage.

The muscles in the previous paragraph relax. The **palatoglossus** and **palatopharyngeus** muscles pull in a downward direction on the velum.

3.8.2   Muscles of the tongue

The tongue's primary biological function is in mastication, the chewing of food. The tongue pushes the food around so that it comes between the molar teeth in chewing, and then it plays a role in directing food toward the back of the mouth for swallowing, and in swallowing itself.

To perform these functions, and also for speech articulation, the tongue must be able to change shape and to move around within the oral cavity (and even to project beyond the mouth to lick the lips). While these two functions (changing shape and moving within the oral cavity) are often intertwined and performed simultaneously, and cannot be fully separated, in large measure different sets of muscles control the two.

The tongue itself is almost entirely made up of muscle tissue, the only other large amount of tissue being the mucosa – the outer surface tissue of the tongue found within the mouth.

There are muscles that make up the tongue body itself, collectively called the *intrinsic tongue muscles*, and those muscles that connect the tongue to outside structures, collectively called the *extrinsic tongue muscles*. The intrinsic muscles are largely responsible for the shape of the tongue, and the extrinsic muscles for the position of the tongue relative to surrounding structures, primarily the mandible (lower jaw).

Keeping this distinction in mind will help you to understand the functioning of tongue muscles described and illustrated in several of the following sections.

3.8.3   Tongue shape – arched and raised tip

Initially in this section, we are addressing the shape of the tongue as seen in a sagittal view (i.e., from the side) rather than in a coronal view (from the front). Two major tongue forms are used in speech: arched and tip raised. If you say a k-sound, you will note that the tip of the tongue is low but the tongue dorsum is raised. The position is slightly different, but the same is true when you say an ee-sound ([i]). This configuration, with the tongue dorsum the highest point on the tongue, is an *arched configuration.* If you say a t-sound, d-sound, n-sound and some others, the tip of the tongue is the highest point

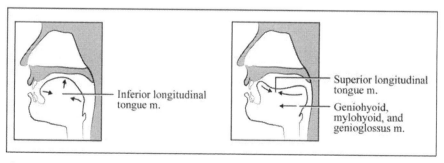

Figure 3.18 Action of intrinsic tongue muscles

and the tip is pointed somewhat upwards. We will call this the *tip-raised configuration*. These two configurations are basic to a very large portion of individual speech sounds. These configurations are shown in Figure 3.18.

As can be seen in Figure 3.19B, there are two large muscles that run the length of the tongue, back to front, with their fibers likewise oriented back to front. These intrinsic tongue muscles are the **superior longitudinal tongue muscle** and the **inferior longitudinal tongue muscle**. Remember that a muscle can contract – get shorter – in the direction of its fibers. So if both these muscles are contracted at the same time, the tip of the tongue will be drawn backwards into the mouth. But if one of these is contracted, but not the other, the tongue will change shape.

Figure 3.19A shows a folded piece of paper held flat between the palms of two hands. If the top part is drawn backward (as if it were shortened), then the front of the sheet is drawn upwards in the tip-raised configuration. On the other hand, if the bottom fold of the sheet is drawn backward (as if it were shortened), then the upper surface of the sheet takes on an arched configuration. The sagittal and coronal cross-sections of the tongue in Figure 3.19 show the location of the superior and inferior longitudinal tongue muscles.

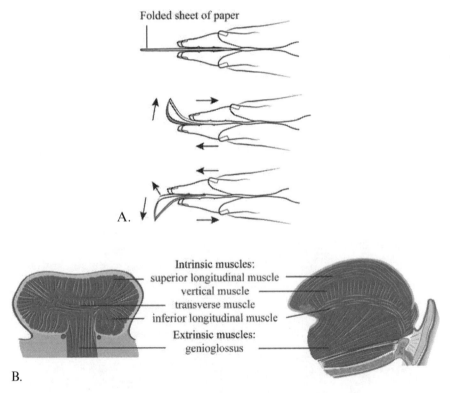

Figure 3.19 A. Tip-raising and arching demonstrated with a piece of folded paper
B. Intrinsic tongue muscles, including the superior and inferior longitudinal tongue muscles, as well as the genioglossus muscle

3.8.4 Narrowing and widening the tongue

If you place your tongue in position to say an l-sound ([l]) and, instead of saying the l-sound, you blow air out of your mouth while holding your tongue in position for the l-sound, you'll observe that your tongue has been *narrowed* so that air can flow by both sides.

If you say "to to to" ([tu tu tu]) and pay attention to the position of the sides of the tongue while you say the t-sounds, you will notice that the sides of the tongue are pressed against the upper molar teeth. The tongue is *widened* in order to make a seal along the sides.

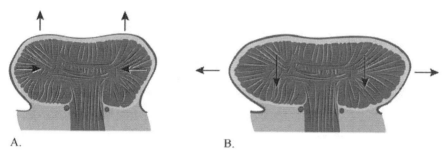

A.   B.

Figure 3.20 Changing the shape of the tongue in coronal cross-section. A. The **transverse tongue muscle** has been contracted, making the tongue narrower side-to-side to make a sound such as [l]. The tongue is thicker top-to-bottom as a consequence. B. The vertical tongue muscle has been contracted, making the tongue thinner top-to-bottom. That makes the sides bulge out – the tongue is wider in cross-section – and the sides may reach the molar teeth to make a seal against them as in the pronunciation of a [t] or [d] sound.

These gestures are illustrated in outline in Figure 3.20. In Section 3.7.3, we saw how a muscle, when squeezed in one direction will bulge in another direction. With the exception of its external layer, the tongue is entirely muscle, and it reacts the same to being compressed in one direction: it expands in another.

Observe the orientation and extent of the **transverse tongue muscle** and the **vertical tongue muscle** in the coronal section of Figure 3.19. Both of these are intrinsic tongue muscles. If the *transverse tongue muscle* contracts, the tongue will become narrower for sounds like the l-sound mentioned above. The tongue will also become thicker top-to-bottom, but this is not particularly relevant to this articulation.

If the *vertical tongue muscle* is contracted, the tongue will become thinner top-to-bottom, but it will become wider as its edges are squeezed out to the sides. This is the gesture needed for the t-sound mentioned above.

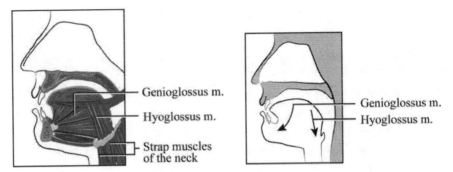

Figure 3.21 Lowering the tongue body

3.8.5   Lowering the tongue

The tongue needs to be lowered within the oral cavity for low vowels (this may be combined with lowering the jaw slightly as we shall see in Section 3.8.8). The *vertical tongue muscle* (Figure 3.20) can pull the tongue surface down (making the tongue wider). While intrinsic muscles will also control the shape of the tongue surface, extrinsic muscles will exert a downward pull on the tongue body. The **genioglossus muscle** pulls down and forward on the tongue while the **hyoglossus muscle** pulls down and slightly backward on the tongue. A balance of forces between these two muscles will pull downwards without significant movement forward or backward. See Figure 3.21. Not illustrated in Figure 3.21 is a *pharyngeal constrictor muscle* that may help to counter the forward pull of the genioglossus muscle so that the tongue lowers without moving forward.

3.8.6   Raising the back of the tongue

Raising the back of the tongue may be done with or without arching of the tongue. The back of the tongue can be arched using the *inferior longitudinal tongue muscle* as described previously.

To raise the back of the tongue without arching the center portion, there are a number of extrinsic tongue muscles that insert into the tongue and that originate in the skull: the posterior end of the hard palate for the **palatoglossus muscle** and the **styloid process**[11] of the skull for the **styloglossus muscle**. The position of the base of the tongue is influenced fundamentally by the position of the hyoid bone, so upward movement of the hyoid bone can serve to help raise the back of the tongue. See Figure 3.22.

---

[11] In anatomy, a process on a bone or a cartilage is a part that protrudes. The styloid process, whose name comes from the same root as stylus, is indeed very pointed. It is situated on the skull below the ear canal.

The blade and tip of the tongue are raised as described in Section 3.8.3. The back of the tongue does not need to be high for the tip to be high. For instance, the l-sound requires the tongue tip to be raised. The l-sound in the word *lock* is produced with the back of the tongue relatively low, but the l-sound in *Luke* is produced with the back of the tongue relatively high.

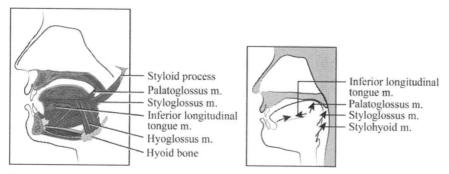

Figure 3.22 Raising the back of the tongue

3.8.7   Lip-rounding and lip-spreading

Some speech sounds such as the vowel "ee" ([i]) require spreading the corners of the mouth more widely. Others such as the vowel "oo" ([u]) or the r-sound require the lips to be rounded. Sounds in many languages require more rounding than these English sounds.

The muscles responsible for these articulations belong to a group known as the *muscles of facial expression*. These muscles share the characteristic of not being attached to any bone or cartilage; their origin and insertion are situated very shallowly under the skin.

The bulk of the lips is made up of muscle tissue, collectively called the *orbicularis oris muscle*. The reality is that this is a group of muscles that function independently, not as a single entity, but the single label is convenient. Additionally, some facial muscles at the corners of the mouth intertwine with the *orbicularis oris*, but again, labeling them separately is convenient.

Contraction of the *orbicularis oris muscle* rounds and purses the lips.

There are two principal paired muscles that are located at the corners of the mouth that, when contracted, pull back (and in the case of one slightly upward) on the corners of the mouth. These are the *risorius muscle* and the *buccinator muscle* (whose names were commented on above) and they serve to spread the lips. They also function in this capacity in smiling and laughing. See Figure 3.23.

3.8.8   Mandible (lower jaw) raising and lowering

The *mandible* (lower jaw) does not change its degree of opening very much during speech, but if you observe people talking, you will notice that there

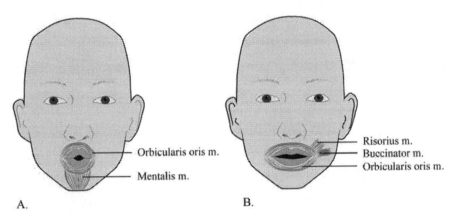

Orbicularis oris m.

Mentalis m.

Risorius m.
Buccinator m.
Orbicularis oris m.

A.

B.

Figure 3.23 Muscles of facial expression in speech articulation. A. The *orbicularis oris muscle*, possibly with the aid of the *mentalis muscle*, helps to round and extend the lips. **B.** The *risorius muscle* in combination with the *buccinator muscle* pulls back the corners of the mouth to produce sounds having a spread configuration of the lips.

is usually some movement. The primary biological function of movement of the mandible up and down is for mastication (chewing) of food, and closure for swallowing. The mastication of food into smaller bits and mixing them with saliva starts the digestion process and allows more complete extraction of nutrients than in animals that swallow food whole.

In order to successfully chew tough food, the muscles that raise the mandible are very powerful, much more powerful than required for speech. Additionally, there are a number of movements that can be invoked for chewing, such as protruding the mandible and moving it side to side, that are not relevant to typical speech production. (These movements can be seen clearly in animals, such as cattle, that eat a diet of highly fibrous vegetation.)

The joint between the mandible and the *temporal bone* of the skull is a complex one that allows the kind of movements mentioned in the previous paragraph. This is the *temporomandibular joint* (the *TMJ*). Within the joint itself are a couple of muscles, the *lateral* and the *medial pterygoid muscles*. Their functions are quite complex in elevating and moving the mandible and these will not be described here.

Primary elevators of the mandible (closing the mouth) are the *temporalis muscle* and the *masseter muscle*. Depressing the mandible requires much less force in chewing, and the muscles responsible require a complex pattern of contraction in order to accomplish the task. Muscles of mandibular depression (opening the mouth) include the *digastric muscle* (particularly its anterior belly), *mylohyoid muscle, geniohyoid muscle, genioglossus muscle*, and the *lateral pterygoid muscle*. Some authors include the *platysma muscle*. See Figure 3.24 for a view of some of these muscles.

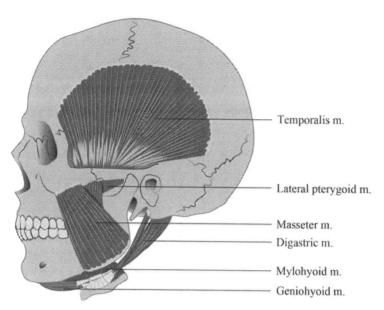

Figure 3.24 Some mandibular muscles

3.9   Vocabulary

abdominal cavity
abduction, to abduct
adduction, to adduct
alveolar ridge
anatomy
apex (tongue)
apical
arched configuration
arytenoid cartilages
back (tongue)
bilabial
blade (tongue)
body planes
bronchus, bronchi
buccinator muscle
conus elasticus
cricoid cartilage
dental
diaphragm
digastric muscle
dorsal
dorsum (tongue)

epiglottis
esophagus
expiration, expiratory
F_0 (fundamental frequency)
false vocal folds
frequency
front (tongue)
frontal (coronal) plane
functional residual capacity
fundamental frequency (F_0)
genioglossus muscle
geniohyoid muscle
glottis
hertz, Hz
hyoglossus muscle
hyoid bone
inferior longitudinal tongue muscle
inferior pharyngeal constrictor muscle
insertion
inspiration, inspiratory
intercostal muscles, internal, external
labial

laminal
laryngopharynx
larynx
levator palati (levator veli palatini)
    muscle
lingual
lips
lungs
mandible
masseter muscle
mentalis muscle
middle pharyngeal constrictor
    muscle
mode of vibration
muscle
muscle fiber
muscles of facial expression
mylohyoid muscle
nasal cavity
nasopharynx
oral cavity
orbicularis oris muscle
origin
oropharynx
overlaid function
palate, hard, soft
palatoglossus muscle
palatopharyngeal constrictor muscle
parietal pleura
pharyngeal
pharynx
phonation
physiology
platysma muscle
pleural cavity
process (on bone or cartilage)
pterygoid muscle (lateral, medial)
recoil (elastic recoil)
residual capacity
respiration
rib
rib cage

risorius muscle
root (tongue)
sagittal plane
sternohyoid muscle
sternum
styloglossus muscle
stylohyoid muscle
styloid process
superior horn (thyroid cartilage)
superior longitudinal tongue muscle
superior pharyngeal constrictor
    muscle
supraglottal
teeth
temporalis muscle
temporomandibular joint (TMJ)
tensor palati (tensor veli palatini)
    muscle
thorax, thoracic cage
thyrohyoid membrane
thyroid cartilage
tongue (tip, blade, front, back,
    dorsum, root)
tongue muscles: intrinsic, extrinsic
trachea
tracheal cartilages
tracheal rings
transverse (horizontal) plane
transverse tongue muscle
turbinates
uvula
uvular
velar
velic
velopharyngeal port/passage (VPP)
velum
ventricles of Morgagni
ventricular folds
vertical tongue muscle
visceral pleura
vocal folds (vf, vfs)
voicing

4 Air Pressure and Aerodynamics

4.1 Speech production requires a movement of air

The production of speech involves a flow of air, whether for vowels or consonants, whether speech is whispered, spoken in a normal voice, or shouted.

The production of consonants often involves modifying the flow of air, building up and releasing air pressure (thereby creating a small explosion), reducing and releasing air pressure (creating a small *implosion*), forcing air through a small opening (generating noise), or some combination of these. For certain kinds of speech sounds, the speech articulator is moved by the flowing air, not by the muscles. So it is useful to review the principles that govern the behavior of pressure and moving air in order to understand better how the medium of air is involved in the production of all types of speech sounds.

4.2 Air fills all spaces

Evangelista Torricelli (1608–47) showed great insight when he stated, "We live at the bottom of an ocean of air." That ocean of air covers the entire surface of the earth. Close to sea level, air has a particular pressure, and the farther one goes upward, the less and less air pressure there is.

Because the air around us is under pressure, it spreads out evenly and enters and fills all cavities and spaces to which it has access. See Figure 4.1. The only time a cavity or space is not filled is when that space is separated from the surrounding *atmosphere* and there is no passageway for air to flow into it.

The vocal tract is filled with air at all times. When air flows out of the lungs and up through the bronchi and trachea, through the larynx and out through the pharyngeal, oral and nasal cavities, the air from the lungs *displaces* air that is *already in those locations*. So it is not correct to say that air "enters" the airway from the lungs as if it were entering an empty space; air already fills the airway. It is accurate to say that air flows through the airway and that "newly arrived" molecules of air displace the "old" molecules of air that were already there. See Figure 4.2.

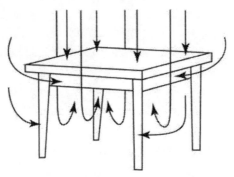

Figure 4.1 Air pressure is exerted in all directions. There is as much pressure on the bottom and sides of a table as there is on the top surface. That is why this table is not crushed by the 23,247 kg or 51,250 pounds of force (equivalent to 3 of the largest bull elephants) pressing down on the top of the table. (This number is based on the table having dimensions of 1.5 meters by 1.5 meters (giving a surface area of 2.25 sq. meters). This is explained further in Section 4.3.3.)

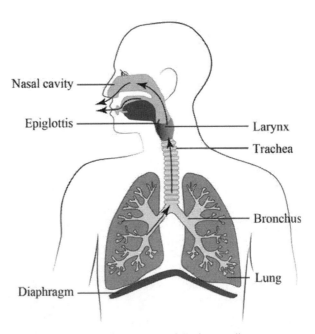

Figure 4.2 All air passageways are full of air at all times.

4.3 Air pressure

The air that surrounds us is under pressure. It is squeezed like a sponge that you grip tightly with your hand. If that pressure were released, the air would greatly expand in volume, just as releasing that sponge would cause it to expand. What causes air to be under pressure?

4.3.1   Gravity creates air pressure

There is air all around the earth – an "ocean" of air in Torricelli's observation. What keeps it there, and squeezes it against the surface of the earth? It is the force of gravity, the force that causes matter to be attracted to other matter. The mass of the earth is immense, so the earth exerts a great gravitational pull on matter around it. That is why a dropped ball falls to the earth, and that is why a great mass of air sticks to the earth's surface, and why the air near the surface of the earth is under considerable pressure, being *pulled down* by gravity and *pushed down* under the weight of the "ocean" of air above it that is likewise pulled by gravity.

The higher one rises off the surface of the earth (for example, by climbing a mountain or traveling to a place of higher altitude), the lower the pressure is. The force of gravity diminishes with distance from the earth and, higher up, there is a smaller "pile" of air above us than there is on the surface of the earth.

4.3.1.1   Temperature, a variable we can largely ignore with speech

If air in a confined space is heated, its pressure increases. Since our topic is the production of speech, we can safely ignore the effects of temperature on air pressure in the rest of this discussion.

4.3.2   Measures of air pressure

Normal air pressure at sea level in SI or metric units (see Sidebar 4.1) is 101.325 kilopascals (kPa), which can also be expressed as 101,325 pascals (Pa).[1] This pressure can also be expressed as 1013.25 millibars, a metric (but not an SI) unit.

In the United States customary system of measures (USCS), normal sea-level air pressure can be expressed as 29.92 inches of mercury (inHg) or 14.696 pounds per square inch (psi) or lbs/in². See Table 4.1.

The US customary / Imperial unit *pounds per square inch (psi)* makes very clear the fact that air pressure exerts a force (in pounds) on a surface. You can think of a pile of 15 one-pound packages

> **SIDEBAR 4.1 Not all metric units are SI units**
>
> A *metric* unit is one having steps that are multiples of 10.
>
> Most of the world uses a metric system of measures that is usually called "the metric system" in English-speaking countries. More correctly, this is the *Système international*, abbreviated as **SI**, or the *International System of Units*.
>
> The pressure units pascal (Pa), kilopascal (kPa), micropascal (μPa), etc., are SI units, part of "the metric system."
>
> The pressure units *bars, millibars*, and so on are metric units (based on multiples of 10) but are not SI units.

---

[1] In the metric system, the prefix *kilo-* means that the unit is multiplied by 1,000. That is why 101,325 pascals equals 101.325 *kilopascals*.

Table 4.1 Normal air pressure at sea level: standard units

	All the values in the table show exactly the same pressure. These examples illustrate different units and systems of measure			
	SI units	Metric units, not SI	United States customary units / Imperial	Generic units (not tied to a system of measures)
Normal air pressure at sea level	101.325 kPa (kilopascals) 101,325 Pa (pascals)	1013.25 mbar (millibars)	29.92 inHg (inches of mercury) 14.696 psi (pounds per square inch)	1 atm (atmosphere)

of butter or margarine stacked on top of a piece of wood that is 1 inch by 1 inch, and that lets you get a good sense of the pressure involved.[2] Similarly, the unit *inches of mercury (inHg)* states explicitly that air pressure will support a column of mercury of a certain height.[3]

In the SI system, the units *pascal (Pa)*[4] and *kilopascal (kPa)* – thousands of pascals – refer to the same concept as US units, but they don't explicitly state that a surface receives pressure in terms that can be easily imagined.[5] While the book will generally use metric units, as befits a work of science, metric units of pressure don't have the "feel" of pounds per square inch; it is hard to imagine how much a pascal or a kilopascal is. It is good to remember that pascals represent a certain force on a certain area, just like psi (pounds per square inch), even though the SI unit isn't as explicit about what it represents.

4.3.3   At the bottom of the ocean of air …

A fact about the air pressure on the surface of the earth under this ocean of air is that air presses not only down, but sideways and, because air is a gas (a fluid as conceived by physicists), upwards and in all conceivable directions (as shown in Figure 4.1). This is a surprise to many, but it is essential to the functioning of a great many everyday events.

---

[2] For readers who use the metric system routinely, think of 6.7 kg on top of a block of wood measuring 2.54 cm x 2.54 cm. Or: 1.03 kg resting on 1 cm². This produces a better mental picture than pascals.

[3] Mercury is a dangerous substance, so don't try this at home!

[4] In the metric system, units such as *pascal* that are named for people are written with a lower-case letter, but abbreviations such as *Pa* (which means *pascal*) have an upper-case or capital letter.

[5] Technically, the unit *pascal* is a derived unit. That is, like *miles per hour*, it is made up of other units. Ultimately, it is defined in terms of a unit of force, the *newton*, just as *pounds per square inch* involves *pounds* as a unit of force.

A quick calculation will reveal that the air pressure on the surface of a table 1.5 meters by 1.5 meters (about 4 feet 10 inches square) is 23,247 kg[6] or 51,250 pounds[7] (more than 3 very large bull elephants)! It seems that the table would be crushed flat in an instant. And if you thought about the equivalent pressure on your body, it is hard not to imagine that the breath – and the life – would be squeezed out of you in an instant.

The reason that neither the table nor we ourselves are crushed by air pressure – despite the enormous forces involved – is that air pressure operates equally and simultaneously in all directions. Tons of pressure pressing upward from underneath the table equals and counteracts the tons of pressure bearing downward on the upper surface of the table, and thus the table is not flattened onto the floor. Just as air pressure presses inward on our torso, there is the pressure of air within the lungs pressing *outward*, equalizing the *inward* force and preventing our chest from being squashed flat.

On the Internet, it is easy to find videos of people experimenting with air pressure. In one common scenario, a large oil drum has the air pumped out of it and the drum suddenly and violently implodes (see Sidebar 4.2). What this demonstrates is that normal air pressure exerts a huge force on objects, and it is only the fact that air pressure presses in all directions that saves those objects from being crushed – that is, an oil drum is not normally crushed by air pressure because there is equal air pressure inside, pushing back out. Removing or reducing the air inside allows the tremendous pressure on the outside of the drum to crush it.

Keep this fact in mind when considering how air and air pressure behave in the production of speech, and then in the workings of the ear.

SIDEBAR 4.2 Video demonstrations of normal air pressure, in which a metal drum implodes violently

In most of these experiments, the drum is filled with steam, sealed, and then cooled. When cooled, the steam turns back into water, which has a tiny fraction of the volume of the gaseous steam. Cooling the drum full of steam effectively evacuates most of the gas in the drum, creating not a perfect vacuum, but a greatly diminished air pressure in the drum. Normal air pressure outside the drum is then free to crush it, which it does suddenly and violently, making a dramatic demonstration of the enormity of air pressure on the surface of the earth. Don't try this at home.

---

[6] A kilogram (kg) is not a unit of force the way the pound is. However, if we agree that we are making the comparison on the surface of earth with normal earth gravity, and if we understand that we are taking liberties with SI units, this example makes the point that a simple dining table takes an enormous pressure of air on its surface.

[7] This is calculated in US/Imperial units by making the conversion of units, finding the surface area of the table in square inches (it is very close to 3100 sq. in.) and multiplying by 14.7 pounds per square inch.

4.4   Air pressure equalizes itself

Molecules of air – like any kind of gas – distribute themselves so that they are all about the same distance apart from one another on average. Greater pressure means that molecules are squeezed closer together and lower pressure means that molecules are farther apart. Therefore, if all the molecules are approximately the same distance apart, then the pressure is equal everywhere.

If, for any reason, air pressure is greater in one place (molecules squeezed closer together), then molecules will move (pushed by the force of higher pressure) to areas of lower pressure until equilibrium is reached. The flow of molecules is very rapid.

4.4.1   Air pressure is equalized except …

As noted, air fills the space that contains it so that the molecules are spaced evenly – the pressure equalizes so that pressure is the same everywhere. This statement is true as far as it goes. But the air around us does not have the same pressure everywhere, for a number of reasons.

The following explanations do not change anything for a person speaking at a given moment in a given place. However, they are intended to help you understand how air behaves, and thus how it behaves in the production of speech.

4.4.1.1   Altitude

Air at different altitudes has different pressures. The air pressure in Denver is considerably less than the air pressure in New York City.[8] The air pressure outside your window when you're sitting at home is very different from the air pressure outside your window if you are in an airplane flying at 35,000 feet (10,668 meters).

The reason is that the air on the surface of the earth has a very tall "pile" of air on top of it. The higher one goes, the less that is true – there is a taller "pile" of air above your head in New York than in Denver. The higher the pile of bricks on a scale, the heavier the weight shown by the scale, and the same goes for air. Additionally, the atmosphere (air) stays on the surface of the earth because the force of gravity holds it there. The force of gravity becomes less and less as the distance from the earth increases. Air pressure in Denver is less than in New York City, and it is even less at an altitude of 35,000 feet, a common altitude for commercial jets to fly. Average air pressure in New York City is 101.3 kPa or 14.7

---

[8] The average elevation of New York City is a little above sea level; that of Denver is in the range of 5,400 feet or 1,650 meters, slightly more than a mile or 1.65 kilometers.

psi; in Denver it is 84 kPa or 12.2 psi. Outside your airplane window at 35,000 feet, the air pressure is 23.9 kPa or 3.46 psi (insufficient to maintain life).

Differences of pressure due to altitude are not important in relation to the production of speech sounds.

4.4.1.2   Weather

A very large component of weather has to do with differences in air pressure covering large areas of the earth's surface. Winds are a manifestation of air pressure equalization: winds are air pressure equalizing – that is, air molecules traveling from areas of higher pressure to areas of lower pressure.

Why do large areas of the surface of the earth have different air pressure than neighboring areas? Why doesn't the pressure equalize and stay equalized? This is not a book on meteorology, so let us simply note that one major factor is temperature. As air is heated, directly or indirectly, by the sun, the molecules move farther apart and the air becomes less dense, so pressure lowers. Because the warm air is lighter, it rises, and other air moves in to fill the gap and equalize pressure. That movement of air is what we call *wind*.

Differences of pressure due to weather are not important in relation to the production of speech sounds, of course, except if you are trying to make your voice heard above the noise of a strong windstorm. However, the principle of air moving from an area of high pressure to one of low pressure is basic to speech.

4.4.1.3   Disturbances of a local nature

Air pressure varies locally because of local disturbances. These local disturbances are like objects dropping into water, causing waves or ripples on the surface. As a door swings closed, it causes a rise in pressure on the side that it is moving toward, and a reduction in pressure on the side it is moving away from; normally the pressure quickly equalizes on the two sides of the door. As a truck hurtles down the highway, air pressure in front of it is greatly increased and air pressure behind it is greatly reduced.

Air pressure can also be increased when a lot of air is squeezed into a small space. The air in a balloon is under higher pressure: the air in it is squeezed into a smaller space because air was pushed in at a higher than normal pressure, acting against the elastic walls of the balloon itself. When you pump up a bike tire with a hand pump, the pump is designed so that when you push the handle down, you are making the space that contains a quantity of air smaller: same number of air molecules forced into a smaller space makes the air pressure higher. And that higher pressure will flow toward an area of lower pressure in order to equalize the pressure. In this instance, it flows into the bike tire because you have deliberately made the air inside the pump have higher pressure than the air in the tire.

4.4.1.4   Respiration and speech

Respiration and speech create local variations in air pressure. In certain cases, speech sounds involve creating sufficient air pressure differences for an audible pop to be created when the air pressure is permitted to equalize. As we examine the production of speech sounds, paying attention to the differences in pressure at different points in the vocal tract will help greatly in understanding the processes and movements involved in speech production.

4.5   Airflow from higher to lower pressure

Air molecules flow naturally from areas of high pressure to areas of low pressure, just as water naturally flows downhill. The area of higher pressure has more potential energy than the area of lower pressure, so it impels air molecules toward the low-pressure area.

An example of a powerful flow of air is the standard vacuum cleaner. The motor and fan inside the power unit of the cleaner constantly and rapidly lower the air pressure inside the machine's canister. The only way the pressure can equalize is for air to flow in from the surrounding atmosphere through the nozzle and into the hose. That creates a powerful wind that blows dust and dirt particles, hair, or – in the case of wet–dry shop vacuums – water into the canister.

4.5.1   Two common misconceptions
4.5.1.1   Suction

The low-pressure area is often said to "suck" air or objects toward it and we certainly speak of suction in relation to vacuum cleaners. While this terminology creates a mental image that helps us to see what is happening in a practical sense, it actually misleads us as to what is truly going on in

---

SIDEBAR 4.3 Compress and rarefy

The word *compress* is familiar to most of us. When a certain amount of air is made to occupy a smaller space, it is *compressed*, and the result is *compression*.

When the opposite occurs, i.e., a certain amount of air is moved to a larger space, it is *rarefied*. To *rarefy* is to reduce the pressure and the density of a gas. The process is called *rarefaction*.

a deeper sense. A low-pressure area is not like gravity; it does not act from afar to "attract" air or dust toward it.

We can see how absurd this is if we think of the ultimate low-pressure area: a complete vacuum, an area that contains absolutely nothing. If you say that the vacuum "sucks" objects toward it, you are saying that the absolute absence of anything is capable of doing work: attracting objects from a distance. The absence of anything – material, energy, *anything* – can't do work; there is nothing there to *do* any work. On the other hand, if there is an area of higher pressure nearby, that pressure *is* something and it *can* do work – the work of pushing.

The fact is that the area of higher pressure *pushes* air toward the lower pressure area; air that is under pressure has the power to do work. As the air is pushed along, small, light objects are carried along with it. If the **airflow** is fast and strong enough (as in a hurricane), big heavy objects are carried along with the wind.

Once again, vacuum cleaners aren't speech producers, but the principles involved in air movement are equally present. Applied to human respiration and its role in speech, the lungs don't suck air in when we inhale; rather, muscles act on the lungs, causing them to expand, causing a lowered air pressure inside them. So air is *pushed into* the lungs through the mouth and nose by the air around the person now that the air pressure inside the lungs has been reduced.

4.5.1.2   Vacuum

A vacuum is an area in which there is absolutely nothing. But we often use the word, imprecisely, to mean an area of lower pressure. For instance, the cleaning device is called a *vacuum* cleaner, even though there is nothing remotely approaching a vacuum inside the machine. (If there were a real vacuum inside the cleaner, its canister would be crushed flat in a millisecond by air pressure.) While this is common usage of the word *vacuum*, we need to be careful that we are not led into believing that what we casually call a "vacuum" truly is a vacuum. We're not saying that the everyday sense of the word *vacuum* ought to be avoided,[9] but we are saying that to understand how speech production works, you need a better grasp of the concepts.

The term "partial vacuum" is commonly used in conversation for an area of moderately low pressure. The word *partial* prevents this term

---

[9] This is an example of the fact that the technical meaning of a word is different from the everyday meaning. Both meanings are fine in their place, but it is important not to confuse the two.

from being outright wrong (though still usually exaggerated) and, because "partial vacuum" is a familiar expression, we will use this phrase in a non-technical way to refer to spaces in which the air pressure is considerably lower than normal air pressure. For instance, when you smack your lips (making a sound that is called a *click* in phonetic terminology), you reduce the air pressure inside the mouth (i.e., you rarefy the air in your mouth), and then you release the blockage at the lips so the higher pressure outside the mouth pushes air into the mouth[10] rapidly and noisily. We could say that you make a "partial vacuum" in your mouth, and then release it. In a more technically accurate turn of phrase, however, we would say that you reduce pressure in the mouth, or you rarefy the air in your mouth, then release it so that the higher pressure outside suddenly (and noisily) pushes air into the mouth to equalize the pressure.

4.5.2   Two types of airflow: laminar and turbulent

As air moves from one area to another, it can do so in different ways. Air can move smoothly, so that the molecules do not collide very much, and so that the movement of all of the individual molecules is in as direct a line as possible from starting point to ending point. Such a flow is called *laminar*, and it creates very little noise.

On the other hand, air can flow in such a way that there are many collisions among the molecules, and many of the molecules are moving in directions that do not get them from start to finish in the most direct way; sometimes they are moving at right angles to a path that would get them to their destination, sometimes they are moving in the opposite direction. Such a flow is called *turbulent*. One of the characteristics of turbulent flow is that it generates noise; turbulent airflow is *noisy* airflow. This fact is exploited in the production of some types of speech sound.

In simple terms, turbulence is created by two important factors: speed and change of direction (and change of direction can be caused by air being forced through a small opening, for example). The faster airflow is, the more likely it is to be turbulent (and therefore noisy), and slower airflow is less noisy than rapid airflow. When flowing air is forced to change direction, its flow is likely to become turbulent, and the more abrupt the change of direction (and the faster the flow), the more turbulent and noisy the flow. Pronounce an s-sound and think about the airflow passing through a narrow slit and then hitting the back of the upper incisors and having to change direction abruptly.

---

[10] You would have said "sucked into the mouth" until you had read the preceding section.

4.5.2.1   A water analogy

In comparing laminar to turbulent airflow, think about different rivers or different places on a river you have seen. Imagine a place where the river is quite wide, relatively straight, and with smooth banks on both sides having nothing protruding into the flow of the river. The flow of the water at this point will be relatively *laminar*. Note that the flow of water does not create much noise.

Where the river goes through rapids, where it is narrow and rocky, and where the water goes down a steep slope,[11] the water moves more randomly; it has swirls and eddies; it changes direction often and irregularly; the flow makes a lot of noise. This is *turbulent* flow.

4.6   Local air pressure disturbances in the production of speech

4.6.1   Flow in and out of the lungs

Airflow out of the lungs supports the production of a majority of speech sounds. (As we will see in Chapter 9, other parts of the vocal tract can generate air pressures and air movement, but the majority of sounds of the world's languages are supported by air from the lungs.)

Airflow into the lungs (breathing in) is an *ingressive* airflow, and airflow out of the lungs is an *egressive* airflow; when the lungs are the motivator of air movement, we refer to the airstream as being *pulmonic*. Most speech occurs on an *egressive pulmonic* airflow, though speech on an ingressive pulmonic airflow may occur in some exceptional circumstances.

Air flows *into* the lungs when the muscles of inspiration (Chapter 3) increase the space inside the *thoracic cage* (chest). This increase in volume of the thorax pulls the lungs along with it, and therefore the lungs expand. The result is that there is greater space inside the lungs. The same number of air molecules in a space that is now larger means that the air pressure inside the lungs becomes lower, or slightly rarefied. As long as the upper airway is not blocked (vocal folds are open and at least one of the mouth and the velopharyngeal port is open), then air will flow from the area of higher pressure (outside the body) to the area of lower pressure (inside the lungs) until the pressure is equalized. See Figure 4.3.

Air flows *out of* the lungs when the lungs contract in size (in speech, typically because the muscles of *inspiration* relax a little). This contraction in size slightly compresses the air in the lungs, so the air pressure

---

[11] Think white water kayaking or rafting.

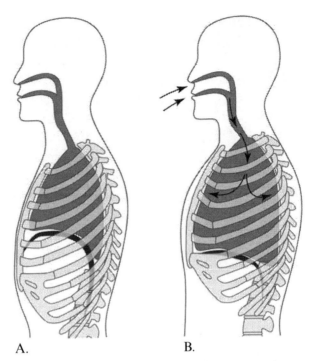

A.   B.

Figure 4.3 Inhaling as airflow from high pressure to low pressure. Inhaling involves increasing the volume of the lungs, as in the change from A to B. The same number of air molecules then occupy a greater volume, so they are less closely packed together, which is another way of saying that the pressure has been lowered. So air flows from outside the body, where pressure is now greater, into the lungs to equalize the pressure inside and outside.

in the lungs will be higher than the air pressure surrounding the person. As long as the upper airway is open, air will flow out of the lungs, equalizing the pressure in the lungs with that of the air surrounding the individual.

Air flowing out of the lungs pushes air already in the airway ahead of it as it makes its way up the bronchi, through the trachea, into the larynx, between the vocal folds, into the pharynx, and then into the oral and/or the nasal cavities. If airflow is gentle and there are no obstructions, there will not be a great deal of difference in air pressure along the length of this passage. However, the act of speaking in part involves creating differences of air pressure at different points along this pathway.

The amount of air pressure just below the glottis (just below the vocal folds) is called *subglottal pressure*. It can be adjusted rapidly by control of the muscles of respiration. Increased subglottal pressure increases the amplitude of speech sounds (i.e., how loud they are), and there are frequent adjustments related to stress and emphasis in speech.

4.6.2   Absolute and relative air pressure

In 4.4.1.1, it was stated that the average *air pressure* in New York City is 101.3 kPa or 14.7 psi and in Denver it is 84 kPa or 12.2 psi. It follows from this that it requires a greater amount of pressure inside the lungs to exhale in New York than it does in Denver. In either city, it requires a little more air pressure inside the lungs than in the surrounding atmosphere in order to exhale, and that is a bigger number in New York than in Denver.

In a similar way, the pressures required for speech production will vary depending on the atmospheric pressure around the talker. A discussion of the processes involved would become very complex if we had to account for the local air pressure.

In discussions of the production of speech sounds, when reference is made to pressure, it is a matter of *relative pressure* and not *absolute pressure* that is meant. To exhale, the pressure inside the lungs must be higher than the air surrounding the person (that is, the *pressure* is higher in the lungs *relative to* outside the person). This fact does not change from New York to Denver, even though the *absolute pressure* involved would change.

4.6.3   Impounding then releasing air in the production of sounds: plosives

One of the ways that airflow and air pressure are changed in the production of speech is by *impounding*[12] the airflow by a closure somewhere in the oral cavity (with the velopharyngeal port also closed). For instance, say "Pa pa pa pa." To make the p-sound, you need to impound the air in your mouth with your lips (the velopharyngeal passage must be closed so the extra air pressure does not leak out through the nose). This stops the airflow and allows the air pressure inside the mouth (behind the lips) to rise to the same – or nearly the same – level as the air pressure in the lungs. The air pressure is suddenly released when you start to say the vowel sound that follows the p-sound. This sudden release of pressure makes a kind of popping sound. As we shall see in Chapter 5, consonants like these are called *plosives* or *occlusives*.

Figure 4.4 shows that if the velopharyngeal passage (VPP) is open, a plosive (occlusive) sound such as [p] cannot be produced, but when the VPP is closed, air is impounded and a plosive can be produced.

---

[12] *To impound* is to enclose and hold inside. The police might impound a car that is illegally parked and blocking traffic. The car is placed in a "pound," an enclosed area that holds impounded vehicles. Here, we are using the term for the enclosure of air in the mouth and pharynx.

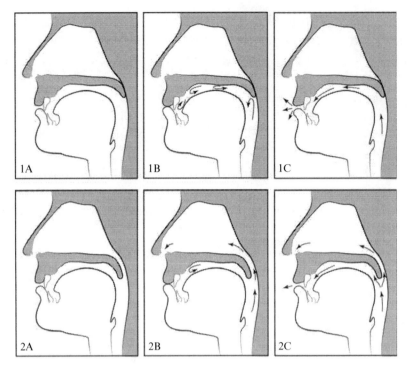

Figure 4.4 Impounding air for plosives. In sequence 1, the talker prepares themself, then says [po]. In part 1B, air is pushed upward by the lungs, but the pressure cannot escape because the air is impounded behind the closed lips and the closed VPP. In part 1C, when the lips part, there is an explosion of air, which we hear as a [p] sound. In sequence 2, the talker tries to do the same thing, but this time leaves their VPP open. As they try to build up air pressure behind the lips, this time the extra air does not build up pressure, but rather escapes through the open VPP. In this case, there would be no [p] sound and no explosion of pressure. Instead of a [p], the talker would produce a voiceless [m̥], which would sound a bit like a snort.

4.6.4 Forcing air through a constriction: fricatives

When air is forced under pressure to pass through a small passage, its flow becomes turbulent. As we have seen, this also occurs when the direction of airflow is abruptly changed. This generates a noise.

The exact quality of the sound depends on a number of things. Among these are the size and shape of the small passage, the relative pressure of the flow, and the larger cavity (i.e., the oral cavity) in which this occurs, as the larger cavity will modify the noise through resonance.

Compare an s-sound with a z-sound by producing a prolonged example of each. The z-sound is produced with vibrating vocal folds, whereas the s-sound has an open glottis and no vibration. Notice that the noise component (the part of the sound that is not generated by the vibration of the vocal folds, the part that is not a regular buzzing sound) is softer in the z-sound. Airflow must make the vocal folds vibrate for the z-sound, and this reduces the air pressure that is available to generate noise through turbulence. This is a general pattern, as we shall see.

4.6.5   Pressure variation across the glottis

When the vocal folds vibrate, the periods of closure or near-closure of the glottis create an obstacle to the flow of air. Since the pressure is generated below, at the level of the lungs, the *subglottal* pressure will be greater than the *supraglottal* pressure (pressure above the glottis). Indeed, a **pressure differential across the glottis** is necessary for the vocal folds to vibrate because there must be airflow for this to happen. If the air pressure is the same above and below the glottis, then the vocal folds won't vibrate because air won't flow if the pressure is the same everywhere.

Try this experiment (you must say it aloud for it to work). Say "rapid" and hold the p-sound for a long time. Don't repeat the p-sound; just hold the mouth closed for 3 or 4 seconds so that the p-sound creates a long silence or pause. It may seem strange to do this, but it is not difficult to do.

Now say "rabid" and hold the b-sound for a long time. You will quickly reach a limit of how long you can make the b-sound – if you keep your lips and velopharyngeal port closed, you'll be unable to continue the b-sound. What is happening? Why can you prolong the p-sound indefinitely, but you can't prolong the b-sound very long at all? The b-sound, unlike the p-sound, requires the vocal folds to be vibrating; if the vocal folds are not vibrating, then it's a p-sound, not a b-sound. For the vocal folds to vibrate, the pressure must be greater below than above the vocal folds,[13] and air must flow between the folds. When you make a b-sound, the air flows through the glottis and makes the folds vibrate. Where does the air go? It goes into the pharynx and oral cavity, but it cannot leave during the production of the b-sound because the lips and velopharyngeal passage are closed. So more and more and more air builds up in the supraglottal cavities. The cheeks may expand a bit to accommodate this increased volume of air, but pretty soon a limit is reached and the cavity can't get bigger. At that point, air pressure rises in the oral cavity and pharynx. Eventually, the pressure above the glottis is as high as the pressure below the glottis, and the vocal folds stop vibrating.

Notice that if you try this experiment with different medial consonants, say "t" and "d" rather than "p" and "b," in the words "matter" and "madder," it is even more difficult to prolong the d-sound than it was to prolong the

---

[13] The vocal folds will vibrate with the opposite pressures and opposite airflow, but that is not a normal part of speech.

b-sound. This is because there is a lot of space in the mouth behind the lips, and the cheeks can easily bulge.[14] However, behind the point on the alveolar ridge where t and d form occlusions, there is less space for the air to build up. Additionally, for these latter consonants, the cheeks cannot bulge to accommodate the extra air.

4.7   Bernoulli principle

One principle of aerodynamics is responsible for a range of ordinary and seemingly unrelated events in everyday life. These include the force that keeps airplanes from falling down, the force responsible for the patterns of fallen leaves and scraps of paper on the ground among tall buildings in downtowns, flags flapping in the wind, and, more to the point for our purposes here, the vibration of the vocal folds.

The principle is called the **Bernoulli principle** (also called the *Venturi Effect*) and it has a number of effects in the production of speech. The principle itself seems counterintuitive – which is to say that, to many people, it seems as if it is the opposite of what "should" be true.[15]

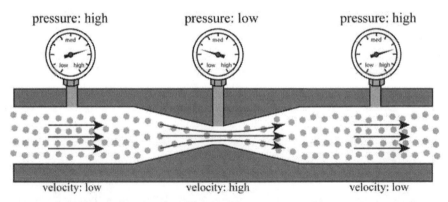

Figure 4.5 The Bernoulli principle. Air flowing through the constriction (narrowing) has lower pressure than the air flowing through the wider pipe

[14] The technical term for the ability of a system to expand a bit to accommodate the additional air is *compliance*. The upper airway is more *compliant* when producing a b-sound than when producing a d-sound. This is because the production of the b-sound allows the cheeks to inflate fully (bulge outwards), whereas there is less room for expansion with the d-sound because the blockage is farther back in the mouth.

[15] In answer to an exam question asking for a description of the Bernoulli principle, a student of mine once wrote, "What the professor wants us to say is [and here she wrote the correct answer], but everyone knows that this is not true." Well, yes, it is true, even though it may not be intuitive.

The essence of Bernoulli's principle is that, when a gas[16] flows through a narrowing (a *constriction*), the pressure of the gas is lowered at the narrowing (Figure 4.5). It might seem that this makes no sense; it may seem that the air would be "squeezed" at the narrowing and therefore of higher pressure, but in fact the pressure is lower at the constriction. One way of making sense of this in your mind is to realize that the individual molecules of air must be travelling much faster at the narrowing than at the wider spots in the passageway. Think of a group of people moving through a narrowing; the faster the people move, the farther apart they are. The molecules of air would bump into one another more, the faster they are moving, and so they would space themselves farther apart. Since the distance between molecules is related to pressure, the farther the molecules are apart, the lower the pressure.

Do you have trouble seeing why the molecules are moving faster at the constriction? Examine Figure 4.5. Think of it as showing three zones: (1) the larger tube to the left with air molecules going in the direction of the constriction; (2) the constriction; and (3) the larger tube leading away from the constriction.

Think of the situation in which the air has been flowing long enough for everything to have stabilized. In that condition, the number of molecules of air that pass a point in Zone 1 each second must be the same as the number that pass a point in Zone 3 each second. If that is true, then the same number of molecules of air must pass a point in Zone 2 each second. But in Zone 2, there is a narrower passageway – therefore, in order for the same number of molecules to pass per second, the individual molecules must be traveling faster. As we saw above, the faster they move, the farther apart they must be, and, therefore, the lower the pressure.

The upshot of the principle is this: As air flows through a narrowed passage, the pressure is less, and in turn that might mean that there is insufficient pressure to support an object that might be supported if the air were flowing through a larger passage. We will see how this affects various aspects of the speech production apparatus in the following section and following chapters.

4.8   Vocal fold vibration

The vibration of the vocal folds is essential to the production of speech, though not for all speech sounds – some are produced with no vocal fold vibration. We will examine vocal fold vibration in greater detail in Chapter 8,

---

[16] It applies to all fluids, meaning both gases and liquids, but our interest here is the flow of air.

and at this point we will look briefly at the role of aerodynamics and air pressure on their vibration.

The *myoelastic aerodynamic theory* describes the functioning of vocal fold vibration. Let us look at these words to see what they mean:

- *myo*: this refers to muscles
- *elastic*: this refers to the elasticity of muscles and other tissues
- *aero*: air
- *dynamic*: in motion, not static

Thus, the *myoelastic aerodynamic theory* takes into account muscle activity, the elasticity of tissues, and principles of air in motion.

Implicit in the name of the theory is a precise balance among the forces, particularly muscular and aerodynamic. The muscles of the larynx adduct (draw together) the vocal folds with a precise degree of contact and tension. The respiratory system pushes air upward and against the adducted vocal folds.

Given the relative strengths of the tension of the vocal folds and the pressure of air from below, the air pressure forcibly separates the vocal folds. As the vocal folds separate, a number of forces that would bring them back together increase:

1. The muscles hold the vocal folds in the same position, so they separate by stretching under the pressure of air. Tissue being elastic, the more it is stretched, the stronger the force pulling it back to its original shape and position.
2. The air pressure that separated the vocal folds was a static pressure when the vocal folds were closed. But as soon as the folds separate, there is a flow of air and thus the physics governing airflow comes into effect. As the air flows through the constriction of the vocal folds (which are still narrower than the trachea below), the Bernoulli principle serves to reduce the air pressure between the vocal folds. This lesser air pressure is not sufficient to keep the vocal folds separated.
3. As the vocal folds start to return to the closed position, air above the glottis continues to flow away from the ever-smaller glottis, further reducing pressure immediately above the vocal folds.

These forces bring the vocal folds back together. That stops the airflow, so, once again, there is a static pressure of air pressing against the vocal folds. Once again, this is sufficient force to stretch the vocal folds open. As soon as that happens, elastic recoil and aerodynamic forces work together to return them to the closed position, and the cycle repeats.

4.9   Vocabulary

air pressure
airflow
atmosphere (unit) (atm)
Bernoulli principle
compress, compression
constriction
egressive
impound
inches of mercury (inHg)
ingressive
International System of Units
kilogram (kg)
kilopascal (kPa)
laminar

millibar (mbar)
myoelastic aerodynamic theory
pascal (Pa)
pounds per square inch (psi)
pressure, absolute, relative
pressure differential
pulmonic
rarefy, rarefaction
SI (Système international)
subglottal pressure
suction
turbulent
vacuum

5 Consonants

5.1 Consonants

The word *consonant* means 'with (a) sonant' – that is, *with a vowel*: consonants are sounds that are produced with accompanying vowels (though there are exceptions). Effectively, the very word for consonant says "speech sound that isn't a vowel, but is accompanied by one." In the next chapter, we will see that vowels are produced without obstruction in the vocal tract – that is, with a vocal tract that is open at least as far as for the vowel [i] (the vowel of the word *beet*).

Consonants are speech sounds made with:

1. *a **blockage** of the vocal tract (such as for the p-sound),*
2. *a considerable **narrowing** of the vocal tract (such as for the s-sound), or*
3. *a **diversion** of the sound and airflow through the nasal passages (such as for the m-sound). By contrast, vowels do not constrict airflow.*

Consonants have a greater narrowing of the vocal tract than the vowel /i/ ("ee"). We are considering consonants before vowels because it is easier to describe and to intuit consonant articulation than vowel articulation: when we articulate consonants, generally one of our articulators is in contact with another or very close to another. It's relatively easy to feel where an articulator (particularly the tongue) is making contact or positioning very close to another articulator. With vowels, the tongue takes up a position within the oral cavity without touching other articulators. It's much harder by introspection to know where the tongue is.

The analogy can be made to a musical instrument. Saying consonants may be likened to playing an instrument that has specific keys, like a piano keyboard, a xylophone, or many wind instruments. You press the right key, you get the right note (as long as the instrument is in tune). Vowels are more like playing a slide trombone or a violin: there are not specific defined places on the instrument that produce specific notes; the player has to know where, in an undefined space, to make the desired note.

5.2 Articulation, terms, and consonant naming conventions

5.2.1 Articulate, articulation, articulators

Articulation is the term used to mean making the movements necessary to produce speech sounds. The talker **articulates** the sounds of speech. Articulation of connected speech is a continuous process of movements by the "organs of speech," also known as the **articulators**.

5.2.2 Approximate, approximation

A term that will be used repeatedly in describing the articulation of consonants is that the articulators will **approximate** one another. To *approximate* is to get close to something. We usually think of it in a metaphorical sense, such as an approximate number, but the word means *physical proximity* just as much.

When one articulator approximates another, it means that it approaches – gets physically close to – the other articulator. There are different degrees of approximation, including right up to full contact with considerable pressure. Different degrees of approximation result in different types of speech sounds. The **approximation** of two articulators means that the two articulators are brought very close to one another.

5.2.3 The articulators, active and passive

Articulation of speech sounds most typically involves two articulators that either come into contact or come into close proximity[1] – that is, that **approximate** one another. It is possible for there to be 3 articulators that are relevant, but the default case is 2. In discussing articulation, we normally distinguish the **active articulator** from the **passive articulator**. Pronounce a d-sound a number of times in a row. You will notice that the blade of your tongue rises up to the alveolar ridge behind the upper front incisors (teeth), and the tip of the tongue touches the interior surface of those teeth (you may notice slight variation depending on your native language, and perhaps dialect).

In this instance, a particular part of the tongue has moved to contact parts of the roof of the mouth. Those parts of the roof of the mouth (*alveolar ridge* and *incisor teeth*) have not moved; they just sit there, attached, as always, to the rest of the skull. The tongue has moved; thus, the tongue is the *active articulator* and the alveolar ridge and teeth are *passive articulators*. In a sense, the alveolar ridge is not an "articulator" at all: it doesn't do anything.

---

[1] It would be a good idea at this point to review Chapter 3, "Anatomy and Physiology of Speech," and/or to refer back to that chapter and its illustrations as the discussions of consonant articulation proceed.

But the critical facts in articulatory phonetics involve *the specific place where the articulation is made*. Therefore, the alveolar ridge is extremely important. Indeed, a sound such as the d-sound is called simply an *alveolar* sound; normally we don't even mention the tongue in its articulation.

5.2.4   Consonant "targets"

In discussing consonants, it is well to keep in mind the idea of articulatory "targets." This term reminds the student of phonetics that when speech sounds are articulated in the context of connected speech, the standard textbook descriptions of the position of the articulators in the production of a given sound may not be fully attained. Therefore, rather than thinking of those as static positions, it is better to think of them as targets that may be more fully or less fully (even considerably less fully) attained.

5.2.5   Naming conventions for consonants

There is a standard way of providing a basic articulatory description of consonants, and this provides us with a "name" for them. These descriptions are of the following type:

- *voiced alveolar lateral*
- *voiceless dental fricative*
- *voiced palatal glide*
- *voiceless bilabial plosive*

There are three terms in a specific order. Sometimes additional terms are used.

1. *voiced or voiceless*, a specification of whether or not the vocal folds are vibrating;
2. a *place of articulation* term, indicating where in the vocal tract the articulation takes place; and
3. a *manner of articulation* term, indicating the nature of the modification of the airstream (cf. second paragraph of 5.1).

Some commentary on each of these terms is necessary.

5.2.5.1   Voicing

Most basically, voicing is a matter of whether or not the vocal folds are vibrating during the production of the consonant. However, the situation is a little more complicated than that: There are both different **modes of voicing** and different **degrees of voicing**. These two are among the topics of Chapter 8, "Voice, Phonation, and Nasality," but here is a very brief preview.

Modes of voicing involve different ways that the vocal folds can vibrate; these differences may be phonemic (phonologically significant) in some languages, though they are not in most varieties of English, nor in most European languages. You've probably heard someone with a very breathy voice, or one that you might describe as a "husky" voice; these differences involve different modes of vocal fold vibration. In some languages, a word said with a breathy voice and the "same" word said with a normal voice would have different meanings to the speakers of that language.

The *degree of voicing* is particularly relevant to speech sounds such as [p b t d k g], called *plosives*. These sounds can be more than simply voiced or voiceless; they can have different degrees of voicing.

5.2.5.2   Place of articulation – tongue involvement is assumed

The place of articulation is the location in the vocal tract where the articulation occurs – that is, where the airflow is blocked, constricted, narrowed, or diverted toward the nasal passages.

Given that the large majority of speech articulations involve the tongue, the naming conventions do not mention the tongue except under special conditions, noted below. Think of the d-sound that you repeated above. It is a *voiced alveolar plosive* (at least for most native speakers of English in most dialects). Notice that, while it is the tongue that makes the articulatory gesture and creates the blockage of the airstream, the tongue is not even mentioned in the term for the sound. What is mentioned is only the passive articulator, the alveolar ridge. So, something is implicit here: we write "alveolar," but we mean that *the tongue does something*, and what the tongue does *is in the region of the bony alveolar ridge*. The alveolar ridge has done nothing, nor can it "do" anything, to articulate a sound.

The typical classification name of the sound mentions only one articulator, assuming that the other is the tongue. However, there are three circumstances in which more than one articulator is named.

1. *Neither articulator is the tongue.* The p-sound is bilabial (two lips, no tongue), neither articulator is the tongue, so both are named (bi-labial, 'two lips'). The f-sound is labiodental (lip and teeth, no tongue), so both are named. Neither sound directly involves the tongue.
2. *An unexpected part of the tongue is used.* Calling a consonant *dental, alveolar, palatal, velar, uvular*, etc., implies that the active articulator is the tongue. But it implies more than that: it implies that the nearest part of the tongue is used. So, if a sound is described as alveolar, it is assumed that the *blade* of the tongue is used; if dental, that the *tip* of the tongue is used, and likewise with the parts of the tongue that, at rest, lie below the palate, the velar region, and so on.

   Try making a t-like sound by placing the tip of your tongue on the palate (curl your tongue back so the tip points vertically upward).

Thinking about using the tongue to dislodge a bit of food that is stuck to the palate may help you to make this gesture. If you were making a consonant this way, it could be called an **apico-palatal** consonant. The tongue is named (the apical part of it) *because an unexpected part of the tongue contacts the palatal area.*

3. There is a third circumstance in which it might appear that two articulators are named. The sh-sound is usually classed as a **voiceless alveopalatal fricative.** In fact, the term alveopalatal does not name two (passive) articulators; it names only one: the middle of the region of the roof of the mouth where the alveolar area meets the palatal area. So the tongue (unmentioned in the terminology) meets a region of the roof of the mouth: the alveopalatal region. The **alveopalatal region** is also called the **postalveolar region.**

The various places of articulation used in the world's languages are discussed in Section 5.3.

5.2.5.3   Manner of Articulation
The **manner of articulation** is the way in which the airstream is modified in consonant production. The discussion of consonants below is organized by manners of articulation (beginning in Section 5.6).

5.2.5.4   Other terms
The three terms mentioned above in consonant classification – voicing, place of articulation, and manner of articulation – are supplemented by other terms whenever it is necessary to make further distinctions or when a full articulatory description is required.

5.3   Principal places of consonant articulation (PoA)

Consonants are typically produced in a range of "places" in the vocal tract. English consonants are produced in a number of these places, though not in all the places used by languages of the world. The principal places of articulation are shown in Figure 5.1. It is to be remembered that intermediate places exist as well; the arrows in the figure show typical positions. *PoA* means "place of articulation."

5.3.1   Bilabial PoA (1 in Figure 5.1)
The two lips are brought together in the production of bilabial consonants (bi = two, labial = lips). English [p] and [b] are bilabial. The lower lip moves farther than the upper lip, and may involve small changes in the jaw position, as it rises to make the approximation of the lips possible.

5.3.2   Labiodental PoA (2 in Figure 5.1)

In typical labiodental articulation, the lower lip is raised and drawn inward to approximate the upper front teeth (the incisors). English [f] and [v] sounds are labiodental. In a word such as *inferior*, the nasal sound spelled with the letter <n> may be labiodental.

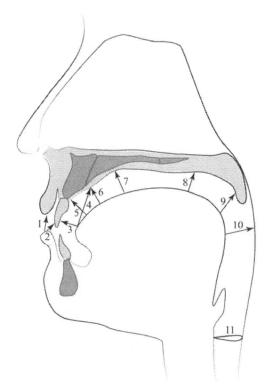

Figure 5.1 Places of articulation

5.3.3   Dental or Interdental PoA (3 in Figure 5.1)

When the tip of the tongue approximates the inner surface or lower edge of the incisors, this is known as a **dental articulation**. If the area of the blade of the tongue just slightly behind the tip approximates the lower edge of the incisors, this is known as an **interdental articulation**. The English th-sound [θ] is typically interdental in that the tip of the tongue is between the upper and lower teeth (incisors). However, since the approximation is with the lower edge of the upper teeth, and the lower teeth do not contribute significantly to the sound generated, this articulation fits the IPA definition of **dental**, though you may see the term *interdental* used elsewhere.

5.3.4   Apico-postalveolar PoA: retroflex consonants (4 in Figure 5.1)

If the tip (apex: apico-) of the tongue is raised upwards, curling the tongue back, and approximates the postalveolar region, we can say that the articulation is apico-postalveolar. Variants of this position have the tongue bent less far back and contacting the alveolar region (apico-alveolar) or the palatal region (apico-palatal). Sidebar 5.1 provides information about the combining forms of these place-of-articulation terms.

Such articulations are called *retroflex* (retro = backwards, flex = bend). In North American English, some speakers pronounce the <tr> of *train* and the <dr> of *drain* as retroflex consonants, though many speakers do not.

5.3.5   Alveolar PoA (5 in Figure 5.1)

If the blade of the tongue is approximated to the alveolar ridge (typically, but not necessarily, with the tip touching the inner face of the upper incisors), this is an alveolar place of articulation. English [t], [d], [l], and [n] are typically alveolar.

5.3.6   Postalveolar PoA (6 in Figure 5.1)

If the blade of the tongue (or the intersection between the blade and the dorsum of the tongue) approximates the area on the border between the alveolar ridge and the palate, this is called a *postalveolar articulation*. It has been common to call this an alveopalatal articulation as well.

5.3.7   Palatal PoA (7 in Figure 5.1)

When the front part of the tongue dorsum approximates the palate, this is a palatal articulation. The English y-sound as in *yes* ([j] in the International Phonetic Alphabet [IPA]) is palatal.

5.3.8   Velar PoA (8 in Figure 5.1)

If the mid to back portion of the tongue dorsum approximates the soft palate or velum, this is known as a **velar articulation**. English [k] and [g] are typically velar, though their PoA can be drawn quite a distance forward when near certain vowels. More on this in Chapter 10, "Speech Dynamics."

5.3.9   Uvular PoA (9 in Figure 5.1)

If the back portion of the tongue dorsum (or upper part of the tongue root) approximates the uvula, this is called a **uvular articulation**.

5.3.10   Pharyngeal PoA (10 in Figure 5.1)

Some languages have speech sounds that involve the tongue root approximating the posterior wall of the pharynx. These are pharyngeal sounds.

5.3.11   Laryngeal PoA (11 in Figure 5.1)

There are a couple of speech sounds that are made directly at the location of the vocal folds. In English, the [h] sound as well as the glottal stop [ʔ] are made there. The glottal stop occurs in the middle of the negative expression *uh-uh.*

5.3.12   The PoA is not the whole story

As we will see in greater detail in Section 5.7.1.2, naming the place of articulation (PoA) does not provide a full description of a sound's articulation. Consider the articulation of the d-sound (pronounce it several times). Indeed, the blade of the tongue is on the alveolar ridge, but this does not capture the fact that the edges of the tongue play a critical role. Alternate saying the d-sound and the l-sound, paying attention to the configuration of your tongue. You will notice that the edges of the tongue are in different positions for the two consonants. So, in order to *describe* the articulation of these sounds, it is important to mention what the sides of the tongue are doing, even though the *classification* of the sound – voiced alveolar plosive – does not mention the sides.

5.4   Types of movement in consonant articulation

The active articulators (primarily the tongue, lips, and velum) undergo movement in the articulation of consonants, but, unlike what you might think, the motivating force for the movement is not the same in all cases.

Section 5.2.3 introduced the idea of the active versus passive articulator. In this section, we will examine movement of the active articulator.

To articulate a speech sound, there is movement of at least one articulator. The movement may be any of the following types:

1. deliberate (both directions)
2. ballistic
    a. rebound
3. elastic recoil / gravity
4. aerodynamic
5. "way station"

Let us look at these in turn.

5.4.1   Deliberate movement in both directions

Pronounce the syllable "ga," repeating it several times in quick succession, paying attention to the movement of your tongue. It is evident that the talker makes a deliberate muscular movement of the back of the tongue toward the velum, followed by a deliberate muscular movement pulling the back of the tongue away from the velum. Your jaw may move up and down a little as well.

In this instance, the active articulator is deliberately moved toward the point of articulation, then deliberately moved away from the point of articulation, and toward the position needed for the following sound or sounds. In both directions, the movement is motivated by contraction of muscles.

It's likely that anyone who gives any thought to speech-sound articulation assumes that this is the way all articulation proceeds. In fact, however, there are a number of different mechanisms by which the active articulators are moved.

5.4.2   Ballistic movement of the active articulator (flap, part 1)

If you are a native speaker of North American English, and you say, in a casual tone, "What's the matter?" it is likely that the t-sound of *matter* has been articulated in a different way, called a **ballistic movement**.

The term *ballistic* normally refers to the movement of a bullet or other projectile. When a bullet is fired, there is an initial explosion that propels it down the barrel of the gun, but once it leaves the barrel, the bullet no longer has any external force pushing it forward. It moves by its own inertia (momentum), gradually slowing down. There is an initial force, then nothing more; the bullet coasts the rest of the way.

In a similar way, a ballistic articulatory gesture involves an initial force by rapid muscle contraction, followed by a relaxation of the muscles. The only articulator to which this applies is the thin anterior part of the tongue, the blade.

5.4.2.1   Rebound (flap, part 2)

When the tongue blade is given a rapid, sharp input of energy to move upward, it quickly hits the alveolar ridge area, and because it still contains some of its energy of movement, it may bounce off (or rebound from) the alveolar ridge and be propelled in the downward direction. This is aided by elastic recoil and gravity (following section).

5.4.3   Elastic recoil / gravity (flap, part 3)

The soft tissues of the body have the property of elasticity to varying degrees. When stretched, tissues have potential energy (like a stretched rubber band), and return to a previous configuration such that they are no longer stretched. In the case described in the two previous sections, elastic recoil may have an influence on the return of the tongue from the alveolar region.

Likewise, because the tongue is relaxed after the initial pull, it is subject to the force of gravity, and gravity will have an effect in lowering the tongue blade. However, it is a good idea not to exaggerate the role of gravity; it is possible to produce normal-sounding speech with the head on its side (as in a lying position) or even upside-down, and so other forces must be able to replace the role that gravity plays.

5.4.4   Aerodynamic movement (trills)

Some articulatory gestures are powered by the flow of air. Think of a flag flapping in the wind: it's clear that the wind – the movement of air – is driving the movements of the flag. You wouldn't think that something inside the flag is making it move back and forth; you know that the force of the wind is responsible.

There are three speech articulators that can be made to vibrate by a stream of air blowing over them. These are the lips, the blade of the tongue, and the uvula. Making the lips vibrate with airflow is like the sound that is typically written *Brrrrr* (made to say how cold it is) – this is an exceedingly rare sound among the world's languages and we won't consider it again. The other two sounds are much more common.

The tip and blade of the tongue can be made to vibrate, and this is the r-sound in Spanish when written with a double <rr> (even the single <r> at the beginning of a Spanish word is sometimes pronounced this way). The uvula can be made to vibrate, and this sound is a kind of r-sound that occurs in a number of languages.

5.4.5   "Way station"

The informal term "way station" is not a description of a kind of force that moves articulators, and it is not a technical term in this field. It is listed here simply as a reminder that, in connected speech, the articulatory gesture for a given sound might be little more than an intermediate point as articulators move from the target of the previous sound to that of the following sound.

5.5   The International Phonetic Alphabet

As we saw in Chapter 3, the *International Phonetic Alphabet (IPA)* is the alphabet used internationally by phoneticians, phonologists, linguists, speech pathologists, and others to write the sounds of language in

SIDEBAR 5.2 Voicing

It is important to understand that in almost no instance is the difference between the voiced and voiceless variety of the sounds in a single IPA cell based on voicing alone. There are other important differences. We will look in greater detail later, but, for the moment, consider this: when we whisper, sounds are not voiced at all, but we don't often confuse the voiced and voiceless sounds having the same place and manner of articulation. That is because there are important phonetic differences between them other than just voicing.

SIDEBAR 5.3 Attested sounds

A sound that has been *attested* is one that has been found, and verified by experts, to be present in the phonetic inventory of at least one language.

a consistent and unambiguous way. The IPA has undergone periodic revisions and updates.

For the most part, we will present consonant sounds in a way that is consistent with the IPA table of consonants. However, some concepts are clearer for students new to phonetics if they are presented in an order that differs from the official table.

Figure 5.2 shows the main table of consonants in the official IPA; Figures 5.3 and 5.4 show tables of additional consonants.

Examine the main IPA consonant table in Figure 5.2. The *columns* represent *place of articulation* (PoA), the topic of Section 5.3 and Figure 5.1. The *rows* represent the *manners of articulation*.

Note that there are four sorts of cells in this table: cells with 2 symbols, cells with 1 symbol, blank cells, and gray cells. This is how to interpret the cells:

1. **Cells with 2 symbols:** this particular combination of place and manner of articulation has been *attested* (see Sidebar 5.3) in both voiceless and voiced varieties among the languages of the world. The voiceless sound is represented on the left and the voiced sound on the right. Note also the sidebar on voicing (see Sidebar 5.2).

2. **Cells with 1 symbol:** The sound is attested, but only a voiced or a voiceless version, not both. Looking at Figure 5.2, you will notice that, in almost all cases, the one sound is on the right, meaning it is voiced. Only in the instance of the glottal stop [ʔ] is the single symbol on the left, meaning voiceless.

3. **Gray cells:** The gray cells represent combinations of place and manner of articulation that are deemed impossible to articulate. Not only have we not attested these sounds in any language – more than that, we believe that they will never be attested because they cannot be pronounced.

4. **White cells**: Confusingly, the white cells represent two different situations in the official IPA charts: attested sounds that are written with a base symbol plus a diacritic (see Sidebar 5.4), and those that are not attested but are deemed to be possible speech sounds.

   a. *Sounds written with a base symbol and diacritic.* Look at the column "Dental" in the IPA table (Figure 5.2). The plosive and nasal rows are blank, despite these being common sounds in many languages, including western European ones. In fact, the Plosive row should show [t̪, d̪] and the Nasal row should show [n̪]. However, the practice with the IPA is not to show symbols with diacritics in the main table.

   b. *Sounds not attested but deemed possible.* Some blank cells represent sounds that could exist, but which have not been attested. For example, a labiodental plosive is possible (so the cell is white), but the cell is blank because it is not attested.

> ### SIDEBAR 5.4 Diacritics
>
> Diacritics or diacritical signs are often called *accents* or *accent marks*. The following letters, used in French and other languages, have diacritics: é, è, ô, à. In the IPA, as well as in the spelling of several languages, consonant letters have diacritics as well: [t̪, ɫ].

Important: For reasons having to do with the teaching of phonetics in a way that makes sense to students starting out in phonetics, and with an emphasis on consonant groups important in English, a different order of these manners of articulation will be used in the discussion that follows. In some cases, we present an additional manner of articulation and bring material from Figures 5.3 and 5.4 into the main categorization.

The equivalent of Figure 5.2, as reorganized for this chapter, can be found at the end of the chapter. The individual rows as reorganized for this chapter are found individually in sections devoted to each row in the following.

THE INTERNATIONAL PHONETIC ALPHABET (revised to 2020)

CONSONANTS (PULMONIC)   ©⊕⊜ 2020 IPA

	Bilabial	Labiodental	Dental	Alveolar	Postalveolar	Retroflex	Palatal	Velar	Uvular	Pharyngeal	Glottal
Plosive	p b			t d		ʈ ɖ	c ɟ	k ɡ	q ɢ		ʔ
Nasal	m	ɱ		n		ɳ	ɲ	ŋ	N		
Trill	ʙ			r					R		
Tap or Flap		ⱱ		ɾ		ɽ					
Fricative	ɸ β	f v	θ ð	s z	ʃ ʒ	ʂ ʐ	ç ʝ	x ɣ	χ ʁ	ħ ʕ	h ɦ
Lateral fricative				ɬ ɮ							
Approximant		ʋ		ɹ		ɻ	j	ɰ			
Lateral approximant				l		ɭ	ʎ	L			

Symbols to the right in a cell are voiced, to the left are voiceless. Shaded areas denote articulations judged impossible.

Figure 5.2 The International Phonetic Alphabet (consonants). IPA Chart: www.internationalphoneticassociation.org/content/ipa-chart

CONSONANTS (NON-PULMONIC)

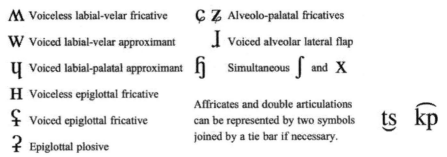

Clicks	Voiced implosives	Ejectives
⊙ Bilabial	ɓ Bilabial	' Examples:
ǀ Dental	ɗ Dental/alveolar	p' Bilabial
ǃ (Post)alveolar	ʄ Palatal	t' Dental/alveolar
ǂ Palatoalveolar	ɠ Velar	k' Velar
ǁ Alveolar lateral	ʛ Uvular	s' Alveolar fricative

Figure 5.3 The International Phonetic Alphabet (non-pulmonic consonants). IPA Chart: www.internationalphoneticassociation.org/content/ipa-chart

OTHER SYMBOLS

ʍ Voiceless labial-velar fricative   ɕ ʑ Alveolo-palatal fricatives

w Voiced labial-velar approximant   ɺ Voiced alveolar lateral flap

ɥ Voiced labial-palatal approximant   ɧ Simultaneous ʃ and x

ʜ Voiceless epiglottal fricative

ʢ Voiced epiglottal fricative

ʡ Epiglottal plosive

Affricates and double articulations can be represented by two symbols joined by a tie bar if necessary.   t͡s k͡p

Figure 5.4 The International Phonetic Alphabet (other [consonant] symbols). IPA Chart: www.internationalphoneticassociation.org/content/ipa-chart

5.6   Manners of articulation of consonants

Reading down the left side of the IPA consonant chart, we see the following manners of articulation:

1. Plosive
2. Nasal
3. Trill
4. Tap or Flap
5. Fricative
6. Lateral fricative
7. Approximant
8. Lateral approximant

There are also additional consonants under the headings "Non-pulmonic consonants" (Figure 5.3) and "Other symbols" (Figure 5.4).

As we examine various kinds of consonants in the sections that follow, we will not follow the 8 groupings shown here, for reasons explained above.

5.7   Plosives

Plosives are consonants like those at the beginning of the words *paw*, *ball*, *tall*, *doll*, *caw*, and *gone*. Repeat *paw* several times. Notice that you close your lips together to form the sound, you hold them together momentarily, then you pull them apart suddenly. These actions describe the three phases of plosive production.

1. The *closing phase*, during which the articulators are moving toward the closure (sometimes called the *approach* or *shutting phase*).
2. The *closure phase*, which is a period during which the vocal tract is completely closed (it is impossible to breathe). Note that, for closure to occur, the velopharyngeal passage must be closed as well so that air and sound do not escape through the nasal passages.
3. *Release*, which is a moment during which the closure is opened abruptly, and both sound and air may escape. If pressure has built up in the vocal tract, release may be accompanied by a burst of airflow out of the mouth.

5.7.1   Closing and closure

There are a couple of very important aspects of the closing and closure phases that are often overlooked, but that are very fundamental to the production of plosives.

5.7.1.1   Velopharyngeal port

As noted above, bilabial plosives, for example, do not simply have closure at the lips. It is absolutely essential for the production of any oral plosive for the velopharyngeal port to be closed, blocking both airflow and the radiation of sound through the nose. If you are asked how a bilabial plosive is produced and you answer with the lip closure but not the velopharyngeal closure, your answer is incomplete in a fundamental way.

> **SIDEBAR 5.5 Other terms for plosives**
>
> *Plosives* are also called *stops* or *occlusives*, but we will use only the term *plosive* because there is the possibility of ambiguity in these latter terms. Some authors use one or both terms to refer also to nasal consonants, because, like plosives, nasals require closure in the mouth. Additionally, the term *occlusive* may imply a phonological usage rather than a phonetic one.

5.7.1.2   Edges of the tongue

Closure is often more complex than a simple place-of-articulation view-point would suggest. Pronounce a series of d-sounds: *dah, dah, dah*, etc. If you are a native speaker of English, you placed the blade of your tongue on the alveolar ridge, and, given the naming conventions, that makes [d] an alveolar plosive.

So, if you were asked how you articulate a d-sound, a typical answer might be "you place the blade of the tongue on the alveolar ridge." You already know that that response is inadequate in one way; you need to mention that the velopharyngeal port is closed, otherwise the air pressure would leak out of the nose. But it's more complex than that. It's possible to plant one's tongue blade on the alveolar ridge but continue to breathe in and out through the mouth, and that is not possible when producing a plosive. *Putting one's tongue against the alveolar ridge does not, in itself, block the mouth.* Put your tongue in the position to say a [l]: you can still breathe in and out through your mouth.

So, what else is required? The sides or edges of the tongue, from the blade back, press sideways against the upper molars and premolars (the upper "side teeth"). If teeth are missing, the edge of the tongue will press against the palate and velum or gums. Toward the region where the mouth meets the pharynx, the tongue presses to the sides of the pharynx.

This action along the edges of the tongue serves to complete the seal. Plosives require a momentary complete closure of the vocal tract, and that means that air must be prevented from escaping through the center of the oral cavity, through the velopharyngeal port, or over the edges of the tongue. See Figure 5.5.

Review also Section 3.8.4 and Figure 3.19.

5.7.1.3   Release

As noted above, the closure at the place of articulation is typically re-opened at the moment of release. However, a plosive can be released by opening the velopharyngeal port. This typically happens when a plosive is followed by a nasal consonant. For example, pronounce the word *helpmate*. The p-sound is not released by opening the lips; rather the velopharyngeal port is opened for the production of the m-sound that follows, as the lips stay closed for the duration of the [m]. The lips are parted for the vowel follow-ing the [m], but this is not how the pressure built up for the [p] is released – that occurs by opening the velopharyngeal port.

In the word *door*, the [d] is released by lowering the blade of the tongue, and release occurs over the center of the tongue. But in the word *paddle*, how is the [d] released? The edges of the tongue are drawn toward the center of the oral cavity to form the [l], and air escapes over the edges.

5.7.2 Aspiration

English is one of many languages that produces at least some voiceless plosives with *aspiration*. Aspiration occurs when the release of a plosive is accompanied by a significant outward puff of air, a kind of mini explosion of air.[2] This involves the buildup of a greater pressure of air in the mouth during closure just before release than is required for non-aspirated voiceless plosives.

In English, strong aspiration is produced when a voiceless plosive ([p t k]) is the first sound of a strongly stressed first syllable of a word: p̲ass, t̲oss, c̲ase. If the voiceless plosive is not the first sound, but is preceded by a [s], then the plosive is not aspirated: sp̲am, st̲ill, sk̲ull.

In English, voiceless plosives in word positions other than the first sound in the word are not generally aspirated. There may be exceptions, especially when there is unusual emphasis. For example, if a person says "impossible" in a dramatic way, stretching out the first syllable and then pausing slightly before saying the rest of the word very forcefully, then the [p] may be aspirated.

Voiceless plosives other than the three in English can be aspirated as well, in the languages in which they appear.

Voiced plosives are not aspirated in the way that voiceless ones are, so the term is generally not applied to voiced plosives. Occasionally, a voiced plosive is described as aspirated, but generally this refers to a very different phenomenon – namely, where the voicing of the plosive is of a special type. There is more on this topic in Section 8.6.2.1.

5.7.2.1 Diacritic for aspiration

The symbol for aspiration is a small raised <h> following the symbol for the plosive: [pʰ tʰ kʰ].

> **SIDEBAR 5.6 Why do we write "a [s]" and not "an [s]"?**
>
> The reader might have noticed in the second paragraph of Section 5.7.2 the following phrase: "... but is preceded by a [s], then the plosive ...." You might have wondered why we did not write: "... but is preceded by an [s], then the plosive ...."
>
> The reason is a fundamental one in phonetics. When we write *[s]*, where the symbol s is between square brackets, the s represents a *sound*, and should not be called by the name of the English letter. So the phrase means: "... preceded by a [sssss] ...," where you would read the *sound* the letter makes, represented here as "ssss." What is in the square brackets is pronounced "sssss," not "esss."
>
> In the same way, we will write "**an** [u]" and not "**a** [u]" because what is in square brackets is the sound of the vowel, not the name of the letter as used in English.
>
> There are many more cases that are similar throughout the rest of the book.

---

[2] *Aspiration* is the correct technical term for this phenomenon, but it's a terrible choice of term. The basic meaning of "aspiration" (outside of phonetics) is an inward drawing of air, an inward flow. Phonetic aspiration is precisely the opposite: an outgoing puff of air.

5.7.3   Plosives and languages

In the following table, the Plosive line of the IPA chart has been repeated, with empty columns deleted. We have added IPA letters that require diacritics or "accent" marks, something not done in the official IPA, so this chart includes columns that are blank in the official IPA. Remember that where there are 2 symbols in a cell, the left one is voiceless (no vocal fold vibration) and the right one is voiced (vocal fold vibration).

	Bilabial	Dental	Alveolar	Retroflex	Palatal[a]	Velar	Uvular	Glottal
Plosives	p b	t̪ d̪	t d	ʈ ɖ	c ɟ	k g	q ɢ	ʔ

[a] Note that the symbol for a voiced palatal plosive is an upside-down <f>: ɟ.

- *Bilabials* [p b]: Bilabial [p] and [b] occur in English and in all European languages. They are very common in the world's languages. They are spelled <p b> in English as well as in most other languages using the latin alphabet.
- *Dentals*: [t̪ d̪]: The dental [t̪] and [d̪] are not shown on the IPA table because, where the symbol requires a diacritic, the IPA chart leaves the

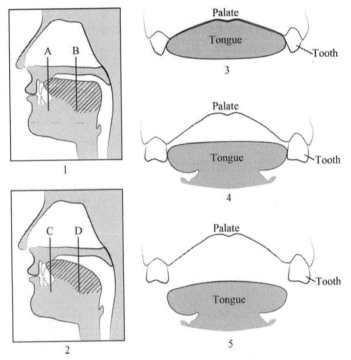

Figure 5.5 Tongue seal along the molars. 1. Sagittal section showing the tongue in the production of [t d]. 2. Sagittal section showing the tongue in the production of [l]. 3. Coronal section at Line A, essentially the same for [t d] and [l]. The tongue creates a seal at the alveolar ridge with the canine or premolar teeth. 4. Coronal section at Line B in Part 1. The tongue creates a seal along the molar teeth so that air cannot escape over the sides of the tongue. 5. Coronal section at Line D in Part 2. The tongue is narrowed, and its sides do not create a seal with the molars. Air passes freely over the sides of the tongue.

cell blank. These sounds are common among European languages and languages around the world. These occur in both French and Spanish rather than the alveolar type that is typical of English.

- In English, the dental varieties may occur when a [t] or [d] occurs next to the th-sound ([θ] or [ð]). For example, in "both Tom and I" or "both David and I," the plosive at the beginning of each man's name may be more dental than alveolar.
- *Alveolar* [t d]: These sounds are both part of the inventory of English, as well as many other languages. There are very few languages that have both dental and alveolar plosives in contrast, although many, like English, have the two as positional variants.
- Both dental and alveolar plosives are typically spelled <t d>. In English, the [t] sound is occasionally spelled <th>, as in *Thomas* and *Thames*.
- *Retroflex* [ʈ ɖ]: Retroflex sounds involve curling the tongue back so that the tip points upward, touching the roof of the mouth in the post-alveolar region. Many languages have retroflex plosives, including many of the major languages of India (Hindi, Punjabi, Gujarati, etc.).
- In English, some talkers make retroflex [ʈ] and [ɖ] at the beginning of words when the plosive is followed by the r-sound. This occurs in words such as *train, drain, drag, trout*, and so on.
- When languages having distinctive retroflex consonants are latinized (i.e., written with the latin alphabet), the retroflexes are often written with a dot under the symbol: <ṭ ḍ>. In the IPA, the curly "tail" (descender) shows a retroflex articulation: [ʈ] and [ɖ].
- *Palatal* [c ɟ]: English does not have palatal plosives that contrast with other plosives. However, like many languages that have velar plosives, those sounds move forward in the mouth with vowels pronounced farther forward. So, in English words such as _keep_, _kin_, _cape_, _geezer_, _gill_, _gape_, and so on, the initial consonants are often [c] and [ɟ] rather than [k] or [g].
- *Velar* [k g]: These sounds are both part of the sound inventory of English, in words such as _copper_, _goon_, and so on. Note that the correct IPA symbol for the voiced velar plosive is [g] and not [ɡ] (though the latter is often seen).
- The velars are usually written with the letters <k g>. In English, the k-sound is sometimes written <ch>, as in *chaos*, and [g] is sometimes written <gh> as in *ghost* and *ghoul*. One peculiarity of the spelling of [k] in English is that, at the end of a word, the spelling <ck> is usually used. As to spelling, not sounds: at the end of a word simple c, such as in *music* or *traffic*, is not very common, and a simple <k>, as in *trek*, is very rare, as is the double <k> in *trekking*.
- *Uvular* [q ɢ]: English does not have the uvular plosives in its inventory but many languages do. Inuktitut, the language of the Inuit, has only voiceless plosives, but [q] counts among them. Both uvular plosives

are in the inventory of most varieties of Arabic.

- When languages having a voiceless uvular plosive are written in the latin alphabet, the sound is usually written <q> (without a <u>), as in the country name Qatar.

- *Glottal stop* [ʔ]: Note that this sound is called a *stop* rather than a *plosive*, essentially for historical reasons. The glottal stop is not a contrastive sound in English, but it does occur. In most varieties of English, the negative expression *uh-uh* is pronounced with a glottal stop at the start of both syllables. In many varieties of English, glottal stop replaces [t] in words such as *but̲ton*. In parts of Britain, the glottal stop replaces many instances of [t].

- Many languages around the world count glottal stop among their inventory of sounds, including Arabic, Hebrew, and Hawaiian (it is represented by a reversed apostrophe[3] in the word *Hawaiʻi*). In languages that have this sound and that use the latin alphabet, it is written in a wide variety of ways because this alphabet has no history of writing that sound;[4] most often it is represented with an apostrophe. In the latinization of Squamish, an indigenous language spoken near Vancouver, Canada, the numeral 7 is used to represent the glottal stop (see Sidebar 5.6).

5.7.4 Plosive contrasts in English

English contrasts 6 plosives: voiceless and voiced bilabials, alveolars, and velars, /p b t d k g/. English contrasts these sounds in all positions within words: at the beginning of words, in the middle of words, and at the end.

5.7.5 Voicing in English plosives

In Chapter 8, we will examine voice and voicing more closely, but for the moment let us say that voicing in plosives is more complex than just voiced or voiceless. However, that simple categorization – voiced versus voiceless – captures an important contrast in English.

---

[3] Reversed apostrophe or opening single quotation mark: ʻ.
[4] Our letter <A> came from a Phoenician symbol that represented a syllable made up of a glottal stop followed by a vowel that we can write as "ah." The Greeks borrowed the symbol but, not having a glottal stop in their language, they used the letter to represent only the vowel.

5.8   Nasals

Nasals are consonants like those at the beginning of the words *might* and *night*, and at the end of the word *sing* (in most varieties of English). Say an m-sound and prolong it, as if you were humming. Notice that you hold the lips together, that the velopharyngeal port is open (sound and airflow are radiating from the nostrils), and that your vocal folds are vibrating. (If you place a finger on your thyroid cartilage, you will feel the vibration.)

5.8.1   Closure and the velopharyngeal port

5.8.1.1   Velopharyngeal port

Nasal consonants require the velopharyngeal port to be open so that airflow and sound may radiate out through the nose.

5.8.1.2   Oral cavity closure

Nasal consonants require that the oral cavity be blocked completely at the place of articulation. This means that for alveolar, palatal or velar nasals, the edges of the tongue make a seal along the upper teeth or palate along the sides, as described for plosives in 5.7.1.2.

Note that in the nasal row of the IPA chart, the Pharyngeal and Glottal cells are gray. Nasals cannot be produced at these locations because nasals require that airflow be diverted through the nasal passages. If airflow were blocked in the oropharynx, no flow could reach the velopharyngeal port, and thus a pharyngeal nasal could not exist, nor a laryngeal one. (Pharyngeal and laryngeal sounds could be nasalized, however, meaning that there could be a nasal element to their articulation, as there is in nasalized vowels: Section 6.8.)

> **SIDEBAR 5.7 Phases of sound production**
>
> With consonants other than plosives, we do not usually refer to the three phases of articulation (closure, production, release), even though these phases could be observed in the m-sound of the word hammer. While the phases are not explicitly discussed, it is important to keep in mind that with all consonants (indeed all speech sounds), there is: (1) a movement toward the target; (2) reaching or being near the target; and (3) moving away from the target. Note that the third phase of one sound blends with the first phase (or more) of the next sound in connected speech.

5.8.2   Nasal consonants and languages

In the following table, the Nasal line of the IPA chart has been repeated, with the same modification mentioned above for plosives. The nasal consonant symbols are all to the right of their respective cell, meaning that they are voiced. While nasals might lose their voicing when in contact with other voiceless sounds, nasal consonants are normally voiced.[5]

	Bilabial	Labiodental	Dental	Alveolar	Retroflex	Palatal	Velar	Uvular
Nasals	m	ɱ	n̪	n	ɳ	ɲ	ŋ	N

- **Bilabial [m]:** The bilabial nasal occurs in English and is very common among the languages of the world. In the latin alphabet, it is spelled with the letter <m>.
- **Labiodental [ɱ]:** In English, the labiodental nasal may occur when it is followed immediately by a labiodental fricative, as in *in*ferior.
- **Dental [n̪]:** As seen with the dental plosive, an alveolar nasal in English may be dental following the th-sound [θ ð]: " ... both <u>N</u>ancy and I ... ". Many European languages (as well as languages all over the world) have dental nasals in their inventories. The letter spelled <n> in Spanish and French, for example, tends more to be dental than alveolar.
- **Alveolar [n]:** The alveolar nasal is a contrastive sound of English, usually spelled <n> (not followed by <k> or <g>).
- A reminder that it is not enough to note that the blade of the tongue contacts the alveolar ridge, without noting that the sides of the tongue form an airtight seal all the way back to the pharynx. This is true of all lingual nasals, from the dental nasal back.
- **Retroflex [ɳ]:** This nasal consonant is made with the tongue tip pointing upwards and contacting the roof of the mouth in the postalveolar region. Languages that have retroflex nasals include many languages of India, as well as numerous others. When such languages are written in the latin alphabet, it is most usual to denote the retroflex nasal with a dot under the letter, thus: <ṇ>. The name of the great Sanskrit grammarian of the fourth century BCE, Pāṇini, is usually written in English this way (with the dot under the <n> to show retroflexion).
- **Palatal [ɲ]:** When the front part of the tongue dorsum creates an occlusion against the palate, a palatal nasal is created. This sound occurs in English as a variant of [n], particularly when the [n] is followed by the y-sound,[6] as in *ca*nyon. Many languages have this sound in their inventories, and this includes romance languages such as French, Spanish, and Italian. In French and Italian, this sound is normally spelled <gn>,

---

[5] There are rare exceptions among the world's languages – for example, Icelandic has voiceless nasal consonants. A voiceless nasal is written with the normal voiced symbol, with a voicelessness diacritic written underneath: [m̥ n̥]. Where the nasal consonant symbol has a descender, the voicelessness diacritic may be written above: [ŋ̊].

[6] This is written [j] in the IPA, as we shall see in Section 5.11.4.

as in *agneau* ('lamb' in French) or the equivalent *agnello* in Italian. The same sound is spelled with a tilde over the <n> in Spanish, thus: <ñ>.

- **Velar [ŋ]:** When the back part of the tongue dorsum makes an occlusion in the velar region, the velar nasal is articulated. Note that the velum must remain lowered somewhat so that the velopharyngeal passage remains open. This sound is common in English and is spelled <ng> as in *sing*. Notice that the sound written <n> is pronounced as [ŋ] when followed by a velar sound: *think, tank, mangle,* and so on.

- Unlike the plosives and the other nasal consonants, there is a restriction on the possible positions of the velar nasal in English. It must always follow the vowel in the syllable, never precede it. While *shong* could be a possible English word, *ngosh* could not (if the <ng> represents [ŋ]). But in many languages, this sound is found before the vowel in a word. For example, the basic currency unit in the country Bhutan is the *ngultrum*. Practice saying [ŋ] at the beginning of a series of nonsense words: *ngo, ngall,* etc.

- **Uvular [ɴ]:** The uvular nasal is less common than other nasal consonants but occurs in a number of languages. In Afrikaans, Dutch, and Spanish it occurs as a variant of [n] before a uvular fricative. Again, notice that, while the back of the tongue is pressed against the uvula, the velum remains lowered far enough to ensure that the velopharyngeal passage remains open.

5.8.3 Nasal contrasts in English

English contrasts 3 nasal consonants: bilabial, alveolar and velar /m n ŋ/. English contrasts the first two sounds in all positions within words: at the beginning of words, in the middle of words, and at the end. The last, the velar, occurs only after vowels, so never at the beginning of a word.

5.9   Fricatives

Starting with the fricatives, we are presenting consonant manners of articulation in a different order from that found on the IPA consonant chart; the order here takes into account how common sounds are in English.

Fricatives[7] are sounds that are produced by forcing air under a certain amount of pressure through a narrowing or constriction in the vocal tract. The flow of air becomes turbulent and therefore noisy, and this contributes to the particular characteristic sound of the fricatives.

---

[7] In the past, the term *spirant* was often used for what are now generally called *fricatives*.

For fricatives made in the oral cavity (which is all the fricatives of English and other European languages), leaving the velopharyngeal port open will bleed away a significant portion of the air pressure needed to create the fricative; the air would escape through the nostrils. In the cases of those fricatives requiring the highest pressure (such as /s/ and /ʃ/), an open VPP will likely result in the fricative not being produced at all because the air pressure would be insufficient. For fricatives requiring less air pressure than these, an open VPP will still allow some air pressure to leak away. The fricative produced in this way will be less loud and will have a nasal quality, but it may still be audible. For fricatives made in the pharynx or at the glottis, the state of the velopharyngeal port does not change the nature of the sound generated at the constriction, though it will contribute to the overall sound.

5.9.1   The nature of the constriction

Fricatives are produced, as we noted, at a constricted point in the vocal tract, leading to turbulence and the generation of noise. Again, we need to consider more than simply the place of articulation. As with other manners of articulation, we need to understand that the tongue will seal along its sides to direct airflow to the place of articulation.[8]

But, with fricatives, there is an additional factor: the shape of the small opening. In the production of some fricatives, the tongue is grooved along the centerline. That is, the edges are raised so that the center creates a groove. When the tongue is placed against the passive articulator, the shape of the small opening will be approximately round. By contrast, the tongue can be held relatively flat, so that the small opening will be more the shape of a wide oval rather than round. Much of the difference in sound between the s-sound and the sh-sound has to do with the shape of the constriction.

5.9.2   The wide range of fricative sounds

A quick glance at the IPA table of consonants shows that there is a far greater number of different symbols for fricatives made at different places of articulation than any other manner of articulation. This has to do with the fact that this manner of articulation leads to very distinctive sounding phones at only slightly different places of articulation, where the same does not happen with other manners of articulation. Let us take the example of plosives: [t̪] and [d̪] do not sound a lot different from [t] and [d], and languages do not typically contrast them. However, fricatives made at these places of articulation, [θ] and [ð] contrasted with [s] and [z], sound very different and are often contrasted, as they are in English. The fact is that small

---

[8] There is an exception to this, and that is where the fricative is made over the edges of the tongue, not in the center of the vocal tract. See Section 5.11.3.

differences in place of articulation make significant differences in sound and are exploited by the world's languages, so there are more different fricatives than other types of consonants. Note that several of the columns of the standard IPA consonant table contain only fricatives; in addition, several fricatives shown in the "Other symbols" chart are not included in the standard table (two of them have been added to the one-line table below).[9] Additionally, the standard table has a row "Lateral fricative," another type of fricative. So, the fricative row below is actually two columns wider than the way it is typically charted.

5.9.3 Voiced and voiceless

It is common for relative beginners in phonetics to feel that voiced consonants are just the same as the voiceless one having the same place and manner of articulation, simply with the addition of voicing (vocal fold vibration). But the situation is more complicated than that. We will have more to say about this later in the chapter (Section 5.15, and more in Section 8.4), but for the moment let us just consider voicing in fricatives. When a sound is voiceless, the vocal folds are separated enough for air to flow between them quite easily. Therefore, voiceless fricatives can be made with quite high air pressure. When a sound is voiced, however, the airflow from the lungs must make the vocal folds vibrate, and this slows down the flow of air considerably; in addition, it restricts the amount of air pressure possible.

Try this experiment. Put your hand over your mouth, so close that your hand is touching, but allow small spaces for air to escape. Now produce a prolonged s-sound as loud as you can. You can feel air flowing over your hand. Now produce a prolonged z-sound as loud as you can. You will feel that the airflow is much less.

The lower air pressure and airflow possible with voiced fricatives means that the generation of turbulence is less in the voiced fricatives than the voiceless ones, and that therefore the amount of turbulent noise is reduced in the voiced ones. The sound of voiced and voiceless fricatives is very different, and not simply because one is voiced and the other not.

5.9.4 Fricatives and languages

In the following table, the Fricative line of the IPA chart has been repeated, but modified as noted previously. A column has been added for alveo-palatal fricatives in the "Other symbols" section of the IPA chart (called alveolo-palatal in the official chart).

---

[9] In the IPA chart under "Other symbols," the following sounds are shown as fricatives: /ɕ/, /ʑ/, /ʍ/, /ɦ/, and /ʕ/. /ɕ/ and /ʑ/ are the two that have been moved to the Fricatives table in Section 5.9.4. The next of these, /ʍ/, will be considered below under Approximants (Section 5.11). The other two are mentioned in Section 5.9.4.2.

	Bilabial	Labiodental	Dental	Alveolar	Alveolar Lateral	Postalveolar	Alveopalatal	Retroflex	Palatal	Velar	Uvular	Pharyngeal	Glottal
Fricatives	ɸ β	f v	θ ð	s z	ɬ ɮ	ʃ ʒ	ɕ ʑ	ʂ ʐ	ç ʝ	x ɣ	χ ʁ	ħ ʕ	h ɦ

Because there are so many fricatives, for this one row of the IPA table, we have done something different to reduce possible confusion. We have marked in gray those columns that are of no relevance to English. We will consider first the plain columns in order (sounds relevant to English), then consider the gray columns in order, left to right. The palatal column does not contain a contrastive sound in English, but does contain one sound that occurs with some frequency in English.

5.9.4.1 Fricatives relevant to English (including one variant sound)

SIDEBAR 5.8 Spelling of [θ] and [ð]

Modern English spells both of these sounds <th>. In Old English, these sounds did not contrast with one another, but there was a special letter that was used to write this sound. It is called *thorn*, and is derived from the ancient north European Runic alphabet. In Old English, *the* was pronounced pretty much as it is today, but was written <þe>. Thorn was usually used at the beginning of words, where a <d> with a bar through it, called bar-d, was used in other positions, such as old English *eorðe*, meaning 'earth.' Thorn and bar-d are still used in Icelandic; the upper-case forms are <Þ> and <Ð>.

- *Labiodental* [f v]: The lower lip is placed against the upper incisors to create the labiodental fricatives. These sounds are quite common in the world's languages.
- In English, they are spelled with the letters <f v>. The spelling <ph> is quite common for [f], as in *phonetics* and *pharynx*. One peculiarity about spelling [v] in English is that the letter <v> is rarely doubled, even to show the pronunciation of the preceding vowel as is done with other consonants. The letter <w> represents [v] in some languages, and <v> represents [f] in some.
- *Dental* [θ ð]: The dental or interdental fricatives are common sounds in English in all word positions.
- English spelling does not distinguish these sounds, spelling both <th>. Many speakers of English are unaware that these are two different sounds. The

voiced [ð] occurs in the words *thy* and *either*, where the voiceless [θ] occurs in *thigh* and *ether*. The voiceless [θ] occurs in European Spanish, where it is spelled with a <c> or a <z>. The voiced [ð] is articulated where a <d> occurs between vowels in most varieties of Spanish (see also Sidebar 5.8).

• *Alveolar* [s z]:

With respect to spelling, it is important to note that in English, the sound [z] is often spelled with the letter <s>, as in the word *is*. These two phones are not only alveolar, but they are *grooved* as well. That is to say, the center of the tongue is lowered with respect to the sides, making a smaller, rounder space for the air to pass through.

• *Postalveolar* [ʃ ʒ]: First, there is a potential for terminological confusion here. These phones have traditionally been called *alveo-palatal/alveopalatal*. However, in the current version of the IPA, these are called *postalveolar* (meaning just behind the alveolar region), and the term *alveopalatal* (or *alveolo-palatal*) is reserved for the relatively rare phones described below in Section 5.9.4.2).

We will conform to current IPA practice and use the term *postalveolar*, but note that you may come across the term *alveopalatal* for these phones, and your professor may prefer the latter term.

These phones are quite common among the world's languages and both count among the sounds of English, as in *sheep* and *vision*. [ʃ] is quite consistently spelled <sh> in English, though in a few words borrowed from

We have all seen signs in fake "Old English" (in fact, fake Early Modern English) saying things like "Ye olde tea-shoppe." *Ye* has never been the word for *the* in English. Its use is an error that occurred when the letter thorn was no longer used, and people not familiar with thorn saw *þe* in older writings and thought that the strange letter must be a <y>. So if you see a sign that writes *the* as <ye>, pronounce it just like *the*; that's close to how it's always been pronounced.

SIDEBAR 5.9 Spelling of voiceless and voiced fricatives in English

We have noted in this section that, in the spelling of English, voiceless and voiced fricatives are not consistently distinguished the way that plosives, for example, are. While we use the letter <z>, it is actually uncommon; most [z] sounds are spelled <s> in English, such as in the words *is* and *busy*. Likewise, English uses the letter <v>, but rare instances of the sound [v] are represented by the letter <f>, as in *of*. In general, though, the use of a distinct letter (<v>) for the voiced fricative is the most consistently spelled voiced fricative in English.

[θ] and [ð] are never distinguished in English spelling, both being spelled <th>. And there is no consistent spelling at all for [ʒ], as in *garage*, *leisure*, *genre*, *beige*, *déjà vu* (there is considerable dialect variation in the pronunciation in these words, so they may not contain [ʒ] in your speech).

In Old English, voiceless and voiced fricatives were not distinguished; they were positional variants. This has led to the present situation where vocabulary has been added since Middle English times, making the voiceless and voiced fricatives distinct, but the spelling has not kept pace.

It would be very straightforward to use <th> versus <dh> and <sh> versus <zh>, but spelling reform for a language as widely used as English is a nonstarter.

French, it may be spelled <ch>.[10] By contrast, [ʒ] is very inconsistently spelled in English, as in *vision, genre, beige*, etc. When languages that do not use the latin alphabet are transliterated,[11] the spelling <zh> is often used, by analogy with <sh>, for example, the former Soviet premier Leonid Brezhnev. The letter <j> is used for the transliteration of this sound from other languages that use the latin alphabet; this sound is spelled <j> in French, as in some borrowed words or expressions such as *déjà vu*.

Farsi (Persian) has the sound [ʒ] and it is usually spelled with a <j> when written in the latin alphabet.

- *Palatal* [ç j̊]: Neither of these sounds is a contrastive sound in the English inventory, but the voiceless sound is pronounced by many speakers. In words that start with <h> followed by a pronounced "you" [ju], the tongue is in the position for a [ç] and the high rate of airflow typical of [h] creates this sound in words such as *huge, humungous, human*, etc. Other talkers de-emphasize the voiceless [h] in these words, and some produce a short, weak [j̊] at the beginning of these words.

- *Glottal* [h ɦ]: The sound spelled <h> in English at the beginning of a word or the beginning of a stressed syllable is a fricative made at the glottis, between the vocal folds. Typically, the articulators are held in position for the following vowel when [h] is produced. The configuration of the glottis is similar to that for whispering, so the initial [h] is like a whispered version of the following vowel.

  The phone [ɦ] is a voiced [h]. Because the sound is a fricative, there must be a frictional sound as the air passes through the glottis, but there must be voicing as well. The result may be akin to noisy breathy voicing (see Chapter 8). In some varieties of English, this phone is how the <h> in a word like be<u>h</u>ind is pronounced. Because the sounds on both sides are voiced, the [h] is voiced as [ɦ]. This is not a distinctive phoneme in English.

---

[10] For example, the word *chassis*, though the initial sound is pronounced as [tʃ], not [ʃ] in many regions of the US.

[11] To transliterate is to write a word from one language in the writing system of another language. It does *not* mean to translate. So, when a Russian, an Arabic, or a Japanese word is written in the latin alphabet, it has been *transliterated*.

5.9.4.2   Fricatives that do not occur in English

*   *Bilabial* [ɸ β]: Pull the corners of your mouth back (as in a slight smil-ing gesture) while keeping the lips close together or touching. Blow air through the slight opening: this is the voiceless [ɸ]. If you produce voicing while doing this, you'll pronounce the voiced [β].

    The voiceless [ɸ] is a sound in the inventory of Japanese. When Japanese is written with the latin alphabet, this sound is represented by the letter <f> but it is usually not the [f] sound as in English.

    In Spanish, the sound written as <v> is often pronounced as [β] in word-initial and word-medial positions, thus, *vamos* [βamos]. There is much variation in this sound among dialects.

*   *Lateral fricatives* [ɬ ɮ]: It may seem unnecessary to write *fricatives* in this heading, but the word *lateral* alone can be mistaken for the much more common *lateral approximants* (which we will examine below in Section 5.11). So, to be clear: these are *lateral fricatives*.

    Place your tongue in position to say an l-sound (that is, L). Now blow air out through your mouth while keeping your tongue in position for the [l]. The air passes noisily over the sides of the tongue, creating the sound [ɬ]. The word *lateral* refers to the side of something, and lat-erals are sounds that are created at the sides of the tongue, not over the center of the tongue, as is typical of other speech sounds.

    If you say that same sound again, but make your vocal folds vibrate while doing so, you will create the voiced lateral fricative [ɮ]. One lan-guage that has a voiceless lateral fricative is Welsh; in Welsh, the double <ll> spelling is a lateral fricative, thus the name *Lloyd* in Welsh starts with a fricative, not the kind of l-sound that English has.

*   *Alveopalatal* [ɕ ʑ]: Again, a terminological comment: the term *alveo-palatal* has been used for years in reference to [ʃ] and [ʒ]; however, following the official IPA, we are calling those sounds *postalveolar*, and are using *alveopalatal* for [ɕ] and [ʑ]. As noted above, your professor may wish to use the term *alveopalatal* in the traditional way, for [ʃ] and [ʒ], and may have no reason to refer to [ɕ] and [ʑ].

    These sounds are relatively uncommon; they are pronounced slight-ly back of the postalveolar region but still on the border between alve-olar and palatal regions. Polish has an unusual set of contrasts: in both voiceless and voiced sets, it distinguishes dental, retroflex and alveopal-atal fricatives – [s̪ ʂ ɕ] and [z̪ ʐ ʑ].

*   *Retroflex* [ʂ ʐ]: As with the retroflex plosives above, curl the tongue backward so that the tip is pointing upwards. Blow air gently through to make a sound that is similar to [s]. Same for the voiced [ʐ], with voicing. As noted above, these are both sounds of Polish. As noted

elsewhere, many of the languages of India have retroflex consonants – for example, Marathi has the voiceless [ʂ].

Velar [x ɣ]: Velar fricatives are quite common among the world's languages. To pronounce [x], place your tongue in position to say a [k], but do not press the tongue hard against the velum. Blow air through the constriction you've created, and the sound generated is [x]. As with the other fricatives, do the same but producing voicing in order to produce [ɣ].

[x] is the sound spelled <ch> in Scottish *loch*. [x] is a common sound in German, also spelled <ch>, as in *lachen*, 'to laugh.' In Spanish, this is the sound spelled <j> or <g> before <i> or <e>. Occasionally, this sound is spelled <x> in Spanish: *Mexico*.

- [ɣ] occurs in Spanish when a [g] occurs between vowels, as in *amigo* [amiɣo]. This sound is also common in Dutch.
- *Uvular* [χ ʁ]: These fricatives are produced slightly farther back than velars; the arch of the tongue more directly contacts the region of the uvula. Note the difference between the symbols for the voiceless velar and uvular fricatives: [x χ]. The uvular [χ ʁ] are sounds in classical Arabic, but in most modern vernaculars, they have been replaced by velars.
- *Pharyngeal* [ħ ʕ]: These fricatives are produced by retracting the root of the tongue, narrowing the pharynx; in effect, the tongue root approximates the back wall of the pharynx. These consonants are present in Arabic.
- *Epiglottal* [ʜ ʕ]: These fricatives are very rare and involve the epiglottis in their production. One or both appear in one variety of Arabic, in Chechen, Haida, and Somali, among other languages.

5.10 Affricates

There is no row in the IPA consonant table for affricates because affricates are the combination of other sounds that are listed in the table. However, these sounds are distinguished from simple sequences in that they have a consistent structure and have phonological status in a given language.

Affricates are the combination of a plosive followed by a fricative having the same voicing and the same place of articulation. In English, the two affricates are [tʃ] as in *church* and [dʒ] as in *judge*. In these affricates, the fricative part is postalveolar where the symbols [t d] are understood to represent alveolars. In reality, the plosive part is retracted to the postalveolar area. Technically, it might be more correct to mark the plosive with the diacritic for retraction: [t̠ d̠]; in practice, this is almost never done.

Affricates are to be distinguished from a simple sequence of plosive plus fricative by a number of factors, including the status of the affricate in the sound system of the language and the details of the articulation. For example, consider the expression _chocolate shop_. There is an affricate [tʃ] at the beginning of _chocolate_, but the [t] at the end of _chocolate_ combines with the [ʃ] at the beginning of _shop_ to create a similar sequence. However, there are both phonetic differences between the two [tʃ], sequences and differences in how speakers of English would perceive the two.

If it is necessary to distinguish an affricate from a sequence, there are a couple of ways this can be done. The two characters in an affricate can be connected with a ligature (also called a tie-bar), thus: [t͡ʃ]. Or a digraph may be used if available with the font one is using. A digraph is a single character made up of the combination of 2 individual letters: [ʧ ʤ].

Affricates are quite common among the world's languages. German has [p͡f], as in _Pfeffer_ 'pepper.' It also has one of the most common affricates, [ts], spelled <z> as in _spazieren_, 'to walk.' The same affricate, spelled also with a <z>, occurs in Italian, as in the familiar words _pizza_ and _piazza_. Quebec French has both [ts] and [dz], which are generally lacking in French spoken elsewhere; they are not explicitly reflected in the writing system, thus _tu_ [tsy] 'you (singular/familiar).'

5.11 Approximants

Approximants are a class of sounds with some consonant characteristics and some vowel characteristics. Most of them are voiced (like vowels). The name comes from the fact that the articulators are **approximated** (brought close together) in their production, but not so much that a consonant-like noise is generated, or that air is diverted through the nose.

There are two basic types of approximants, namely **laterals** and **glides**. In the Approximant row of the official IPA table, the sounds are glides, and this term has been added in the portion of the table shown below.

5.11.1 Liquids: important note on classification and terminology

The sounds in this section include the English l-sounds [l ɫ] and the North American English r-sound [ɹ]. These sounds are classed as **approximants**, in keeping with the classification of the official IPA (table in Section 5.5). It has been traditional to classify these sounds as **liquids**, a term with a long history but which has been applied to different groups of sounds.[12] Classing

---

[12] The term goes back to a Latin translation of a term meaning 'moist' in ancient Greek, and which referred to _r_, _l_, _m_, and _n_ as they related to the meter of Greek poetry.

[ɹ l ɫ] together under a single exclusive label does capture the similarities among these sounds, but it fails to capture their similarity to the *glides*, and the fact that [ɹ] actually acts as a glide in most varieties of English. The term *approximant* captures all these similarities and is in keeping with official IPA usage.

We will make no further reference to the term *liquid* here, but your professor may prefer to use this term that has long been used to group these sounds.

Further, the term *glide* does not form part of the terminology of the IPA, but this term is useful in categorizing a distinct subclass of approximants. The term *glide* will be used throughout the book.

5.11.2   Approximants and languages

In the table below, three symbols, [ʍ], [w], and [ɥ] have been moved from the "Other symbols" section of the IPA consonant page to the Approximant row. They each appear in two columns (bilabial and velar) because there are relevant articulatory gestures related to both columns.[13] As above, we have also added the dental articulation, which is normally not shown in the IPA table because of the diacritic. Finally, we have added a second alveolar lateral, which is repeated in the velar column, for reasons that will be made clear below. Phones that appear in more than one column of this table are shown with shading to draw your attention to the fact that they appear twice. Remember that when an entire cell is grayed out, it means that the articulation of such a sound is impossible. In this table, we have emphasized individual symbols to remind the reader that these symbols appear in more than one column.

	Bilabial	Labio-dental	Dental	Alveolar	Post-alveolar	Retroflex	Palatal	Velar
Approximant (Glide)	ʍ w ɥ	ʋ			ɹ		ɻ	j ɥ	ʍ w
Lateral approximant			l̪	l ɫ		ɭ	ʎ	ʟ ɫ

---

[13] The fact that they would appear in two columns is the reason why the compilers of the IPA table did not place these symbols within the main table, but in the "Other symbols" section.

5.11.3   Lateral approximants

As noted above under the heading of *lateral fricatives*, *lateral* sounds are made with the tongue blocking the center of the vocal tract, but air and sound are free to move over the sides of the tongue and out of the open mouth. In the case of the lateral fricative, air is forced out at sufficient speed to generate noise as it passes over the sides of the tongue.

In the case of *lateral approximants*, there is voicing, and the airflow is not rapid enough to cause noisy turbulence.

Remember that we emphasized for earlier types of speech sounds – plosives, fricatives, and so on – that just giving the place of articulation is not a complete articulatory description of the sound. It is necessary to specify that the edges of the tongue contact the palate or molars in order to make a complete seal. In the case of lateral approximants, the sides do not seal. In general, the open area along the sides is toward the front; there remains a seal at the back end of the mouth.

- *Dental lateral approximant* [l̪]: This sound is produced similarly to the English l-sound, except with the tongue contacting the upper incisors rather than the alveolar ridge. Spanish and French tend toward dental, rather than alveolar, articulations.
- *Alveolar lateral approximant* [l]: This is the l-sound that is typical of English, particularly where the [l] is at the beginning of words and associated with certain vowels (namely high front vowels[14]), for example, in a word like *lip*.
- *Velarized alveolar lateral approximant* [ɫ]: The symbol for this sound has been added to the table above, but is not found on the IPA table, again because it uses a diacritic. In a section below, there will be reference to the concept of *velarization*. For the moment, this is essentially the same as the [l] above except that the back of the tongue is raised – and makes a kind of approximant – with the velar region. This sound is the English l-sound at the ends of words and associated with back vowels, for example, in the word *full*. Russian makes a distinction between these two types of l-sound; English has both but does not distinguish them (see also Section 1.6.3).
- *Retroflex lateral approximant* [ɭ]: We have seen other retroflex consonants in previous sections, and the tongue movement and posture are the same except for the opening on both sides of the tongue. In the same way, this

---

[14] This topic will be treated in Chapter 6, so you may be unfamiliar with this terminology. It is stated here for when you are reviewing and for those readers who are familiar with vowel classification.

is an l-sound made with the tip of the tongue pointed vertically upwards. This sound occurs in Marathi and Gujarati, among many other languages.

- *Palatal lateral approximant* [ʎ]: Place your tongue in position for the ee-sound. Now raise the center of the tongue to contact the palate, while leaving space on both sides of the tongue. This is the sound spelled with a double <ll> in Spanish.
- *Velar lateral approximant* [ʟ]: To produce this sound, the center line of the tongue makes contact with the velar region (as for [k] and [g]), but the edges of the tongue are drawn in so that air passes on the two sides. This sound is notoriously difficult for individuals whose native language does not have this sound.

5.11.4   Glides

We are using the term *glide* to characterize the sounds in the row called *approximants* in the IPA. The use of the term *glide* has particular implications: it suggests a *movement* of the articulators.

To be clear, all *glides* are *approximants* but there may be approximants that are not glides (depending on how the author defines *approximant*).

A glide is an approximant sound that involves movement of the articulators, either *away from* the sound preceding or *toward* the sound following. One might counter this definition by saying that all phones in the context of connected speech involve movement from the previous sound and toward the following sound. What is different in the case of glides is that it is the fact of movement that characterizes the glide sound; if the movement is too slow, a glide will sound like a vowel. When a person speaks at a very slow rate, phones will be prolonged to various degrees, but glides must maintain a minimum speed of movement to be perceived as glides.

- *Labiovelar glides*[15] [ʍ w] (found in both the bilabial and velar columns):
  - o *Voiceless labiovelar glide* [ʍ]: Note first that the symbol [ʍ] is not an <M>; it is an upside-down <W>. This phone is produced with the back of the tongue approximating the velum while the lips are rounded, thus the term *labiovelar*. This phone occurs in some varieties of English, appearing as the first phone of *which*, for those speakers who pronounce *which* differently from *witch*. These two words are pronounced the same in most varieties of English, while the distinction is maintained in parts of the United States.
  - o *Voiced labiovelar glide* [w]: This phone is produced similarly to [ʍ], but with voicing and with a lesser flow of air than [ʍ]. This is the sound at the beginning of most English words that start with the

---

[15] We will comment below on the use of the term *labiovelar*, which seems to contradict what was said in Section 5.2.5.2.

letter <w>. In most of the English-speaking world, words starting <wh> are also pronounced [w], but <wh> words are pronounced with [ʍ] in some regions. In a small number of French borrowings in English, this sound is spelled <ou>, such as *bivouac*.

- *Labiopalatal glide* [ɥ] (found in both the bilabial and palatal columns): Note that the symbol [ɥ] is not a <y>; it is an upside down <h>. This glide involves tongue approximation in the palatal area and rounding of the lips. Like other glides, the movement of the articulators to or from this position is distinct and quite rapid. This sound occurs quite commonly in French, spelled <u>,[16] such as in the word *puis*, meaning 'then.'
- *Alveolar (bunched, rhotic) glide* [ɹ]: This is the type of r-sound that is common to North American varieties of English. The term *rhotic* comes from the word *rho*, the name of the Greek letter that represents the r-sound. This sound also has the characteristic of being "bunched." *Bunched* refers to the fact that the tongue is tightened up into a rounder shape than at rest. This distinctive shape can be seen in Figure 5.6.
- *Retroflex glide* [ɻ]: This is the type of r-sound that occurs in some speakers of North American English, especially when the r-sound follows an initial [t] or [d], as in *train* or *drain*. See Figure 5.7.
- *Palatal glide* [j]: This is the glide that is usually spelled with the letter <y> in English, as at the beginning of *yes* and *yellow*. Note that the IPA symbol is [j] ([y] is the symbol for a particular vowel).

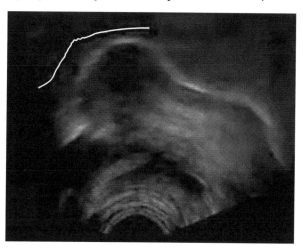

Figure 5.6 An ultrasonic image of an American English bunched [ɹ]. The white line shows the location of the palate and alveolar ridge. This image has been reversed left-to-right so that the front of the mouth is on the left, to match the orientation of Figure 5.1 and others in this book.

---

[16] In French, the spelling <u> represents both a vowel and the labiopalatal glide, depending on the syllable structure of the word.

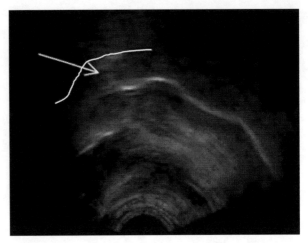

Figure 5.7 An ultrasonic image of a retroflexed [ɻ]. The arrow points to the blade of the tongue pointing upward. The white line shows the location of the palate and alveolar ridge. This image has been reversed left-to-right.

5.12   Flaps

Flaps are created with a ballistic movement of the tongue (or, in one rare phone, the lower lip). This type of articulation is explained in Sections 5.4.2, with Sections 5.4.3 and 5.4.4 detailing the subsequent tongue movement. Briefly, to produce a flap, the tongue (or lip) is made to move abruptly in the direction of the closure and is then relaxed so that the rest of the movement occurs through momentum and rebound.

5.12.1   Flaps and languages

In the table below are the flaps recognized in the IPA.

	Bilabial	Labiodental	Dental	Alveolar	Postalveolar	Retroflex
Flap		ʋ		ɾ		ɽ
(Nasal, lateral flap)				(n) (l)		

In the IPA chart, the *Flap* row is labeled "*Tap* or *Flap*." In fact, the distinction between taps and flaps is somewhat inconsistent, and most phoneticians do not make the distinction at all. Additionally, there are not separate IPA symbols for taps and flaps. For these reasons, the distinction will not be made here; we will use the term *flap*.

In the table above, it will be seen that another row has been added, one that is not present in the IPA table, but that the symbols in this row are not different from those for the alveolar nasal and alveolar lateral approximant. This addition will be explained below.

- *Labiodental flap* [ⱱ]: This flap of the lower lip against the upper incisors is relatively rare among the world's languages, but is present in a number of Central African languages.
- *Alveolar flap* [ɾ]: This flap occurs in North American English where a [t] or a [d] occurs in intervocalic position (i.e., between vowels) and after a stressed syllable; that is, in words such as *ma<u>tt</u>er* and *la<u>dd</u>er* (see also Sidebar 5.10).
- *Rhotic alveolar flap* [ ]: There exists a flapped r-like sound that is also alveolar, but the IPA does not have a symbol that is distinct from that for the non-rhotic alveolar flap. The flapped r-sound occurs in many languages such as Spanish (spelled with a single <r>) and British English between vowels (such as a British pronunciation of the word *ve<u>r</u>y*).
- *Retroflex flap* [ɽ]: The production of this sound is very similar to that of the alveolar flap, but the tongue goes farther up and back to the retroflex position that we have seen in a number of other manners of articulation.

The nasal and lateral flaps are shown in a row of the table above, but are not shown in the IPA table, nor do they have particular symbols. In the same situations where North American English makes a flap of [t] and [d], it makes a flap of [n] and [l], as in *ma<u>n</u>y* and *be<u>ll</u>y*.

5.13 Trills

Trills are speech sounds produced when the airflow over a particular articulator causes it to vibrate back and forth. This was explained in 5.4.4. There are three articulators that can be made to vibrate in this manner: the lips, the forward part of the tongue, and the uvula. All three types of trill are attested among the world's languages.

5.13.1   Trills and Languages

Bilabial trill [ʙ]: This sound is made somewhat like the sound we make to indicate that we are very cold; this sound in English is usually written *Brrrrrr.* This is a speech sound of a relatively limited number of languages.

	Bilabial	Labio-dental	Dental	Alveolar	Post-alveolar	Retroflex	Palatal	Velar	Uvular
Trill	ʙ			r					ʀ

- *Alveolar trill* [r]: This sound is produced by the aerodynamic vibration of the tip and blade of the tongue. The Spanish r-sound written with a double <rr> is such a trill, and sometimes the single <r> at the beginning of Spanish words is pronounced as a trill.
- *Uvular trill* [ʀ]: This sound is produced by the aerodynamic vibration of the uvula. Some languages have this sound in their inventory, and some European languages have an r-sound that contains aspects of both a uvular fricative and a uvular trill: [ʁ] and [ʀ] – that is, while the uvula is trilled, there is considerable frictional noise generated between the back of the tongue and the uvular region.

Note that all the trills are voiced.

5.13.2   The movement of trills is aerodynamic

It might be natural to think that the multiple movements of a trill are created through multiple muscular contractions, but this is not the case. Muscles cannot repeatedly contract as fast as the vibrations of a trill. Production is a matter of placing the articulator in a position where airflow will cause vibration. In the case of the uvular trill, it is a matter of raising the back of the tongue such that airflow is directed over the uvula.

5.14   Secondary articulation and double articulation

5.14.1   Secondary articulation

A *secondary articulation* involves a second place of articulation that has less constriction than the primary place of articulation. (If the two constrictions are equal, it is a *double articulation*: Section 5.14.2.) Secondary articulations of consonants are relatively common among the world's languages.

The clearest example in English is the l-sound. In English, where the l-sound occurs after vowels, particularly the vowels of words like *fool, full,* and *foal,* the l-sound is produced with a secondary articulation in the velar region. This kind of l-sound is sometimes called *dark l*, but the proper term is *velarized l*, or, more specifically, ***velarized alveolar lateral approximant***. By contrast, the l-sound in words like *lip*, *leek*, and *late* are not velarized; there is no secondary articulation in the velar region.

One diacritic for velarization is [~] written though the symbol for the non-velarized sound, so velarized [l] is written [ɫ] in the IPA – but note the table below.

5.14.1.1   Secondary articulation terminology

The terminology for secondary articulations is very specific. The place of articulation of the secondary articulation is turned into an adjective ending *-ized*, and this term is given before *voicing* or *place* or *manner of articulation*.

Table 5.1 Secondary articulations

Place of secondary articulation	Term	Symbol and example	
lips, labial	labialized	ʷ	tʷ
palate, palatal	palatalized	ʲ	tʲ
velum, velar	velarized	ˠ	tˠ
pharynx, pharyngeal	pharyngealized	ˤ	tˤ
either velarized or pharyngealized		~	ɫ

5.14.1.2   Other secondary articulations

Speech sounds may have secondary articulations in a number of different places of articulation, as shown in Table 5.1.

Note from the table that the usual way of transcribing a velarized [ɫ] is with a diacritic that is ambiguous as to whether it means velarized or pharyngealized or both. This is done as a matter of tradition.

5.14.2   Double articulation

Some languages have phones that have double articulation – that is, the phone has two places of articulation simultaneously. For instance, the language Igbo, spoken in a region of southern Nigeria, has doubly articulated plosives that combine a bilabial with a velar: [k͡p ɡ͡b]. (The ligature tying the two characters together may be placed over or under the individual letters.) The name of the language, Igbo, does not contain a [g] followed by a [b]; rather, it contains one consonant that is a simultaneous [g] and [b].

In North American English, the word *potato* is often produced with a doubly articulated plosive: [p͡teiɾo]; the vowel of the first syllable is dropped and the [p] and the [t] are produced simultaneously in casual, rapid speech.

5.14.2.1   Manners of double articulation

The example above showed a doubly articulated plosive. There is some doubt as to whether doubly articulated fricatives or approximants exist. (The IPA "Other symbols" section shows the IPA letter [ɧ] for the [ʃ͡x] phone, a doubly articulated fricative. Despite this, there are claims that this sound in Swedish is either a sequence of fricatives or is the result of a secondary articulation (previous section).

5.15   Fortis versus lenis and other differences

Consonants may differ from one another in a range of characteristics beyond those that we have seen so far. A principal one is what might be characterized as "strength" differences, and the terms that are used are *fortis* and *lenis*, Latin terms for '*strong*' and '*weak*,' respectively.

The notion is that some sounds in some languages, sounds that might be characterized with the same IPA character, are in fact quite different in terms of the amount of energy put into the articulation.

It is very common for voiced consonants to be produced with less articulatory force than voiceless ones. For instance, in English, voiceless plosives in word-initial position tend to be fortis, whereas voiced plosives are lenis. In words such as *span*, *Stan*, and *scan*, the plosives tend to be lenis.

There are no diacritics in the IPA for fortis and lenis; nonetheless, it is easy to show this characteristic. Since voiceless sounds are generally fortis, a fortis voiced sound can be shown as a voiceless consonant with voicing: [p̬, t̬, k̬] – in other words, this represents a fortis (voiceless) sound that is voiced. In the same way, a voiceless lenis sound can be shown as a devoiced voiced sound: [b̥, d̥, g̥] – in other words a lenis (voiced) sound that is not voiced.

5.16   Other types of consonants

5.16.1   Airstream mechanisms

There are other types of consonants than those outlined in this chapter. Specifically, there are *ejectives* (also called *glottalized plosives*), *clicks*, and *implosives*. These will be addressed in Chapter 9, *Airstream mechanisms*, along with the production of speech by talkers whose larynx has been surgically removed.

5.16.2   Syllabic consonants

Some consonants may play the role in the syllable that vowels normally play. These are called *syllabic consonants*. A number of the consonants that we have examined earlier in this chapter can be syllabic, including nasal consonants and lateral approximants in English, and even fricatives in some other languages. These phones will be examined in Chapter 6, "Vowels," where we examine the relationship between glides and vowels and between consonants and syllabic consonants, since syllabic consonants essentially *act* as vowels.

5.17   Diacritics introduced in this chapter

The following table shows the diacritics (diacritical marks, "accents") introduced in this chapter. Your professor may wish to advise you which are important for you to know.

Diacritic	Example showing position	Meaning	Remarks	English
̪	t̪	dental articulation		allophone
.	ʈ	retroflex	not official IPA, use official symbols without diacritics[a]	a few allophones
ʰ	pʰ	aspirated	plosive released with accompanying puff of air	In English, voiceless plosives in word-initial position
͡ or ͜	t͡ʃ	shows that two symbols represent single phone	Called ligature or tie-bar Not really a diacritic, but a symbol used with IPA symbols	affricates and diphthongs
~	ɫ	velarized or pharyngealized	Not official IPA symbol but commonly used for English velarized l	velarized ɫ
ˠ	tˠ	velarized	As noted above, English velarized l more usually transcribed [ɫ]	
ˤ	tˤ	pharyngealized		
ʷ	tʷ	labialized, rounded		allophone

Diacritic	Example showing position	Meaning	Remarks	English
ˇ	ǩ	voiced (fortis)	These symbols represent voiced and voiceless, respectively. They *imply* fortis and lenis when used with consonants of the opposite voicing, as discussed in Section 5.15.	
˚	b̥	voiceless (lenis)		

ᵃ In the IPA, retroflex consonants have a symbol, that of the alveolar consonant, but with a descender (tail) that curls to the right: [ɖ ʈ ʂ ʐ ɭ ɳ]. The dot symbol shown in the table is sometimes seen in a range of sources because it was once standard usage, and it is sometimes used when writing words in one of the languages of the Indian subcontinent with the latin alphabet.

5.18   Consonant table as introduced in this chapter

Table 5.2 shows the consonants tabled in the manner shown in the various sections of this chapter, rearranged slightly from the official IPA (following the text of this chapter) for reasons of clarity.

Table 5.2 The consonant table as described in this chapter, slightly modified from the official IPA table shown in Figure 5.2. Shading is used differently from the IPA table, and some phones that are written with a diacritic are included in this table. Sounds that are said to constitute the phonemes of American English are shown in table cells that are enclosed with a double border, but note that in several instances such a cell contains an English phoneme that might be a variant sound in English, or one of the sounds in that cell does not occur in English, as detailed in the preceding sections. Shaded symbols are those whose characteristics lead them to be listed in more than one column – these are listed in a separate part of the official IPA table.

	Bilabial	Labiodental	Dental	Alveolar	Alveolar Lateral	Postalveolar	Alveopalatal	Retroflex	Palatal	Velar	Uvular	Pharyngeal	Glottal
Plosives	p b		t̪ d̪	t d				ʈ ɖ	c ɟ	k g	q ɢ		ʔ
Nasals	m	ɱ	n̪	n				ɳ	ɲ	ŋ	ɴ		
Fricatives	ɸ β	f v	θ ð	s z	ɬ ɮ	ʃ ʒ	ɕ ʑ	ʂ ʐ	ç ʝ	x ɣ	χ ʁ	ħ ʕ	h ɦ
Approximant (Glide)	w ɥ	ʋ		ɹ				ɻ	j	w			
Lateral approximant			l̪	l ɫ				ɭ	ʎ	ʟ ɫ			
Flap		ⱱ		ɾ				ɽ					
(Nasal, lateral flap)				(n) (l)									
Trill	ʙ			r							ʀ		

5.19 Vocabulary

aerodynamic
affricate
airstream mechanism
alveolar
alveopalatal
apico-postalveolar
approximant
approximate
approximation
articulate
articulation, primary, secondary, double
articulator
articulator, active, passive
aspiration
ballistic
bilabial
closing phase
closure phase
consonant
constriction
degree of voicing
deliberate
dental
diacritic
elastic recoil
flap
fortis
fricative
glide
glottal
glottal stop

gravity
interdental
International Phonetic Alphabet (IPA)
labiodental
laryngeal
lateral approximant
lateral fricative
lenis
liquid
manner of articulation
mode of voicing
nasal
palatal
pharyngeal
place of articulation (PoA)
plosive
postalveolar
recoil
release
retroflex
secondary articulation
syllabic
target
trill
uvular
velar
velarized
velopharyngeal port (VPP)
voiced
voiceless
voicing

6 | Vowels

"Lost in space"

6.1 Vowels and consonants

The basic distinction in types of speech sounds is that between *consonants* and *vowels*. As we have seen, in consonant production, the flow of air – and the transmission of sound – is blocked (plosives), constricted (fricatives), or diverted through the nose (nasals). There are also approximant consonants (Section 5.11), and they share a number of important characteristics with vowels, as we shall see in Section 6.14.

Vowels have no more constriction than for approximant consonants (though there may be *as much as* for approximant consonants), and there is no sound of friction. While in some languages (such as Japanese), vowels may be devoiced, it is usual for vowels in almost all languages to be mostly voiced in ordinary speech, although they may be devoiced if adjacent to voiceless consonants (and all sounds are devoiced in whispering).

Vowels (or vowel-like sounds) are required for the existence of syllables; a vowel is said to be the *nucleus* of a syllable. More on this topic in Section 6.13.

6.1.1 Consonants and vowels as musical instruments

It might help to understand some of the essential differences between consonants and vowels, at least in articulatory terms, by comparing them to the production of sounds with different kinds of musical instruments.

Creating a consonant sound might be likened to playing a keyboard, in the sense that hitting the right key produces the right note. The right place in consonant production is a matter of contacting (or closely approximating) the correct articulators: for example, placing the lower lip against the upper front teeth or the blade of the tongue on the alveolar ridge.

Creating vowel sounds is different in that the tongue does not contact any other articulator. The tongue is held – in a particular shape – in a three-dimensional space, but without touching other articulators that would give guidance as to where the tongue is located. This may be thought of as something like playing a slide trombone or unfretted string instrument: there are no keys or marked places to hold the slide; knowing where to place it is a matter of "muscle memory" and feedback of the sound created.

Vowels, then, are "lost in space." It is more difficult to describe what to do with the articulators in order to create a certain vowel sound than it is to describe how to create a consonant sound, due to the lack of reference points of tongue contact in the case of vowels. For these reasons, it may be easier to teach an individual to pronounce an unfamiliar consonant than an unfamiliar vowel.

SIDEBAR 6.1 Speech sounds versus letters

Again, as has been pointed out elsewhere, the latin alphabet letters that are called *vowels* in English generally represent vowel sounds in English spelling, though there are exceptions. The first sounds of *Europe* and *use* are not vowels. <Y> sometimes represents a vowel and sometimes a consonant (glide) in English spelling. Often letters called vowels represent no sound in English or may indicate what sound another letter represents, such as the <e> in *site* and similar words. Usage may be different in other languages using the latin alphabet. In Welsh, for example, <w> often represents a vowel, as it does in borrowed word *cwm*. Also, there are some patterns of spelling in English in which letters we call consonants are part of a group of letters representing a vowel sound: *right, might, high*. Sometimes we call those "silent consonants" but in fact the <gh> indicates how the letter <i> is to be pronounced, so they help the reader to know what the vowel sound is.

6.1.2   Some terms

In everyday speech, the word *vowel* typically refers to a letter of the alphabet. As we have emphasized a number of times, in this book and throughout phonetics *vowel* means a type of speech sound, not a letter (see Sidebar 6.1).

From the Latin word for vowel, **vocalic** is the adjective form of *vowel*. A *vocalic sound* is a vowel. *Postvocalic* means 'following a vowel' – for example, *The word* car *contains a postvocalic* [ɹ]. The word **prevocalic** means 'before a vowel' – for example, *The word* ham *has prevocalic aspiration*.

The particular characteristic sound of a vowel is its **quality** or **timbre**. *The letter <e> represents vowels each having a different quality in the words* b<u>e</u>t *and* b<u>ee</u>t. The word **timbre** is occasionally spelled <tamber> and that is how *timbre* is pronounced. It is not pronounced like the word *timber*. The word is French and "tamber" represents the English pronunciation that imitates the sound of the French word's first vowel.

Vowel length and the terms **long vowel** and **short vowel** are used in a different way in phonetics in comparison to how they are used in the context of teaching reading and the sound–letter correspondence in English (i.e. phonics). The usage of these terms is explained further in Section 6.9.

6.2   IPA vowel table

Figure 6.1 shows the table of vowels in the official International Phonetic Alphabet (IPA). In Figure 6.1, the terms in the column on the left have been changed from the official IPA, as shown in Table 6.1. This change is explained in Section 6.3.

Table 6.1 Terms in the IPA vowel chart

Terms in Figure 6.1	Terms in official IPA chart
High	Close
Upper mid	Close-mid
Lower mid	Open-mid
Low	Open

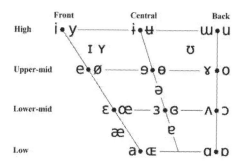

Figure 6.1 The International Phonetic Alphabet vowel table. The terms for height have been modified from the official IPA, as explained in Section 6.3 and listed in Table 6.1. IPA Chart, www .internationalphoneticassociation.org/ content/ipa-chart.

6.3   Cardinal vowels and the vowel quadrangle

As a means of trying to describe tongue placement in the production of vowel sounds, phoneticians have developed a system of classifying vowel sounds by tongue positions. There is a set of 8 vowels that are considered *primary cardinal vowels*, and another set of 8 *secondary cardinal vowels*.

These *cardinal vowels* are not intended to represent a set of vowels that exists in any one language, but rather as a set of extreme vowel articulations that can be used to locate the production of vowels within a 2-dimensional space. Other dimensions of vowel production (such as nasalization) are considered as well, but not directly in the cardinal vowel system.

The idea of "cardinal" points that permit orientation of other points is familiar to us from the points of the compass: North, East, West, and South are cardinal directions, and other directions, such as north–north–east, are defined by comparison to the cardinal points. Similarly, the set of cardinal vowels define positions in vowel space, and provide reference points to describe other vowels.

6.3.1   Other vowel dimensions

As we introduce vowels in this chapter, we are starting with the basic classi-fication shown in the IPA vowel table. This classification is based on *vowel height* and *vowel frontness*, vowel dimensions to be explained in the following section. This basic classification does not account for a number of other dimen-sions of vowel articulation that create important distinctions in many lan-guages, including English. These dimensions include *rounding, tenseness/ATR, nasalization, duration*/length, *diphthongization,* and *syllabicity.*

Each of these other vowel dimensions will be treated in its own section after cardinal vowels.

6.3.2   Primary cardinal vowels

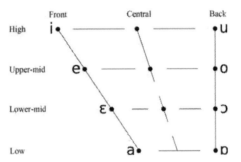

Figure 6.2 Primary cardinal vowels

The primary cardinal vowels are shown schematically in Figure 6.2. The terms *Front, Central, and Back* refer to tongue placement within the mouth, whether it is more toward the front, more toward the back, or between these extremes. This is the horizontal dimension in Figures 6.1 and 6.2, and this particular trait of the vowel is referred to as its *degree of frontness* (occa-sionally *backness*). Notice that the front of the mouth is toward the left and the back toward the right, so the orientation of the vowel quadrangle is the same as the orientation of the head in various drawings in the anatomy and consonant chapters.

The terms *High, Upper mid, Lower mid,* and *Low* refer to how high the tongue is within the oral cavity – in other words, how much space there is between the roof of the mouth (that is, the palate or velum) and the upper surface of the tongue. With high vowels, the top surface of the tongue is very near to the palate or velum; with low vowels, there is quite a distance between them. This is the vertical dimension in Figures 6.1 and 6.2, and this trait of vowels is referred to as its *height.*

Outside of North America, the height terms may be replaced by *Close*, *Half-close*, *Half-open*, and *Open* for *High*, *Upper mid*, *Lower mid*, and *Low*. These latter terms are the ones used in the official IPA but are not the usual terms in North America.

6.3.3   The vowel quadrangle

The shape of the four-sided figure defined by the cardinal vowels is referred to as the *vowel quadrangle*.[1] A quadrangle simply means a four-sided fig-ure (squares and rectangles are quadrangles, but those shapes have more specific names). The term *vowel space* is also used, not to describe the shape, but rather to indicate the space within the mouth where vowels can be articulated – the space within the quadrangle.

The vowel quadrangle is intended to represent the *entire* space in which vowels can be articulated. Consonants may be more front or more back than the quadrangle, but vowels cannot be. Again, the cardinal vowels are at the extremes of the vowel space.

We will examine in Section 6.4.3 where in the mouth this quadrangle or vowel space lies.

6.3.4   A cautionary note on key words

In a written work on phonetics, one difficulty is communicating to the reader what sounds are intended, and the way this has traditionally been done is with **key words**. The concept is very simple; it is a matter of presenting a word (in written form) that is familiar to readers, and saying simply "The symbol in question represents the sound in this word."

The difficulty (discussed previously in Chapter 1 and elsewhere) is that the word is very likely pronounced at least a little differently by different readers of the book, due to regional differences in pronunciation or even because the reader is not a native speaker of the language. The situation is worse for vowels than for consonants because there is typically much more regional and social variation in vowels than in consonants. *It is therefore very important that the reader does not rely too heavily on thinking they know the pronunci-ation that is intended by a given key word.* We are sometimes quite surprised to find how a very familiar word is pronounced in another region or country.

Fortunately, the Internet provides a way to overcome this problem. Versions of the International Phonetic Alphabet (IPA) with symbols that can be clicked in order to hear the sounds in question can be found online.[2]

---

[1] *Vowel quadrilateral* is a term that is sometimes used, and more rarely the term *trapeze* or *trapezoid*.

[2] At the time of writing, one can be found at www.internationalphoneticalphabet.org/ipa-sounds/ipa-chart-with-sounds.

6.3.5 Pronunciation of the primary cardinal vowels

Let us look at how the primary cardinal vowels are pronounced, taking into account the caution above. But there is another caution necessary with the cardinal vowels: the closest vowels in English are not the same as the cardinal vowels. But many are quite similar, so we will use key words to demonstrate those pronunciations. The pronunciations intended are General American pronunciations.

Table 6.2 begins with the high front vowel, moving down, then the high back vowel, moving down.

Table 6.2 Pronunciations close to the primary cardinal vowels		
IPA symbol	Closest English word	Descriptive term
	Comment on true cardinal vowel	
i	heap	high front tense spread vowel
	higher and more front than the English [i]; "pure" vowel, not diphthongized	
e	hate	upper mid front (tense) vowel
	more front than the English [e]; "pure" vowel, not diphthongized	
ɛ	bet	lower mid front (lax) vowel
	more front than the English [ɛ]	
a	No key word. The first vowel of *father* in certain US Midwestern pronunciations	low front vowel
u	hoot	high back rounded vowel
	higher, more back and more rounded than the English [u]; "pure" vowel, not diphthongized	
o	boat	upper mid back rounded vowel
	more back and more rounded than the English [o]; "pure" vowel, not diphthongized	

Table 6.2 (Cont.)		
IPA symbol	Closest English word	Descriptive term
	Comment on true cardinal vowel	
ɔ	caught (except in varieties that do not distinguish *caught* and *cot*)[a]	lower mid back rounded vowel
	more back and more rounded than the English [ɔ];	
ɒ	No key word. The vowel of *cot* is similar, but would need to be pronounced with rounded lips	low back rounded vowel

[a] This vowel does not occur in the speech of most Canadians or most Americans living in north central parts of the 48 contiguous American states.

6.3.5.1 The case of [æ]

In Chapter 1, we discussed the fact that certain conventional uses of phonetic symbols contravene the official IPA, but are nonetheless traditional in discussions of particular languages. It is our intention throughout this book to respect the official IPA, while at the same time acknowledging traditional ways that English phonetics are described.[3] Your instructor will give you guidance as to their preferred usage (see Sidebar 6.2).

It has been traditional in textbooks of English phonetics to show the low front vowel on the quadrangle as [æ]. This is the vowel of such English words as *bat*, *hat*, *mast*, and so on. Other material you read may reflect this usage.

The classification of cardinal vowels recognizes 4 degrees of height, and since it classifies [a] as low front, [æ] is not strictly a cardinal vowel, but it is an important vowel of English.

SIDEBAR 6.2 The vowel [æ]

Examine Figures 6.1 and 6.2 showing the official chart of the IPA. Note the location of [æ], at the front between lower mid and low.

Traditionally, especially in works summarizing English phonetics, the vowel [æ] has been shown as low front, thus:

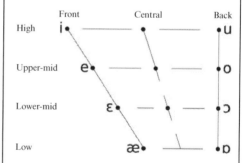

Your instructor may direct you to use the traditional English-language categorization, but we will present the IPA as currently established.

[3] For instance, the discussion of the term *liquid* in Chapter 5.

6.3.6   Secondary cardinal vowels

The secondary cardinal vowels are shown schematically in Figure 6.3.

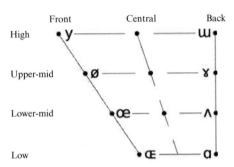

Figure 6.3 Secondary cardinal vowels

6.3.7   Difference between primary and secondary cardinal vowels – the effect of lip rounding

Figure 6.2 shows the primary cardinal vowels. All of the front primary cardinal vowels are produced with the lips either spread[4] (as for [i]) or neutral (neither spread or rounded), as for [ɛ]. All of the back primary cardinal vowels are produced with the lips rounded, as for [u].

The secondary cardinal vowels, shown in Figure 6.3, have the opposite lip rounding. Front secondary cardinal vowels are rounded, and back secondary cardinal vowels have either spread lips or neutral lips.

Modern Standard American English has only two of the eight secondary cardinal vowels, so Table 6.3 will show examples from languages other than English for the most part. Again, you can hear these vowels pronounced by using internet resources.

To pronounce the front rounded vowels, say the primary vowel at the same frontness and height (for example, to say [y], first say [i]), then, *without changing the position of your tongue*, round your lips as if to whistle.

To pronounce the back unrounded vowels, say the primary vowel at the same frontness and height (for example, to say [ɯ], first say [u]), then, *without changing the position of your tongue*, spread your lips as if to smile (although try to pull back on the corners of the mouth without pulling them upwards as in a smile).

---

[4] This is the origin of the expression "Say cheese" when a photo is taken. The vowel sound of *cheese* is [i], which is produced with spread lips, like a smile. Spreading the mouth for [i] uses the risorius muscle, literally the 'smile muscle.'

Table 6.3 Pronunciations close to the secondary cardinal vowels with examples from a variety of languages

IPA symbol	Example word	Descriptive term
	Comment on true cardinal vowel	
y	French <u> as in *rue* 'street' German <ü> *as in müssen* 'must'	high front tense rounded vowel
ø	French *feu* 'fire' German *können* 'can, be able'	upper mid front (tense) vowel
œ	French *seul* 'only, alone'	lower mid front (lax) vowel
Œ	*Occurs in some varieties of Swedish and Danish*	low front vowel
ɯ	*Found in a number of varieties of Chinese. Say "oo" (IPA [u]) and spread the lips as in a smile while keeping the tongue in the position of [u]*	high back rounded vowel
ɣ	*Say "oh" (IPA [o]) and spread the lips as in a smile*	upper mid back rounded vowel
ʌ	*cut* *The English sound tends to be more central than the cardinal vowel*	lower mid back rounded vowel
ɑ	cot	low back rounded vowel

6.3.8   Why primary and secondary?

What is the reason for distinguishing primary from secondary vowels? Are "primary" vowels truly primary in some way? It has been suggested that, given that most vowels in English are primary, the categorization is simply a matter of ethnocentricity. But there are valid reasons for the categorization that have to do with how vowel systems work universally, across languages, and have nothing to do with specific characteristics of the English language.

6.3.8.1   Frequency of occurrence of primary and secondary vowels

Across languages, primary vowels are much more common than secondary vowels. A majority of languages have few or no secondary vowels, but every language has primary vowels.

6.3.8.2 Order of acquisition

Children acquiring language tend to acquire primary vowels before the corresponding secondary vowels. For instance, imagine a language such as French or German that has both [i] and [y] (high front) in its inventory. Children acquiring these languages will learn to say [i] consistently well before they learn to say [y] consistently. Another way to look at this is to say that acquisition of the secondary vowel seems in some sense to be dependent on acquisition of the primary vowel having the same height and frontness.

6.3.8.3 Languages having a given secondary vowel have the corresponding primary vowel

If a language has a secondary vowel in its inventory, it is very likely to have the primary vowel with the same height and frontness in its inventory as well. For example, both French and German have the vowels [y] and [ø] in their inventories. This implies that they will both have [i] and [e] (the primary counterparts of these two secondary vowels) in their inventories as well, and this is indeed true.

This is not a hard and fast "rule"; rather, it is a very strong tendency. There are exceptions. Japanese has 5 vowels, of which [ɯ] (secondary) is one, but it does not have [u], the corresponding primary vowel. Most varieties of English have both [ʌ] (secondary) and [ɔ] (primary) in their inventories, as expected. But Canadian English and English spoken in the north central US have [ʌ] but not [ɔ], so they have only the secondary vowel at this height and frontness.

One way of looking at this is to realize that the rounded–spread distinction in lip posture is not absolutely binary in phonetic terms. [ɯ] in Japanese may not be rounded, but it is not particularly spread either.

Having [y] in a language's inventory almost guarantees that [i] will also be in its inventory, but most languages that have [i] do not have [y]. The implication is in one direction only.

6.3.8.4 Primary and secondary

The reasons above combine to demonstrate that primary cardinal vowels truly are primary in a very real sense, and secondary vowels are indeed secondary.

To reiterate: the *primary vowels* are **front unrounded** and **back rounded** vowels, and the *secondary vowels* are **front rounded** and **back unrounded**.

6.4 Where are front and back? What is high or low?

The vowel quadrangle is intended to represent a real physical space within the mouth, and to permit the designation of particular places within that space. But what, exactly, does it represent?

6.4.1 What is it that is high or low or front or back?

With an individual in an upright position – that is, standing or sitting erect – the "thing" that is represented within the quadrangle *is the highest point on the surface of the tongue during the production of the vowel.*

That is, the tongue is somewhat arched in the middle in vowel production, such that the part of the tongue below the palate or velum is more elevated than other parts of the tongue, and that high point is the point of reference.

In front vowels, the highest point on the arch of the tongue is below the palate. Say the vowel [i] ("ee") and press the tongue against the roof of the mouth without changing the shape of the body of the tongue. It will touch first at the palate, showing that the point that was highest on the tongue surface was below the palate.

In back vowels, the highest point on the arched surface of the tongue is below the velum. In low vowels, the tongue is quite flat, and it may be more difficult to locate the point where the high point on the arch is located, but moving back and forth between the vowels [æ] and [ɑ] will demonstrate that your tongue moves forward and back to produce the two vowels.

It would be helpful at this point for you to pronounce a series of cardinal (or near-cardinal) vowels, paying attention to the position of your tongue as you say each one.

6.4.2 It's the same place on the surface of the tongue

Pronounce the sequence [i u i u i u], etc. Initially, you will notice the change in lip posture rather than tongue position. We are more consciously aware of what is happening at the front of the mouth than the back.[5] But stop paying attention to the lips as you alternate between the two vowels.

It will become apparent that the shape of the tongue remains quite constant; that is, the place on the surface of the tongue that is highest for [i] is the same place that is highest for [u]; what has primarily changed is the position of the body of the tongue, which is drawn forward for [i] and backward for [u].

In physical articulatory terms, the muscles that control the *shape* of the tongue don't change position or tension much in going from [i] to [u]. However, the muscles that control the *position* of the tongue move it forward or backward for the two kinds of articulation.[6]

Now produce a sequence of vowels with the same frontness but different degrees of height, such as [i e ɛ æ]. Notice as you move from the high vow-

---

[5] As long as we're not feeling the presence of a foreign object at the back, which gets our attention immediately.

[6] These are the *intrinsic* and *extrinsic* tongue muscles, respectively.

el through intermediate vowels to the low vowel that the tongue changes from strongly arched for [i] to flatter for [æ].

So, the difference between front and back vowels (at the same height) is the *position of the tongue.*

The difference between different heights of vowel (with the same frontness) is the *shape of the tongue,* and, in slow, deliberate pronunciations, the degree of jaw opening as well.

6.4.3   Where is the quadrangle situated?

The vowel quadrangle is situated in the oral cavity as indicated in Figure 6.4.

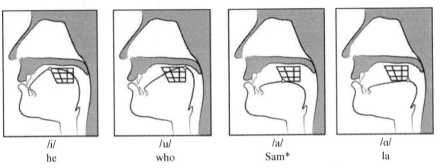

/i/	/u/	/a/	/ɑ/
he	who	Sam*	la

Figure 6.4 Vowel quadrangle in place. English does not have true cardinal vowels, so the English vowels in the key words are not exactly at the extreme points of the quadrangle, but are close.

* Particularly, the vowel of "Sam" is generally characterized as /æ/, not /a/, but the two are very close together on the IPA chart (Figures 6.1 and 6.6).

It is often mistakenly believed that front vowels are produced forward of the palatal region, such as in the drawings in Figure 6-5A and B. This may come about because we are more consciously aware of the front part of the mouth, so we may feel the tip of the tongue when we ask ourselves "where is my tongue?" when pronouncing a front vowel.

6.5   Non-cardinal vowels

There are a number of vowels that are neither primary nor secondary cardinal vowels. The non-cardinal vowels are shown in Figure 6.6. To the left, the full IPA vowel table is shown again for reference. To the right, the same table is shown, but the primary and secondary cardinal vowels, which we have already seen, have been deleted in order to emphasize the new material, though [ɤ] and [ʌ] are still shown.

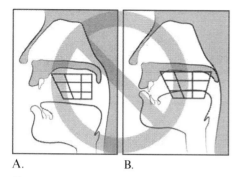

A.   B.

Figure 6.5 Inaccurate vowel quadrangles as seen in various reference works.

It is relatively common for reference materials to exaggerate the size and the position of the vowel quadrangle, as shown in these two drawings.

In both, the vowel quadrangle is shown too far forward, and too far back as well in B. In A, the quadrangle is too low, and the tongue and jaw position far too low. In B, the tongue would have to be lowered too far for low vowels. Part A shows all vowels as nasalized, as the velopharyngeal port is open, while nasalized vowels (Section 6.8 and Figure 6.7) are generally less common than non-nasalized ones.

There may be some pedagogical value to exaggerating the vowel quadrangle, particularly in works destined for second language teaching. However, as we explore the production of speech sounds, it is important to realize that the smaller quadrangle in Figure 6.4 is much closer to reality, as long as we understand the definition of the points shown in the quadrangle as explained in Section 6.4.1.

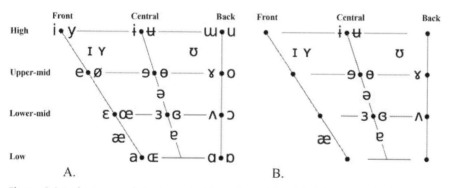

A.   B.

Figure 6.6 A. The IPA vowel chart, repeated from Figure 6.1. B. All of the non-cardinal vowels for which there are special IPA symbols

6.5.1   English non-cardinal vowels
6.5.1.1   Lax vowels [ɪ] and [ʊ]

English has a couple of vowels, usually characterized as *lax* (Section 6.7), that are quite high in place of articulation. These are:

IPA symbol	Example word	Descriptive term
ɪ	bit, zipper, sip, hill	high front lax unrounded vowel
ʊ	could, book, hood	high back lax rounded vowel

6.5.1.2   Mid-central schwa [ə]

The vowel in the mid-central position in the vowel quadrangle – that is, the vowel that is midway on both the frontness and height dimensions – is called *schwa*. While schwa can be stressed, in English this vowel normally occurs in unstressed syllables, and only in unstressed syllables, and so it tends to be very short and indistinct in English (more in Chapter 11).

6.5.1.3   Lower mid / low front unrounded [æ]

The *lower front vowel* [æ] is often referred to as being *low front* in sources related specifically to English, but is correctly halfway between lower mid and low. We will call it "lower front" to distinguish, and to avoid a long explanation each time it is referred to. Your professor may wish to use the term *low front*.

IPA symbol	Example word	Descriptive term
æ	bat, cast, attic, pal	Lower mid / low front unrounded vowel; for economy, "lower front"

6.5.1.4   High central vowels [ɨ] and [ʉ]

The high central vowels are not phonemes of English, but they – and more particularly [ɨ] – are said to be variants of some English high vowels.

6.5.2   Schwar [ɚ]

The vowel of the words *bird*, *shirt*, *her*, and so on has a distinctly r-like quality. Note that in most standard dialects, there is no consonant [ɹ]. In the word *bird*, for example, the /b/ is not followed by a vowel having no r-like quality, which is then followed by /ɹ/. After the /b/ and all the way to the /d/, there is just one single vowel, one that has an r-like quality.

This vowel has the same articulatory characteristics as the English consonant [ɹ], the same place of articulation and the same bunched tongue shape, as noted in Section 5.11.4.

The symbol / ɚ / is made up of two parts. It is a schwa [ə] plus the dia-critic [˞]. Since vowels other than the mid-central schwa can have what is called r-coloring (an r-like timbre), the symbol [˞] is seen in the IPA as a diacritic that can be added to any vowel.

6.5.3   Non-English non-cardinal vowels
6.5.3.1   [ʏ]
The same difference exists between [i] and [ɪ] as between [y] and [ʏ], which is to say that [i] and [y] are tense, whereas [ɪ] and [ʏ] are lax (Section 6.7).

6.6   Rounding

Rounding, also called *labialization*, refers to the movement whereby the lips are drawn into a circular formation and slightly protruded. This move-ment greatly affects the vowel sound produced.[7] Therefore, rounding is an important descriptor for vowel sounds.

Recall from Chapter 1 the brief discussion of phonetics versus phonology or phonemics. When discussing the phonemes of a language, it is sufficient to distinguish **rounded vowels** from **unrounded vowels**. However, at the phonetic level, there is considerably more detail that is required to describe the articulation of sounds.

- The vowel of the English word *heat* has a **spread** lip posture. That is, the corners of the mouth are drawn back, spreading the lips wide.
- The vowel of the English word *hat* has a **neutral** lip posture. That is, the lips are neither spread nor rounded.
- The vowel of the English word *hoot* has a **rounded** lip posture. That is, the lips are rounded. However, even rounded vowels in English such as [u] are not really very rounded. The [u] sound in many other languages is considerably more rounded than in English.

So, for purposes of describing articulation (which may be important in help-ing someone learn how to say the sounds of a particular language), it may be necessary to provide more information than simply saying **rounded** or **unrounded**.

6.6.1   Rounding contrasts
Where a language has a contrast based on rounding alone, the degree of rounding may be greater than where there is no contrast.

---

[7] It can also cause a change in the sound of a number of consonants.

For example, most varieties of English have both [ɔ] and [ʌ] in their vowel inventories. There appears to be a tendency to round [ɔ] more fully than [u] or [o], at least among some talkers. If [ɔ] is unrounded, it may sound like [ʌ], causing misidentification of words. So speakers emphasize the rounding.

6.7   Tense and lax; ATR

The English vowels [ɪ] and [ʊ] were characterized above (6.5.1) as being *lax* (as opposed to *tense*). This raises an issue of some controversy. Let us begin by invoking your intuition (if you are a native speaker of a major variety of English[8]).

Pronounce the pair [i ɪ i ɪ] while lightly touching the tip of your fingers just above the larynx, at approximately the point where the horizontal bottom of the mandible meets the vertical line of the neck. You will notice a slight pressure forward on your fingers when you say [i], but not when you say [ɪ]. Now try the pair [u ʊ u ʊ]. You will feel the slight pressure for [u] but not for [ʊ], though the effect may be less marked than for the [i ɪ] pair.

This extra muscular activity for [i] and [u] led to the traditional classification *tense* for these vowels, and the absence of this muscle contraction led to the term *lax* for [ɪ] and [ʊ] (plus at least one other vowel, as we shall see).

Many schools of phonology in the latter twentieth century and into the twenty-first have taken as a starting point the idea that there are only 3 vowel heights, not 4.[9] In order to account for the difference between [e] and [ɛ] and between [o] and [ɔ], they have used *tenseness* or *ATR* (see below) to account for these distinctions in their classifications. So [e] was considered tense and [ɛ] lax; [o] was considered tense and [ɔ] lax. This solves the classification problem, but it does not answer the question as to whether the difference between, for example, [o] and [ɔ] is based on the same phonetic adjustment as the difference between [i] and [ɪ]. This may not make a difference within some approaches to phonology, but it leaves the impression that there is an overarching phonetic principle at work where there may not be.

---

[8] The particular feature under discussion here is one of the most difficult phonetic details of English for speakers of many other languages, so even the second language speaker of English who is highly fluent and relatively accent-free may not produce this feature in the way that native speakers do. There are also a number of varieties of English, besides those with the largest numbers of speakers, that do not make the same distinction.

[9] Remember that phonology may have as its goal to account only for the *contrasts* of sounds in language, not necessarily to provide finely grained phonetic descriptions. Contrasting only 3 vowel heights made it possible to characterize all 3 of those heights with two binary features ([± high] and [± low]). But this made it necessary to use another feature to capture the contrast among what are classed phonetically as upper mid and lower mid vowels.

In many of these classifications, *tenseness* gave way to *Advanced Tongue Root (ATR)*. The idea is that the root of the tongue (facing into the pharynx) is drawn forward (advanced) in the articulation of vowels such as [i] and [u], accounting for the pressure felt in the experiment above. By contrast, vowels such as [ɪ] and [ʊ] are articulated with the tongue root in a neutral position or even retracted (moved backward), thus creating no feeling of tension and resulting in the absence of the tension felt in the experiment noted above.

The position of the tongue root, including *retracted tongue root (RTR)*, plays a role in the phonetic–phonological systems of a number of languages, and in particular in *vowel harmony* (see Section 10.10.2) in a number of West African languages, among others. Research on these phenomena has resulted in many scholars claiming that ATR and tenseness are different phenomena, while others say that they are essentially the same phenomenon, at least within the vowel system of English.

6.7.1 Another lax vowel

A high front rounded lax vowel [ʏ] exists with the same tongue position as [i] and [y]. In Laurentian French, spoken in Quebec and Ontario, the lax [ʏ] replaces the tense [y] of international French in certain circumstances. The vowel [i] is also replaced by [ɪ] and [u] by [ʊ] in similar environments in this North American variety of French.

6.8 Nasalization; nasalized vowels; nasal vowels

As a matter of classification, an oral vowel is produced with the *velopharyngeal port* (VPP) firmly closed. No airflow passes out through the nose, and, more importantly for the sound of the vowel, there is no acoustic influence coming from the nasal passages. When a vowel symbol is written in the normal way, without a diacritic, it means that the velopharyngeal port is closed.

If the velopharyngeal port is open to a reasonable degree while a vowel is being produced, then sound waves will enter the nasal passages, and the nasal cavities will acoustically alter the sound of the vowel. Such a vowel is said to be *nasalized* (Figure 6.7).

Nasalized is a phonetic term that simply describes the condition of the vocal tract while the vowel is produced. However, some languages distinguish between nasalized and *non-nasalized (oral)* vowels. In those languages, the nasalized state of the vowels is phonological or phonemic, and in that case, these vowels may be called *nasal vowels*. This latter term means that the nasal quality of the vowel is phonologically distinctive in that language. Therefore, we can say that all *nasal vowels* are *nasalized*, but not all *nasalized vowels* are *nasal*.

Nasal vowels occur in a large number of languages, including French, Portuguese, Polish, Yoruba, and Cherokee and many languages around the world.

In the IPA, a tilde [~] written as a diacritic above the vowel shows that the vowel is *nasalized*. That nasalized vowel might be distinctively nasal, but the IPA symbol shows its phonetic character, not its phonology.

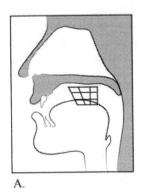 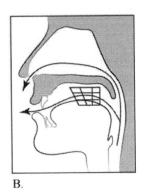

A.   B.

Figure 6.7 Oral and nasalized vowels, [ɛ] and [ɛ̃]. A. Oral, non-nasalized vowel [ɛ].
Note that the velopharyngeal port (VPP) is closed so that the nasal passages do not influence the sound produced. **B.** Nasalized vowel [ɛ̃]. Note that the VPP is open, and air as well as sound waves can pass through both the oral cavity and the nasal cavities.

When nasal consonants are produced, the VPP must open, and for oral consonants, the VPP must close. But, in fact, the movement of the VPP is quite slow relative to the rate at which individual speech sounds can be produced in connected speech. Therefore, in words spoken in connected speech, for instance the word *can*, the movement to open the VPP for the consonant [n] starts very early in the vowel so that the opening can be complete when it is time to say the [n]. The result is that the vowel in this word is strongly nasalized: we say [kæ̃n], not [kæn].

We will see more about nasalization from surrounding nasal consonants in Chapter 10.

In languages such as French, Portuguese, and Polish – and many other languages besides – nasalization of the vowels potentially makes a difference to the meaning of the word that is spoken. Therefore, talkers of a language such as these attend to avoiding unwanted nasalization on vowels that are not phonemically nasal.

In a language such as English, the meaning of a word will not change as a result of a vowel being nasalized or not. Therefore, in such a language, talkers may not make much of an effort to avoid nasalizing vowels. Whether they do or not, it doesn't change the meaning of the word.

Speakers of English in North America (and particularly in regions of the American southwest), tend to talk with the VPP at least a little bit open for all sounds except ones that require it to be closed. Those sounds are plosives and high-pressure fricatives such as [s] and [ʃ]. Therefore, there is pervasive nasalization.

6.9   Vowel duration ("length")

Vowel length can be difficult to explain to native speakers of English because the terms "long vowel" and "short vowel" are commonly used in everyday English (and when teaching English to second-language learners as well as native English-speaking school children) in a sense that is quite different from what we mean in phonetic science.

In reference to English spellings and the sounds represented, the letter <e> in the word *met* is called "short e," and the letter <e> in the word *meet* is called "long e." Historically, these terms originated for excellent reasons, and the vowel sound of *meet* is indeed a little longer in duration than that of *met*. However, the principal difference between the two sounds [i] and [ɛ] is that they are *different vowel sounds*, not long and short versions of the same vowel sound. Remember, the terms "short e" and "long e" refer to *letters*, and to *spelling conventions in English*, but in phonetics the word *vowel* means a kind of sound regardless of how it is written. These two vowel sounds represented by the letter <e>, that is, [i] and [ɛ], are different – *they have different vowel quality – and occur at different places in the vowel quadrangle:* [i] *and* [ɛ].

To reiterate: the vowels [i] and [ɛ] are different vowels, *not* long and short versions of the same vowel, despite the fact that they are usually represented in English orthography as being written by what is commonly called "long <e>" and "short <e>."

In the discipline of phonetics, the term *vowel length* is understood to refer to the duration of the vowel and *not to its quality*. In this terminology, long and short versions of the same vowel would have *identical timbre*, and would be different only in duration.

The length, which is to say the duration, of vowels is variable, and different languages use vowel length in different ways.

6.9.1   Contextual duration

The duration of vowels is influenced by position in a word and by the voicing of the following consonant. Voicing of the following consonant tends to lengthen a vowel. The duration of the vowel in "mate" is shorter than that of the vowel in "made." The vowel in "may" is longer than that in "mate" as well.

As we will see in Chapter 11, a vowel in a stressed syllable is longer than a vowel in a syllable with reduced or with no stress.

6.9.2   Language-specific rules

In English, vowels such as [ɪ ɛ æ ʌ] tend to have shorter duration than vowels such as [i e o u]. In Section 6.11, we will see that these latter vowels have another characteristic in addition to their length.

There is nothing inherent in these different vowel sounds that makes them longer or shorter. It is just a feature of the English language that this difference exists, and for spoken English to sound natural, the different lengths must be articulated. The relative duration of these two groups of vowels could conceivably be reversed in another language; in other words, it would be possible for a language to have [ɪ ɛ æ ʌ] that are longer in duration than [i e o u].

Speakers of other languages who learn English often have difficulty making the distinction between [i] and [ɪ]. If they cannot make the difference in quality or timbre between these two vowels, they may focus on their duration. Many second language speakers of English don't distinguish [i] and [ɪ] in their speech; they distinguish [i] and [ĭ] (that is, they distinguish [i] from a short version of [i]). This does not sound natural in English and may lead to errors in perception.

The diacritic [˘], as in [ĭ] or [ŏ], indicates that the vowel is short, so [ĭ] means a short [i]. The [˘] symbol can be called a *breve*. Again, "short" means short in duration and does not refer to vowel quality.

6.9.3   Contrastive vowel length

Many languages make a distinction among words by vowel duration alone, which is to say that length is phonemic in these languages. For example, examine the following words from Finnish:

Short vowel		Long vowel	
Pronunciation	Spelling and meaning	Pronunciation	Spelling and meaning
[tili]	tili 'account'	[tiili] or [tiːli]	tiili 'brick'
[tuli]	tuli 'fire'	[tuuli] or [tuːli]	tuuli 'wind'
[tɑkːa]	takka 'fireplace'	[tɑɑkːa] or [tɑːkːa]	taakka 'burden'
[mutɑ]	muta 'mud'	[muutɑ] or [muːtɑ]	muuta 'other'

These examples show that the duration of the vowel is phonemic in Finnish – that is, whether a vowel is long or short changes the meaning of a word.

In the examples in the table, the long vowels have been written two different ways in the IPA. Both ways are acceptable.

- Showing a double vowel ([uu]). Such a vowel is called **geminate**.[10] Symbolizing the long vowel in this way does not indicate that the short vowel is pronounced twice; rather it shows that the vowel is approximately twice as long.
- Showing the length mark ([uː]). The length mark [ː] shows that the duration of a vowel is approximately double.

There is also a symbol in the IPA for a "half-long" vowel, which is to say, a vowel that is one and one-half times longer than a "normal" vowel: [ˑ] – for example, [ɑˑ].

These various methods of showing a longer vowel do not show the status of the additional length, whether it is phonemic in the particular language (as in Finnish) or not (as in English).

In some regions of the United States, there may be a case where phonetic vowel length can distinguish words. In many places on the eastern seaboard and in the South, postvocalic [ɹ] sounds – r-sounds following a vowel, as in the word *car* – are not pronounced. In some of these areas, the "missing" r-sound makes the vowel a little bit longer. *Car* may be pronounced [kɑˑ], with a slightly lengthened vowel. In such a region, the name *Carter* will not have r-sounds but the first vowel will be lengthened. The name *Kotter* will not have an r-sound at the end, but the first vowel will not be lengthened. In these regions the sole difference between *Carter* and *Kotter* may be the length of the first vowel, and speakers of this variety will hear the difference.

6.10   Diphthongs

Note: Several times throughout this book, readers are cautioned that key words used as a guide for readers may be pronounced differently in their own speech as compared to the "General American" pronunciation intended, and that the reader should consider the

---

[10] From the same root as the astrological sign Gemini, meaning 'twin.'

General American pronunciation, not their own pronunciation, if it is significantly different.

A special caution is required for diphthongs. In many regions of the American South, diphthongs are pronounced very differently from in the rest of the country, and differently from the same sounds in most dialects of English around the world. In fact, in the speech of many individuals in this region, diphthongs of English *may not be diphthongs at all*. For such speakers, any attempt to self-examine their own pronunciation will not help with understanding what a diphthong is. Again, I emphasize that the intended pronunciations associated with examples and descriptions are General American.

A *diphthong* is a vowel whose *quality* or *timbre* changes considerably during its articulation. For example, the vowel of the word "my" is pronounced by starting with the tongue in a low position and then moving the tongue up to a high front position. You can feel the movement if you pronounce this vowel slowly while paying attention to your articulators.

Because this sound is usually spelled with a single letter and forms one phoneme (contrasting sound) in English, some students have trouble hearing that it is actually made up of two parts. The easiest way to hear it is to prolong the pronunciation of the diphthong. As you prolong it, you will hear that you can prolong the first part or the second part, but that at no time are you producing the whole vowel sound.

The standard transcription of diphthongs is intended to show the approximate starting and finishing points of their articulation. So a diphthong whose articulation starts in the neighborhood of [a] and finishes up in the neighborhood of [i] is transcribed [ai].

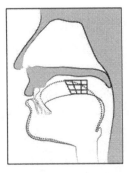

Figure 6.8 The diphthong /ai/.
The figure shows the movement of the tongue in the articulation of the diphthong /ai/. The solid outline of the tongue is the starting point and the broken line the ending point.

Figure 6.8 shows a stylized drawing of the articulation of a sample diphthong.

More than other vowels in English, the precise quality of the diphthongs varies enormously with surrounding sounds and with dialect. The diphthong /ai/, for example, may be pronounced [ɑi], [aɪ], [ɔi], etc. If we wish to transcribe the precise quality of a particular diphthong, we must carefully indicate its starting and finishing points. However, for purposes of broad or phonemic transcription, standardized transcriptions are often used. These are satisfactory as long as the user understands that they are broad, not precise, reflections of the pronunciation. The following shows conventional ways of transcribing English.

Vowel	Example words
/ai/	my, buy, eye, I, might, hide
/au/	cow, loud, found, howl, pout
/ ɔi /	boy, foil, hoist

It should be reiterated that the quality of diphthongs varies greatly and is not reflected in these standardized phonemic transcriptions. For example, in my own speech, the vowels of "lout" and "loud" are very different, both in length and in quality. Use of the standard transcription [laut] and [laud] does not come near to reflecting this difference. Nonetheless, if the specific quality of the diphthong is not the focus, then using standard transcriptions allows one to read the transcription without drawing unnecessary attention to the details of the diphthong pronunciation.

6.10.1   Use of the ligature or tie bar in transcribing diphthongs

When two vowels are juxtaposed in separate syllables, they do not form a diphthong. In the word "doing," for example, the [u] is in one syllable and the [ɪ] in another, so no diphthong is formed. Normally, transitional glide (Section 6.15) will be inserted between.

The word *knife* contains the diphthong /ai/, but the words *naïf* and *naïve* have the sequence of /a/ followed by /i/. Making a broad transcription of *knife* and *naïf* would both yield /naif/. The same broad transcription, but the two words are pronounced very differently – it is obviously a problem if we use the same transcription for words that are pronounced differently.

This is why the ligature is used: it helps to clarify the transcription: [na͜if] shows a one-syllable word with a diphthong; [naif] shows a two-syllable word without a diphthong. Nonetheless, common practice omits the ligature. For the rest of the chapter, ligatures will not be used.

6.10.2   Transcriptions of diphthongs

There are a number of different ways that are commonly used for transcribing diphthongs.

1. as shown above, two vowel symbols connected with a ligature: [na͜iv]
2. a vowel followed by a glide: [maj]
3. a vowel followed by a superscript vowel: [maⁱ]

The first and third of these permits showing the phonetic quality very precisely. The second shows a general direction of tongue movement, but is often entirely adequate for general transcription.

6.10.3   Rising and falling diphthongs

It is common practice to use the term *diphthong* as in the previous section and to mean a vowel complex in which the initial element is fully vocalic and the second element is a glide or glide-like element – for instance [aj].

Some sources indicate a distinction between the type of vowel complex noted in the previous paragraph – called a *falling diphthong* – and one in which the initial element is a glide and the second is fully vocalic, for instance [ju], called a *rising diphthong*.

As was done in the title of Section 6.10, we are using the simple term *diphthong* to refer to falling diphthongs.

6.11   Diphthongized vowels

The vowels [i, e, o, u] are identified as long vowels in English, since they are usually quite a bit longer in duration than other English vowels such as [ɪ ɛ ʊ æ]. This prolongation goes hand in hand with another characteristic of these vowels as they are pronounced in most dialects of English.[11] The long vowels in English tend to be slightly diphthongized. This means that their point of articulation changes slightly as they are pronounced. Pronounce the word "say," prolonging it a little bit, and carefully observe your articulatory gestures. Notice that the jaw or tongue is not in a constant position throughout the pronunciation of the vowel – the vowel becomes higher as its articulation progresses. Try the words "see," "sue," and "so" and observe the changing quality in them.

It is useful to compare the way a native speaker of French, Italian, or Spanish pronounces the closest vowels in those languages with the way

---

[11] Some varieties of English spoken in parts of Ireland have relatively long vowels that are not diphthongized.

you pronounce the English vowels. In English, the articulators move considerably during the production of the vowel; in the other languages mentioned, there is very little or no movement during the production of the vowel.

Vowels articulated with very little to no movement of the articulators during the production of the vowel are referred to as ***monophthongs***.[12] The term *pure vowel* is sometimes used, though it is a term that can be misunderstood as having a positive sense. Languages have the vowels that they have; there is nothing better about a monophthong as compared to a diphthong or diphthongized vowel, as might be implied by the term *pure.* Another, more neutral, term that is sometimes used is a *simple vowel* as opposed to a *complex vowel*, which is diphthongal or diphthongized.

While the long vowels in English are generally slightly diphthongized, the short vowels are more monophthongal. The vowels [ɪ ɛ ʊ æ] and the other short vowels do not typically change much in quality (timbre) during production. There are dialects, such as those of the American South, in which short vowels are *complex* or *diphthongized*: "bit," for example, might be pronounced [bɪət] or [bijət] in parts of the South.

The transcription conventions that were introduced earlier in this chapter for vowels such as [i, e, o, u] do not indicate the diphthongized nature of these long vowels but represent them as if they were pure vowels. For the most part, this is a satisfactory phonemic transcription system for English; many manuals of transcription use simple transcriptions such as these.

Several systems of transcribing English vowels more precisely are in use, however. One system was devised by Jones (1972) in England, another by the team of Trager and Smith (1951) in the United States. A comparison is shown in the following table.

Simple	Jones	Trager–Smith	Trager–Smith updated to conform to IPA use of [y]
/i/	/iː/	/iy/	/ij/
/e/	/ei/	/ey/	/ej/
/o/	/ou/	/ow/	/ow/
/u/	/uː/	/uw/	/uw/

The "updated" symbols in the last column reflect the fact that the IPA uses the symbol [j], not [y], for the palatal glide (approximant). Many

---

[12] *Diphthong* comes from two roots: *di*, meaning 'two,' and *phthong*, meaning 'sound.' 'Two sounds' refers to the changing timbre as the tongue moves from the first position to the second (end) position. *Mono* means 'single, one' and that characterizes a *monophthong*, a vowel having a single sound, sometimes called a "pure" vowel.

authors use these updated standard transcriptions that are based on the Trager–Smith system.

There are other differences among the systems, but for our purposes it is enough to point out the quality of the long vowels and to be prepared for a possible variety of transcriptions of the same sounds. In all cases, it is best to pick one system for one's own use and to stay with it consistently, except where the focus of the transcription is on the particular characteristics of the vowels in question. Enclosing the IPA symbols in slash marks (/ /) as opposed to square brackets shows that these are generic transcriptions of these phonemes in English and that they are not intended to be precise transcriptions of all of the exact details of a given pronunciation.

Of course, it is always possible to use IPA symbols to transcribe accurately the details of the articulation. For example, the English phoneme [e] of "bay" may, in different dialect areas, be pronounced [ei], [eɪ], [ɛi], etc.

In this discussion of transcription of English long vowels, let us not lose sight of the practical significance of their diphthongal nature. Once again, if we wish only to distinguish /i/ from /ɪ/ from /e/, we can safely ignore their diphthongal quality. But in an accurate description, their phonetic quality, their diphthongal timbre, is important. While the difference between [eː] and [ei] may be subtle, it is important; pronouncing the word "say" as [se] or [seː] rather than [sej] sounds strange or non-native (or, as we noted above, it may be normal for a speaker from some parts of Ireland).

6.12   Terminology

In this brief section, we will see how vowels are normally described in articulatory terms. Relate these descriptors to the articulatory positions shown in Figure 6.1. The terms shown in the table represent standard articulatory descriptions of vowels.

Height and frontness		
	Height first, frontness second	
	/i/	High front vowel
	/u/	High back vowel
	/e/	Upper mid front vowel
Rounding		
	Rounding term follows height and frontness	
	/i/	High front (spread) vowel

	/y/	High front rounded vowel
	/ɯ/	High back spread (or unrounded) vowel
Nasalization		
	Nasalization term follows height and frontness	
	/ɛ̃/	Lower mid front nasalized vowel
	/ã/	Low front nasalized vowel
Length (duration)		
	Length term generally comes before height and frontness	
	/oː/	Long upper mid back (rounded) vowel
	/eˑ/	Half-long upper mid front vowel
Tenseness		
	Tenseness term follows height and frontness	
	/i/	High front tense vowel
	/ɪ/	High front lax vowel
Diphthongization		
	Diphthongization term generally follows height and frontness	
	[ij]	High front diphthongized vowel

The inclusion of terms in the description depends on what is relevant in a particular context. It may not be relevant to specify rounding in a given instance, for example. However, it is important to recognize that *high front vowel* is by no means a complete phonetic/articulatory description of a vowel.

6.13   Vocoids and syllabicity

You may see the term *vocoid* used to refer to vowels. This term includes vowels and some sounds classified as consonants in Chapter 5, sounds like [l, ɹ, w, j]. All of these sounds (including vowels) are sounds that are produced without the noise of friction in the mouth, and no complete blockage of airflow.

A *syllable* comprises a single sound or a group of sounds clustered around a *nucleus*, defined as having high *sonority*. In English and a majority of languages across the world, the nucleus of a syllable is most often a vowel. However, sounds such as [l, ɹ, m, n] may form a syllable nucleus in English. Additionally, in the English interjection "Pssst," the voiceless fricative [s] is the nucleus.

SIDEBAR 6.3 Sonority

Speech sounds are placed on a *sonority hierarchy,* based on factors such as amplitude and resonance. Most languages use only the most sonorous sounds as syllable nuclei. The following list shows speech sounds ordered from most sonorous to least sonorous:

- low vowels
- mid vowels
- high vowels
- glides
- flaps
- laterals
- nasal consonants
- voiced fricatives
- voiceless fricatives
- voiced plosives
- voiceless plosives

This particular order is a common one, but not the only one proposed by scholars.

The IPA allows for phones that are normally *syllabic* to be marked as *non-syllabic.*

The mark [̯] under a normally syllabic sound shows that the sound is non-syllabic, as in [kino̯a] for *quinoa.* Most English speakers would pronounce the <o> of *quinoa* as a [w], but if the articulatory position is closer to [o] for speakers of Spanish, then the symbol [o̯] can show that. See also Section 6.14 and Sidebar 6.3.

6.13.1 Syllabic consonants

Under the topic of syllabicity, we will revisit consonants briefly. Consonants are typically considered to be non-syllabic and to require a vowel to create a syllable.[13] However, there are exceptions, as noted in Section 5.16.2.

The diacritic [̩] under a normally non-syllabic sound shows that the sound is syllabic, as in [hm̩m̩] for the interjection "Hmmm." The consonants that are most commonly syllabic are those that are voiced and sonorant.

6.14   Glides and approximants

In Section 5.11.4, we examined glides as consonants. The initial sound of the word "yes" (for example) acts as a consonant. The sound /j/ is non-syllabic; the word "yes" consists of a single syllable and the only vowel in it is /ɛ/, so the glide at the beginning is not the vowel nucleus of the syllable: it must be a consonant.

However, glides also have vowel-like characteristics, and those are what we will examine in this section. Let us start by performing a little

---

[13] *Con-sonant* means 'with vowel.'

experiment. Say the word "eat." Now prolong the first sound, the vowel, for a long time: [iːːːːːːːːːːːːt]. As you are saying the long [i] sound, listen to it. At any point during the pronunciation, the vowel sounds like [i]. There is no surprise here. Now say the word "yes." Prolong the initial glide the way you prolonged the vowel previously. Don't prolong the vowel /ɛ/, prolong the glide /j/. If you listen to a prolonged /j/, you'll notice that it sounds like the vowel /i/, so the word sounds like [iːːːːːːːːːjɛs].

In Section 5.11.4, we noted that these sounds are called *glides* for a very good reason: these sounds are articulated with a movement ("gliding") of the articulator. When you prolong a glide, you stop the movement, and the glide no longer sounds like a glide; it sounds like a vowel.

Each of the glides we saw in Chapter 5 has the articulatory position of a vowel. To be a glide, the sound is produced with the articulators moving away from – or toward – another vowel sound, as we saw in the word "yes." The equivalent articulatory positions of vowels and glides are as follows.

Vowel	Equivalent glide	Sample English word	Remarks
/i/	/j/	yes	
/u/	/w/	want	
/ŭ̥/	/ʍ/	where	voiceless; use of the voiceless glide /ʍ / is geographically restricted and is replaced by /w/ in many regions of the English-speaking world
/y/	/ɥ/	French *tuile* 'tile'	Not a sound in most varieties of English

Glides are called **semivowels** or **semiconsonants**, terms that demonstrate the link that exists between the vocalic and consonantal character of glides.

While it is not the usual way of considering these sounds, the type of r-sound ([ɹ]) in English acts as a glide, and shares with other glides in having a vocalic equivalent. So we could add another line to the table above:

Vowel	Equivalent glide	Sample English word	Remarks
/ɚ/	/ɹ/	run	

In a similar way that prolonging the [j] in "yes" produces the vowel [iːːːːːː], prolonging the [ɹ] at the beginning of "run" produces the vowel [ɚːːːːːː].

6.14.1   Glides are non-syllabic vowels

These same facts could be expressed by saying that *glides are non-syllabic vowels*. Vowels normally form the nucleus of a syllable, and so they are said to be syllabic. Another way of saying that a vowel is syllabic is to say that it can stand on its own as a syllable. A segment that is like a vowel, but that does not form the nucleus of a syllable – that is, another vowel accompanies it that does form the nucleus – is a non-syllabic vowel, or a glide. The diacritic [̯] is used to indicate non-syllabicity, so writing [i̯] amounts to the same thing as writing [j], and [u̯] amounts to the same thing as writing [w]. No one is suggesting that these more complicated transcriptions should be used routinely; rather, they are mentioned in order to help you think about the articulatory nature of glides.

Furthermore, some languages have glides whose articulatory positions correspond not to [i] and [u], but a bit lower, to [e] and [o] or elsewhere in the vowel quadrangle. There are no glide symbols that indicate these exact articulatory positions. They can be symbolized thus: [e̯ o̯] and so on. For example, the second sound in many people's pronunciation of "coincidence" may be a velar glide lower than [w], corresponding to [o] in articulatory position: i.e., [o̯]. The same may be true of the <o> in *quinoa* in varieties of Spanish.

6.15   On-glides, off-glides, and transitional glides

Pronounce these words and pay a lot of attention to the transition from the vowel to the final consonant: "peak" and "peel"; "kook" and "cool." In the words "peak" and "kook," the vowel seems to end abruptly where the final consonant begins. But in the words "peel" and "cool," there is vowel-like transition from the vowel to the final consonant. The actual sound of this transition is like a schwa ([ə]), but there seems to be a glide transitioning between the main vowel and the schwa.

The combination of glide plus [ə] is often called an ***off-glide*** of the main vowel. It is typical of English for the vowel to have an off-glide before the consonant [l] in the same syllable. Since this transitional sound is typical of the [l] rather than the vowel itself, it could be considered an ***on-glide*** to the [l]. In either case, it is a transitional glide, facilitating the movement from one sound to the next. By "facilitating the movement from one sound to the next," we do not mean that universal phonetic constraints demand such a transitional glide; rather, we mean that it is typical of English and it facilitates the transition for English speakers, and similar phenomena occur in many other languages.

If we compare the English word *pool* with the French word *poule* (meaning 'hen'), we could say that each contains a similar sequence of three phonemes. However, the French word makes the transition from the vowel to the following [l] as simply as English makes the transition from vowel to [p] in the word *hoop*. The complex transitional glide to the [l] found in English is absent from French. English speakers learning French (or other languages) tend to put in these complex English transitions before [l], and it forms part of their foreign accent, and vice versa.

English also inserts transitional glides when two vowel sounds come together in words. In a word like "going" there tends to be a [w]-glide between vowels, and in a word like "seeing," a [j]-glide is typically inserted.

6.16   Diacritics introduced in this chapter

The following table shows the diacritics (diacritical marks, "accents") introduced in this chapter. Your professor may wish to advise you which are important for you to know.

Diacritic	Example showing position	Meaning	Remarks	English
~	õ	nasalized vowel		man
ː	oː	long vowel		
ˈ	oˈ	"half-long" vowel	longer than unmarked vowel but shorter than long vowel; between /o/ and /oː/ in length	
˘	ă	short in duration	called a *breve*	
‿	ai͡	ligature or tie bar	shows that a sequence of two vowel symbols represents a diphthong, a single syllable	
ˌ	m̩	syllabic		
˯	o̯	non-syllabic		
˞	ɚ	having a rhotic quality		bird

Diacritic	Example showing position	Meaning	Remarks	English
The following are some consistent patterns in the IPA symbols rather than actual diacritics. Taking note of these may make some symbols easier to remember.				
-	i ʉ	central articulation	Not a general diacritic for central; use restricted to i, u.	
small upper case	ɪ ʊ ʏ	lax vowel	small upper-case letters are also used for some vowels that are lax	

6.17 Vocabulary

approximant
ATR (advanced tongue root)
back
backness
cardinal vowel
central
close
close-mid
consonant
diacritic
diphthong
diphthong, falling
diphthong, rising
diphthongized, diphthongization
duration
front
frontness
geminate
glide
half-long
height
high
International Phonetic Alphabet (IPA)
key word

labialization
lax
length (duration)
ligature, tie bar
long
long vowel
low
lower mid (open-mid)
mid-central
monophthong ("pure" vowel)
nasal vowel
nasalization
nasalized vowel
neutral (rounding)
non-nasal
non-syllabic
nucleus
off-glide
on-glide
open
open-mid
oral (non-nasal)
order of acquisition
postvocalic
prevocalic

primary (cardinal vowels)

quadrangle, vowel
  quadrangle

quality

rounded

rounding, lip rounding

RTR (retracted tongue root)

schwa

schwar

secondary (cardinal vowels)

semivowel

short

short vowel

sonority

syllabic

syllabicity

syllable

tense

tenseness

tie bar

timbre

transitional glide

unrounded

upper mid (close mid)

vocalic

vocoid

vowel

vowel length

vowel space

VPP (velopharyngeal port)

7 Sounds of North American English

NOTE regarding the order of chapters. At the beginning of Chapter 3, it was noted that some instructors may wish to skip ahead to the present chapter in order to begin practice with transcription.

If your instructor is taking the chapters in order, then you will find parts of this chapter are a review of concepts introduced in Chapters 4, 5, and 6.

If your instructor has asked you to start Chapter 7 before reading the preceding chapters, then you will require coaching to advance in this chapter. It uses terminology and concepts from preceding chapters. On the other hand, it is entirely possible to begin transcription of speech before fully understanding the theory behind it.

Your instructor will decide whether you skip ahead to this chapter, and they will provide the required coaching.

7.1 The sounds of General American English

This chapter summarizes the sounds of English (with emphasis on General American). In earlier chapters, we have examined the production of these and other sounds in much greater detail. We have looked at the modifications of these sounds in words and in connected speech, and we have examined the effects of stress and intonation on them.

7.1.1 General American English

General American English is a kind of idealized variety of American English, most closely related to the English of the American Midwest and west coast. It is different in important ways from that of New York City, of New England, from American English spoken across the South, but should be familiar to people from these regions. With the exception of a handful of phonemes, it is similar to General Canadian English, with which it shares a larger number of features, both phonetically and in terms of vocabulary, than with English elsewhere in the English-speaking world.

In addition, there is socially related dialect variation, whose boundaries are defined not geographically but by membership in particular social groupings. The most significant of these in the United States is *African-American Vernacular English* (AAVE).

By presenting General American English – again, a somewhat artificial, idealized concept – there is no intent to suggest that this variety is superior, or a model to be emulated; it is not "better" than the dialect you speak. The purpose of this book is to elucidate principles of phonetics (speech production), mainly for students in North America, using the example of a familiar, major variety of English. It is not our purpose to systematically describe varieties of English spoken in the United States.

The phonetic differences between General American and major national dialects of English spoken in other countries should not be exaggerated. What is presented here remains a mostly accurate description of the sound inventories of other major varieties of English, though vowels differ among dialects of English considerably more than consonants do.

7.1.2 Phonemes of General American

Essentially, this chapter will present the inventory of basic phonemes of General American English, without delving into the variations that occur in different phonetic environments.

7.1.3 Caution regarding key words

In a written work, speech sounds are communicated by providing key words – that is, words that contain the particular sound when it is pronounced in the dialect being described. This works well when the reader and the writer speak the same dialect of the language. It works less well where there are important differences in the way the words are spoken. Readers should be vigilant in using key words, understanding that (unless otherwise stated) the pronunciation intended is General American, which may differ from the reader's usage.

Online resources may be used to find key words in General American.

7.2 Consonants and vowels

In later chapters, we will define consonants and distinguish them from vowels in a technical way. For the moment, your intuitions are probably generally correct. However, there is likely a very important way in which the terminology is different from the way you use it in casual speech.

7.2.1 The meaning of the words *consonant* and *vowel*

*The words **consonant** and **vowel** refer to different kinds of speech sounds, not to letters of the alphabet!* These words, *consonant* and *vowel*, will never be used to mean letters in this book, and, in phonetics generally, the words *consonant* and *vowel* never mean letters, but rather two main categories of speech sounds.

This will not require a great change in the way you think about these concepts. Usually, in the spelling of English, the consonants are represented by letters that you're used to calling "consonants," and vowels are represented by letters that you're used to calling "vowels." However, this is not always the case. The first sound in the words *Europe* and *use* is not a vowel, and the first sound in the word *honor* is not a consonant, nor is the last sound in the word *though*.

7.2.2   Classification of consonants and vowels

In the following listing of the phoneme inventory of General American English, sounds will be classified using standard phonetic terminology but without explanation. The purpose here is to present the inventory of sounds rather than to explain them in detail. That detailed explanation appears in the chapters devoted to consonants and vowels (Chapters 5 and 6).

7.3   Sound inventory of General American English[1]

This section provides a quick overview of the categorization of speech sounds in General American and their equivalent symbols in the International Phonetic Alphabet (IPA).

Key words have been provided, *but it is important to understand that the key words work only in General American.* There is considerable geographic and social variation in the pronunciation of particular words and/or particular classes of words within the United States, and even greater variation within the English-speaking world as a whole. If your own pronunciation differs from General American, then the key words will be misleading. If you can, think of the General American pronunciation of the words when using them to guide you. There is generally far greater variation in the pronunciation of vowels and r-sounds than there is in consonants.

Even if you do speak a variety close to General American, pronunciations may differ slightly depending on the formality of the speaking situations, referred to as the speech *register*. The key words are intended to be pronounced with neither a hyper-formal nor a highly casual register.

Symbols of the IPA are placed between slash marks (/ /) or between square brackets ([ ]). The difference between the use of slashes and of square brackets is that square brackets enclose fine or detailed phonetic

---

[1] From Section 7.3 forward, this chapter is reprinted from *Acoustics in Hearing, Speech and Language Sciences: An Introduction,* by Ian R. A. MacKay. Used by permission.

transcription and slashes designate broader, phonemic transcription. In reality, one is almost always transcribing somewhere in the middle. In that instance, follow the instructions.

As noted in Chapter 1, angle brackets (< >) enclose normal spelling, to indicate that the letters are not IPA symbols but regular spelling.

Sounds and spellings that often lead to errors in transcription are listed under the heading "Transcription trouble spots" in each of the sections below.

7.4 Consonants

7.4.1 Most varieties of English have the following plosive consonants:

[p t k b d g]

key words: pot, tot, cot, bought, dot, got.

The voiceless plosives are aspirated [pʰ tʰ kʰ] (i.e., released with a puff of air) when they are the initial sound in a stressed syllable, particularly at the beginning of a word. This may be mitigated when followed by a glide, lateral, or rhotic (r-like) sound: there may be less aspiration in "plate" than in "pate." If the stressed syllable is not word-initial, there may be considerably less aspiration than in word-initial position.

In utterance-final position, American English often fails to release plosives. This is transcribed with the nonrelease diacritic [̚], so [stɑp̚].

English has a glottal stop (it is not usually called a plosive), [ʔ], which does not occur as part of the usual inventory of consonants (though it does in many languages). It is used in American English in a couple of interjections and as a replacement for [t] in specific environments, particularly before unstressed syllabic [n], as in a word like *button*. Some varieties of British English substitute [ʔ] for [t] in a wide range of environments. American English has the negative interjection "uh-uh," [ʔʌʔʌ].

Transcription trouble spots: The letter <g> often represents a sound other than [g], and it is easy to write down [g] corresponding to the letter <g> when it represents a different sound. For instance, compare the word *get* as opposed to *gem*, *gym*, and *gist*. The letter <g> is also used in combination with other letters in English spelling to represent quite different sounds or no sound, such as *laugh* and *through*.

7.4.2 English has the following fricatives

[f v θ ð s z ʃ ʒ h]

key words: fin, vent, thin, then, sin, Zen, shin, vision, help.

The sound [h] has a different status than the others; it is a fricative made at the glottis (between the vocal folds) – which is in a configuration similar to that for whispering. You may see [h] classified in a different grouping than fricatives, often for phonological rather than phonetic reasons.

Transcription trouble spots: Most English consonants are spelled in one or two consistent ways. There are exceptions for a number of the fricatives.

[θ ð ʃ] are usually spelled with two letters.

[ʒ] is spelled in a number of different ways: genre, garage, vision.

[z] is often spelled with the letter <s>, not <z>: busy.

[θ ð] are never differentiated in spelling, and for this reason, speakers have difficulty distinguishing the two. Here are a couple of minimal pairs: ether-either, thy-thigh.

7.4.3   English has the following affricates

[tʃ dʒ]

key words: church, judge.

Transcription trouble spots: Again, inconsistent spelling can influence transcribers to write down the wrong IPA symbol because they're thinking of spelling, not sound. [tʃ] is usually spelled <ch> or <tch>, but <ch> represents [ʃ] in some words ("chaise") and [k] in other words ("chaos").

7.4.4   English has the following nasal consonants

[n m ŋ]

key words: gnat, mat, tan, tam, tang.

Note that [ŋ] occurs only in postvocalic position – that is, after a vowel in the same syllable.

Transcription trouble spots: [ŋ] often occurs where it is not spelled with the expected <ng>. It occurs in words such as *sink, rank*.

7.5   Approximants

7.5.1   English has the following approximants

[ɹ l j w]

key words: ray, lay, yay!, way.

[ʍ] is present in some varieties and not in others; it is the first sound of "which" only for those speakers who pronounce "which" and "witch" differently.

[ɹ]: Note that the sound transcribed [r] does not occur in American English. It is common in British English and other varieties. In most North American varieties of English, the rhotic (i.e. r-like) sound is transcribed [ɹ]. When [ɹ] is prevocalic (before a vowel), it acts as a glide – that is, a vowel-like sound that transitions into another vowel. Like other glides, if a speaker "holds" this sound, it turns into a vowel. A prolonged [ɹ] is an [ɚ].

[j]: In prevocalic position, normally spelled <y> in English. Note that the IPA symbol [y] represents a high front rounded vowel as in French "*tu*." While some phonetics or phonology books use "y" for [j], it is contrary to the IPA. The symbol [j] is used postvocalically to represent the last element in a diphthong (see Chapter 6, "Vowels").

The name of this letter of the IPA is usually said as *yod*. Calling it by the name of the English letter that has the same shape can cause confusion. When you say *yod*, the meaning is clear (at least to other people familiar with phonetics).

Transcription trouble spots: In many English words, [j] precedes the vowel [uw], but it is not represented in spelling, so it may escape notice. Notice the difference between *fuel* and *fool*, *beauty* and *booty* (meaning a pirate's treasure, not what you are thinking). This includes other spellings of the vowel and those in word-initial position: [j] is the first sound in *Europe* and *use*, for example.

[l]: The English lateral has two main allophones [l] and [ɫ]. The first of these is commonly called a "light" or "clear" [l]. The second of these is commonly called a "dark" [l], but more properly called a velarized [ɫ].

In American English, "light" [l] typically occurs at the beginnings of words and when in the environment of short front vowels. The velarized variety tends to occur at the ends of words or of syllables, and in the environment of all back vowels other than low ones. So in a word such as "loose," the initial lateral tends to be velarized (due to the vowel [u]), even in initial position.

Another feature of the postvocalic [l] or [ɫ] in English is that, if the preceding vowel is either long (diphthongized) or a diphthong, there is what is called an "on-glide" to the lateral.

[w]: The English labio-velar glide generally causes little problem, as it is usually spelled consistently in English. Note that this glide is used to mark the diphthongal quality of vowels, a topic to be discussed under vowels. Note that, for speakers who do not distinguish the pronunciation of "which" and "witch," the sound [w] is also spelled <wh>.

Transcription trouble spots: there are some words in which the sound [w] is spelled with letters other than <w>. The most common words in this group are borrowed from French, in which the letters <ou> are used to designate the [w]-sound, as in the word (as pronounced in English) *bivouac*.

[ʍ]: This is the voiceless [w] produced with noisy airflow. At an earlier stage of English, this was the initial sound of most words that are spelled <wh> at the beginning. Many varieties of American English retain this sound (unlike most non-American varieties), but there is considerable variation.

7.6   American English has a non-rhotic flap

"Non-rhotic" means that this flap does not have an r-like sound.

[ɾ]

key words: matter, madder, bitter, bidder.
The flap may replace [t] or [d] in intervocalic post-tonic position. That is, this occurs where the [t] or [d] is between vowels and following a syllable having primary stress.

Flapping is optional; speakers may do it or not. However, if it is used or not used where social convention says it should not be or should be, the result will sound odd. Flapping intervocalic [t] and [d] is a feature common to North American (American and Canadian) English, but does not occur widely in English spoken in other parts of the world.

7.7   The relationship between glides and vowels

There is a particular relationship between glides and vowels. In effect, glides are vowels whose timbre changes rapidly and which are not syllabic. Unlike a vowel, a glide cannot be the nucleus of a syllable. In most cases in English, glides precede vowels, but there are exceptions, such as the second element in diphthongized vowels and diphthongs.

The terms *on-glide* and *off-glide* are sometimes used. In the word *Yeah*, the [j] is an on-glide to the vowel, whereas in *bee*, the [j] is an off-glide to the vowel.

In the following, we will speak of "prolonging" the pronunciation of a glide. In practical terms, this is sometimes what we do in order to dramatically emphasize a word. For example, instead of saying simply "Yes" we might draw it out and say, "Yyyyyyyyyyyes!" This shows the prolongation of the [j] sound of *yes*.

If [j] is prolonged, you get the vowel [i].
If [w] is prolonged, you get the vowel [u].
If [ɹ] is prolonged, you get the vowel [ɚ].
While it is not a glide, if the approximant [l] is prolonged, you get the syllabic [l̩].

7.8 Vowels

7.8.1 Most varieties of English have three types of vowels
In common with almost all other dialects, General American English has:

- short vowels (monophthongal or "pure" vowels) such as [æ];
- long vowels (diphthongized vowels) such as [ow]; and
- diphthongs such as [aj].

7.8.2 American English has the following short vowels

Front	Central	Back
ɪ	ɚ	ʊ
ɛ	ə	ʌ
æ		ɔ
		ɑ

Key words in American English:

bit	bird	book
bet	about	but
bat		caught
		cot

7.8.3 American English has the following long (diphthongized) vowels
There is a variety of standard ways to transcribe these vowels; one is shown in the table. These standard transcriptions don't capture the fine phonetic detail of these vowels.

Front	Central	Back
ij		uw
ej		ow

Key words in American English:

beet	boot
bait	boat

7.8.4   American English has the following diphthongs

There is a variety of standard ways to transcribe these diphthongs; one is shown below. These standard transcriptions don't capture the fine phonetic detail of these vowels.

The timbre (sound) of these diphthongs may be somewhat different in syllables closed by a voiceless consonant as opposed to open syllables and syllables closed by a voiced consonant. The standard transcription does not capture this important fact.

Diphthong	Example words
aɪ	buy, might, sigh, ride, kite
aʊ	cow, bout, bowed
ɔɪ	boy, rhomboid, adroit

7.9   Word stress

Like other major varieties of English, American English has word stress. This is an important aspect of the pronunciation; inaccurate stress can render words unintelligible to other speakers of the language.

Stress is a matter of the **prominence** given to the syllable, which is to say a combination of loudness, duration, and articulatory precision. The greater the level of stress, the more of each of these dimensions is present in the syllable.

Note that word stress affects the syllable (not the whole word): the grammatical level at which word stress functions is that of the word (or word equivalents[2]). It does this by giving different prominence to the various syllables of the word.

In almost all varieties of English, isolated words have up to three levels of stress. That is to say, in an isolated English word, there may be as many as three different levels of stress given to the various syllables of the word.

---

[2] Here is what is meant: what is critical is not what English orthography spells as a single word; what matters is the phonological shape of the word. In essence, "White House" is a single word, phonologically, even though it is spelled as two.

The three levels of stress are identified as follows, from greatest to least:

1. primary stress, marked in the IPA with a raised short vertical stroke: [ˈ]
2. secondary stress, marked with a lower short vertical stroke: [ˌ]
3. unstressed (also called tertiary stress), unmarked in the IPA.

The stress mark is written before the first sound of the syllable.

An isolated word has at least one primary stress. The number of additional primary, secondary, and tertiary stresses in a word is highly variable; don't make up rules of thumb for yourself that will invariably turn out to be wrong. There is no rule that says there have to be a certain number of primary, secondary, or tertiary stresses, other than the rule in the first sentence of this paragraph.

7.9.1 Example

The word "pimento" as usually pronounced in English has this pattern of stressed syllables: unstressed, primary stress, secondary stress – [pəˈmɛnˌto].

8 | Voice, Phonation, and Nasality

8.1 Voice and phonation

In Chapter 5, "Consonants," we saw that some consonants are voiced (produced with vocal fold vibration) and some are not. In Chapter 6, "Vowels," we saw that vowels are nearly always voiced. In Chapter 3, "Anatomy and Physiology of Speech," we briefly discussed voicing (Section 3.5). And in Chapter 4, "Air Pressure and Aerodynamics," we examined a principle of aerodynamics (the Bernoulli principle) that plays a basic role in voice.

In the present chapter, we will examine *voice* and *phonation* specifically.

8.1.1 Terminology

There is quite a bit of inconsistency in the use of terms related to voicing and phonation. This is understandable, given the different focuses of such disciplines as general linguistics, phonology, phonetics, speech–language pathology, singing, and oratory, to say nothing of medical concerns.

To reduce possible confusion, we will set out how we will use the terms in this chapter. While the usage described below represents common usage in this field, it is important to remember that when you see these same terms in other material – books, lectures, and online – they may not refer to exactly the same concepts.

8.1.1.1 Voice
Voice refers to the generation of sound through the vibration of the vocal folds as a component of making speech sounds.

8.1.1.2 Voicing, voiced, voiceless
Voicing and the related terms *voiced* and *voiceless* refer to the fact of a particular phoneme being or not being produced with voice (as defined above). The term *voicing* also refers to the *process of producing* voice – that is, voicing can be a property of a speech sound, and it can also be a process occurring as a human speaks.

8.1.1.3   Phonation

Phonation is the creation of speech-related sounds within the larynx. This includes the production of voicing. It also includes the production of the sound of **whispering**; whispering is not voice because the vocal folds do not vibrate, but it is phonation. As some authors use the terminology, phonation also includes the glottal stop.

The term *phonation* is often defined as meaning voice or voicing, as used above, but we will maintain the distinction whereby phonation includes the production, within the larynx, of both voicing and speech sounds unrelated to voicing as such.

8.1.1.4   Voice again

In the field of speech–language pathology, the term **voice** is often used to include **nasality** in speech; in other words, it refers to an important aspect of speech resonance, divorced from the action of the vocal folds. For this reason, the present chapter includes a short section on nasality. However, this is not the definition typically used within the discipline of phonetics, so within the rest of the text of this chapter and elsewhere, the term *voice* is restricted to its definition above.

8.2   The glottis

As noted in Chapter 4, the **glottis** is the name given to the space between the vocal folds. The glottis is not a structure; it is a space defined by what surrounds it. When the vocal folds are pressed together along their entire length, the glottis disappears.

The glottis is the space through which air passes going into and out of the lungs. For respiration to occur, there must be a glottis to create an airway. But, given the other functions of the larynx, the size and shape of the glottis is variable to a considerable degree. The primary function of the larynx is to protect the airway and lungs from the entry of food and liquid during swallowing, and to aid in ejecting such material if it does enter the airway. Secondarily, all terrestrial mammals and a number of aquatic ones have developed the ability to make the vocal folds vibrate in order to vocalize.

The *vocal folds* are attached at the anterior end to the same point on the *thyroid cartilage* (Section 3.4). At the posterior end, they are attached to the *arytenoid cartilages*, which have the ability to pivot, tilt, and slide – by doing so, they have the ability to modify the glottis greatly, changing its size and shape. Because the vocal folds are attached together at the anterior end and separately at the posterior end, the glottis is usually roughly triangular in shape.

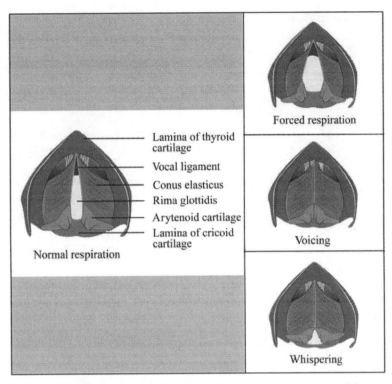

Figure 8.1 Positions of the arytenoid cartilages and consequent positions of the vocal folds and size and shape of the glottis. View from above. The point of the thyroid cartilage (the Adam's apple) is at the top of each view.

In forced respiration, such as when one is winded from heavy aerobic exertion, the glottis is as wide as it can be. In quiet respiration, the glottis is open, but less wide. When producing voice, the vocal folds are together along their length, rapidly vibrating, with or without a small triangular gap at the posterior end. In the production of voiceless sounds, the vocal folds are separated just enough to cause vibration to stop while allowing a quick movement back together to allow voicing to be reinitiated. In whispering, the vocal folds are held together so that they do not vibrate, but there is a triangular gap between the arytenoid cartilages through which air passes noisily. See Figure 8.1.

8.3   Production of voice; voicing

8.3.1   Voice production, basic

Voicing is the vibration of the vocal folds; they move together and apart rhythmically. This movement is described as *quasi-periodic*, meaning that each cycle of movement of a vocal fold away from and back toward the other vocal fold takes close to – but not precisely – the same amount of time as the cycle before and the cycle after. This vibration creates a buzzing sound that is fundamental to producing the sounds of speech. The buzzing sound is always filtered through the pharynx (throat) and oral and/or nasal cavities of the talker, so you have never heard this sound all by itself. If you did, it would sound somewhat like a kazoo.

The production of voice proceeds essentially in this fashion:

- The vocal folds are brought into contact (*adducted*) along their length (though not necessarily their entire length). This is accomplished using the muscles that move the arytenoid cartilages, including the *vocalis muscle* located within the vocal folds themselves.
- The tension of the vocal folds and the force holding the two vocal folds adducted are adjusted to balance the pressure of the air that rises from the lungs; this precise balance of forces is critical to voice production.
- Air pressure in the lungs is raised so that this pressure is sufficient to push the vocal folds up and apart.
- The balance of forces is, as we said, critical: the air pressure is not sufficient to hold the vocal folds apart. The elasticity of the tissue of the vocal folds, in addition to aerodynamic forces, brings the vocal folds together again.
- The vocal folds are again in contact along their length, blocking airflow. But their tension is still in a fine balance with the air pressure from below, so that air pressure is sufficient to force the vocal folds apart, but not to hold them apart.
- The vocal folds fall back into contact, and the cycle repeats.

A series of photographs of the glottal cycle can be seen in Figure 8.2.

CLINICAL NOTE 8.1 Anomalies of the vocal folds

The vocal folds themselves are subject to abuse, injury, disease, and a range of physical anomalies. All of these will affect to some degree the ability to produce voice and/or the quality of the voice that is produced.

A simple case of laryngitis or the difficulty talking after spending 3 hours shouting at a football game are a couple of everyday examples.

The field of *voice disorders* is a subfield of speech–language pathology. Voice clinicians deal with, among others, singers and other professional voice-users whose voices may show signs of overuse.

Anything that affects the flexibility of the vocal folds will change the quality of the voice; anything that affects the way that the vocal folds come together and seal the airflow will likewise affect the voice. A common example of both is *vocal nodules*, callous-like tissue on the contact surface of the vocal folds.

Many other conditions affect the voice, including swelling caused by a respiratory disorder such as a cold, or by gastric reflux.

8.3.2   Fundamental frequency (F_0)

In reference to the production of voice, the term *fundamental frequency* refers to the number of times per second that the vocal folds complete a cycle of vibration (together – apart – back together). It is measured in a unit called **hertz**, abbreviated **Hz**,[1] which is the number of these cycles per second.

Human speech is comprised of many sound frequencies, so the term *fundamental frequency* is used exclusively for the frequency of vocal fold vibration to distinguish it from other frequencies contained in speech.

Typical fundamental frequencies for women, men, children, and infants are shown in Table 8.1. Fundamental frequency is often abbreviated F_0 or F0 (the second character is the number zero, not the letter O).

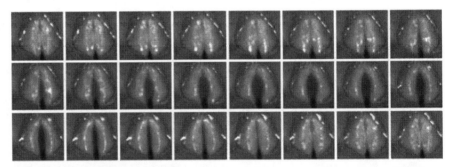

Figure 8.2 The glottal cycle. This series of photographs shows the state of the glottis (seen from above) through a single cycle of vibration. The arytenoid cartilages are situated at the bottom of each frame. Note the gradual opening, then closing, of the glottis. The entire series lasts 6 milliseconds or 0.006 seconds. There is an interval of 0.25 milliseconds (0.00025 seconds) between each frame. The talker's fundamental frequency is approximately 167 Hz.

---

[1] In the international system of measures that we informally call the *metric system* in English, units named after people are spelled with a lower-case letter when spelled out in full, but with an upper-case (capital) letter when abbreviated: *hertz* and *Hz*. This unit is named for the German scientist Heinrich Hertz who lived from 1857 to 1894 and who made important contributions to the study of electromagnetic waves.

Table 8.1 Fundamental frequencies for different talkers and a singer

Talker	Fundamental frequency
Adult woman	165 to 255 Hz
Adult man	85 to 155 Hz
Infant	250 to 650 Hz
Extreme infant vocalization	As high as 1000 Hz
10-year-old girl or boy, pre-puberty	Approximately 400 Hz
Singer's "Soprano C" (C6)	1046 Hz

8.3.2.1 Modal frequency

In order to understand the meaning of Table 8.1, we need to examine the concept of *modal frequency*. We can briefly define the modal frequency as the most "natural" frequency for a particular talker. Producing voice at the modal frequency causes the least vocal fold strain for the individual talker.

8.3.2.2 Fundamental frequency range

The first three rows of Table 8.1 show a range of frequencies for each group of talkers. The range shows the possible modal frequencies for different individuals within the group. For example, the range of 165 to 255 Hz for women indicates that one woman may have an F_0 of 170 Hz, another 210 Hz, and still another 240 Hz. The table indicates that it would be quite unlikely – though not impossible – for a given woman to have an F_0 of 285 Hz. The range of values shows the possible values for *different individuals within each group*.

This is different from the *frequency range of a given individual*. Every person is capable of changing the pitch (F_0) of their voice to frequencies higher or lower than their modal frequency. This is that individual's *personal vocal range*.

The woman from the paragraph above, whose F_0 is 240 Hz, may have a personal vocal range from 180 to 340 Hz (this is a little less than an octave). If she has a professionally trained voice, her personal range will be greater.

Note that the *personal vocal range* of a single individual may include frequencies above or below the range of modal frequencies for that person's cohort.[2] In the example in the previous paragraph, the woman's personal range goes up to 340 Hz, which is outside the typical range of modal frequencies for adult women.

---

[2] That is, the group to which they belong: adult women, adult men, children of a certain age range.

Be sure to keep separate in your mind the ideas that:

- there is a range of typical modal fundamental frequencies for men or women or children as groups;
- each given individual has their own modal frequency; and
- each individual's voice is capable of a range of frequencies, which may go beyond the typical modal frequencies for their cohort.

8.3.3   Other frequencies in voicing

The production of speech depends upon there being a wide range of frequencies produced in the larynx in addition to the fundamental frequency. These other frequencies set up resonance within the cavities of the vocal tract, creating the sounds of vowels and many consonants.

For reasons to be explained in Section 8.5 and in Chapter 12, the vibrating vocal folds produce what is called a **harmonic series** of frequencies. This is a series of frequencies that are whole number multiples of the fundamental frequency.

What does this mean in practice? Let us take the example of a talker whose fundamental frequency is 100 Hz. The frequencies produced by that talker's voice will include 100 Hz, 200 Hz, 300 Hz, 400 Hz, 500 Hz, and so on, up to quite high frequencies. In speech, harmonic frequencies up to somewhat less than 4000 Hz are important in producing the identifying characteristics of vowels and some consonants.

8.4   Voice onset time

As we saw in Chapter 5, "Consonants," some speech sounds are *voiced* and some are not (they are *voiceless*). It may appear that voiced or voiceless is a binary choice, that is, a speech sound is either voiced or not voiced – and that there is no in-between.

The actual facts are different, in particular for plosive consonants. There are *degrees of voicing*, not just voice or no voice. While this may not seem intuitive, in fact it is easy to understand when the following is taken into consideration.

- The production of a plosive consonant is performed by muscles in the tongue, velum, or lips, while voicing is performed by muscles within the larynx (combined with respiration).
- Because producing the plosive and producing voice are performed by different muscle groups and anatomical structures, the two events can be coordinated in different ways.

○ If you are entering text with a keyboard or a touchscreen, and tapping your foot at the same time, the movements of your fingers and foot can be coordinated or not coordinated.

8.4.1   Release is the reference point for plosive voicing

If we are to quantify voicing in plosives, we will do so on a *timeline:* how long does it take before voicing is initiated? We start measuring time at one specific moment and continue timing until another event (the start or onset of voicing).

The reference point for the start of timing is the **release** of the plosive (cf. Section 5.7, and particularly 5.7.1.3). This is done both because it makes sense, but also for practical reasons: it is generally very easy to identify the point of release on an audio recording, especially with a spectral analysis (Chapter 12). The moment where closure begins is very often impossible to determine in an audio recording and would require complex equipment to determine reliably.

Recall from Chapter 5 the phases of plosive production: the **closing phase** (also called **approach** or **shutting phase**), followed by the **closure phase (occlusion)** during which there is no airflow, and finally **release.**

You might think, logically, that a voiced plosive should have voicing during the entire closure phase, and voiceless plosives should have no voicing until just after the release of the plosive (since, once the plosive is released, the talker is producing the next phone). The reality in English – and many other languages – is quite different.

8.4.2   How to measure voice onset time

Voice onset time (VOT) is the time taken – starting at plosive release – until voicing is initiated. If voicing starts *after* release, the VOT value is positive because you're measuring forward in time. On the other hand, if voicing starts *before* release, the value is negative because you're measuring from a point later in time (release) back to an earlier time when voicing was initiated. If voicing is initiated at precisely the same moment as plosive release, then there is no delay and the VOT value is zero.

Voice onset time, like other events in speech, is measured in *milliseconds* (*ms* or *msec*): thousandths of a second.

Figure 8.3 provides a graphic representation of different ranges of voice onset time. In this figure, time runs from left to right. The vertical line represents the moment of release of a plosive consonant, so the plosive consonant is shown to the left of that vertical line, and the following vowel at the right.

The start of the zigzag part of the horizontal lines shows where voicing starts, and the continued zigzag shows voicing continuing. The ranges of voice onset time, as shown in the figure, are **long lead**, **short lead**, **zero**, **short lag**, and **long lag.**

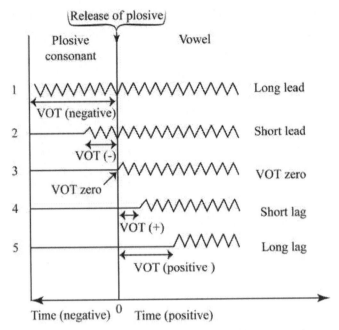

Figure 8.3 Voice onset time. This table shows 5 different ranges for voice onset time. Each time range is shown on a different row, each identified by number. The straight vertical line represents the release of the plosive, so the closure phase of the plosive is to the left of the vertical line, and the following vowel is shown to the right of the vertical line.

In each row, the straight horizontal line represents time during which the vocal folds are not vibrating. The zigzag line represents time during which the vocal folds are vibrating.

In *long lead VOT*, the start (onset) of voicing *leads* (goes before) the release of the plosive by a long period of time. In *short lead VOT*, the onset of voicing *leads* the release of the plosive by a short period of time. When the onset of voicing leads release, the exact number of milliseconds is shown with a negative sign (for example, -30 msec).

In *zero VOT*, the start (onset) of voicing occurs simultaneously with the release of the plosive. There is no lead and there is no lag; both events occur together. The VOT value is 0 (zero).

In *short lag VOT*, the start (onset) of voicing *lags behind* (occurs after) the release of the plosive by a short period of time. In *long lag VOT*, the onset of voicing occurs a long period of time after the release; in other words, it *lags behind* by a long time. When the onset of voicing lags release, the value of the VOT is shown with a positive sign (for example, +15 msec, though the plus sign is not obligatory).

The terms *long lead, short lead,* and so on are general terms to describe a particular VOT, or to characterize voice onset times in a particular language or dialect. Precise values can be provided instead of these categories.

8.4.3   Utterance-initial VOT

VOT is generally measured and reported for utterance-initial plosives. Utterance-initial means that the plosive in question is the first thing said – the first sound in the utterance. It is preceded by silence.

If one attempts to measure VOT for plosives in other positions in the word or utterance, other aspects of the articulation generally get in the way. For example, consider a voiced plosive between vowels in a word such as the [b] in *rabbit*. There will be voicing in the preceding vowel, the [b] is voiced, and the following vowel is voiced. Therefore, no separate onset of voicing occurred for this [b], and so the term VOT is meaningless.

8.5   Voice production in greater detail

The details of voice production matter because the specific qualities of the human voice are basic to the production of normal-sounding speech. The vibration of the vocal folds is not a simple back-and-forth motion, but a complex undulatory[3] motion, required in order to generate the rich harmonic series that creates resonance in vowels and some consonants.

8.5.1   Videostroboscopy of the vocal folds

Figure 8.2 showed images that together illustrate a **glottal cycle** – that is a vibratory cycle – of the vocal folds. Let us imagine that this is the voice of a woman whose F_0 is hypothetically 200 Hz. That means that the entire set of images shows 1/200 of a second or 0.005 second(s). But the cycle was divided into 24 parts, so each image represents 1/24 of 0.005 s, or 0.0002083 s. This is an extremely short space of time.[4]

Cameras exist that can take photos at the required speeds, but they are extremely expensive and very bright light is required to capture images that fast. It is not a practical way to capture these images of the human vocal folds in vibration.

What is done instead is to make use of the **stroboscopic effect**. This is the effect that makes the wheels of vehicles in movies and videos seem to stop turning or to turn backwards. It is a question of the timing of taking pictures as compared to the speed of rotation of the wheels, or, for our purposes, the frequency of vibration of the vocal folds.

---

[3] Moving like a snake, a wave, or a rope that is shaken at one end
[4] In phonetics, milliseconds (ms) – one thousandth of a second – are a commonly used unit. So 0.005 seconds would be expressed as 5 ms. The value of 0.0002083 seconds could be expressed as 0.2083 ms.

In videostroboscopy of the vocal folds, a fiber-optic device is inserted through the nose, through the nasal cavity, and past the velum so that it is looking downward in the pharynx, with the vocal folds in view. See Figure 8.4. A video camera is attached.

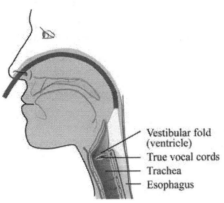

Vestibular fold (ventricle)
True vocal cords
Trachea
Esophagus

Figure 8.4 Fiber-optic viewing of the vocal folds. A camera is attached to the fiber-optic scope, and a microphone detects vocal fold vibration in order to synchronize light flashes that give the illusion of slowing the vibration through the stroboscopic effect. The image that is seen is like those shown in Figure 8.2, except that the orientation is different, as described in relation to Figure 8.2.

Using a microphone, the system detects the fundamental frequency so that it can synchronize a flashing light to capture steps in the movement. The light flashes very slightly later in each cycle. When the video is viewed, it appears to capture the vocal fold movement in slow motion, but each image was taken during a separate cycle of vocal fold vibration.

8.5.2   Anatomical structure of the vocal folds in cross-section

Let us turn our attention to the anatomical make-up of the vocal folds. The reason for this close examination is that the different layers of tissue each have different properties, and it is the interaction among them that generates the particular quality of the human voice and makes speech clear and intelligible.

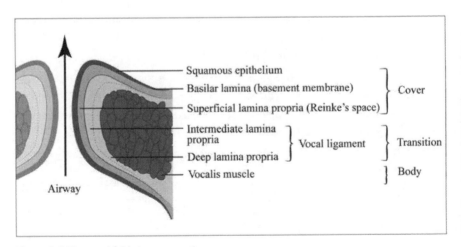

Squamous epithelium
Basilar lamina (basement membrane)
Superficial lamina propria (Reinke's space)   Cover
Intermediate lamina propria
Deep lamina propria   Vocal ligament   Transition
Vocalis muscle   Body
Airway

Figure 8.5 The vocal folds in cross-section

Figure 8.5 shows the internal structure of the vocal folds.

The deepest layer is the *vocalis muscle*, a muscle making up much of the body of the vocal folds. It is one of a complex of muscles in the larynx that can swivel the *artytenoid cartilages* and thus adjust the *glottis*. In a later section, we will see why it is identified as the *body* of the vocal folds in Figure 8.5.

Moving toward the outer surface, the next layer is the *vocal ligament*, which in turn is made up of two layers, the *intermediate* and *deep layers of the lamina propria*. Together, these form the *transition layer* between the *body* and the *cover*.

The outer layers of the vocal folds, which collectively form the *cover*, include the *squamous epithelium*, the *basilar lamina* and the *superficial lamina propria* (also known as *Reinke's space*).

8.5.3   Myoelastic aerodynamic theory of voice production

The *myoelastic aerodynamic theory of voice production* has been known for a century and a half and has been widely accepted for a long period. Titze (1980) noted that the theory originated with Mueller in 1848, then was "formulated explicitly" by van den Berg in 1958, and has been widely accepted since that time as *the* mechanism by which the vocal folds vibrate.

The name of the theory points to its major elements:

- *Myo-*: in compound words in English, *myo-* refers to *muscles*. Muscles of the larynx are involved in positioning the vocal folds. Respiratory muscles are involved in providing airflow and air pressure from the lungs.
- *Elastic*: this term refers to the *elasticity* of the tissues involved, mostly the vocal folds themselves. As this tissue is stretched, it bounces back like a stretched rubber band.
- *Aerodynamic*: There are two parts here: *aero-*, referring to *air*, and *dynamic* referring to *movement*, so this term addresses *airflow* and physical laws governing airflow, topics we addressed in Section 5.7.

We will see how these various elements come together in normal vocal fold vibration.

8.5.4   Additional detail concerning the vibration of the vocal folds

Review the steps in vocal fold vibration we saw above in Section 8.3.1; this section will provide additional information.

The upper surface of the vocal folds, as seen in typical videos of vocal fold movement, have a rippling motion across them while in vibration. This comes from three principal factors:

- migration of vocal fold opening and closure, forward and back, undulatory movement in the horizontal dimension

SIDEBAR 8.1 Mass and inertia

Physics recognizes the existence of *mass* and *inertia*, which combine to affect the way objects move. *Mass* is the amount of "stuff" or material, and it remains constant. You would *weigh* less on the moon than on earth because the force of gravity is less on the moon, but *your mass would be the same in both locations* – you'd still be made of the same amount of stuff on the moon as on the earth.

Inertia is the resistance of mass to acceleration or deceleration. It takes a lot of energy to accelerate your bicycle (or car) up to the speed you would like to go. If you have to stop suddenly, you recognize that it takes a lot of energy to stop your bike and yourself. A mass at rest requires a lot of energy to get it moving, and a moving mass requires a lot of energy to stop it – that is inertia.

If an object like a vocal fold oscillates back and forth, it must accelerate up to speed, then decelerate to a stop, then accelerate in the opposite direction, then decelerate to a stop. It is important to understand that inertia constantly works against this back-and-forth movement.

- a small amount of vertical (up-and-down) movement of the vocal folds, particularly the contact edges
- the fact that the upper and lower contact edges of the vocal folds do not oscillate synchronously

Let us look at these in turn.

8.5.4.1   Rippling closure, forward then backward

Figure 8.2 shows a series of still pictures during a vibration cycle of the vocal folds. Note that the movement together and apart is not symmetrical. There is movement from the posterior (back) end to the anterior (front) end, and back again. In some frames the glottal space can be seen in more than one place. The important lesson here is that the vocal folds do not move together and apart like two hands clapping. Rather, there is a wavy ripple that moves forward and back along the length of the folds in the horizontal dimension.

The pattern of the closure moving forward and the opening moving toward the back is typical. However, there are variations of this pattern among some individuals with healthy vocal folds. The pattern can be very different in certain vocal fold pathologies.

8.5.4.2   Up-and-down movement of the vocal folds

As we saw in Section 4.8, the closed vocal folds are forced to open by a heightened air pressure below the folds. They are pushed up and apart as they open, and then, as they close, they return downwards and together, as seen in the vertical dimension. This is shown in Figure 8.6.

The effect of this is to raise the surface of the vocal fold close to the line of contact between the two folds, which then returns downward, rippling the upper surface of the vocal folds.

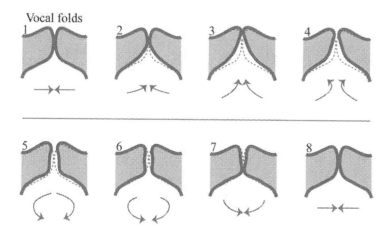

⟶ = Direction of movement of the mass of the vocal folds

Figure 8.6 Up-and-down movement in vocal fold vibration. This movement changes the shape of the upper surface of the vocal folds, spreading a ripple across the upper surface.

8.5.4.3 Upper and lower contact edges of vocal folds do not move synchronously

It might be natural to think that, as the vocal folds move together and apart, the entire body of the vocal folds moves as a single unit. Such a hypothetical movement is shown in Figure 8.7. *But in fact, this is not true.* Despite the small size of the vocal folds themselves, their flexibility allows them to move in a more complex way.

Figure 8.7 The vocal folds do *not* move apart and together this way. The image shows the vocal folds in cross-section. They are moving apart, then together as if each was a single mass whose shape does not change. But we will see that the movement is more complex than shown here; two flat hands clapping together is very different from the movement of the vocal folds.

Imagine holding an object in your hand and swinging it back and forth with your arm. The object you imagine should be heavy enough that it requires energy to get it moving and to stop it. Now imagine that a second object like the first is suspended by an elastic cord below the first. As you swing the upper object back and forth, the one below will also swing back and forth, but its movement will always lag behind the upper one. For example, at each end of the swing, the upper object will change direction before the lower object.

Indeed, the upper and lower edges of the contact face of the vocal folds act like these two weights, attached together by an elastic cord. In an effort to describe technically how this motion occurs, scientists have formulated the *two-mass model of vocal fold vibration* and the *cover–body model*.

These models attempt to take into consideration: (1) the effect of inertia on the motion of the vocal folds; and (2) the different properties of the epithelial layer and the interior body of the vocal folds.

8.5.4.4   The two-mass model

The *two-mass model* addresses the fact that separation of the vocal folds starts with the inferior edge and then works up to the upper edge, acting as if there were two masses. This is like the analogy of swinging a pair of weights, one hanging below the other, except that in the vocal folds it is the lower mass that leads. This movement is shown in Figure 8.8.

This two-mass model is often shown as two blocks (masses) attached by a spring, in order to demonstrate the motion shown in Figures 8.6 and 8.8. An image of this type is shown in Figure 8.9.

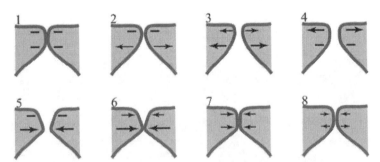

Figure 8.8 Vocal fold vibration in cross-section, showing that the lower edge separates first, followed by the upper edge, and the lower edge comes back together first, followed by the upper edge. The edges of the folds do not act as a single unit (shown in Figure 8.7). This image does not show the slight upward movement described in Section 8.5.4.2. This illustration was influenced by Story (2002).

8.5.4.5   The cover–body model

The cover–body model makes reference to the complex anatomical structure of the vocal folds, which we saw in Section 8.5.2. The outer layers, the epithelium, basilar lamina, and the superficial lamina propria have greater flexibility than the stiffer inner parts, particularly the vocalis muscle. This allows the outer layers to move as described above while the inner parts are less subject to changing their shape. In Figure 8.9, m_1 and m_2 are part of the superficial layers, while **m** represents inner layers.

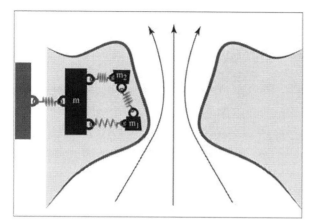

Figure 8.9 A mechanical 2-mass model. The small blocks with the letter **m** are masses; m_1 and m_2 are the two masses of the model. They are attached together with springs, allowing movement but exerting a force if stretched or compressed. The internal structure of the vocal folds is the mass marked simply **m**. At the moment this image is taken, the lower edges of the vocal folds are beginning to come back together, corresponding to frame (5) in Figure 8.8. (This illustration was influenced by www.ling.fju.edu.tw/hearing/ishizaka.htm. Helpful animations are shown on that site.)

Imagine a toy balloon filled with gelatin. The gelatin would not move in the same way as it would without the balloon (sitting on a plate, for example). The movement as you squeeze the balloon will result from a combination of the properties of the stretched balloon "cover" and the gelatin "body." The whole balloon would behave differently from one filled with air or another filled with water. In this analogy, the cover is quite stiff and the body is quite soft and flexible. In the vocal folds, the opposite is true, with much greater flexibility in the cover and a rigid body. Still, this analogy of a cover–body model allows you to think about different parts of a complex structure interacting to create the behavior of the overall object.

8.5.4.6 The mucosal wave

The complex movements of the vocal folds when producing voice, which we have seen in the preceding sections, leads to a rippling motion along the upper surface of the vocal folds. This movement is easily visible in videostroboscopy of the vocal folds, and many videos can be found online. This rippling motion of the superior surface of the vocal folds is called the *mucosal wave*.

This rippling is fundamental to normal vocal fold voice production. It is used diagnostically: if the diagnostician sees an absent or abnormal mucosal wave, they will be alerted to possible pathology. However, it is not the ripple itself that produces normal-sounding voice. It is the complex movements discussed above – when those movements are normal, a typical mucosal wave is produced.

8.5.5   The role of Bernoulli's principle in voicing

We have seen how movement of the tissue, based in part on its physical properties and elasticity, and how it is acted upon by inertia, contribute to the very particular movement of the vocal folds in vibration. This particular movement in turn generates the distinctive sound of the voice.

In Section 8.3.1, we saw the basics of vocal fold vibration. We said that air pressure from below forces the vocal folds up and apart and that the vocal folds come back together due to elasticity of the tissue and an aerodynamic principle. That principle is the Bernoulli principle, detailed in Section 4.7. Review that now.

When the vocal folds are together, ready to produce voicing, there is a static pressure of air pressing against the vocal folds – there is no aerodynamic process because the air is not moving. The moment that the vocal folds are pressed apart, air flows between them – that is an aerodynamic situation. As the air flows through the narrowing between the vocal folds, pressure drops in accordance with Bernoulli.

So, the vocal folds fall back together for two reasons: they have been stretched and so elastic recoil acts, but the air pressure that was sufficient to push the vocal folds apart is now lower and is unable to keep the vocal folds separated.

The moment the vocal folds return together, air stops flowing. There is no aerodynamic principle at work because the air is static. The pressure rises to the amount that is sufficient to force the vocal folds apart. As soon as that happens, air pressure is reduced between the vocal folds, and the pattern repeats.

8.5.6   Jitter and shimmer

As we noted above, normal voice is quasi-periodic. Each cycle is very similar to the one before and the one following, though not identical. Two types of variation that are important in voice studies are *jitter* and *shimmer.*

8.5.6.1   Jitter

Jitter is frequency variation. Where there is jitter, the duration of each glottal cycle is different. A certain amount of jitter is entirely normal. There are formal measures of jitter.

8.5.6.2 Shimmer

Shimmer is amplitude variation in voice. It can also be measured and quantified.

Jitter and shimmer together, if sufficiently strong, can give an impression of harshness or hoarseness to the voice.

8.6 Modes of vocal fold vibration: types of voice

8.6.1 Modal voice

Up until the previous couple of paragraphs of this chapter, we have addressed *modal voice*. Modal voice is the "natural" mode of vocal fold vibration.

Additionally, modal voice is the most efficient, in the sense that it uses the breath stream to the best effect in producing voice, using the least air to produce the most sound.

8.6.2 Breathy voice, murmur

In *breathy voice*, the glottis is configured so that considerable air escapes during voicing. Typically, this means that, while the vocal folds vibrate, there remains a triangular gap between the arytenoid cartilages that allows air to pass noisily. The contact pressure between the vocal folds themselves may also be reduced as compared to modal voice, and this means that the open phase of each glottal cycle is a little longer relative to the closed phase, and this allows more air to escape with each cycle.

Some individuals tend toward a breathier voice, others more nearly modal. In English-speaking societies, among others, there is a tendency for girls' and women's voices to be breathier than boys' and men's, though there is great individual variation.

In English, h-sound in a word such as *ahead* may be produced with breathy voice; this "voiced h" is symbolized [ɦ] in the IPA. The voicing for the vowel preceding and following the /h/ may not be stopped and the breathy [ɦ] results.

8.6.2.1 Murmur

The term *murmur* is usually used for breathy-type voice used to distinguish words for other grammatical functions.

SIDEBAR 8.2 Murmur and retroflexion

The IPA symbol for *murmur* is two dots under the symbol for the sound that is murmured: [b̤ ɑ̤].

As noted in Chapter 5, retroflex consonants are symbolized with a descender (tail) curling to the right attached to the alveolar symbol: [ʈ ɖ]. However, in typical transliterations of languages having retroflex consonants, a single dot is used under the letter: <ṭ>. Be sure not to confuse /t̪/ with <ṭ>.

For example, a number of the languages of India make a 4-way distinction among plosives:

1. Strongly aspirated voiceless plosives (long lag)
2. Voiceless plosives (short lag)
3. Voiced plosives (short to long lead)
4. Murmured plosives (breathy voice or murmur)

See Table 8.2 for examples.[5]

Table 8.2 Contrast between murmured and modal plosives

Language	Aspirated voiceless	Voiceless	Voiced	Murmur
Hindi	[pʰɑl] 'knife blade'	[pɑl] 'nurture'	[bɑl] 'hair'	[b̤ɑl] 'brow'
	[ʈʰɑl] 'lumber shop'	[ʈɑl] 'postpone'	[ɖɑl] 'branch'	[ɖ̤ɑl] 'shield'
	[kʰɑl] 'skin'	[kɑl] 'span of time'	[gɑl] 'cheek'	[g̤ɑl] 'confusion'
Nepali	[pʰɑl] 'throw away'	[pɑl] 'rear'	[bɑl] 'burn'	[b̤ɑl] 'forehead'

Some authors use the term *whispery voice* for *murmur*, and there is some controversy concerning the mechanism by which murmur is created. However, it is generally accepted that a reduced tension in the vocal folds during production is an essential part of murmur (Butcher, 2016). There may be some difference among languages, with different laryngeal configurations producing a similar sound.

8.6.3   Creaky voice

Creaky voice or *laryngealization*[6] is voice produced with high tension of the vocal folds combined with increased subglottal pressure (Butcher, 2016). Occasionally it is called *vocal fry* or *glottal fry* because the sound reminds some people of the sound of frying bacon. The symbol for creaky voice is a tilde underneath the segment: [a̰ b̰].

There has been recent attention to this phenomenon in popular media, and these sources exaggerate the degree to which this is a brand-new

---

[5] Examples from www.phonetik.uni-muenchen.de/~hoole/kurse/artikul/multi_voice.pdf from Sounds of the World's Languages.

[6] The term *laryngealization* is sometimes used for other phenomena, such as replacement of a segment by – or insertion of – a glottal stop. Since there is the possibility of ambiguity, this term is not recommended for *creaky voice*.

phenomenon in the speech of many young women (Yuasa, 2010), especially urban and upwardly mobile young women. The phenomenon is also found in men's speech and the speech of older women.

To the extent that Yuasa's findings represent something of a trend, it is a sociolinguistic phonetic phenomenon – that is, a phonetic phenomenon related to a particular social or geographic group. It does not change the meanings of words, and it is therefore not phonemic in nature.

Danish provides an example of phonemic use of creaky voice – that is, where modal versus creaky voice signals a change in the meaning of the word. It is important to note, however, that there is considerable variation in the realization of creaky voice in Danish, and it may be realized as a glottal stop. Phonemic creaky voice is called *stød* in Danish. See Table 8.3.

Table 8.3 Creaky voice in Danish (after Riad, 2003)

Meaning	Pronunciation	Normal spelling
she	[hun]	hun
dog	[hun̩]	hund
reader	[lɛ:sɐ]	læser
reads	[lɛ̰:sɐ]	læser
painter	[mæ:lɐ]	maler
paints	[mæ̰:lɐ]	maler

The language Zaiwa, spoken in parts of China and Burma, also provides an example of phonemic creaky voice. For instance, Zaiwa has pairs of verbs that are the same except for the fact that one member of the pair has creaky voice and the other doesn't. The one with creaky voice has a causative or directive meaning, as shown in these examples: 'to be attached' versus 'to attach'; 'to move (intransitive)' versus 'to move (something)'; 'to explode (intransitive)' versus 'to explode (something)' (Lustig, 2010).

8.7 Whisper

In order to produce audible vowels and other sonorant sounds, there needs to be a source of sound containing a broad spectrum of frequencies. (More detail will be seen in Chapter 12.) In normal speech, voicing serves this function.

Normal voiced speech is too loud in certain situations where one wants not to be overheard or not to disturb others. But you can't simply stop voicing in order to speak more quietly – if you did that, your speech would be completely inaudible.

In order to produce a less-loud background sound of broad spectrum, we whisper. Whispering is essentially producing a fricative-like sound at the glottis, which is filtered in the oral and pharyngeal cavities just as voiced speech is.

8.7.1   Maintaining voicing distinctions in whispered speech

Normal speech in most languages requires making the distinction between voiced and voiceless vowels. In whispered speech, nothing is voiced. So how is it that whispered speech continues to be intelligible – we can still hear a difference between [t] and [d], [p] and [b], [s] and [z]?

As we stressed in Chapter 5, the difference between voiced and voiceless consonants is not found only in voicing. For instance, in normal speech, the vowel is longer in *mad* than in *mat*. This timing difference is maintained in whispered speech, and so the two words remain distinct. In normal speech, [s] has a stronger fricative element than does [z], and this is maintained in whispered speech. These are examples of how phones differ from one another in ways that are not normally part of phonetic classification systems.

8.8   Nasality

Nasality is not an aspect of *voice*, as we have been using the term in this chapter (consistent with its meaning in phonetics). However, terminology differs among fields, and in the field of communication disorders – speech–language pathology – nasality is often included in a clinical definition of voice. For this reason, we will examine nasality briefly here.

A good place to start is to review the **velopharyngeal port** (Section 3.3), nasal consonants (5.8) and nasal vowels (6.8). Only brief aspects of those discussions will be repeated here.

Fundamentally, nasality occurs when the velopharyngeal port (VPP) is open, permitting sound waves from the vocal folds to rise into the nasal cavities and produce a characteristic sound. Nasality can occur with the oral cavity closed, producing **nasal consonants**, or with the oral cavity open, producing **nasalized vowels**.

Anomalous hypernasality can also occur when there are openings between the oropharynx or oral cavity and the nasal cavities in addition to normal opening of the VPP. The structures involved in closing the VPP (the velum plus others) may be inadequate, or there may be anomalous openings in the palate. See Section 8.8.3.

8.8.1 Effect of hypernasality

Review Section 4.6.3 and Figure 4.4.

When the VPP is open, not only can sound waves pass into the nasal cavities, but air can also pass from the pharynx and oral cavity into the nasal cavities. This flow of air prevents the normal production of many consonants by making it impossible to produce a relatively high air pressure within the oral cavity and pharynx. The production of plosive consonants (especially voiceless ones) and fricatives (especially voiceless ones) is rendered impossible.[7] The resulting speech will have extremely low intelligibility if the air is unrestricted in its passage to the nasal cavities. If air can pass, but only slowly, then the intelligibility of those consonants will be reduced, but it will not necessarily be impossible to produce them.

CLINICAL NOTE 8.3
Hypernasality and hyponasality

Speech difficulties involving nasality are quite common, especially due to congenital structural anomalies of the palate and velum associated with cleft palate. These congenital defects occur quite frequently and require intervention from a range of specialists, including speech–language pathologists, as well as surgical intervention.

Without intervention, the individual's speech can be of very low intelligibility. Hypernasality affects the production of many sounds, especially consonants requiring high air pressure or a high rate of airflow. While hyponasality is rarer, it causes issues with intelligibility of speech as well.

8.8.2 Development of the palate

The oral and nasal cavities form one large opening in the face of the early-stage embryo. The palate develops as two shelves of bone (palatine processes) grow from the sides of the opening toward the centerline. This is called the *secondary palate* when speaking of embryonic development. At the same time, the *primary palate* develops in a series of steps and it forms a triangular area at the front of the palate and *maxilla* (upper jaw).

These three parts (both the bones and their overlying soft tissue) fuse together in normal development. (See Figure 8.10.) If anomalies occur during the developmental process, there may be openings (clefts or fistulas) along the lines of fusion.

Development of the velum and its associated musculature occurs within the same time frame.

---

[7] In a language having distinctively nasalized vowels, there may be intelligibility issues with vowels as well. The distinction between nasalized and non-nasalized vowels will be lost.

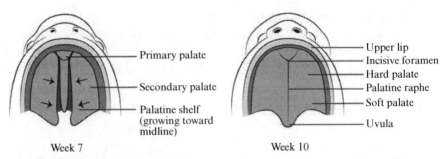

Figure 8.10 Development of the palate. The palatine shelves grow toward the midline as the primary palate develops in a roughly triangular shape. The parts fuse by the end of the first trimester. If the normal process is interrupted, there may be openings (a cleft or fistulas) along the lines of fusion.

8.8.3   Causes of air leakage

If there is air leakage into the nasal cavities when it is not desired, there may be any of several causes.

8.8.3.1   VPD–VPI

Velopharyngeal dysfunction (VPD) is a generic term[8] for failure of the velopharyngeal mechanism to function properly. In the field of communication disorders, this has traditionally been called **VPI**, which is variously said to stand for *velopharyngeal insufficiency* or *velopharyngeal incompetence.*

VPD may occur for a number of reasons:

• The amount of tissue in the velum or its size (width or length) may be insufficient to close off the velopharyngeal port fully to make an airtight seal.
• There can be problems with the musculature such that a sufficiently large velum cannot be moved or stretched to close the passage fully. (Muscles of the pharyngeal wall also come into play in the closure or lack thereof.)
• As in the previous item, with essentially the same consequences, a neurological problem can prevent normal closure by failing to signal the muscles.
• An individual without physical anomaly can have failed to learn to use the velopharyngeal port appropriately in speech production. This may occur, for example, in instances of profound hearing impairment since birth.

VPD/VPI may be part of a cleft lip and/or cleft palate anomaly.

It is to be noted that VPD/VPI can affect swallowing as well as speech.

---

[8] www.ncbi.nlm.nih.gov/pmc/articles/PMC3706038.

8.8.3.2   Palatal fistula

A *fistula* is an abnormal passageway connecting two anatomical areas that are not normally connected, or are not normally connected at that particular location. As part of the same anomaly that gives rise to cleft palate, there may be one or more fistulas connecting the mouth, through the palate, to the nasal cavity, along the developmental suture lines.

8.8.3.3   Cleft palate

In gestational development, the oral and nasal cavities start out as a single opening in the head. Then two shelves of bone (the secondary palate), one from each side, grow toward the midline and fuse. Along with an additional small bone (the primary palate), the fused bone "shelves" form the hard palate.

   In cleft palate, the palatal bones have not fused entirely. This could result in a fistula, as we saw above, or could result in a cleft (gap) running the length of the palate. If the maxilla (upper jaw) and/or lip are also cleft, that cleft will either be double, or, if single, it will be to the right or the left of the midline, due to the configuration of the primary palate that normally fuses to the secondary palate.

8.8.3.4   Not learning to control the velopharyngeal port

If a child with cleft palate or a palatal fistula lacks treatment for their condition, they may fail to acquire the normal movements of the VPP. In essence, if there is a gap in the palate, then it does not matter whether the velum is raised or lowered; air and sound waves will move directly between the nasal and oral cavities irrespective of the state of the VPP.

   A profoundly hearing-impaired child learning to talk may not be aware of the difference in sound produced with the VPP open versus closed. Again, in this situation, the individual with normal functioning of a sufficiently sized velum and associated structures may nonetheless fail to control nasality without special intervention.

8.9   IPA symbols introduced or mentioned in this chapter

Murmur: [b̤ ɑ̤]
Retroflexion: [ʈ ɖ]
Creaky voice: [a̰ b̰]

8.10   Vocabulary

adduct
airflow

arytenoid cartilages
aspiration

basilar lamina

Bernoulli's principle

breathy voice

body (of the vocal fold)

cleft palate

cover

cover–body model

fiber-optic

fistula

fundamental frequency

glottal cycle

glottis

harmonic, harmonic series

hertz, Hz

hypernasality

inertia

jitter

lag, voicing lag

lamina propria, deep, intermediate, superficial

laryngealization

larynx

lead, voicing lead

long lag

long lead

mass

maxilla

millisecond, ms, msec

modal voice, modal frequency

mode of vibration

mucosal wave

murmur

myoelastic aerodynamic theory of voice production

nasality

palate, primary, secondary

periodic

phonation

quasi-periodic

Reinke's space

shimmer

short lag

short lead

squamous epithelium

stroboscopic effect

thyroid cartilage

transition

two-mass model

velopharyngeal dysfunction (VPD)

velopharyngeal port

vocal folds

vocal ligament

vocalis muscle

voice

voice onset time (VOT)

voiced

voiceless

voicing

VPD, VPI

whisper, whispering

whispery voice

Airstream Mechanisms: Clicks, Implosives, Ejectives, Esophageal Speech

9.1   Different types of airstream

Speech sounds are generated by a column of air, either moving or static, and, if static, under pressure.[1] Speech is most commonly produced on a stream of air that is pushed from the lungs, up through the larynx, into the pharynx, from which it exits through the mouth, the nose, or both. All languages of the world use that type of airflow for at least most – if not all – of their sounds. Previous chapters on consonants, vowels, and voice have implicitly assumed that all airflow is of this type.

Among the world's languages, there are phones that are made through other types of airflow or air pressure. Many speakers of English use a couple of these phones as interjections. Additionally, persons having undergone certain types of surgery that make the usual airstream mechanism impossible use an airstream that is different from any used in natural human languages.

The term **airstream mechanism** is used to designate the mechanism[2] by which the air is set into motion to flow or to create pressure in a particular direction. We will turn our attention now to looking at the range of airstream mechanisms, looking first at those used in languages and then at those used by persons with surgically modified vocal tracts.

The various airstream mechanisms are named for two parameters: the *direction of airflow* and the *initiating mechanism*, or *initiator*. The two directions of airflow are outgoing (from the inside of the body to outside), called *egressive*, and incoming, called *ingressive*. The terms that refer to the different initiators are *pulmonic* (the lungs), *glottalic* (the larynx or

---

SIDEBAR 9.1 Occurrence of pulmonic sounds

Egressive pulmonic phones occur in 100 percent of the world's languages.

Ingressive pulmonic phones occur distinctively in 0 percent of the world's languages.

---

[1] As you'll remember from Chapter 4, "under pressure" means that the pressure is higher than normal atmospheric pressure.

[2] The word *mechanism* refers to the means by which a particular action or process is achieved. The different airstream mechanisms are different groups of functions that serve together to create airflow or air pressure.

glottis), *velaric* or *lingual* (the tongue at the velum), and *esophageal* (the esophagus). The last of these four is used for speech only by those having undergone surgical modification of their vocal tracts. Finally, there is the *buccal* airstream mechanism that is not used in the typical production of any language.

Section 9.8 has a summary table of all the mechanisms described below. You may wish to consult the table occasionally while reading about individual mechanisms.

9.2 The pulmonic airstream mechanism

The *pulmonic airstream mechanism* is powered by the lungs. All languages use the *egressive pulmonic airstream*, although a good number of languages use other airstream mechanisms in addition.

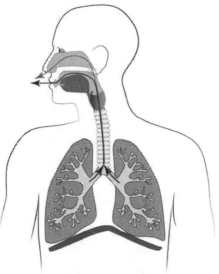

Figure 9.1 Pulmonic egressive airstream mechanism. Air flows outward from the lungs through the larynx, the pharynx and the oral cavity (and/or through the nasal cavities).

— Air passes through mouth only
— Air passes through nose only
═ Air passes through both nose and mouth

9.2.1 Egressive pulmonic airstream

The *mechanisms of respiration* were described in Chapter 3; as a quick reminder, recall that it is primarily the *diaphragm* and the *intercostal muscles* that power inspiration, or airflow into the lungs; these are the *abdominal* and *thoracic respiratory mechanisms*,[3] respectively. Outflow (egressive flow; expiration) may occur strictly by elastic forces resulting from the elastic

---

[3] Or, less technically, *belly* (or *tummy*) *breathing* and *chest breathing*.

recoil (contraction) of the lungs and of the thoracic cage after they have been stretched during inhalation. Exhalation may also be powered by muscle forces, but quiet conversational speech tends to be powered exclusively by elastic recoil forces, resisted by muscles in *in*halation. See Figure 9.1.

9.2.2 Phones produced by the egressive pulmonic airstream mechanism

All of the phones of English – with the exception of a couple of interjections – are produced with the *egressive pulmonic airstream mechanism*. All of the phones of European languages, and of a very large proportion of the other languages of the world, are also produced exclusively with this airstream mechanism. Additionally, in every language of the world, most speech sounds are produced this way.

All phones that we have considered in previous chapters are produced with the egressive pulmonic airstream mechanism.

9.2.3 Ingressive pulmonic airstream

The *ingressive pulmonic airstream* is a variant of the pulmonic egressive airstream that may occasionally be used when an individual is in a highly emotional state or is speaking when out of breath as, for example, when they are distraught and reporting an emergency after running a distance.

> **CLINICAL NOTE 9.1 Signs for direction of airflow**
>
> Extensions of the IPA for clinical uses include signs for the direction of pulmonic airflow.
>
> [a↑] **egressive** (normal) airflow
> [a↓] **ingressive** (anomalous) airflow
>
> **Caution**: arrow symbols are used to mark tones in the official IPA.

9.2.4 Phones produced by the ingressive pulmonic airstream mechanism

The only sounds produced by the ingressive pulmonic airstream mechanism are idiosyncratic instances of speech sounds normally produced with an egressive flow. (In Section 9.3.5, we will see one possible exception to this statement.)

9.2.5 Symbols for pulmonic sounds

All letters shown in the IPA tables – with the exception of those in the section titled "*Consonants (Non-Pulmonic)*" – represent sounds that are produced with the egressive pulmonic airstream mechanism.

> **CLINICAL NOTE 9.2 Airflow direction in some hearing-impaired children**
>
> Sometimes profoundly hearing-impaired children use an ingressive pulmonic airstream where an egressive one would be appropriate. Occasionally, normally hearing children do the same in the early stages of acquiring linguistic skills.

There are no IPA symbols for ingressive pulmonic sounds, given their non-linguistic status. As mentioned in Clinical Note 9.1 above, extensions of the IPA for clinical purposes include a downward-facing arrow to show ingressive flow.

Figure 5.2 in the "Consonants" chapter – the main consonant table of the IPA – shows the entire set of (egressive) pulmonic consonants.

9.3 The glottalic airstream mechanism: ejectives and implosives

The *glottalic airstream mechanism* uses the larynx and vocal folds as the initiator (hence the name *glottalic*, from *glottis*, the space between the vocal folds). This mechanism is used for consonants only, primarily plosives (though there are rare fricatives produced by this mechanism as well).

9.3.1 Egressive glottalic airstream

The *egressive glottalic airstream* relies on the ability to move the larynx up and down, independent of other movements. As a speaker of English or another language using only the pulmonic airstream, you may not have learned to make this motion independently; however, you can demonstrate to yourself that it is possible by placing your fingers on the area over your larynx and swallowing. You will note that the larynx moves up and down a considerable distance. This vertical movement can be learned separately from swallowing.

> **SIDEBAR 9.2 Occurrence of ejectives or glottalized consonants**
>
> *Ejectives* occur in 20 percent of the world's languages (Ladefoged, 2005, p. 148). However, ejectives are contrastive in a smaller number of languages.

To produce a consonant by the egressive glottalic mechanism, the larynx is lowered with the vocal folds open. The vocal folds are then closed tightly. Simultaneously, the oral articulation is made for the plosive in question (bilabial, alveolar, palatal, etc.). The velopharyngeal port is closed so that the space between the glottal and oral occlusions is sealed at both ends, and air may not "leak" into or out of the nasal passages.

Now the talker raises the larynx in their throat; by raising the larynx, the speaker compresses the air enclosed between the two occlusions: the one in the oral cavity (the articulation) and at the vocal folds. The talker then releases the oral occlusion, just as for any other plosive, producing an explosive release sound. The glottal occlusion (i.e., the closure of the vocal folds) is released *after* the oral occlusion is released. See Figure 9.2.

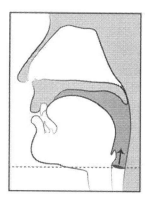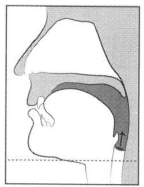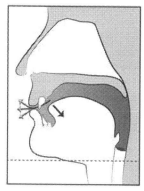

Figure 9.2 Glottalic egressive airstream mechanism (ejectives or glottalized consonants). Air is trapped between an oral occlusion and the closed vocal folds; this air is compressed by raising the larynx (containing the vocal folds), and then the oral occlusion is released.
The glottalic ingressive airstream mechanism (implosives) is produced in the opposite direction: the larynx is lowered, creating lower pressure between the oral occlusion and the vocal folds.

9.3.2   Phones produced by the egressive glottalic airstream mechanism

Plosives produced with this mechanism are known as *ejectives* or as *glottalized consonants*; the two terms mean the same thing. They are transcribed with the symbol ['] as in [p', t', c', k', s'] and are shown in the non-pulmonic table of the IPA.

In order to hear phones of this type, go to one of several IPA tables on the Internet that have clickable links to sound files with each symbol of the IPA.

9.3.3   IPA symbols for ejectives / glottalized consonants

	Bilabial	Labiodental	Dental	Alveolar	Retroflex	Palatal	Velar	Uvular
Ejectives or glottalized consonants	p'		t̪'	t'		c'	k'	
Glottalized fricatives				s'				

9.3.3.1   Steps in producing glottalized consonants / ejectives

It may help your understanding of the production of ejectives / glottalized consonants if we review the steps in their production in the form of a list. However, *note that steps 2, 3, and 4 could occur simultaneously or in a different order and the results would be the same.*

1. Lower the larynx in the neck.
2. Close the glottis (press vocal folds together).
3. Close the velopharyngeal port as for any plosive.
4. Create an occlusion as for any other plosive (e.g., bilabial, alveolar, palatal, etc.).
5. Raise the larynx in the neck
   - this compresses the air trapped between the vocal folds and the occlusion.
6. Release the occlusion at the place of articulation (like releasing any plosive)
   - the compressed air bursts egressively from behind the occlusion.

9.3.4 Ingressive glottalic airstream

The *ingressive glottalic airstream mechanism* essentially works in reverse. An oral occlusion is made (bilabial, alveolar, palatal, etc.) at the same time as the vocal folds are closed. This time, however, the vocal folds are brought together *with the larynx high in the throat* (it is at its highest in mid-swallow; you can feel it by putting your hand on your throat as you swallow). As with the egressive type, the velopharyngeal port is closed so as not to allow airflow through the nasal passages.

SIDEBAR 9.3 Occurrence of implosive consonants

Implosives occur contrastively in about 13 percent of the world's languages (Maddieson, 2008).

To produce an ingressive glottalic sound, the larynx is *lowered* in the throat during the articulation. This reduces air pressure between the two points of occlusion – one in the oral cavity, the other at the glottis. When the oral occlusion is released, a sound like a plosive in reverse is created (but see the next section).

9.3.5 Phones produced by the ingressive glottalic airstream mechanism

Plosives produced with this mechanism are known as *implosives*. Implosives are most commonly produced with accompanying voicing. The act of voicing allows airflow across the glottis, and therefore affects the pressure difference between the air in the pharynx and the air surrounding the talker, so implosives typically have distinctly less of a "popping" sound than ejectives. Burnett-Deas (2009) reports that implosives in three languages have long negative VOTs, indicating that voicing occurs throughout all or most of the period of oral occlusion. There is variation among languages, but implosives are associated with voicing in most languages that have them.

symbols for implosives

Bilabial	Labiodental	Dental	Alveolar	Retroflex	Palatal	Velar	Uvular
ɓ		ɗ̪	ɗ		ʄ	ɠ	ɠ̌

.ols for implosives have a hook curved toward the right at the top
.ol for the voiced plosive having the same place of articulation.

Steps in producing implosives
. your understanding of the production of implosives if we review
.y making a list. However, *note that steps 2, 3, and 4 could occur*
.usly or in a different order and the result would be the same.

.he larynx in the neck.
.he glottis (press vocal folds together).
.the velopharyngeal port as for any plosive.
. an occlusion as for any other plosive (e.g., bilabial, alveolar, pal–
.tc.).
. the larynx in the neck
.is reduces the pressure of the air trapped between the vocal folds
.nd the occlusion
.onal, but typical of most languages with implosives.) Set the vo-
.olds in the configuration for voicing, thus initiating voicing as air
.s across the glottis to equalize pressure in the oral cavity; note that
.vill flow across the glottis in the reverse direction as compared to
.nal voicing.
.ase the occlusion at the place of articulation (like releasing any
.sive).

.s no separate figure showing implosive sounds, but you can map the
.bove onto Figure 9.2.

The ingressive velaric/lingual/oral airstream mechanism: clicks

.elaric airstream mechanism (also called the *lingual airstream mech–*
.n or the *oral airstream mechanism*) uses the tongue as its chief initia-
.he tongue acts in the region below the velum and this is the reason it
.lled *velaric* – however, the articulation may include the posterior end
.e hard palate. Speech produced with an *egressive* velaric airstream is
.1 called *buccal speech* in speech pathology textbooks – see Section 9.5.

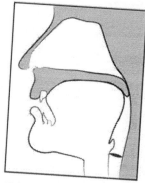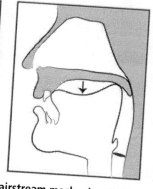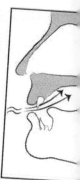

Figure 9.3 Velaric ingressive airstream mechanism (clicks). Air pressure betwe
points on the roof of the mouth is reduced and then the anterior occlusion is releas

In natural languages,[4] only the *ingressive velaric airstream m*
is known (though there may be one exception as mentioned in Sic
The mechanism of articulation is as follows. The oral cavity is bl
from the pharyngeal cavity in the velar region (this accounts for
velaric). The velum may be raised or lowered, but, if lowered, i
the speaker to breathe normally while making speech sounds
mechanism. A second occlusion is made at a point forward of th
occlusion: because of the velaric occlusion, it is not possible to a
sounds posterior to the alveopalatal region. See Figure 9.3.

SIDEBAR 9.4 Occurrence of clicks

Clicks occur in a relatively small number of languages in southern and eastern Africa, not all from the same language family. There is one Australian language that has several clicks, including an egressive one. Clicks occur in other cultural groups, but, as in English, these are interjections or sounds associated with a particular meaning, not as part of the repertoire of speech sounds making up ordinary words.

At this point, there are two occ
one velar and one in the labial, a
or alveopalatal region, corresp
to the *place of articulation*. Now
maintaining both points of oc
and maintaining tongue contact
the sides, the speaker lowers the
body between these two points, cr
a space of low pressure. The front
sion is then released, and air rush
creating the speech sound; the occl
along the sides of the tongue are re
first in the case of a lateral sound.

Such phones are known as
They are part of the inventory of ph
of some languages, in particular

---

[4] Natural language: as explained in Chapter 1, any naturally occurring human languag
spoken as a first or mother tongue. Invented languages such as Klingon or Esperanto
not natural human languages.

of southern and eastern Africa, such as Zulu, Nama (the
uage), and Xhosa, which belong to two different language

kers, and speakers of a wide range of languages, produce
ections. One way that some people smack their lips is by
oial click. The sound of disapproval often written <tsk-tsk>
s a dental or alveolar click. The sound made to encourage
giddy-up" sound) is a click as well; it is released laterally.
lveolar occlusion is maintained on release, but the sides of
e lowered to release the sound. A postalveolar click is some-
oy humorists as a kind of vocal "exclamation mark" to their

al Latin orthography of languages using clicks, the letters <c>,
d <q> (alone or in combination with other letters, sometimes
often used to represent clicks, as in the language name *Xhosa*,
sound is similar to the "giddy-up" click in English. In latin writ-
languages, an exclamation mark (!) is used in the spelling to
click sound, sometimes for a click other than the particular one
is used in the IPA (the postalveolar click). The language Taa, a
nguage, is also written !Xóõ.

A symbols for clicks

	Bilabial	Dental	Alveolar	Postalveolar	Palatoalveolar
				!	ǂ
	⊙	ǀ			
h lateral release			ǁ		

nat the IPA symbols for the dental and alveolar lateral clicks have
rs and no serifs (see Chapter 3). Here we compare them to other
(surrounded by non-click vowel symbols) so you can see how they
ted on the line: [u | e ‖ o ⊙ a ǂ i]. As can be seen, two of the click
have descenders.

Steps in producing clicks
help your understanding of the production of clicks if we review the
their production in the form of a list.

ce the tongue flat against the roof of the mouth (normally over the pal-
l and velar regions, but the exact location varies with different clicks).
sure that the edges of the tongue all around form a tight seal with the
of of the mouth.

3. While maintaining the seal around the edges, lower the
the tongue, creating an area of low pressure between th
of the tongue and the roof of the mouth.
4. Release the contact between the edge(s) of the tongue a
the mouth
   - the location of the release – whether the sides or the tip,
   on the particular click sound.
5. Air rushes into the space that held the low pressure, ma
"clicking" sound.

9.5 Laryngectomees

A *laryngectomee* is a person who has undergone the surgica
called a *laryngectomy*. This involves the surgical removal of a
the larynx, usually due to cancer. As we saw in Chapter 3, the l
primary biological function that is unrelated to voice or speech
the lungs from food and liquid – failure to do so would resul
lung damage, and continued failure would result in death.
   The larynx performs its protective magic on two levels: in
swallow, and when a speck of food or liquid enters the laryngea

9.5.1 Normal swallow

In normal swallowing, the larynx rises in the neck, and as it doe
glottis folds down over the entrance to the larynx and creates a
for food and liquid to pass over the larynx and to enter the e
behind, such that the swallowed material is directed toward the
and away from the trachea and lungs.

9.5.2 Cough reflex: when a speck of food or liquid gets pa
epiglottis

If food or liquid starts to enter the *laryngeal vestibule*,[5] whether
swallowing or not, an emergency protective reaction occurs: *cough
effect is to eject foreign material from the larynx and upper trachea
this by generating a blast of air with an abrupt start – that is, a cou
   The difficulty is that, for there to be an egressive blast of air,
must first be drawn in. There is a risk that the air being drawn
pull the foreign matter farther into the larynx or even into the tr
The cough reflex thus involves a rapid (but not too rapid) intake

---

[5] The entrance to the larynx as seen from the pharyngeal end; that is, from above

followed by an explosive expulsion of air. After the intake of air, the expiratory muscles contract, building up a greatly increased air pressure, but, initially, the vocal folds remain closed, preventing the air from flowing. An instant later, after air pressure is heightened even more, the vocal folds separate, and an explosive blast of air passes through the narrowing, normally pushing material adhering to the walls of the cavity outward. This is repeated as necessary to rid the larynx and trachea of any foreign material.

This explains the existence of vocal folds: in terms of their evolutionary presence in the mammalian larynx, they are primarily for closing the top of the trachea and for coughing, not for creating voice. Voice is very much a secondary function, though one used by most mammals and further refined in human voice.

9.5.3   If there is no larynx, then what?

If there were no larynx in the throat, then a person's lungs would quickly be inundated with chunks of food and liquid.

Therefore, in the case of the laryngectomee, the connection between the lungs and mouth must be severed, for – with the larynx gone – there is no way to protect the lungs. Laryngectomees breathe through a surgically created hole low in the neck, below the level of the shoulders, called a *stoma*.[6] The trachea connects to the stoma. See Figure 9.4.

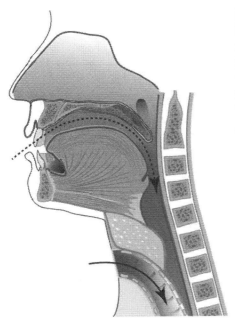

Figure 9.4 Respiration in a laryngectomee. The trachea is connected to a stoma (surgically created opening) in the front of the neck. Breathing is not connected to the mouth. The solid arrow shows inspiration (breathing in) through the stoma. The dotted arrow shows the path for food and liquid.

[6] The word *stoma* means a 'mouth' or 'opening' and is used for other surgically created openings, not only the one laryngectomees use for breathing.

It is very important to understand that, once the laryngectomy has been performed, the patient's lungs are no longer connected with the oral cavity; breathing cannot occur through the mouth or nose. The mouth is then for food and liquid only, not for breathing. The vocal folds are no longer present to create voice. The issue is how to create a substitute for normal voice to allow the laryngectomee to produce intelligible speech. Sounds generated as a substitute for voice are known as *pseudovoice*. We will examine several forms of pseudovoice, though they must not be considered equivalent in practicality.

9.6   Buccal speech

9.6.1   General buccal speech

The term *buccal* refers to the (inner surface of the) cheeks or to the mouth in general. For example, dentists refer to two faces of the teeth: the *lingual* and the *buccal*. The lingual side of a tooth is the side facing the tongue, and the buccal face of the tooth is that touching the cheeks or the inside of the lips. The Latin root of this word, while originally meaning 'cheek', has become the word for 'mouth' in a number of languages: *boca* (Spanish), *bouche* (French).

Buccal speech, then, is speech in which the force of the air (the airstream) is generated inside the mouth. There are various means by which an airflow can be generated within the mouth, generally using pressure created by the tongue. Pseudovoicing can be generated by pushing this flow of air through a constriction and this creates *buccal speech*.

In general, buccal speech cannot be used to generate intelligible speech, for the very simple reason that when the tongue is occupied creating a flow of air, it is not free to articulate a wide range of sounds. Some specific sounds, namely clicks, can be created, as we saw in Section 9.4. But creating a wide range of sounds is not possible when the tongue is occupied generating the airflow.

9.6.2   The egressive velaric airstream mechanism

One specific type of buccal speech is that created by the *egressive velaric airstream mechanism*. This mechanism suffers from the same constraints as other forms of buccal speech: it cannot create a wide range of speech sounds.

Some laryngectomees speak using an *egressive velaric airstream mechanism*. Its production is just the opposite of the ingressive mechanism used for clicks. There is an occlusion in the region of the velum and one at the point of articulation of the sound the person wants to say, and the tongue between is *raised* to produce an airstream or air pressure.

The velaric egressive airstream is not very satisfactory for producing normal-sounding speech, as you might imagine. No sounds whose place of articulation is palatal, velar, or farther back can be produced successfully – anterior sounds are substituted – and speech produced this way has a "Donald Duck" quality that lowers its intelligibility and its acceptability. However, it may afford certain individuals their only way, or their most comfortable way, of speaking.

9.6.3   Pharyngeal speech

A related mechanism, known as *pharyngeal* speech, uses the root of the tongue and/or constrictor muscles of the pharyngeal walls to produce an airstream originating in the pharynx. Such a mechanism permits a more successful articulation of palatal and velar sounds than buccal speech, but its use is relatively rare.

9.7   The esophageal airstream mechanism

9.7.1   Belch-talking or burp-talking by persons with normal anatomy

As we have seen in Chapter 8 ("Voice, Phonation, and Nasality") and elsewhere, voiced speech is produced with an airstream flowing through the lungs and making the vocal folds vibrate as the air passes between them. The buzzing sound generated by the vibrating vocal folds is a necessary part of the production of speech sounds, and, as we shall see in Chapter 12 ("Acoustics"), that vibration sound is rich and it generates a cascade of acoustic events leading to the normal sound of vowels and many consonants.

> **SIDEBAR 9.5 Occurrence of the egressive esophageal airstream mechanism**
>
> This airstream mechanism is used by laryngectomees, either through the injection of air into the esophagus from the mouth, or through a shunt that allows exhaled air to pass from the trachea into the esophagus.

The acoustic effect of voicing can be substituted by a number of other buzzing sounds (some of which sound more natural than others).

9.7.1.1   Buzzer, electric razor, etc.

For instance, it is possible to hold a device that buzzes against the neck above/beside the larynx and then simply "mouth" the sounds of speech without phonation. Audible speech sounds will result, though their amplitude will be low and the buzzer itself will drown out the effect to some degree. Holding a running electric razor (or other device that makes a buzzing sound) in a similar location will create speech-like sounds in a similar way. There are buzzer devices made specifically for laryngectomees for this purpose, some having a tube that is inserted into the mouth so that the buzz comes mostly from *inside* the mouth so that it contributes more to, and competes less with, the speech-like sound that is produced.

This is similar in principle to the "talk box" used by some singers of pop or rock music (made famous by Peter Frampton), by which the output of a musical instrument is made to conform to the changing frequency patterns of the singer's voice output.

9.7.1.2   Vibration of the esophageal sphincter

Recall that the **esophagus** is the tube running from the back of the throat to the stomach. There is a sphincter muscle and tissue at the upper end, so the tube to the stomach is not normally open except when swallowing. When a person belches or burps, air from the stomach or esophagus forces its way through the closed esophageal sphincter from inside the esophagus to the pharynx.

The sound of the burp is generated as the air flowing through this narrowed area makes the tissues vibrate. This vibration is not as regular as laryngeal voice, and it has a muffled quality and a very low pitch, but substitutes for voice and creates audible and intelligible speech sounds. It is often described as sounding as if the talker is hoarse.

Children and even some adults find it funny to talk using the sound of a belch. Some have contests to see how long they can sustain talking, counting to 10 or beyond with esophageal speech. Some contests involve chugging a soft drink and thus producing impressively long periods of belch-talking.

The fact that belch-talking is a matter for contests among children points to an essential aspect of this type of pseudovoice: the supply of air in the esophagus is very limited (much less than the air held in the lungs) and so only short phrases can be spoken with it before the air supply in the esophagus must be replenished. Therefore, being able to produce more syllables on a single supply of air is a contest-winning skill among those who are amused by this.

This form of **pseudovoice** is successful in producing speech of good intelligibility and acceptability. The sound is generated at a similar place in the throat and so its acoustic effect is similar to true voice. This is the **esophageal airstream mechanism**, which is exclusively egressive.

9.7.2   Esophageal speech

The **esophageal airstream mechanism** does not form a normal airstream mechanism in any natural language. For the purpose of sustained communication, it is used exclusively by laryngectomees. As laryngectomees lack both the mechanism for laryngeal voicing and any pulmonary airstream through the mouth, the esophageal airstream is used as a substitute for both by many such individuals. As we have seen, such speech is produced with a controlled belch that sets tissue in the lower pharynx and upper esophagus (the *pharyngoesophageal junction*) vibrating in a way that simulates voicing. Air is injected into the esophagus with the tongue; this *charge* of air, as it is called, permits the accomplished esophageal speaker to utter a number of syllables.

There are a number of difficulties, including psychological ones, inherent in mastering esophageal speech. One difficulty is that a single charge of air produces far fewer syllables than a lungful of air does, even in the case of an accomplished esophageal speaker who makes very efficient use of the air supply. The result is that speech is slower and more laborious than the speaker is used to, and it contains frequent interruptions as air is injected into the esophagus (sometimes with an audible clunking sound). It may also be interrupted or masked by the noise of injecting the charge of air. A second potential problem is that the frequency of vibration of the tissues is around 50 to 80 hertz, a very low frequency even for a male voice. Accomplished male esophageal speakers simply sound hoarse, but female esophageal speakers may worry that their voices sound masculine. However, differences between male and female speech reside in many aspects of the speech signal – acoustic, phonetic, lexical, and syntactic. This has been demonstrated experimentally: blind identification of taped esophageal voices shows a high level of correct identification of the gender of the talker. Finally, many people, having been brought up to believe that belching is rude, worry that others will find esophageal speech unaesthetic. However, accomplished speakers simply sound hoarse, and they find that their speech is both acceptable and intelligible. Roughly two-thirds of those who attempt to learn esophageal speech achieve functional speech and are variably successful in overcoming the problems inherent in it.

The problem of the small air supply that requires frequent renewal is perhaps the most serious difficulty of esophageal speech. A number of surgical techniques and prosthetic devices have been developed in an attempt to use the pulmonary air supply for esophageal speech. All these methods have in common a *tracheoesophageal puncture* – that is, a passageway between the trachea and the esophagus. The trick is to permit exhaled lung air to enter the esophagus when needed for speech, but to prevent any food or liquid from passing through the puncture from esophagus to trachea (and from the trachea to the lungs). One device designed to accomplish this is the Blom–Singer prosthesis, essentially an acrylic tube that is inserted into the stoma, through the tracheoesophageal puncture, and into the esophagus. The design of the tube is intended to prevent food or liquid from entering the trachea, and normal stomal breathing is not interfered with. However, when the individual blocks the stoma on exhalation, the exhaled air is channeled into the esophagus through the prosthesis. This provides a more constant esophageal airstream for speech. See Figure 9.5.

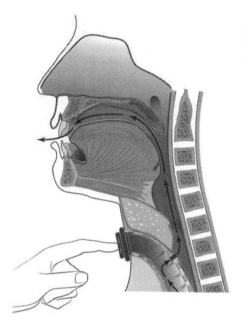

Figure 9.5 Laryngectomee's airway and a tracheoesophageal shunt for producing esophageal speech

For the student of phonetics, one of the more interesting aspects of esophageal speech involves voicing and its perception. In normal speech, voicing is often initiated and terminated (switched on and off) very rapidly. When one says the word "hippopotamus," for example, voicing is switched on four times and off four times (five times if the preceding word ends with a voiced sound), all in a very short space of time. This rapid switching on and off of voicing is more difficult in esophageal speech, and the result is that many supposedly (i.e., phonemically) "voiceless" segments are in fact pseudovoiced.

The table in Section 9.9 summarizes the various airstream mechanisms.

9.8   Table of consonants introduced in this chapter

		Bilabial	Labiodental	Dental	Alveolar	Postal-veolar	Palatoal-veolar	Retroflex	Palatal	Velar	Uvular
Ejectives	Ejectives or glottalized consonants	p'		t̪'	t'				c'	k'	
	Glottalized fricatives				s'						

		Bilabial	Labiodental	Dental	Alveolar	Postalveolar	Palatoalveolar	Retroflex	Palatal	Velar	Uvular
Implosives	Implosives	ɓ		ɗ̣	ɗ				ʄ	ɠ	ʛ
Clicks	Click	ʘ		ǀ		ǂ					
	Click with lateral release				‖						

9.9 Airstream mechanism summary table

	Known in some or all human languages
	Unknown in any human language
	Possible only with surgical modification

	Direction of airflow	
Body system	Egressive	Ingressive
Pulmonic	Mechanism: the lungs expel air or draw it in. Used across the board for vowels and consonants, except the specialized types listed below.	
	Ordinary consonants and vowels. Used in all languages (universal).	A variant of the egressive pulmonic speech production. Used rarely, generally in specific circumstances, such as speaking in a panicked, out-of-breath situation.
Glottalic	Mechanism: the vocal folds are closed and the larynx is raised (to push air ahead of it, pressurizing) or lowered (to pull air behind it, creating a partial vacuum). Generally restricted to plosive consonants, not to vowels or other classes of consonants	
	Glottalized plosives, also called *ejectives*. Occur in a subset of languages, not very common	*Implosives* Less common than ejectives, reasonably rare.
Velaric	Mechanism: the tongue, acting against the roof of the mouth, is used to create suction (ingressive) or push air (egressive). This mechanism is separated from respiration, unlike the others – you can breathe in and out through the nose while making these types of sounds.	

	Direction of airflow	
Body system	Egressive	Ingressive
	This creates the "Donald Duck" type of speech. Not used in any language. Usually included in the category *buccal speech*, below.	*Clicks*. Used in a number of southern African languages (of more than one language group) and in a few others. Interjections or commands to animals in some other languages such as English. Rare.
Buccal	**Mechanism:** air is squeezed out between the cheek and oral structures including the teeth. Vibration of tissues makes a kind of pseudovoicing	
	Idiosyncratic	Does not exist
Pharyngeal	**Mechanism:** air is squeezed from the pharynx into the oral cavity.	
	Usually included in the category *buccal speech*, above.	Does not exist
Esophageal	NOTE 1: Esophageal speech is used routinely only by persons who have lost their larynx. It is also sometimes used jokingly by youngsters, particularly after chugging a can of soft drink. NOTE 2: Esophageal speech can be created with or without a prosthetic device. The mechanisms differ in the two cases. **Mechanism without prosthesis.** Air is injected into the esophagus by increasing pressure in the oral-pharyngeal cavity with the articulators and simultaneously reducing intra-thoracic pressure with respiratory muscles. **Mechanism with prosthesis.** Blocking a valve on the front of the throat causes air exhaled by the lungs to inflate the esophagus through a surgically created shunt between the remaining upper end of the trachea and the esophagus. **Creation of esophageal "voice":** air is released in a controlled manner from the esophagus into the pharynx. As the air leaves the esophagus, it causes the tissue at the level of the esophageal sphincter to vibrate in a voice-like manner.	
	Used to substitute for laryngeal voice in individuals who require a substitute. There is no term for consonants or vowels produced this way, other than with the adjective "esophageal." This is a clinical matter, not strictly a phonetic–linguistic matter.	Not used.

9.10   IPA symbols

1. Introduced in this chapter:

   Glottalized consonants, ejectives: ['] as in [p']
   Implosives: [ɓ ɗ ɗ ʄ ɠ ʛ]
   Clicks: ʘ | ! ǂ
   Click with lateral release: ‖
   Clinical extensions of IPA:
   Egressive airflow: [a↑]
   Ingressive airflow: [a↓]

2. A range of IPA extensions used in clinical situations may be found at: https://en.wikipedia.org/wiki/Extensions_to_the_International_Phonetic_Alphabet.

9.11   Vocabulary

abdominal
airstream
airstream mechanism
buccal speech
click
diaphragm
egressive
egressive pulmonic airstream
ejective
epiglottis
esophageal speech
glottalic
glottalized consonant
implosive
ingressive
ingressive pulmonic airstream
initiating mechanism

initiator
intercostal muscles
laryngeal vestibule
laryngectomee
laryngectomy
lingual airstream mechanism
mechanism
oral airstream mechanism
pharyngeal speech
pharyngoesophageal junction
pseudovoice
pulmonic
respiration
stoma
thoracic
velaric

10 Speech Dynamics

10.1 Introduction

In Chapters 5 and 6, we examined the articulation of individual segments. Each one was given a description of its articulatory characteristics. While this is a natural way to introduce the subject of speech articulation, it may reinforce a false impression of speech held by many as they embark on learning about phonetics: namely, that speech is made up of a series of individual static postures, the phones or phonemes of the language, with movements in between. It cannot be stressed enough that this is an entirely false impression.

Speech is a *dynamic* rather than a *static* phenomenon, and the articulators are in a state of constant movement during speech. The idealized positions we have seen in Chapters 5 and 6 are nothing more than target positions at which we aim while speaking. Sometimes those targets are attained, often they are not; as a result, speech is often more a series of approximations than a series of phones that fully realize the ideal. Furthermore, the dynamic nature of speech, and the rapidity with which it is produced, means that our brain must be planning articulations long before they occur.[1] Also, there must be some mechanism for planning the transitions *between* articulations. As a result, we have begun to articulate one segment before completing another; we may be as much as several segments ahead or behind (or both) in our motor activity.[2] The result is that sounds are modified by the surrounding sounds (by their *[phonetic] environment*, as it is called): how a [t] or a [s] or an [i] is articulated depends upon what goes before and what follows. This chapter will look at some of the ways sounds are modified by their environment.

A given segment or phoneme cannot be pronounced in an unchanging way, irrespective of environment. Any attempt to pronounce sounds in a way

---

[1] "Long before": this means a long time in terms of the rate of production of speech segments. Movements for speech articulation often begin 5 segments early and might sometimes occur 7 or 8 segments early. That may be less than a second, but it's "long" before the segment, as measured in speech segments.

[2] *Motor activity* means body movement under the force of the muscles. Most of connected speech is motor activity, though it must be said that *aerodynamic* activity – movement caused by the force of moving air – is also involved in speech.

unaffected by surrounding sounds will result in speech that sounds artificial and stilted – and besides, the attempt will be unsuccessful, since, even with conscious effort, the effects of one segment upon another cannot be avoided.

Not only is the *articulation* of segments affected by the surrounding segments, but – as a result – their *sound* is as well. While speech acoustics and perception will be considered in later chapters, we can say at this point that the actual sound you produce when you say a given segment – for example, [s] – is affected by the surrounding segments: the s-sound of "seep" creates different sound waves than the s-sound of "sweep." If you were to record natural speech, and then cut the recording up into individual phones and splice these together into words, the results would be at best highly unnatural and distorted, and more often incomprehensible. Even if you recorded whole words, either pronounced in isolation or in sentences, and then spliced them together to form new sentences, they would sound strange and would be hard to understand (particularly due to the transitions between words: the final sounds of one word transitioning into the initial sounds of the next word).

It is thus apparent that individual speech sounds are pronounced differently depending on the neighboring sounds. We need terms to discuss this phenomenon.

10.1.1 Terminology

Unfortunately, this area of phonetics has terminology that is used in very different – and sometimes contradictory – ways by different authors and in different resource materials.

In order to keep the following discussion clear, we will define three major terms in the field in precise ways. It is important to understand that this terminology is consistent with some, and contradicts some, of the terminology that is commonly found. When looking at other sources, do not expect these three terms to always be used as they are in this book, but do expect the usage to be consistent within this book. In addition, the concepts defined by the three terms are fundamentally important, even if the terminology is often somewhat fluid.

The three basic terms are *accommodation, assimilation,* and *coarticulation.*

10.1.1.1   Accommodation

In this book, we use the term *accommodation* as the generic term to refer to any changes in the articulation of a segment that are created by the presence of other segments or other phonetic features in the *phonetic environment.*

The phenomenon of *accommodation* will be subdivided in a rough way into *assimilation* and *coarticulation.* Under the heading of *speech dynamics,* we note that other processes than accommodation occur in running speech; these we will look at in the latter part of the chapter.

10.1.1.2   Assimilation

Larger sound changes – that is, larger instances of **accommodation** – will be referred to as **assimilation**. By *larger instances of sound change*, we mean that there is a greater difference between the sound before being changed by accommodation, and the sound after it has been changed by accommodation.

Assimilation is used as well to identify instances where the change in the sound is a change of phonemes, not simply of phones or sounds.

10.1.1.3   Coarticulation

Smaller sound changes – that is, smaller instances of accommodation – will be referred to as **coarticulation**. By shorter instances of sound change, we mean that there is a smaller difference between the sound before being changed by accommodation, and the sound after it has been changed by accommodation.

Coarticulation is used as well to identify instances where the change in the sound is subphonemic – that is, a change in sound that is not a change in phoneme.

10.1.1.4   Accommodation, assimilation, coarticulation

We must reiterate that in other material you may see any of these three terms used in any of the three senses given above, or in other related senses as well.

Additionally, it is always possible to find ambiguous or borderline instances for which one can argue for one term or another. The distinctions being made by the terminology are intended to give the broad strokes.

10.1.1.5   Environment, phonetic environment, context

All these terms refer to the sounds surrounding the segment in question. Note that the environment includes not only the surrounding segments but other features of a phonetic nature as well, such as stress and intonation (Chapter 11).

10.2   The nature of accommodation

When we speak, conflicting demands are made on the articulators: the tongue blade must touch the alveolar ridge for a [t]; the tongue body must be high and back for an [u]; the velopharyngeal port (VPP) must be open for a [m] or other nasal sound; the VPP must be closed for other segments. All these demands are made in far less time than is available to fulfill them: normal conversational English is produced at a rate of between 10 and 20 segments per second, implying a maximum of a tenth of a second (100 milliseconds [ms]) per segment on the average. However, it takes much longer than a tenth of a second to complete any voluntary speech gesture, particularly if one considers the return to the starting point. For example, to lower the velum fully for a nasal consonant and raise it again afterwards may take as much as half a second: the time it takes to say 5 to 10 segments.

Clearly, some adjustment must be made. What happens is that compromise gestures are made and/or there is carryover of some features of the articulation of one segment onto another, or a gesture for a later segment is begun well ahead. In other words, there is an *accommodation* in the articulatory gestures.

10.2.1 Coarticulation

Let us consider a few examples to make the point clear. Consider the nonce[3] words /iki/, /uku/, and /aka/. (Nonce words are used instead of real words in order to provide the precise phonetic environment needed for the example.) The sound /k/ is a velar consonant, so you would expect a dorsovelar contact. The vowel /u/ is a high back vowel, so its place of articulation is essentially velar, although no linguavelar contact is made as it is with /k/. By contrast, /i/ is high front, requiring movement of the tongue body

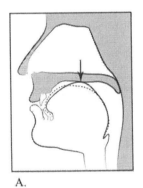 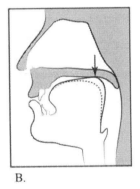 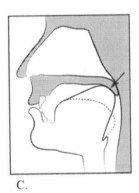

A.   B.   C.

Figure 10.1 Accommodation: coarticulation. A. The nonce word /iki/, pronounced [ici], with a palatal plosive. **B.** The nonce word /uku/, pronounced [uku], with a velar plosive. **C.** The nonce word /aka/, pronounced [aqa], with a uvular plosive. These are typical English articulations; another language might adjust the vowel more than the consonant or find a middle ground. The broken line indicates the approximate vowel articulation and the arrow points to the center of the contact for the consonant.

---

[3] A *nonce word* or *nonce form* is sometimes called a *nonsense word*. It is invented. It should conform to the phonetics and phonology of a given language but is not a real word.

forward, and /ɑ/ is low back, requiring movement of the tongue body back. There would be insufficient time in normal speech to make the movements seemingly required to pronounce /iki/, /uku/, and /ɑkɑ/. What happens, therefore, is that the point of contact for the /k/ changes according to the vowel in its environment, as shown in Figure 10.1.

As shown in Figure 10.1A, if you say /iki/, in fact the contact for the /k/ is not on the velum but is brought forward to the palate, the place of articulation of the /i/. This reduces the amount of movement necessary to articulate the word. So, in saying the word /iki/, in fact what you say is [ici], with a palatal, not a velar, plosive (cf. Section 5.3.7).

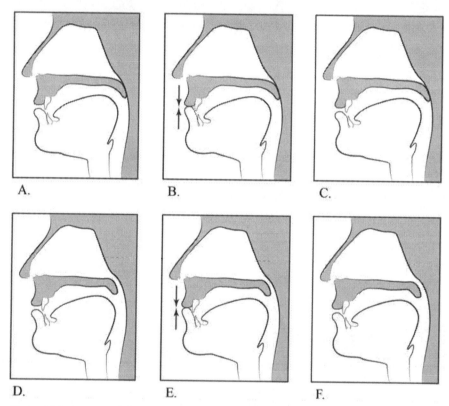

A.

B.

C.

D.

E.

F.

Figure 10.2 Accommodation: coarticulation. A–C. The word /obo/ **D–F.** The nonce word /omo/, pronounced [ōmō]

A similar process occurs with the low back vowel, as shown in Figure 10.1C. Because of the place of articulation of the vowel [ɑ], the point of contact for the /k/ in the word /ɑkɑ/ is farther back on the velum than for a more typical /k/. In fact, what you say when you pronounce /ɑkɑ/ is [ɑqɑ] – that is, there is a back velar, or uvular, plosive instead of a mid-velar one.

In the case of the word /uku/, the vowel's place of articulation is similar to that of the plosive, so in fact you articulate [uku] when you try to say /uku/ (as in Figure 10.1B).

You can feel the different points of articulation noted in Figure 10.1 and the preceding paragraphs by simply saying the three nonsense words in a conversational manner and paying attention to the point of contact between your tongue and the roof of your mouth.

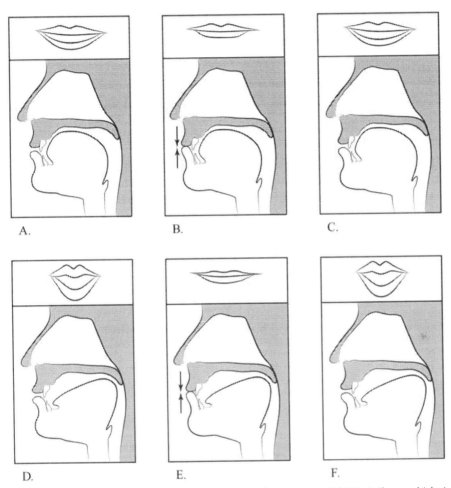

Figure 10.3 Accommodation: coarticulation. A–C. The nonce word /ibi/ **D–F.** The word /obo/. Notice the coarticulation affecting lip-spreading/lip-rounding.

Now turn your attention to Figure 10.2. Here we are dealing with the word /obo/ and the nonce form /omo/. Bilabial consonants have been chosen intentionally for this example, in order to avoid lingual (tongue) coarticulation, allowing us to concentrate on the movements of the velum and the velopharyngeal port.

In the sequence A–B–C of Figure 10.2, we see three stages in the articulation of the word "oboe" (/obo/), corresponding to each of the three phonemes. Virtually no coarticulation in lingual or velic gestures is present, and none has been illustrated. Note particularly that since none of the segments is nasal, there is no opening of the VPP through velic movement.

Now consider the sequence D–E–F of Figure 10.2. Again, each frame corresponds to one phoneme. Again, there is little if any lingual coarticulation, and none is shown. This time, however, the consonant is nasal ([m]). The velum must lower to open the velopharyngeal port for the [m]. Ideally, the port should be closed for the vowels, but there is not enough time for that. So the velum lowers during the first /o/, or even before it, and rises again during or after the second /o/. Thus, both vowels are [õ] rather than [o]. The illustrations are, of course, static and can show only one point in time; you can interpolate the movement between.

Notice the audible difference between the nasalized and non-nasalized /o/'s of the two example words. This trick might help: think of saying /omo/, then start to say it, but interrupt yourself before saying the /m/, and listen to the quality of the vowel. Compare that to an /o/ you say without thinking of a particular word.

Consider now the accommodation shown in Figure 10.3. Here we see the words /ibi/ and /obo/ (oboe). This time we will consider neither the tongue nor the velum, but the lips. The sound [i] is a spread vowel, and [o] is somewhat rounded (lip positions have been exaggerated for illustrative purposes). Notice the lip posture during the closure phase of the [b]. In both cases the lips are *closed* – that is essential to the articulation of a /b/ – but in /ibi/ they are spread and closed, whereas in /obo/ they are rounded and closed. These are two different articulations of the phoneme /b/ – visibly different, although the acoustic effect is minimal.

In these three examples, we have seen **accommodation** in the position or posture of (a) the tongue, (b) the VPP (velum), and (c) the lips. The term *coarticulation* would be appropriate to all three. Literally, *coarticulation* means 'simultaneous articulation, articulation at the same time,' and in each example we saw that two different phonemes were being articulated simultaneously. In the first example, one tongue movement was made for both vowel and consonant. In the second example, the correct velic position for the *consonant* was attained during the articulation of the *vowel* (so that one feature of the consonant was being articulated at the same time as the vowel). And in the third example, the consonant was being articulated with the lip posture appropriate for the vowel (so that both the consonant and one feature of the vowel were being articulated simultaneously).

10.2.2   Assimilation

Now let us consider an example of **assimilation**, as we have defined the term. If someone says "I miss you" in normal conversation, the word "miss" is likely to be pronounced "mish" ([mɪʃ]). This is because the [j] of "you" is palatal and draws the alveolar [s] of "miss" back to an alveopalatal or palatal position.

Or if you say "phonecall" conversationally, the word "phone" is likely to be pronounced "phong" ([foŋ]).

10.2.3   Coarticulation and assimilation

As we noted earlier, there is no absolute line between *coarticulation* and *assimilation*, but it is useful to make a broad distinction. In *assimilation*, there is a major change in the place of articulation, manner of articulation, or voicing of a segment, such that it falls into a different phonemic category. In the foregoing examples, [ʃ] is a different phoneme from [s]; [ŋ] is a different phoneme from [n]. *Coarticulation*, on the other hand, occurs when the various segments are different only to the extent of nonphonemic differences. Whether a plosive is palatal, velar, or uvular (i.e., whether it is [c], [k], or [q]) is not a phonemic difference in English; nor is there a phonemic distinction between a /b/ made with rounded lips and a /b/ made with spread lips.

10.3   The causes of accommodation

Accommodation (that is, *coarticulation* and *assimilation* taken together) is a pervasive phenomenon. What causes it?

It is often explained with reference to a "principle of least effort," which invokes the notion that the least effort possible is expended in the production of speech. This explanation accounts for the phenomenon in part, but not fully.

10.3.1   Time constraints

Accommodations are made because there are more segments to produce in a given period of time than it is possible to produce without some adjustments (i.e., "accommodations") in the articulatory gestures. For example, the instance of velic coarticulation illustrated in Figure 10.2 occurs because there simply is no time to lower the velum at the end of the vowel if one does not wish either a pause or an intrusive consonant. It is a universal physiological constraint: some amount of nasality will "leak" over to a preceding vowel in any language, unless there is an intervening pause or consonant.

But these physiological constraints are not necessarily absolute and cannot be used to explain every instance of accommodation.

10.3.2   Different shortcuts

For example, the lingual coarticulation shown in Figure 10.1 and accompanying text is correct for most speakers of English. That is, we *do* pronounce /k/ on the palate (as [c]) rather than the velum next to a high front vowel. But do we *have* to? The answer is simply "No." Some languages make a phonemic distinction between /k/ and /c/ and maintain this distinction in the environment of /i/ – that is, speakers of these languages would pronounce [iki] differently from [ici]. So, it is *possible* to say [iki] without making the /k/ palatal; it is just that speakers of English *do not*.

Here is an analogy that might be useful in understanding this: on a given route, there are possible shortcuts; whether speakers use a given shortcut depends on the rules of the grammar of that language (a rule in English is that given the sequence /iki/, one takes the shortcut which results in [ici]; a rule in another language might be that one does not take the shortcut). Certain shortcuts may be universally obligatory, such as the nasalization example already mentioned, due to how slow movements of the appropriate structures are. In other cases, there may be more than one shortcut possible. Looking still at the /iki/ example, another shortcut or accommodation that is physiologically possible is to say [ukɯ][4] – that is, to bring the *vowel* articulation *back* to the articulatory position of the consonant, rather than to say [ici], where the *consonant* articulation is brought *forward* to the position of the vowel. But speakers of English do not make this accommodation – not because it is not *possible*, not *because* it is any *less* of a shortcut, but simply because that is not the way that English does it.

In conclusion, then, accommodations are made either because they must be, for universal physiological reasons (an explanation that is true less of the time than you might think), or because the language in question simply functions that way.

It is important also to realize that accommodation is not the result of "sloppiness" or "laziness." While it is true that accommodation reduces movements, and therefore articulatory effort, it does not follow that laziness is its motivating factor. To pronounce each phoneme exactly as illustrated in the drawings of Chapters 5 and 6 would not improve the quality of speech, but it would greatly increase the effort required; a language has a phonetic system with some redundancy, but not too much, because it would simply be inefficient.

An individual speaker says [ici] for /iki/ not out of laziness but because doing so follows the rules of English. It is true that dialects and registers of speech (formal versus informal) differ in the amount of accommodation and the particulars of the accommodations made. So, speakers of one dialect (or who expect a certain register of speech) may feel that the accommodation made in another variety is in some way sloppy or inferior; however, the simple fact of making assimilations or coarticulations is not in itself lazy.

---

[4] [ɯ] is a high back tense unrounded vowel having the same tongue position as [u], but with spread or neutral lip posture like [i] or [ɪ] (see Section 6.3.6).

Indeed, given the primacy of speech over other ways language is used, we recognize that the phonetic codes that languages use maximize the ability to transmit information or meaning in remarkably short periods of time (more on this in Chapter 13). Eliminating accommodation would slow down speech production without improving communication, and would thus make speech *less* efficient.

In fact, since accommodations are rule-governed and are part of the grammar of the language, *making the appropriate accommodations is essential to sounding normal*. The advanced second-language learner often has a hypercorrect pronunciation that sounds strange because it *lacks* the usual shortcuts that native speakers take. In this case, the second-language teacher should *promote* accommodations rather than condemn them.

10.3.3   Accommodations are made because they can be made

Another way of looking at the inevitability of accommodation is to consider that talkers make accommodations in speech because they *can* make accommodations in speech. That is to say, speech remains highly intelligible when accommodations are made, so they should be made in order to communicate information faster and to save the expenditure of unnecessary energy. In an analogy we'll see in the next section, when we walk on smooth ground, we don't lift our feet higher with each step than is necessary to move forward and avoid tripping and falling. For evolution to have brought us to a situation where everyone lifted their feet one and a half times as high with each step would bring us to a world in which huge amounts of energy would be wasted, accomplishing nothing at all, other than to slow down movement from one place to another. Speech works fine with high levels of accommodation, and therefore it makes sense that there should be high levels of accommodation.

Accommodation serves a useful function in speech production in reducing the overall effort required and increasing the number of segments that can be produced in a given amount of time *without loss of clarity*. Speech has a certain amount of built-in redundancy – that is, there is more than one acoustic cue to segments. The "shortcuts" implied by accommodation reduce the amount of redundancy in the speech signal, but in other ways they add new redundancy, such as when a velar consonant accommodates to a front vowel, thus adding new cues. When there is an overall reduction in redundancy, a sufficient level remains for speech to be understood even under less-than-ideal listening conditions. Since a certain level of redundancy remains despite the "shortcuts" – sufficient redundancy for reliable comprehension – there is no virtue whatever in not taking the shortcuts.

10.4   Hyperspeech and hypospeech (H&H Theory)

In Section 10.3, we said that the efficiency of speech (that is, efficiency in terms of information transmitted per unit of time) is enhanced by accommodation. Going further with this idea, we find that the amount of accommodation at any given moment is variable as a result of communicative needs.

Björn Lindblom (Lindblom, 1990) proposed the **H&H Theory** (for *Hyperspeech and Hypospeech Theory*). This theory presents a model for the dynamic nature of speech production processes. In this book, we have concentrated, until this chapter, on the production of individual sounds. At this point, let us consider speech sounds grouped together into a word. If we speak that word, what is the goal? In most situations, we want another person to understand the word we have said. That is, we want the listener to recognize the word as a word they have in their mental *lexicon*[5] of English. While we will consider these matters in greater detail in Chapter 13, we will comment here that recognizing a spoken word depends on more than simply hearing the sequence of phonemes that comprise it. As an example of this fact, Lindblom cites Lieberman (1963) about the predictability of words we might hear spoken. Lieberman asks how predictable (and therefore how easy to understand) the word *nine* is in each of these spoken contexts:

(i) The next word is _____ .
(ii) A stitch in time saves _____.[6]

For the hearer to hear the word *nine* reliably in the second context does not require the same degree of "clarity" as would be required in the first context.

H&H theory says that talkers have an idea of how "clearly" words and phrases need to be spoken for a listener[7] to understand them, and, critically, *the talker makes the necessary adjustments to ensure that the listener hears correctly.*

---

[5] One of the things we know when we "know" a language is a list, a dictionary, of words of that language. Linguists refer to this component of our mental grammar as the *lexicon*.

[6] This expression might be too old fashioned for many readers. The expression is "A stitch in time saves nine." It means that making a sewing repair immediately saves a greater repair later (just 1 stitch is required now, but if you wait, 9 stitches will be necessary, as the hole will have enlarged). It is used metaphorically for taking any action immediately in order to prevent a worse problem later.

[7] We have used the term *hearer* for a person who hears speech. In this instance, we specifically mean a listener: someone paying attention and trying to hear and comprehend.

H&H theory does not talk about "clarity" or "clearly"; rather, it places speech on a continuum from *hyperspeech* to *hypospeech*. Hyperspeech is relatively slow, loud, and very precisely articulated. Hypospeech is quicker (but not excessively so), without extra exertion to increase loudness, and articulated more loosely.

H&H theory does not focus uniquely on what we are calling *accommodation*; however, the degree of accommodation is certainly one aspect – hyperspeech resists some degree of accommodation. But we must emphasize again that a certain amount of accommodation – which is to say, modifications from "idealized" articulations of individual phones when those phones are spoken in words and phrases – is unavoidable. The most hyper of hyperspeech contains modifications that Sections 10.1 and 10.2 have addressed; it is simply that hypospeech has more than hyperspeech.

Hyperspeech and hypospeech are two ends of a continuum, not an either/or choice. Critically for H&H theory, the talker makes adjustments of the point on the continuum they want their speech to occupy at any given moment. Clearly, if the listener frequently asks for the talker to repeat, if the talker knows that the listener has a poor command of the language they are speaking, if the background is noisy, the talker will move in the direction of hyperspeech. As Lindblom says, "Speech motor control is future-oriented." That is, the talker produces speech that they intend the listener to understand, and so the talker takes the steps necessary to make that happen.

Another point that Lindblom makes is that human beings make similar kinds of situationally appropriate adjustments in other motor (i.e., muscle-movement) tasks. Imagine that you are walking on a trail in the woods at night with very little light. The trail has many stones and roots protruding up above the level of the ground. In that situation you will be likely to lift your foot a little higher with each step than you might normally do; you are also likely to move forward more slowly than you might otherwise do. As you leave the woods and continue on an asphalted street, your pace increases and you don't lift your foot so high with each step, even though the lighting is still poor.

This analogy demonstrates that speech uses a similar strategy as other motor activities in increasing effort when necessary, but reducing effort when it can be done without significant cost. In this example, failure to lift your foot high enough with each step will cause *you* to trip and possibly fall, whereas failure to speak in a sufficiently hyper fashion will cause *your listener* to misunderstand or fail to understand. Nonetheless, it is in the talker's interest (in the kinds of situations that are relevant) for the listener to understand.

10.4.1   The Lombard effect

The Lombard effect involves the involuntary increase of "vocal effort" when speaking in loud noise. The effect was first described by Étienne Lombard in 1909. It is clear that what Lombard described comprises a portion of what Lindblom later described under the heading of H&H theory – the talker adjusting to conditions that may affect the listener's ability to decode the speech. However, the Lombard effect recognizes only one motivating factor for increased vocal effort, that of loud noise.

H&H theory recognizes that there are other causes for increased effort: it ties the effect to general principles of motor activity; it ties the phenomenon to principles of speech perception, in particular to *speech invariance* (see Sidebar 10.1); and it proposes a continuum for the manifestation of the effect.

10.5   Do segments exist?

SIDEBAR 10.1 Speech invariance

Speech invariance is the phenomenon whereby the hearer of speech perceives an invariant signal despite the fact that, for a range of reasons – including, but not limited to, accommodation effects – the actual acoustic signal that arrives in the hearer's ear varies according to a wide range of variables. That is, for example, the fact is that the vowel /ɪ/ sounds the same to the hearer despite a great variation in its realization, including possible overlap with neighboring vowels. The articulatory variables that lead to its actual acoustic signal varying include age and sex of the talker, dialect variation, rate of speech, point on the hyper- or hypospeech continuum, background

One of the most basic assumptions we all share about speech is that it is segmentable: that it is made up of a series of individual speech sounds strung together like so many beads on a string. That these individual sounds, called *segments* or *phones*, are present in speech is a notion that is reinforced by our writing system, as well as by the way speech sounds are introduced in phonetics. While the concept of the segment is very useful in talking about the phonetic – and particularly the phonemic – structure of language, it may well mislead us about the dynamic functioning of speech production.

Let us compare a segmental and a nonsegmental approach to a problem of sound change and see what we can learn from the latter approach.

In many dialects of English, the sequence of /VntV/ is pronounced /VnV/ (where V symbolizes any vowel). Thus, the word "winter" sounds like "winner," and the word "twenty" is pronounced as if spelled "twenny."

10.5.1   Sound changes

As languages develop through time, changes occur at all levels of the grammar. A very common change is the type

noise, accentuation, and so on. A great range of sounds with considerable variation will all be heard as [ɪ], and in each case the hearer will say "I heard an /ɪ/." Accounting for this remarkable ability is a central problem in speech perception.

we have seen in the English words *winter* and *twenty*. And the opposite change is also common: a plosive is inserted. Old English *þunor*[8] /θunor/ gives rise to Modern English *thunder* /θʌndɚ/. Notice that the d-sound has been added to the Modern English form in the same environment where the t-sound is deleted in colloquial pronunciations of *winter* and *twenty*.

As we look at this phenomenon more generally, in English and in other languages, we find a common pattern. Where there is a nasal consonant followed by a plosive between vowels, the plosive may be dropped. Where there is a nasal consonant between vowels, a plosive may be inserted after the nasal. More specifically, the plosive is **homorganic** with the nasal consonant. This means that the nasal consonant and the plosive have the same place of articulation. If the nasal is bilabial, then the plosive is bilabial. So the two changes are these:

1. VNV → VNPV
2. VNPV → VNV

where N is any nasal consonant, V is any vowel, and P is a plosive consonant that is homorganic with the nasal.

The examples of *winter* and *thunder*, above, show the phenomenon at the alveolar place of articulation. The dialectal pronunciation [fæmbli] for the word *family* shows the phenomenon at the bilabial place of articulation. In German, the word for *finger* is *Finger*, both English and German words deriving ultimately from the same source word. However, where English says [fɪŋgɚ] (with a [g]), German says [fɪŋɐ] (without a [g]). This shows the phenomenon at the velar place of articulation.

Here are some examples.

---

[8] In the spelling of Old English, the letter <þ>, called *thorn*, was one of two special letters for the <th> sound.

Language	Before change	After change	Change	Remarks
English	/ wɪntɚ/ winter	/wɪnɚ/	Delete /t/ after /n/	Informal pronunciation
English	/twɛnti/ twenty	/twɛni/	Delete /t/ after /n/	Informal
English	/θunor/ þunor	/θʌndɚ/ *thunder*	Insert /d/ after /n/	Historical change
English and German (historically)	*tɛm(b)ra- (*reconstructed form)	English: *timber*; German: *Zimmer*	Insertion or deletion in one of the languages	Either German lost the /b/ or English inserted it historically
Latin to French	*camera* (Latin)	*chambre* (French 'room')	Insert /b/ after /m/	English borrowed the word in the form *chamber*
English (non-standard)	family /fæmli/	"fambly" / fæmbli/	Insert /b/ after /m/[a]	
English and German	finger [fɪŋgɚ] *Finger* [fɪŋɐ]		Historical change from common earlier form	

[a] You may have noticed that the /b/ is followed by /l/, not a vowel. Consonants such as /l/ and /ɹ/ have many characteristics similar to vowels and, as in this example, can participate in this type of sound change. Note that in the previous example, the French word *chambre* has an r-sound following the /b/.

Now that we have seen that this sort of sound change is common, let us return to the examples of *winter* and *twenty*. Assume for the sake of this argument that the pronunciations / wɪntɚ/ and / twɛnti/ are "correct" in the historical sense, and that the pronunciations / wɪnɚ /and /twɛni/ represent changes. How would you characterize the change in pronunciation of these words?

Most people would answer that the /t/ has been "dropped" in each of these words and in others like them. Such an "explanation" most likely will include a comment on the "saving of effort" displayed by the change. This view holds that the word "twenty" is made up of 6 separate phonemes (or beads on a string) and that the change involves the simple dropping of one phoneme or "bead" so that only 5 remain.

A nonsegmental approach to the description of the difference between, for example, "twenty" and "twenny" gives a surprisingly different result. For the purpose of the following analysis, we will use the change between /VmbV/ and /VmV/. By choosing voiced bilabial consonants, we can simplify the example. Bilabials do not affect the position of the tongue, so this hypothetical example allows us to ignore the tongue. The hypothetical example has the same voicing in the nasal and the plosive, allowing voicing to be ignored in the example.

The nonce words we will use for this example are bamab ([bæmæb]) and bambab ([bæmbæb]). The difference between them is in the center of the words /VmbV/ and /VmV/. The sound /b/ starts and finishes each nonce word in order to make a consistent position of the articulators at the start and the end.

Bamab	b	a	m	a	b
Velopharyngeal port (*vpp*)	Closed	Open	Open	Closed	Closed
Lips	Closed	Open	Closed	Open	Closed

Bambab	b	a	m	b	a	b
Velopharyngeal port (*vpp*)	Closed	Closed → Open	Open	Closed	Closed	Closed
Lips	Closed	Open	Closed	Closed	Open	Closed

Examine the sequence of movements during the pronunciation of each nonce form. This may be aided by looking at the row that shows shading: dark for closed and white for open.

Let us look first at the sequence for the *velopharyngeal port*. The table shows the following sequences:

```
VPP
Bamab: Closed – Open – Closed
Bambab: Closed – Open – Closed
```

Now let us look at the sequence for the lips in each nonce word. Here are the sequences:

```
Lips
Bamab: Closed – Open – Closed – Open – Closed
Bambab: Closed – Open – Closed – Open – Closed
```

This sequence can also be seen in Figure 10.4.

As can be seen, the sequences are the same for both relevant articulators for both of the words. The question to ask now is this: In moving from *bambab* to *bamab* (which seemingly has one fewer phones), is the number

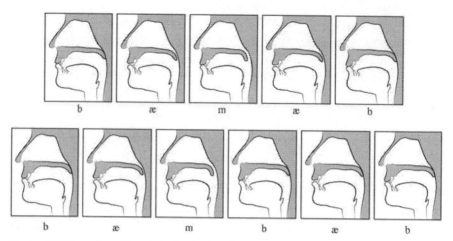

Figure 10.4 Bamab and bambab. Notice that the sequence of steps is the same for each articulator (lips and VPP).

of articulatory gestures reduced? Does it take fewer gestures to say *bamab* than to say *bambab*?

In fact, the answer is "No": *bamab* does not have any fewer gestures than does *bambab*.

Why then does *bambab* have a b-sound after the /m/, but *bamab* doesn't? If they have the same sequence of gestures, why are they different? It has to do with the *timing* of the two sets of gestures, that of the lips and that of the VPP. After the /m/ is pronounced, in *bamab* the lips open *before* the VPP is closed. In *bambab*, after the /m/, the lips open *after* the VPP is closed.

10.5.2   Segments and connected speech

What this example should bring to attention is the idea that, in words and in connected speech, there is considerable overlap between phones. So much so that the gestures involved in one phone are the same gestures involved in another phone.

Thinking of words as being composed of separate units leads us away from thinking about the way the gestures of sounds overlap and involve "compromise" movements. It fails to reveal how an entire "phone" can develop out of nothing but the degree of overlap of the movement of different articulators.

The nature of this overlap has implications for understanding historical sound change as well in therapeutic or language/accent teaching activities.

10.5.3   The segment revisited

It is hoped that this section will have made you question your assumptions about the make-up of speech. The "beads on the string" are not separate – they overlap and interact. We will not abandon the term *segment* in referring to individual speech sounds, but from here on we will use it with a recognition that segments are not autonomous units. We will understand that their articulation represents the overlapping interaction of a number of different articulatory gestures. We recognize that they cannot simply be inserted or deleted like the letters that represent them, without affecting surrounding segments.

10.6 Types of accommodation

Accommodation refers to the phenomenon of sounds becoming like neighboring sounds. Accommodation may affect the *place of articulation,* the *manner of articulation,* the *voicing, other articulatory features* (such as secondary articulations), or any combination of these factors.

10.6.1 Degree of accommodation

Accommodation may be greater or lesser in its effect. It may affect only the voicing or only the place of articulation or only the manner of articulation, or it may affect more than one of these features. The two sounds in question may become identical as a result of accommodation, or they may only become more similar.

Accommodation is called *partial* if the segment that undergoes change retains some separate character. Accommodation is called *total* if the assimilated segment becomes like the assimilating segment in every way.

For example, Italian *Vittorio* corresponds to English *Victor*; *fatto* corresponds to *fact*. In both these words, English retains the original Latin [k] (spelled <c>). In the Italian words, the original [k] has assimilated *totally* to the following [t]. In a similar way, in a casual pronunciation of "nutcracker," most people say [nʌkkɹækɚ]; the [t] is *totally* assimilated to the following [k]. But when someone says [foŋkɑl] for "phone call," a [n] has become a [ŋ] under the influence of the [k]. This is a *partial* assimilation: the place of articulation has changed, but the manner of articulation remains nasal rather than plosive. The [ŋ] is still distinct from the [k].

10.6.2 Direction of accommodation

Accommodation may be divided up into three types according to the direction of its effect. These are known as *progressive, regressive,* and *double accommodation.*

10.6.2.1 Progressive accommodation

In *progressive,* or *left-to-right, accommodation,* a sound affects one that *follows.* For example, in the word "dogs" the final <s> is pronounced [z], while in "cats" the final <s> is pronounced [s]. The [g] of "dogs" is voiced, and that affects the *following* sound; the [t] of "cats" is voiceless, similarly affecting the sound that *comes after it.*

10.6.2.2   Regressive accommodation

In *regressive, anticipatory,* or *right-to-left accommodation,* a sound affects one that *precedes* it. For example, when someone says [mɪʃjə] for "miss you," the palatal glide [j] has modified the articulation of the preceding fricative. When "phone call" is pronounced [foŋkɑl], the [k] has affected the place of articulation of the *preceding* nasal.

10.6.2.3   Double accommodation

Sometimes the segments that precede *and* follow a given segment both exert a similar influence on that segment. In this case the direction of accommodation is said to be *double.* For example, in the word "shear," the vowel is likely to be somewhat rounded. This is because both the [ʃ] preceding the vowel *and* the [ɹ] following the vowel are somewhat rounded. To give another example, the vowels of the words "man," "mat," and "tan" are all likely to be somewhat nasalized. However, the nasalization in "man" is likely to be greater than in the other two words, because the direction of the effect is double. In both "mat" and "tan," the plosive consonant requires the VPP to be closed, so there will be movement of the velum during vowel production in both, either moving *toward* closure or moving *from* closure. In "man," the sounds on both sides of the vowel require that the VPP be wide open, so the vowel will have greater nasalization than in the other two example words.

10.6.3   Diachronic versus synchronic accommodation

In linguistic science, the term *synchronic* refers to contemporary or still ongoing processes. Diachronic means 'through time,' so the term *diachronic* refers to changes that occur over time. A change from Old English (say, the year 1000 CE) to Middle English (say, the year 1400 CE) is a diachronic change. A change from Shakespeare's Early Modern English (approx. 1600 CE) to contemporary Modern English is also a diachronic change.

Accommodations may be of either type, synchronic or diachronic.

To use an example we have employed several times, the pronunciation [foŋkɑl] for "phone call" displays a *synchronic* accommodation, since we pronounce "phone" (when said alone) with a [n], but that sound undergoes the process of accommodation in certain combinations ("pho_n_e call," "pho_n_ebooth").

To take another example we have seen, Old English *þunor* has changed to Modern English *thun_d_er,* with a [d] "inserted" as an accommodation ([θʌndɚ]). This is a *diachronic* or historical accommodation, since it occurred in the past, and the word is no longer undergoing change (at least in the standard dialect) – that is, *thunder* is pronounced with a /d/ in all contexts. This diachronic change happened a long time ago, and there is no longer variation in the general dialect.

Contemporary (synchronic) processes are particularly significant because they produce variant forms, such as the two forms [foŋ], [fom] and [fon] for "phone." Such processes affect other phonetically similar words in a similar way.

10.6.4   Contiguous versus noncontiguous accommodation

Accommodation may affect *contiguous* segments (those next to one another in a sequence), as has been the case in all the examples we have seen. Or it may affect segments that are at a distance from each other. An example of the latter, *noncontiguous*, accommodation is the word *orang-utan*, borrowed from Malay, which is often pronounced (and spelled) *orang-utang* in English, the final [n] becoming [ŋ] under the influence of the [ŋ] in the second syllable.

Because there are a number of special examples of noncontiguous assimilation, the subject will be discussed more fully in Section 10.9.

10.6.5   Types of accommodation

Note that the types of accommodation listed in the preceding subsections are not mutually exclusive categories. For example, *progressive accommodation* could be *partial* or *total*; a *diachronic* accommodation could be *progressive* or *regressive*. Other combinations are equally possible.

10.7   Variants of some English segments

This chapter has discussed various phenomena that occur as sounds "get together" in words, phrases, and discourse generally. Section 10.7 will list a number of examples where there is variation in the sounds of English when those sounds are in combination with others.

It is important to note that not all the following are examples of accommodation – that is, not all have a strictly phonetic cause. However, they do have phonetic effects, and for that reason a number are catalogued here to sensitize the reader to phenomena that occur almost every time we open our mouths to speak.

10.7.1   Release of plosives

In utterance-final position,[9] plosives in English are often unreleased. That is, when no sounds follow the plosive, the final phase of its articulation,

---

[9] Utterance-final position: the position of the last segment in an utterance – that is, before the speaker stops talking. In this position, a segment is not followed by another segment, and thus no articulatory adjustments (such as release) are forced upon that segment by following segments.

the *release* phase, may not be present, and if present, it may or may not be audible. In this case, the accommodation can be seen as being caused by the silence following the segment in question.

For example, if you were to say "Stop!" you might well not release the final [p]. However, if the [p] is followed by another sound (particularly an open sound such as a vowel) – as in "Stop Andy!" – the [p] must be released. Note that nonrelease, like many other accommodations, is not forced on speakers by physiologic necessity, but is optional, determined by rule in English. In French, by contrast, utterance-final plosives are always released, even when silence follows.

The IPA symbol for nonrelease (or for inaudible release) is [']; an unreleased [p] would be indicated thus: [p̚]. Hence, "Stop!" may be [stɑp̚]. In English, utterance-final nasals are also often unreleased: "Who was that?" "Tom" ([tɑm̚]).

When two similar plosives come together, there may be only one release. For example, in the phrase "canned drink" there normally would be only one release for both [d]'s. Single release of two plosives may be transcribed satisfactorily by indicating that the first of the two plosives is unreleased: [kænd̚ dɹɪŋk].

Even when two juxtaposed plosives have different places of articulation, there may be only one release for the two. For example, in saying "locked," talkers usually articulate a velar occlusion for the [k] but do not release it separately from the [t]. That is, they say [lɑk̚t] not [lɑkt]. This phenomenon may occur even if the two plosives are in different words. In the expression "back to nature," the [k] of "back" is likely to be unreleased.

In diachronic (historical) terms, nonrelease may lead to the loss of sounds. Although, as we have noted, all plosives in French are released, this is true of Modern French only. In Middle French, nonreleased plosives were common, and that was the first step in the loss of many word-final consonants. The tendency in English (North American English, at least) toward nonrelease may likewise lead to the loss of final consonants.

10.7.2   Aspiration of plosives

Aspiration is the puff of air accompanying the release of some voiceless plosives; it is associated with a long VOT (8.4.2). In English, voiceless plosives in certain environments are typically aspirated; voiced plosives never are.

To recapitulate, voiceless plosives at the beginning of stressed syllables are typically aspirated in English: for example, the initial plosives in "pan," "tan," and "can." If you check for this by holding your hand in front of your mouth, you will probably feel the aspiration more for [p] than for [t] or [k]. This is because the point of occlusion, and therefore of release, is

farther forward and therefore nearer the hand, in [p] than the other places
of articulation. Voiceless plosives in other positions than at the beginning
of stressed syllables are typically not aspirated in English: for example, the
plosives in "sp̲in," "st̲ing," and "sk̲in."

This is an example from the current list where accommodation is not the
motivating force for this variation in English (as noted in the introduction
above).

10.7.3   Nasal release (nasal plosion)
Plosives are normally released through the oral cavity, either between the
lips (for [p] and [b]) or over the tongue (for [t], [d], [k], and [g]). However, if
a nasal immediately follows a plosive, the plosive can be released nasally.
In the word "ship̲mate," for instance, the [p] is released nasally – that is,
the velum is lowered *before* the lips are parted. This is called *nasal release*
or *nasal plosion.*

Nasal plosion occurs virtually always when the plosive is followed by a
nasal having the same place of articulation. It occurs frequently even when
the plosive and nasal have different places of articulation. So it will occur
in such words as "ship̲mate" and "what̲not"; and it is also likely to occur in
such words as "bat̲man" and "work̲man."

Nasal release is transcribed with this IPA symbol: [ⁿ] – "shipmate" [ʃɪpⁿmet].

10.7.4   Lateral release (lateral plosion)
The plosives [t] and [d] are normally released by opening of the occlusion
that has been made between the tongue blade and the alveolar ridge;
air escapes over the top of the tongue. (Of course, release is nasal if the
plosives are followed by a nasal.) If [t] or [d] is followed by [l], however,
the release is lateral – that is, the laminoalveolar occlusion is maintained
when the plosive is released. Instead of the blade of the tongue being
moved, the sides of the tongue, which have formed a seal along the upper
molar and premolar teeth in the production of the plosive, are pulled
inward; the tongue is narrowed. The plosive release occurs laterally, over
the sides of the tongue. This happens in such words or expressions as
"lit̲tle," "bat̲tle," and "good̲ luck." This is called *lateral release* or *lateral
plosion.*

The IPA transcription symbol is a small raised "l": [ˡ].[10] There is usually
little need to indicate lateral release, since it can be expected whenever

---

[10] This is an unfortunate choice of symbols. It would have been preferable if the IPA had
chosen a small uppercase <L>, not a lowercase <l>. When handwritten, this symbol for
lateral release looks like a small vertical stroke that may be confused with a stress mark
that we will see in a later chapter.

[l] follows [t] or [d] immediately, unless there is a pause between the two sounds.

10.7.5   Place of articulation of [t] and [d]

The plosives classified as alveolars are typically articulated with the blade of the tongue against the alveolar ridge. However, in English, the alveolars may be articulated farther forward under the influence of a dental sound, or farther back under the influence of a back vowel, a palatal glide, or another consonant. For example, in the expression "bo<u>th</u> Tom and me," the [t] of "Tom" follows a dental sound, [θ]. The articulation of this [t] may be advanced to the point that it is dental: [t̪]. The plosives [t] and [d] may be retracted (articulated farther back) before [ʃ] or [j] or some other sounds. Similarly, the /d/ of "bad" may be alveopalatal in the expression "Ba<u>d sh</u>ot."

One can expect similar, but less extensive, changes in the place of articulation of [n], [l], [s], and [z].

The diacritic for dental articulation is [̪]; dentals are symbolized [t̪], [s̪], [n̪], etc. The diacritic for *fronting* is [̟] (thus: [q̟]); this symbol is usually not used with alveolars, since a fronted alveolar is a dental, for which there is a special symbol. However, it may be used with velars and vowels [k̟], for example. The symbol for *retraction* or backing is [̠], so a backed [t], as in "mea<u>tsh</u>op," would be transcribed [t̠]. Where a descender ("tail") of a letter prevents the use of these diacritics, it can be placed after the letter ([g ̠]).

10.7.6   Place of articulation of /k/ and /g/

As we noted in Section 10.2, the place of articulation of /k/ and /g/ varies according to the surrounding sounds. These sounds may be fronted, so that they are palatovelar in place of articulation, or even palatal, as in the examples given in Section 10.2. They may be backed so that they are post-velar or even uvular in place of articulation. A somewhat fronted /k/ may be represented as [k̟]; if it is fronted such that it is clearly palatal, it would be correctly represented by the symbol [c]. If it were backed somewhat, it could be represented as [k̠]; if backed considerably, the symbol [q] would be correct.

10.7.7   The articulation of /h/ and voiceless segments

The consonant /h/ in English is always prevocalic in the same syllable; /h/ accommodates in tongue and jaw position to the vowel that follows it in the same syllable. For example, say "heat" and "hoot." Notice that while you are pronouncing the /h/, your mouth is already in the configuration of the following vowel. Except for the voicing and airflow, the accommodation is total. Indeed, [h] could be considered a voiceless vowel with heightened airflow. The symbol for voicelessness is [̥], so the variant articulations of /h/ could be transcribed as voiceless vowels: "heat" [i̥it]; "hoot" [u̥ut]. This is, of course, not recommended as a normal transcription of /h/, but rather is done here as a means of showing the extent of the accommodation of articulatory features.

The diacritic for voicelessness introduced in the previous paragraph can be used in combination with any IPA symbol for a voiced sound to indicate devoicing, whether the devoicing is due to accommodation, foreign accent, articulation disorder, or other cause. For example, the first vowel in the word "suppose" is often voiceless because of the surrounding voiceless consonants. This pronunciation could be transcribed [sə̥poz]. Or, to take another example, a speaker of French might devoice the final /l/ of "people," as they would do in their native language. This /l/ could be indicated as [l̥]. In the realm of disordered speech, anomalous devoicing, as is common in stuttering, could be indicated with the same diacritic.

The IPA chart "Diacritics" gives a symbol to indicate unusual voicing of otherwise voiceless sounds (we saw this diacritic, [̬], in Section 5.15). For example, the /h/ of "hit" in the phrase "she h̬it it" may be voiced because of the influence of the vowels that surround it.

10.7.8 Vowels

Vowels, like consonants, are affected by surrounding segments. For example, in English as in many other languages, vowels are lengthened before voiced consonants. The /i/ of "feed" is considerably longer, temporally, than the /i/ of "feet." This is likewise true of the other vowels and diphthongs. The /ai/ of "tide" is longer than the /ai/ of "tight." Indeed, as far as the diphthongs are concerned, in many dialects there are differences of quality as well as of length as a result of the voicing of the following segment. Compare the quality of the diphthong /au/ in "mouse" as opposed to "browse," and in "about" as opposed to "proud."[11]

In the preceding example, the increased vowel length is most probably the result of the voicing of the following consonant, so this is likely an instance of accommodation. The difference in vowels in open and closed syllables, described next, is unlikely to be the result of accommodation – but still, the phonetic consequence is evident.

A syllable ending in a vowel is known as an *open syllable*; one ending in a consonant is known as a *closed syllable*. Vowels tend to be longer in

---

[11] Americans tend to think that Canadians say "oot" and "aboot" for "out" and "about." This is not accurate, but it is true that the typical Canadian [au] diphthong has higher starting and ending points than its American counterpart. This is much more marked before a voiceless than before a voiced consonant – hence the examples "out" and "about," but not "loud" and "a crowd."

open syllables than in syllables closed with a voiceless consonant. Those in open syllables are very similar to those in syllables closed with a voiced consonant. The effects on quality as well as length compare with those outlined in the preceding paragraph. Compare "fee," "feed," and "feet"; "tie," "tide," and "tight."

Vowels preceding /l/ in the same syllable tend to have a schwa offglide (Section 6.15). Compare the /o/ of "hope" and "hole," or the /e/ of "bait" and "bail." R-sounds following vowels tend to combine with them and to modify them. For example, the vowel of the word "or" occurs in English only preceding /ɹ/, not in any other environment. While we may transcribe this vowel with the symbol /o/, it is not identical to the vowel in "boat."

10.7.9   Other variants

An exhaustive cataloguing of all variants of phones in English would triple the length of this book and would still not cover the topic. Every sentence spoken provides a multitude of examples of accommodation. Once you are sensitive to this, you discover the almost endless variety of ways in which segments are modified by their context. Before looking at a few further examples, remember the point made in Chapter 1 that, when words are said self-consciously, they are often said in an unnatural way, and assimilations are blocked. The following examples would occur in natural rapid speech.

In saying the word "pine-cone," most speakers pronounce the /n/ as a [ŋ]. But in saying "pine paneling" they probably pronounce that same /n/ as [m]. In "that place" the /t/ of "that" becomes an unreleased [p̚]. The /d/ of "broadcast" is usually an unreleased [g̚]. The /n/ of "inferior" is often pronounced as a labiodental nasal ([ɱ]), as it is in "infer," although stress usually prevents this accommodation in a word such as "infamous" (stressed on the first syllable).

The word *sandwich* is often pronounced "sammich" ([sæmɪtʃ]). The group of 3 consonants /ndw/ is simplified initially by "dropping" the [d] (actually by reordering the gestures such that the /d/ is amalgamated into the /n/, in the manner described in Section 10.5.1); this leaves /n/ followed by /w/. The second step of reducing the number of segments also involves amalgamation: the change of /-nw-/ to [m] involves combining the features of the initial sounds to give those of the resultant sound. [m] is *nasal* like /n/; it is *voiced* like both /n/ and /w/; it is *bilabial* like /w/.

The pronunciation "punkin" ([pʌŋkən]) for *pumpkin* comes about similarly. In precise, unreduced pronunciation, a *bilabial* (the /mp/ complex) is followed by a velar (/k/). In the vernacular reduced pronunciation, there is accommodation of place of articulation: the entire sequence becomes velar.

The old /m/ has its *nasal* feature retained in the new [ŋ], and the old [p] is absorbed into the [k], a *voiceless plosive* like [p].

10.8   Primary and secondary articulations

In Section 10.2, the example was given of a [b] produced with rounded lips as opposed to spread or neutral lips. It's probable that your intuitive reaction to this example was to the effect that such a difference would be of minimal importance. Such aspects of articulation are fittingly called *secondary*, as opposed to the more obvious *primary* aspects. The primary articulation of a [b] is the oral closure at the lips, the plosive manner, and voicing. Additional aspects of articulation are *secondary articulations* – in this case, the /b/ is *rounded* or *labialized*.

   Secondary articulations have a set of labels ending in *-ize* (for the verbs) and *-ization* (for the nouns). We will examine these briefly in this section.

   There are a few points to note with respect to secondary articulations. First, while many start out as accommodations, they may gain a life of their own in the sound system of a given language.[12] So one cannot necessarily find a motivating factor in the phonetic environment when one examines the contemporary language. A second point, related to the first, is that while these are called *secondary* articulations, they are not necessarily *unimportant*. The correct secondary articulation in the correct place is necessary for natural-sounding speech, and languages may distinguish between words on the basis of their secondary articulations alone. And third, note that the terms we use for secondary articulations (those ending in *-ize* and *-ization*) are also used in the sense of a change in the primary place of articulation. Examples follow.

10.8.1   Labialization (Rounding)

If a segment is articulated with a rounding of the lips that is not part of its primary articulation, it is said to be *labialized* or *rounded*. For example, compare the [k]'s of the words "keen" and "queen." In the word "keen," the [k] is pronounced with the lips spread; in "queen," the lips are rounded during the articulation of the [k] (spelled <q>). The latter [k] can be said to be *labialized*. It is transcribed [kʷ]. In English, labialization as a secondary articulation is generally predictable: it occurs when segments are in the immediate environment of a rounded segment.

---

[12] That is, they become *phonologized*: they become part of the phonology of the language.
[13] A reminder that *diachronic* refers to historical language change.

As a diachronic[13] term, *labialization* means the change from a non-labial primary place of articulation to a labial segment.

10.8.2   Palatalization

If a secondary articulation occurs in the region of the palate, the segment is said to be **palatalized**. The symbol for palatalization is [ʲ]. Russian is a language with much palatalization: it contrasts [p] with [pʲ], for example.

As a diachronic term, palatalization refers to a change of the primary place of articulation from a nonpalatal to a palatal one (*palatal* taken broadly to include alveopalatal, postpalatal, etc.). For example, in the history of English, the alveopalatal initial consonants of *sugar* and *sure* came about with the palatalization of the initial [s] sounds when followed by a palatal sound.

10.8.3   Velarization

Velarization occurs when there is a secondary articulation in the velar region. In Chapter 5, you were introduced to the *velarized* ("dark") l-sound /ɫ/, which occurs in the vicinity of high back (i.e., velar) vowels. The official IPA symbol for velarization and for pharyngealization used to be [̴], as in [ɫ]. This way of writing the velarized [ɫ] remains in common use, particularly in reference to English. However, the official IPA now has distinct symbols for velarization and pharyngealization, namely [lˠ] and [lˤ], respectively, shown with the consonant [l]. The small raised symbols in each case are transparent in their source. Looking back at the IPA tables in Chapter 5, you will see that [ɣ] is a velar consonant and that [ʕ] is a pharyngeal one.

What is commonly written as [ɫ] is more correctly written [lˠ], in keeping with updates to the IPA.

As a diachronic term, velarization refers to a change of primary articulation to velar.

10.8.4   Nasalization

When a segment that is normally articulated with the velum raised is articulated with a lowered velum, it is said to be **nasalized**. This topic has been discussed in Sections 5.8 and 6.8. In English, vowels and some consonants are nasalized in the environment of a nasal consonant. In "man," for example, the vowel is nasalized. Note that some languages (French, Polish, Portuguese, and many others) have vowels that are normally pronounced with an opening of the velopharyngeal port. These are often referred to as **nasal**, rather than **nasalized** vowels, as the nasal quality is contrastive in those languages.

Nasalized segments are transcribed with a tilde over the symbol: [ã].

10.8.5　Pharyngealization

Pharyngealization refers to a secondary articulation involving a constriction in the pharynx. The root of the tongue is retracted into the pharyngeal region.

The IPA symbol for pharyngealization used to be the same as for velarization, so in some material it may be unclear whether a given segment is velarized or pharyngealized. As noted above, the current version of the IPA shows pharyngealization with the symbol [ˤ] following the pharyngealized segment.

10.8.6　Glottalization

The *glottis* is the space between the vocal folds. The vocal folds may be used in ways other than voicing, including articulation of a *glottal stop* and production of *ejectives* (see Chapter 9). These are all referred to as *glottalization.*

For example, in many dialects of English, a [t] before an unstressed [n], as in "fatten" and "button," is *glottalized.* What happens is that, since the [t] and the [n] have the same place of articulation, and since the velic movement is slow, the speaker opens the velic port at the same time as making the alveolar occlusion. However, with the velum lowered, it is not possible to produce blockage in the mouth to create the stop necessary for the plosive [t], so that blockage is created at the glottis: the [t] is articulated with a simultaneous [ʔ].

10.9　Noncontiguous (distant) accommodation

In this chapter, nearly all the examples of accommodation that we have seen so far have been of *contiguous*[14] or *contact accommodation.* This simply means that the segment causing the accommodation and the segment affected by it are contiguous – that is, in contact, or next to one another.

By contrast, *noncontiguous accommodation* (also called *distant accommodation*) involves accommodation in which the two segments are not in contact – there is at least one segment between them.

With consonants, *distant assimilation* is relatively rare. When it does occur in English, it is often judged to be an error or "slip of the tongue" rather than an acceptable variant form of the word. Such an error might be "No one answered the front door, sho ([ʃo]) she knocked at the side door,"

---

[14] *Contiguous* means 'in contact.' For example, there are 48 contiguous states in the United States, and 2 noncontiguous states.

in which the /s/ of "so" becomes like the /ʃ/ of "she." In this case, the non-contiguous accommodation is **regressive** or **right-to-left**. This would be seen as an error, not a normal articulation of the word *so*, but the process of distant accommodation can occur in non-erroneous speech as well as in speech errors.

An example of a word that has been changed by noncontiguous accommodation is *orang-utang*. Originally borrowed from Malay as *orang-utan* ('man of the forest'), with /n/ as a final consonant, it underwent modification such that the final sound is pronounced [ŋ] under the influence of the [ŋ] at the end of the first part of the word. In written and reference material in English in recent years, there has been a push back to *orang-utan*.

In Modern Italian, the word for 'bat' (the animal) is *pipistrello*. This developed from Old Italian *vipistrello* (Diez, [1853] 2011). The initial /v/ became /p/ under the influence of the /p/ that followed the first vowel. Both /v/ and /p/ are labial, but to distantly assimilate, the initial /v/ had to lose its voicing and change its manner of articulation from fricative to plosive.

In Modern French, the verb meaning 'to look for / search / seek' is *chercher* [ʃɛʁʃe]. The initial [ʃ] was [s] at an earlier stage of the language (and in Latin from which it was derived). The [s] became [ʃ] as a result of regressive noncontiguous accommodation from the [ʃ] (originally [tʃ]) in the following syllable.

10.9.1   Is it really noncontiguous?

The notion that accommodation "skips" a segment or several – as in the example of *vipistrello* becoming *pipistrello* – is frequently valid only in a superficial sense, even though this Italian example is quite clear-cut.

If one looks at the details of the articulation, particularly in the non-segmental way that was stressed earlier in this chapter, one usually finds that what is really happening is that the particular articulatory gesture is being carried over through the intervening segments, but that it does not change their character noticeably. For instance, in the example "sho she" for "so she," most of the articulatory features of [ʃ], such as the rounded lips, could be maintained through the [o] without adversely affecting the sound of the [o] in context; so these features can hardly be said to "skip" a segment, but rather carry through the intervening segment.

An example of noncontiguous accommodation that is often given is the French word *jusque* [ʒyskə], which is often pronounced [ʒyʃkə] in running speech. The dental [s],[15] which is the third segment, becomes alveopalatal [ʃ] under the influence of the alveopalatal first sound, [ʒ], at the beginning

---

[15] Sounds that are alveolar in English, such as [s], [t], [d], [n], [l], tend to be dental in French.

of the word. So, we ask, has the accommodating factor really "skipped" a segment? In fact, the vowel [y] between the two affected consonants is a high front (i.e. palatal) vowel. The vowel itself will tend to draw the [s̠] back toward the place of articulation of [ʃ]. So the palatal/alveopalatal place of articulation can be largely maintained through the vowel. Therefore, the accommodation is not entirely noncontiguous after all.

To cite another example, the English word "united" is often pronounced as if spelled <uninted>: [junaɪntəd]. An "intrusive" [n] seems to appear one segment away from the /n/ that is its apparent source. However, the nonsegmental view is that the open VPP is maintained throughout the word until the /t/ (for which it must close). The nasality does not "skip" the vowel, but is maintained throughout. Since nasality is not distinctive in English vowels, however, we do not notice it; all we notice, if anything, is the seemingly intrusive [n]. In subsequent examples, direct your attention toward thinking of how the "noncontiguous" accommodation might be explained in terms of some articulatory feature that is maintained throughout the intervening segments, rather than being skipped over. This is not always the case, but is often so.

10.10 Metaphony (distant vowel accommodation)

Noncontiguous (distant) accommodation of consonants is relatively rare, but noncontiguous accommodation of vowels is far more common, although not in Modern English. Any form of *noncontiguous vowel accommodation* is known as *metaphony*.[16] We will examine several specialized forms of metaphony that have their own names. *Metaphony* is the general cover-term.

Since metaphony occurs rarely, if ever, in Modern English, we will examine an example from French. Here are the forms of the present tense of the French verb *laisser*, 'to let, to leave, to permit':

English	French	Pronunciation of verb
(I) let	(je) laisse	[lɛs]
(you [sing.]) let	(tu) laisses	[lɛs]
(he/she/it) lets	(il) laisse	[lɛs]
(we) let	(nous) laissons	[lɛsɔ̃]
(you [pl.]) let	(vous) laissez	[lese]
(they) let	(ils) laissent	[lɛs]

---

[16] It may also be called *vocalic dilation* or *vocalic noncontiguous accommodation* or another such compound term.

SIDEBAR 10.2 Umlaut

In the spelling of German and a number of other languages, a diacritic or accent mark is used, generally, to designate front vowels or vowels that have changed from back to front. For instance, the German word Bach ([bɑx]) means 'creek, brook,' and Bäche ([bɛçə]) means 'creeks, brooks.' The root vowel has changed from back (in the singular) to front (in the plural). The accent mark is called an umlaut.

But the *process* by which this occurs is also called *umlaut*, and it is the process, not the diacritic, that is the meaning of the title of Section 10.10.1. The process can occur without the accent mark; as we will see, lots of Modern English words historically underwent (the process of) umlaut, but are not written with the (diacritic) umlaut.

Incidentally, in an English word (borrowed from French) such as *naïf*, the two dots on the <ï> are a *dieresis*, not an umlaut, even though the two diacritics look the same. The umlaut shows the pronunciation of a single vowel; the dieresis shows that two vowels next to each other represent two separate syllables.

Note that the vowel of the verb stem (*laiss-*) is pronounced the same in all forms except the second person plural (*laissez*). All the other forms have either an unpronounced suffix or a suffix containing the vowel [ɔ]. However, the second person plural has a suffix containing the vowel [e], very close in pronunciation to the vowel of the stem, [ɛ]. The [e] of the suffix modifies the pronunciation of the stem vowel in this case, changing it from [ɛ] to [e].

Such an example – because it is so rare – shows almost random effects of this assimilatory phenomenon; it cannot be said that metaphony is an active, productive process in French, since one has to search quite hard to find rare examples. However, in some languages, metaphonic processes are common and widespread. A couple of these that deserve special mention are *umlaut* and *vowel harmony*.

10.10.1   Umlaut

Umlaut is a form of regressive metaphony specific to the Germanic family of languages, which includes German, English, Swedish, Dutch, and others (see Sidebar 10.2).[17] Umlaut is a productive process in many Germanic languages, and its effects in several modern languages are widespread. In Modern English, by contrast, it is no longer productive, as it was in Old English. However, its effects are still felt in many umlauted forms retained as linguistic fossils; from the modern viewpoint, these may be considered

---

[17] In linguistics, the meaning of the term *umlaut* has been expanded to include similar phenomena in other language families, whether the effect is progressive or regressive. For example, the Chamorro language spoken in the Mariana Islands is described as having umlaut, though it bears no relationship whatever to Germanic languages. Our examples in this section are about English, a Germanic language that shows traces of umlaut in its modern form, and so we are using the term *umlaut* in its traditional sense.

simply "irregular." The most common such forms in English are certain plurals of nouns, such as *goose/geese*.

Essentially, umlaut caused the back vowel in the stem or root of a word to become a front vowel when a suffix was added that contained either a front vowel or a palatal glide. Let us look at the example of the words *mouse* and *goose*.

Some of the following steps occurred in "pre-English," the ancestor language to English before it came to England from northern Continental Europe. Further steps occurred in Old English. Finally, some changes occurred that give us the Modern English forms, but these occurred much more recently, in late Middle English times, and these last steps have nothing directly to do with umlaut.

		mouse	mice	goose	geese
1	Early pre-English	muːs	muːs-i	goːs	goːs-i
2	Umlaut	muːs	myːs-i	goːs	gøːs-i
3	Loss of –i	muːs	myːs	goːs	gøːs
4	Unrounding of front rounded vowels	muːs	miːs	goːs	geːs
5	Great English Vowel Shift (14th to 18th century)	maus	mais	gus	gis

Source: Campbell (2013)

Let us review these steps:

1. In pre-English times (while the ancestor language to English was still located in northern Europe, not England), plurals were marked with the ending [i].
2. **Umlaut occurred.** Under the influence of the front vowel [i] in the plural suffix, [u] in the stem was fronted to [y], and [o] was fronted to [ø]. This is typical regressive noncontiguous vowel accommodation (metaphony). It is given the special name **umlaut** to reflect the fact that this occurred in the Germanic family of closely related languages, but did not occur in the same way in other related languages.
3. (This and subsequent steps are not part of umlaut, but are listed here to show how the umlauted forms became the Modern English words.) The plural ending [i] weakened and then disappeared. However, because the vowels in singular and plural forms were now different, the singular and plural words were still distinguished by their vowel sounds.

4. While the earliest forms of English had front rounded vowels, these were lost. What happened was that the front vowels maintained their articulation except that lip rounding disappeared, so [y] –>[i] and [ø]–>[e].

5. A major change in English vowels, called the Great English Vowel Shift, occurred in southern England, and spread north over many centuries. Upper mid vowels such as [e] and [o] became high vowels [i] and [u], and high vowels [i] and [u] became diphthongs [ai] and [au].

Umlaut is no longer a productive process in English – that is, we do not pluralize new words this way – but it has left its mark on a few words. Note, for example, these pairs: *foot/feet, louse/lice, brother/brethren* (of course, there is also the non-umlauted *brothers*), *old/elder* (again, there is the non-umlauted *older*).

In English, umlaut as an active process ceased many centuries ago, and so there are relatively few affected words left.

10.10.2   Vowel harmony

Vowel harmony is a process unknown in English, but it is an interesting example of the lengths to which accommodation can go. It is a particular kind of **metaphony** that changes some characteristics of vowels so that they are like other vowels.

In a language having vowel harmony, *all the vowels in a phonological unit must be of the same type*. What constitutes a *phonological unit* depends upon the particular language: it might be a single word, a noun plus article, the verb or noun phrase, or some other unit. What constitutes the "same type" of vowel is also defined by the particular language. In one language, the vowels in the unit might have to be either all high or all low. In another language, they might have to be all front or all back; all rounded or all unrounded; all tense or all lax, etc.

A particular vowel determines the type of vowel for all the others in the same phonological unit. So, for example, the vowel of the verb may determine the vowels for all the words in a verb phrase. If that vowel is high, all the others will be high. If it is low, all the others will be low. Generally, then, the morphemes of the language have two forms, one with each of the two types of vowel.

Turkish is a language having vowel harmony. In Turkish, the plural ending on nouns is either *-ler* or *-lar*. Examine the following words to see if you can determine the rule that governs which plural ending is used (the words are given in their usual script, not in the IPA, but you can assume approximately IPA values for the vowels).

TURKISH SINGULAR	ENGLISH SINGULAR	TURKISH PLURAL	ENGLISH PLURAL
diş	'tooth'	dişler	'teeth'
çocuk	'child'	çocuklar	'children'
asker	'soldier'	askerler	'soldiers'
kedi	'cat'	kediler	'cats'
masa	'table'	masalar	'tables'
gece	'night'	geceler	'nights'
baba	'father'	babalar	'fathers'
kuş	'bird'	kuşlar	'birds'

As you can see from these examples, Turkish adds -ler in the plural if the noun stem contains front vowels, and adds -lar in the plural if the noun stem contains back vowels. In terms of vowel harmony, if a noun contains front vowels, then the plural ending contains a front vowel; if a noun contains back vowels, then the plural ending contains a back vowel.

In Akan, a West African language, the verb, the future tense marker (equivalent to English *will*), the object (English *me, it, him, her, them, us, you*), and the subject (English *I, we, you, he, she, they*) are considered together as one unit. So, *I will see them* and *He will find us* are each a single phonological unit, made up of individual units approximately equivalent to similar units in English (except that, in English, we consider these units to be separate words). Depending upon the vowel of the verb, all these units must contain a tense vowel or all must contain a lax vowel. Each other part of the unit, but not the verb, has two forms: one that goes with verbs having a tense vowel and one that goes with verbs having a lax vowel. In this language, the equivalent of *you* is /wʊ/ (lax) or /wu/ (tense), and the equivalent of *I* is /mɪ/ (lax) or /mi/ (tense), and so on.

Vowel harmony is a phenomenon that has become *phonologized* – that is, it has become part of the grammar of the language. Because vowel harmony normally involves the relevant vowels having a number of phonetic similarities, it is likely that phonetic factors played a role in the origin of the phenomenon in the particular language, and also may play a part in maintaining the phenomenon through time (i.e., *diachronically*). However, *synchronically*, in the mental grammar of a contemporary speaker, vowel harmony is just a feature of the language the individual has learned; it is not something spontaneously generated by phonetic principles.

10.11   Stress and accommodation

Accommodation happens most in speech that is rapid and casual. The slower the speech, and the more formal or carefully articulated it is, the less the various types of accommodation occur. Indeed, this is why it is difficult to teach the phenomenon of accommodation to students of phonetics: when the professor or the textbook gives an example, such as the "phone call" example given a number of times in this chapter, the students very often "pronounce" it silently to themselves. But this "pronouncing" is a careful, precise pronunciation: a **citation form**. Being a careful, slow citation form, it does not contain the accommodation the professor or textbook claims is present. At first the students may conclude that their instructor is wrong; finally, I hope, they will recognize that the absence of an assimilatory process in careful speech does not imply its absence in casual speech.[18]

Just as the speed of speech and its formality play a role in the accommodations made, so too does the related phenomenon of *stress*. Stress will be discussed in Chapter 11, along with *emphasis* and *rate*. The effects of stress and other *prosodic elements (suprasegmentals)* upon accommodation will be discussed at that time. At this point, it will suffice to point out that the greater the stress on a syllable, the greater the emphasis on a word, the slower the rate of speech, or the greater the formality of the speech, the less the accommodation which occurs.

10.12   Sandhi

Sandhi is a term that originally meant *accommodation* or *assimilation*, but that has now taken on a special meaning. *Sandhi* is the Sanskrit[19] word for *juncture* ('a place at which 2 things join'), and its use in this context dates from the time of the ancient grammar of Sanskrit written by Pāṇini.[20] *Sandhi* refers to accommodations that occur across word boundaries – that is, those that might affect the final segment(s) of one word and/or the initial

---

[18] Of course, the remarks made in Chapters 1 and 2 concerning dialect apply here: a reader may be completely correct in believing that the example cited does not occur in their own particular dialect.

[19] Sanskrit: /san/ 'together'; / dʰə / 'to put, to hold'; / i / *noun ending*. Hence, 'a putting together' – that is, 'juncture.'

[20] This scholar's name is usually written <Pāṇini> in the latin alphabet. The <ṇ> with a dot under it represents a retroflex, and would be written /ɳ/ in the IPA. The length mark on the vowel would be written [ː] in the IPA.

segment(s) of the following word because of the combination of sounds that occurs when these words are in sequence.[21]

Sandhi certainly exists in English, but not in so widespread a way as in some languages. In French, a sandhi phenomenon called *liaison* occurs. Many words in French have lost their final consonant through historical change, but this "lost" consonant is pronounced when the word is followed within the same phrase by a word starting with a vowel. The specifics are relatively complex and vary with the individual word, the dialect, and the speaker, but two simple examples will illustrate the process. The French plural article meaning 'the' is *les*. It is pronounced [le], except when followed by a word beginning with a vowel, when it is pronounced [lez] (actually the [z] is attached to the beginning of the following word). Thus, the French equivalent of 'the courses' is *les cours* ([le kuʁ]), but that of 'the animals' is *les animaux* ([lezanimo]). What is important to note from this example is not the details of French, but rather the fact that the result of sandhi is that a given word is pronounced differently in different contexts; there may be several pronunciations of the "same" word.

Let us look at a few English examples. The word "you" is often pronounced [jə] in unstressed positions, and in these positions it often combines with a preceding verb, as in "did you" [dɪdʒə]. The [d] and the [j] combine to give [dʒ] by processes that should be familiar to you at this point in the chapter. Other similar examples are "could you" [kʊdʒə], "would you" [wʊdʒə], "had you" [hædʒə], and, with a different consonant, "miss you" [mɪʃjə] or [mɪʃə], as mentioned earlier. Similarly, "wanna" for "want to," "gonna" for "going to," "shoulda" for "should have," etc.

The forms often called *contractions* result from sandhi as well. In English, some of these are optional and depend upon the formality of the speaking situation (the register): "I'll" for *I will*, "won't" for *will not*, "he's" for *he has* and *he is*, "ain't" for *am not*.

The preceding examples of liaison in French are not in fact exotic; English has essentially the same phenomenon – some dialects to a greater degree than others. For example, in all dialects, the indefinite article has a form determined by whether the following word begins with a vowel: "a car" / "an apple." Since, historically, *a/an* is just an unstressed form of the word *one*, you can see that the argument for liaison where a "lost" final consonant "reappears" before a vowel is a valid one, diachronically at least. That is, the [n] of "an" is not *inserted*; rather, in "a," it is *dropped*. In some dialects, the pronunciation of "the" changes depending upon the first sound of the following word: "the car" ([θə]), "the apple" ([θi]). In the latter case, a [j] is likely to appear between the vowels to make the transition.

---

[21] This is called *external sandhi* in some older sources.

In certain nonrhotic ("r-less") dialects, there is another kind of liaison. Word-final [ɹ] or [ɚ] is not present unless the next word begins with a vowel. For example, we find "the ca<u>r</u> came" [θə ka kem] but "the car is" [θə kaɹɪz].

In other nonrhotic dialects a similar, related phenomenon occurs. The details are the same as those just described, except that, in addition to inserting a [ɹ] where it is justified etymologically (i.e., where there is an <r> in the spelling), this dialect also inserts a [ɹ] between any word that ends in a [ə] and any word that begins with a vowel. Thus, "father" is pronounced [fɑðə] (no [ɹ]) but "father is" has a [ɹ]. But so does "ideer is" ("idea is"), where there is no r-sound in the individual words. This is a sandhi phenomenon as well.

Sandhi can go quite far in some dialects. The following story has been told of a number of different places. Two residents meet on the street at about noon. The first asks the second [dʒit] (with a questioning intonation). The second replies [ntʃɛt]. They have had a conversation about lunch.[22]

10.13   Other combinatory phenomena

This chapter has dealt primarily with accommodation, the most pervasive – and therefore the most important – aspect of speech dynamics, and how it occurs as segments combine to form words, phrases, and sentences. Then we looked at some variants of English phones, not all of which are the result of accommodation. In this section, we will briefly consider a number of other phenomena that occur in running speech, or that occur diachronically and thus change the language permanently.

10.13.1   Elision

When a segment or several segments are left out of a word when it is pronounced, we say that the sounds have been *elided*. **Elision** may occur diachronically and alter the word forever; it may have occurred in some dialects; or it may occur synchronically as a function of the speed and formality of speech.

An example of permanent historical change is the words *vehicle* and *article*, which originally had a vowel before the final [l]. This vowel shows up in the related words *vehic<u>u</u>lar* and *artic<u>u</u>late* but has been *elided* in the forms *vehicle* and *article*.

As an example of dialectal differences in elision, take the words *int<u>e</u>resting* and *secret<u>a</u>ry*. In England, both words contain 3 syllables; the marked

---

[22] Try to work out what they said before looking here for the answer. The first asks, "Did you eat?" and the second replies, "Not yet."

vowel is not pronounced. In many regions of the United States both words contain 4 syllables. The marked vowels have been elided in British English. In American English, it is not so much that these vowels were not elided, but rather that the elided vowels were put back again as spelling pronunciations under the influence of Noah Webster.

An example of synchronic processes is the word *police*, which may be pronounced [plis] in rapid speech, eliding the first vowel, and the word *phonetics*, often quickly pronounced as ['fnɛrəks], eliding the first vowel. The same speakers may then pronounce the first syllable with the vowel when speaking more formally.

10.13.2   Haplology

Haplology is like elision in that it involves leaving something out, usually as a diachronic change. In the case of haplology, one of two identical or similar syllables, situated in sequence, is elided. For example, the adverb *probably* is not pronounced "probable-ly"; this is haplology at work. The term for the scientific study of mammals is *mammalogy* and not *mammalology*. We have *mineralogy*, not *mineral-ology*. The linguistic term *morphophonemic* has undergone haplology and exists also in the form *morphonemic*. In this latter case, both haplologized and non-haplologized forms exist, the latter being the preferred form.

The word *Nazism* shows haplology (it is not written *Nazi-ism*), and while dictionaries advocate the haplologized pronunciation ['nætsɪzm], it is common to hear people say ['nætsijɪzm] (not haplologized).

10.13.3   Epenthesis

Epenthesis is the insertion of a sound, without etymological justification (i.e., the sound was not there historically; it has been added), generally to break up consonant clusters[23] or to provide a transition between sounds. Epenthesis may be totally idiosyncratic or dialectal, or it may result in a permanent change in a word (i.e., it may become acceptable and the norm). Epenthesis is also common among language learners who find certain combinations of sounds difficult to pronounce because those sequences do not occur in their native language. Similarly, it may happen in children as they learn their native tongue or in individuals with a certain speech dysfunction.

An example of idiosyncratic epenthesis is that some individuals insert an epenthetic vowel into such words as "film" ([fɪləm] or ['fɪlʌm]) and "athlete" (['æθəlit]).

---

[23] A *cluster* is a group of consonants together in the same syllable (word-initial clusters are often called *blends* by reading teachers).

An example of dialectal epenthesis is the dialect of English that inserts a [ɹ] between a word ending in a vowel and any word beginning with a vowel. In this case, one may say that an epenthetic [ɹ] is separating the vowels.

Learners of English as a second language may make many epentheses, depending upon the phonetic structure of their native language and that of the target phrase. For example, while Old English had such clusters as [kn-] and [gn-] at the beginnings of words (this spelling is still retained in such words as *knight*, *knife*, *gnaw*, and *gnat*), Modern English does not. So the English speaker learning German, a language having these clusters, is likely to separate the consonants of the cluster with an epenthetic vowel. German *Knecht* 'farmhand' should be pronounced [knɛçt], but is likely to be pronounced [kənɛçt] (or [kənɛkt], with a plosive replacing the palatal fricative) by the English speaker. Speakers of foreign languages learning English can be expected to insert epenthetic vowels to break up unfamiliar consonant clusters, or epenthetic consonants to break up unfamiliar vowel sequences. (However, vowels and glides are more often epenthetic segments than are consonants.) What is originally an epenthetic segment may become permanent, particularly in the case of words borrowed from foreign languages. For example, French borrowed the English word *knife* in Middle English times, when the initial [kn] cluster was pronounced and the vowel was [i], not the modern [ai]. The modern French word meaning 'pocket knife' or 'penknife' is *canif*, pronounced [kanif], the [a] originally being epenthetic.

In American English, the most common epenthetic vowel is [ɪ]. For instance, the baseball abbreviation RBI (runs batted in) is often pronounced "ribby." The vowel [ɪ] has been inserted to make the spelling RBI pronounceable in English. Similarly, the automobile manufacturer abbreviation BMW is often pronounced (with the <W> dropped and a suffix added) as "Bimmer"; again, the vowel [ɪ] has been added to make the letter sequence pronounceable.

The term *epenthesis* is also used to describe the transitional sounds that occur as native speakers correctly pronounce their own language. In English, vowels juxtaposed in adjacent syllables are joined by a glide: [j] following a front vowel and [w] following a back vowel. For example, the two vowels of "be̲ing" have a [j] between them; the two vowels of "do̲ing" have a [w] between them. Such sounds, too, may be called **epenthetic** or **transitional**. These transitional sounds might well be described as "making the word easier to say." But, in fact, they are as much a result of arbitrary rule as of physiological necessity. Many other languages have such sequences with no (or far less of an) intervening glide.

10.13.4 Metathesis

Metathesis or *inversion* is said to occur when two adjacent segments are reversed, either as an error, a historical change, or a dialect feature. For example, in some English dialects, the word *ask* is pronounced [æks].[24] Examples of historical metatheses abound; often *both* forms of a word exist, either in different languages or in different dialects. For example, compare the position of the <r> and its accompanying vowel in the following words: the names *Roland*(o) and *Orlando*; Italian *formaggio* ('cheese') with French *fromage*; English *burn* with German *brenn(en)*; English *through* with German *durch*.

While metathesis is traditionally explained as merely the exchange of two segments, it is hoped that your understanding of speech dynamics is such that you question this simple view, understanding that segments overlap articulatorily. When a rhotic sound (any type of r) is next to a vowel, for example, there is a great deal of overlap in the articulation of the vowel and the rhotic sound. One cannot say, in articulatory terms, that the [r] precedes or follows the vowel in an absolute way. They are blended together. Thus, metathesis is not a historical game of leapfrog with speech segments, but rather a slight or a gradual retiming of overlapping motor commands, such that the perception of which "segment" is first changes.

10.13.5 Dissimilation

Another kind of change occurs historically in languages, one that is essentially the opposite of *assimilation*. It is *dissimilation*. It tends to occur more commonly to consonants rather than vowels, and it tends not to occur very frequently. It tends to be noncontiguous or distant.

A good example of this process is the word *colonel*. In this word, the spelling shows the pronunciation before dissimilation occurred, but the pronunciation shows dissimilation. Historically, the two l-sounds in this word really were l-sounds. The first part of the word is related to *column*, as in a column of soldiers. The second l-sound was part of a diminutive suffix (a *little* column of soldiers). The word passed from Latin to French to English. In English, the first l-sound dissimilated from the second l-sound, becoming an r-sound instead. (In fact, the change may have been present in the word already as it was borrowed from French, even though the sound in question is [l] in standard Modern French.)

Latin *arbor* became *arbre* ('tree') in French, but the dissimilated form *árbol* in Spanish. The second r-sound dissimilated from the first, giving an l-sound.

---

[24] In this case, it is interesting to note that the standard form "ask" is the one that has been metathesized; the Old English word was *axian* (where *-ian* was a verb suffix).

The English word *peregrination* (usually plural), meaning 'wanderings, meandering journey,' comes from a Latin word that also had the two r-sounds. But this word root, coming to English by a different route than *peregrination*, gives us the word *pilgrim*. In this word, the first r-sound has dissimilated to [l].

French *marbre* gave English *marble*. French *pourpre* gave English *purple*. In both cases one of two r-sounds (two identical sounds in the same word) *dissimilated* to [l].

To take another example, the Old Germanic (i.e., pre-English) form of the word 'heaven' was *hi<u>mm</u>en*; this was its form in Old English. Note the two similar sounds, both nasals. The modern English form is *hea<u>v</u>en*, in which the first nasal has dissimilated to [v] (still a voiced labial sound). Modern German is *Himme<u>l</u>*, in which the second nasal has dissimilated to [l] (still a voiced alveolar).

10.14   Speech errors

In the previous section, we examined a number of combinatory phenomena not directly related to accommodation. One of the other things that happens when sounds go together to make up words, sentences, and, most importantly, discourse, is that people make speech errors. Such errors have been of academic interest for at least a century; Freudians believed that errors may reveal subconscious wishes, fears, etc. Modern speech researchers are likewise interested in spontaneous errors in running speech, not for their alleged psychopathological content but for what they tell us about the mental process of speech planning.

Speech errors, examined for their phonetic content, fall into a number of types. These include **exchanges, elisions, insertions, perseverations,** and **iterations,** not all of equal frequency. **Exchanges** involve the switching of segments, as in classic Spoonerisms. **Elisions** involve the dropping of segments; **insertions,** the insertion of segments (usually related to exchanges). **Perseveration** involves the prolongation of the articulation of a given segment, and **iteration** its repetition. Perseveration and iteration are found in the speech of persons who stutter, but they are also found quite normally in speech errors of all individuals.

Other types of errors exist, too. These include the **substitution** of whole words or the **blending** of two words, such as when a person is undecided between saying "pretty" and "beautiful" and says instead "prettiful." While interesting for what they show about morphological processing, these errors are not strictly phonetic in nature and will not therefore enter into the present discussion.

10.15   IPA symbols introduced in this chapter

Dental: [̪] as in [t̪]
Fronting: [̟] as in [ɑ̟]
Lateral plosion: [ˡ]
Nasal plosion: [ⁿ], as in [pⁿ]
Nasalization: [̃] as in [ɑ̃]
Nonrelease (or non-audible release): [̚], as in [p̚]
Palatalization: [ʲ] as in [pʲ]
Pharyngealization: [ˤ]
Retraction: [̠] as in [t̠]
Velarization: [ˠ] as in [lˠ]
Velarized [l]: [ɫ] (by older conventions)
Voiced: [̬] as in [h̬]
Voicelessness: [̥] as in [i̥]

10.16   Vocabulary

accommodation
- anticipatory
- contact
- contiguous
- diachronic
- distant
- double
- left-to-right
- noncontiguous
- partial
- progressive
- regressive
- right-to-left
- synchronic
- total

articulation
- primary
- secondary

aspiration
assimilation
blending
coarticulation

context
dissimilation
distant accommodation
dynamic, dynamics
elision, elide
environment (phonetic environment)
epenthesis, epenthetic
fronting
glottalization, glottalized
H&H theory
haplology
homorganic
hyperspeech
hypospeech
insertion
invariance (speech invariance)
inversion
iteration
labialized, labialization
lateral release, lateral plosion
left-to-right

lexicon
liaison
Lombard effect
metaphony
metathesis
nasal release, nasal plosion
noncontiguous vowel
  accommodation
palatalization, palatalized
partial
perseveration
pharyngealization, pharyngealized
phone
phonetic environment

retraction
right-to-left
rounded, rounding
sandhi
segment*
speech error
substitution
syllable, open, closed
total
transitional
umlaut
velarization
velopharyngeal port (VPP)
vowel harmony

11 | Suprasegmentals

"My dear, you have the words, but not the music."

> – Mark Twain to his wife when she tried to embarrass him
> by repeating verbatim a particularly profane curse of his

11.1 Introduction

Previously, we have looked at the sounds of speech as individual "objects," which we called *phones* or *segments*. Then, in Chapter 10, we showed that the articulation of individual phones typically blends into other phones when segments are next to or near one another. That showed us that the domain of articulatory activity is wider than the individual phone. In this chapter, we will see that some phonetic phenomena operate at a much wider level, some attaching to syllables or words and others attaching to phrases or sentences, or even larger aspects of discourse such as turn-taking in conversation.

These phonetic processes are called *suprasegmentals* or *speech prosody*. The word *prosody* has a number of different meanings in different fields, but when referring to language, *prosody* means those elements of speech that affect a range of segments. That is why it is also called *suprasegmentals,* signifying that they are *above* (*supra*) the individual *segments*, affecting many segments at once.

11.1.1 Important reminder

We have noted several times throughout this book that it is necessary to pay careful attention to the *technical terminology* used in phonetics. In the area of speech prosody, this is particularly true, since terms such as *tone, stress, accent, prosody*, and *intonation* are commonly used in everyday speech, but their everyday meanings are either very non-specific or they are used to designate things that are very different from how they are used in a discussion of suprasegmentals. Once again, therefore, we strongly suggest paying close attention to the exact meaning of terms and reviewing the terminology from the lists at the back of each chapter.

Another important factor to keep in mind during any discussion of speech prosody is the grammatical level at which the particular process operates. Some suprasegmentals operate grammatically at the level of the syllable, others at the level of the word, others in sentences and still others in discourse (turn-taking in conversation, for example). In a number of important cases, a very similar adjustment in sound, made by the same physiological and acoustic processes, has a different name if it operates at a different level of the grammar: a particular suprasegmental is given a name in accordance with how it functions grammatically in language. While speakers of English and Mandarin may do similar things with their vocal apparatus, the results may function at the level of the phrase in English, but function in Mandarin at the level of words, and thus the process has a different name.

11.2   Types of suprasegmental elements

Speech prosody involves a number of different phonetic processes. The main types are as follows, with specific suprasegmentals listed below each main prosodic type:

1. *Prominence*, the effort put into the pronunciation 11.3
   a. Stress 11.4
      i. Phrasal stress 11.7
   b. Emphasis 11.8
      i. Contrastive emphasis 11.9
2. *Pitch* (fundamental frequency) of the voice 11.11
   a. Intonation 11.11
   b. Tone 11.13
   c. Pitch accent 11.14
3. *Timing* 11.12
   a. Rate 11.12.1
   b. Pauses 11.12.2
   c. Rhythm 11.12.3
4. *Voice quality* 11.15
5. *Articulatory setting (set)* 11.16
6. According to some authors, such features as *juncture, nasality,* and others

Each of the items above numbered on the left – e.g., *prominence, pitch, timing, voice quality* – involves a particular kind of physical action by the speech production mechanism; that is, they are things the talker *does*. The lettered subcategories – e.g., *stress, emphasis, intonation, tone* – are the names given to the way that physical action functions grammatically in a language. For instance, *stress* and *emphasis* are produced by a similar phonetic mechanism (labeled *prominence*), but provide grammatically different types of information to the hearer – that is, they are perceived as meaningful in different ways.

Items 4 and 5, *voice quality* and *articulatory setting* (or *set*), do not have separate names for the grammatical function and the phonetic adjustment.

In the discussions that follow, phenomena important in English are presented before phenomena that play a lesser role or no role in English. The section numbers on the right of the list above show the order in which the various phenomena are discussed, and the section in which that discussion can be found.

11.3   Prominence

The first type of prosodic element we will consider is **prominence**. The term *prominence* simply indicates that a syllable, group of segments, word, or other spoken language element is made to stand out from the others. This is accomplished by a number of phonetic adjustments such as:

1. an increase in *loudness*
2. an increase in *duration*
3. a reduction of accommodation/coarticulation
4. an increase in the *precision* and *excursion* of articulation, and/or
5. a change in *fundamental frequency*

11.3.1   The mechanism of prominence
11.3.1.1   Increase loudness
The foremost mechanism of prominence is an increase in loudness. This is accomplished by an increase in articulatory effort, and in particular an abrupt increase in subglottal pressure created with the respiratory muscles. The increased subglottal pressure – along with compensatory adjustments in the larynx – generates louder phonation. The increased air pressure will also make fricatives and other types of phone louder.

11.3.1.2   Increase in duration
The increase in loudness involves a gesture (increased subglottal pressure) that takes a little longer to accomplish than maintaining normal subglottal pressure. The adjustments listed under 3 and 4 in the list above also involve additional time to accomplish. For this reason, adding prominence to a group of segments increases their duration. But duration in and of itself is a way to increase prominence.

11.3.1.3   Reduce accommodation/coarticulation

One way to make a sequence of segments (that form a syllable or a word or a longer unit) stand out from others is to reduce the amount of influence the segments have on one another, making each sound more distinct. In effect, this is a matter of producing that specific sequence of sounds in a more *hyperspeech* (and less *hypospeech*) manner (cf. Section 10.4).

11.3.1.4   Increase the precision and excursion of articulation

Reducing accommodation and coarticulation is one of the main factors in increasing the precision[1] of articulation, which can be considered to be a striving toward a kind of "ideal" articulation of the sound in question, regardless of the other sounds nearby. This, like the previous item, is a matter of making the articulation more hyperspeech and less hypospeech (Section 10.4).

Excursion (of the tongue or other articulators) refers to the distance the articulator moves from its rest position or its resting shape. The farther the tongue or other articulatory moves from its central rest position, the greater the excursion. In rapid connected speech, the tongue moves less far from its rest position, and the lips may spread or round less, than in a slower or more deliberate articulation – similarly with the shape of the tongue and movement of the velum or jaw. The effect of excursion is particularly relevant to the articulation of vowels and will be examined in Section 11.4, "Stress," below.

11.3.1.5   Change in fundamental frequency

The rise in subglottal pressure mentioned in Section 11.3.1.1 increases loudness, but also typically affects fundamental frequency (F_0), usually raising it a little (though a change in the opposite direction is not unknown under conditions of prominence).

11.3.2   Linguistic function of suprasegmentals

As noted above, different languages use each particular phonetic phenomenon (not only suprasegmentals, but particular segments, voice type, airstream mechanism, etc.) in their own particular way, including not using some at all. It is not simply that these elements are used "differently,"

---

[1] The term *precision* could be interpreted in some contexts as indicating a value judgment: something that is more precise is *better* in some sense. That is not the sense that is meant here: *precision* means 'exactness.' As we shall see, talkers make (usually unconscious) choices about articulatory precision based on communicative needs, social expectations, urgency, and other factors. In many situations, greater precision would be a bad thing: it would sound strange or pedantic.

but that they function in different ways and at different levels within the grammar of the language. That is, a phonetic element that distinguishes words in one language might distinguish syntactic structures in another, and a third language may not make any use of that kind of element (and that language will make those grammatical distinctions in a different way).

The label *prominence* refers to certain phonetic adjustments that are made as in the list above, but this label does not say *how* a given language uses it. Different names are used, depending on the grammatical role prominence serves. Here is a partial list:

- stress
- emphasis
- phrasal stress
- contrastive emphasis

11.4 Stress

We will deal with stress first because it is very important in English. Its importance is shown by the fact that misplaced stress can render otherwise correct spoken English quite unintelligible.

The following discussion is about stress in major varieties of English, though details may differ in some varieties. Some of the information will be true concerning stress as used in other languages, but some of it is particular to English.

11.4.1 Locating the stressed syllable

The citation form of words of more than one syllable in English contain at least one syllable that is strongly stressed. One-syllable words in English are stressed when they are pronounced alone (the *citation form*), but may have much less stress in the context of spoken utterances.

CLINICAL/PEDAGOGICAL NOTE 11.1 Stress in disorders and language teaching

While stress may be a less tangible phenomenon than consonants or vowels, and while it is only minimally reflected in English spelling, it is nonetheless of great importance. Its correct placement is essential for comprehension. The student of communication disorders should note that stress may be disturbed in certain disorders. The student of linguistics should note the great importance of stress in historical (diachronic) sound change and in contemporary (synchronic) phonological processes. In the realm of second-language learning, misplacement of stress is a common impediment to the intelligibility of speech of non-native speakers of English – and, conversely, English speakers may use stress quite inappropriately when speaking languages of which they are not native speakers.

If you are a native speaker of English, you may never have paid much attention to stress, particularly since English spelling uses no consistent device for recording it. For this reason, many native speakers – who use stress in a completely natural way when they talk – have difficulty locating or identifying stress.

Simply stated, *stress* is an accentuation of, or a giving of prominence to, one syllable (or more) of a multisyllabic word. This accentuation is accomplished with the various processes listed under Section 11.3. For example, if you compare the words "payment" and "invent," you will see that they are stressed differently: "payment" on the first syllable, and "invent" on the second syllable.

If this is difficult for you to perceive, a trick may be helpful to you in locating the stressed syllable. Pronounce the word several times, intentionally stressing a different syllable in the word each time. When you stress the wrong syllable, it will sound strange to you.[2] By a process of elimination, therefore, you can locate the stressed syllable. For example, say "PAYment" and "payMENT," stressing the first, then the second, syllable. When you stress the second syllable, "payMENT," the word will rhyme with "invent." This is obviously the wrong pattern for the word "payment," so the stress must fall on the first syllable. Of course, this trick for locating the stressed syllable will work only if your English is sufficiently good for you to recognize words stressed on the wrong syllable.

Let us look at a 3-syllable word to find out which syllable is stressed: "discover." If you have a good ear for stress, you need only say the word (out loud or, better yet, to yourself) to find the stressed syllable. If you are not used to locating the stress, you will need to use the test of stressing the wrong syllable. Say the word "discover" three times, each time stressing a different syllable: DIScover, disCOVer, discovER. The second one should sound most natural to you. After you have used this technique for a while, you should be able to abandon it and find stress in a word just by saying the word to yourself.

11.4.2   Levels of stress

The degree of stress carried by a particular syllable varies on a continuum from weakest to strongest, and the various components of prominence listed in Section 11.3 each can vary on its own continuum.

---

[2] This instruction is intended for native speakers and extremely fluent speakers of English as a second language. The less fluent you are in speaking English, the less likely this trick will aid in identifying the most stressed syllable.

However, while stress can vary continuously, it is convenient and linguistically relevant to identify a number of levels of stress.[3] For most practical purposes, the continuum from strongest to weakest stress is divided into 3 identifiable **levels of stress.** (A fourth level, which comes into play in phrases and sentences, is distinguishable; we will disregard it in this section as we are dealing with individual words.) The 3 levels are **primary** (the strongest), **secondary** (medium), and **weak** or **tertiary.**[4]

A word like "pimento," for example, has 3 levels of stress in English. The most strongly stressed syllable is the second one, /mɛn/. The last syllable, /to/, has less stress than the second syllable but more than the first. The first syllable has weak stress. Using official IPA symbols, these different levels of stress are marked ['], [ˌ], and [ ] (no mark) before the start of each syllable, respectively, for primary, secondary, and weak (see Sidebar 11.1). The word "pimento" could be transcribed /pəˈmɛnˌto/.

Note that it is a characteristic of English that 3 levels of word stress need to be distinguished. Other languages have different systems of stress (or stress is not a factor at all). For example, Spanish has primary and secondary stress, but not weak, at least in official varieties of the language.

> **SIDEBAR 11.1 IPA stress marking**
>
> The IPA symbols for three degrees of stress are ['], [ˌ], and [ ] (no mark), respectively, for primary, secondary, and weak. Unfortunately, the lack of a mark for weak stress can be ambiguous: the reader does not know whether the writer has not marked stress or has deliberately written that the stress level is weak. In English, this is less of a problem than it might be because of the change in vowel quality that accompanies weak stress, but still ambiguity can result. Some conventions for marking stress that are not official IPA do mark weak stress. The accent marks ´, `, and ^ for primary, secondary, and weak are sometimes used. The marks are placed over the vowel in each syllable, and the syllables do not have to be separated as they do with IPA symbols.

---

[3] Chopping a continuum into discrete units is something that is done by necessity in phonetics. In a similar way, there is an infinite variety of vowels – there is no limit to the number of points between /ɛ/ and /æ/, for example – but we divide the continuum into discrete units. Oftentimes, the cutoff points depend upon the particular language.

[4] Unfortunately, in this area also there has been little standardization of terminology. Some authors use the terms *stressed, unstressed,* and *reduced,* respectively, for what are here called *primary, secondary,* and *weak* stress. Furthermore, if 4 levels of stress are distinguished (as may be required in English sentences where word-level stress and emphasis in the sentence interact), the terms *tertiary* and *weak,* which are synonymous here, must be differentiated in order to have 4 different names to identify the 4 levels. The terms used in this chapter are in widespread use, and they will be used consistently to prevent possible confusion, but these terms may not be the same as you may find in other reading.

11.4.3   Vowel reduction: the phonetic effects of stress on vowels

The various parameters that vary with stress have been enumerated in Section 11.3. A few of these need to be explained a little more fully as they apply to vowels. Often, the effect of reduced stress is greater on vowels than on consonants.

In particular, these 3 factors have a particularly strong effect on the sound of vowels (items numbered as in the list in Section 11.3):

2. an increase in duration
3. a reduction of accommodation/coarticulation
4. an increase in the precision and excursion of articulation

So, as the degree of stress is reduced from primary to secondary to weak, the following effects occur to vowels:[5]

2. a *decrease in duration*
3. an *increase in the amount of accommodation*/coarticulation
4. a *decrease in the precision and excursion* of articulation

11.4.3.1   Vowel reduction and vowels under secondary stress

One of the effects of weak stress is that the vowel tends to be **reduced** to schwa. What is a **reduced vowel**? Following what we have seen above about the effects of weakened stress, a reduced vowel tends to be shorter in duration and to have a less distinctive, mid-central quality. Such a vowel is typically realized in English as schwa [ə] (in some dialects as [ɨ], at least in some phonetic contexts). This results from the fact that in unstressed syllables the tongue movements tend to be more relaxed and not to arrive at articulatory positions distant from the mid-central position.

However, it is not accurate to think of vowels as either reduced to schwa or not reduced at all. There is a continuum, and any point between the extremes may be represented in an actual articulation. Syllables having secondary stress are reduced as compared to those having primary stress, and syllables having weak stress are typically completely reduced to schwa.

11.4.3.2   Vowels under secondary versus primary stress

Are there any differences between vowels in syllables having primary stress and those in syllables having secondary stress? The differences are small, but are important in contributing to a natural-sounding pronunciation of English. For that reason, it is important to pay attention to them. In order to

---

[5] The other 2 effects of stress listed in Section 11.3 apply to vowels as well. However, the point of this section is to emphasize the effects *that most greatly affect* the sound of vowels. These 3 effects also relate to consonants, but that also is not the focus here.

determine what these differences are, a good way to start, as usual, is to listen analytically to some speech sounds. Let us return to the word "pimento"
(as it is pronounced in English) to illustrate.

The syllable /to/ in the word "pime<u>to</u>," as has been shown, is an example
of secondary stress; in the expression "<u>tow</u> truck," the same sounding
syllable has primary stress. When these two are pronounced out loud in a
normal voice, some small difference will be noticed between the syllable
/to/ in "pimento" and in "tow truck." The /to/ syllable in "pimento" is not
as long nor as diphthongized as in "tow truck."

What is occurring is that, for each vowel, there is a point anywhere between
schwa and the full value of that vowel that can be pronounced. We must
therefore make a judgment about which end of the continuum a pronunciation is closer to. In the vowel quadrangle shown in Figure 11.1, the arrows
represent the continua along which each vowel might be pronounced. The
enclosed areas in Figure 11.1 represent the range of pronunciations that would
be clearly and consistently identified as particular vowels.

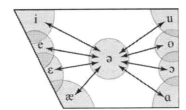

Figure 11.1 The vowel reduction continuum

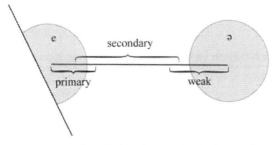

Figure 11.2 A closer look at the vowel reduction continuum

Suppose we consider one vowel, say /e/, in greater detail. Figure 11.2
shows that, depending upon stress, there are numerous realizations of an
English vowel. Although it is not diagrammed, a very important phonetic
change brought about by stress is the fact that /e/ under primary stress is
diphthongized (see Section 6.11), but under secondary stress it is not, or
is less so. All 4 of the English long vowels (/i, e, o, u/) behave similarly.
For example, compare the pronunciation of /i/ in the words "fores<u>ee</u>" and
"pupp<u>y</u>." Further examples will be found below.

11.4.3.3 The reduced forms of vowels

In some varieties of North American English, the high front vowels tend to remain high when they are reduced, resulting in a high central vowel. On the vowel quadrangle, this vowel is located midway between /i/ and /u/, above /ə/; its IPA symbol is /ɨ /. This vowel is present in many speakers' pronunciation of the word "ros<u>e</u>s" (as opposed to "Ros<u>a</u>'s," which has /ə/). Usually the symbol / ɨ / is not used in the broad transcription of English, although of course it is used for detailed transcription as in the case of fine dialect differences or communication disorders. The result of the slightly peculiar behavior of /i/ and /ɪ/ under reduced stress is that a number of different – and therefore confusing – conventions are used in the transcription of these vowels when they do not have primary stress. These conventions will be examined later.

It seems apparent in general that the idealized full articulatory movements for vowels are made only under primary stress (and not excessively rapid speech), and that reduced stress (and a very high rate of speech) leads to articulatory gestures that do not fully reach their target. As noted in our discussion of vowel articulation in Chapter 6, tongue position is not the only factor in vowel articulation. Lip posture and tongue root position play a role as well. It is apparent that each of these features, too, will vary along a continuum and that stress will influence whether or not the idealized articulatory position is reached. For example, an /i/ under secondary stress will have a more neutral (i.e., less spread) lip posture than an /i/ under primary stress. This leads some phoneticians to identify /i/ under secondary stress as an /ɪ/ and contributes to the differences in transcription systems (Section 2.2).

Let us now look at some examples of English vowels under the influence of different degrees of stress. At this time, it would be well to recall a point that is relevant throughout this or any other phonetics book: namely, that the examples may not be appropriate in all dialects.

Table 11.1 shows some English vowels and diphthongs under the three levels of stress. Several ways that stress influences vowels should be noted in the examples. We remind the reader of the precaution from the introduction that there is variation in pronunciation – and in English, this is especially true of stress – so examples may differ from your pronunciation.

1. It may seem arbitrary that a certain reduced vowel is stated to be a reduced form of a particular cardinal vowel, and in some instances it may be. But there is a degree of rationale for most: for example, why is the <e> of *homog<u>e</u>nize* a reduced /i/ and not, say, a reduced /e/? By

Table 11.1 English vowels under primary, secondary, and tertiary stress

Vowel	Primary stress	Secondary stress	Tertiary (weak) stress
i	scheme homogeneous	schematic puppy	homogenize
ɪ	simple morbidity	simplistic morbid	simplistic insipid
ɛ	tempestuous	tempestuous	tempest
e	maintain grade Canadian	maintain gradation	maintenance Canada
æ	nationality extrapolate Canada	extrasensory	nationalism extra Canadian
u	moving	removability	
ʊ	hoodwink	motherhood	
o	photo	photosynthesis	photograph
ɔ	auction	auctioneer	
ʌ	confront	confrontation	
ɑ	monotone	monotonous	
aj	license	licentious	
aw	sauerkraut	sauerkraut	
ɔj	employ	employability	
juᵃ	refute	refutation	

ᵃ As we've seen, [ju] is not typically called a diphthong in English, but rather a sequence. However, there is a traditional distinction between a *rising diphthong* such as [ju] and a *falling diphthong* such as [aj]. In most discussions of English, only the term *diphthong* is used, and it always means a falling diphthong. In any event, it is useful for us to look at what happens to [ju] in English under conditions of different stress.

looking at the word *homogeneous*, a closely related word, we see that when this vowel is stressed, it is pronounced /i/.

2. Note that the long vowels (/i, e, u, o/) are fully diphthongized under primary stress, but are shorter and less diphthongized under secondary stress. And, like the short vowels, they are reduced to schwa under weak stress. Let us take the vowel /e/ from Table 11.1 and look at it in greater

detail. Under primary stress, as in "gr<u>a</u>de" and "Can<u>a</u>dian," the vowel /e/ is highly diphthongized. It might be symbolized [ei], [eɪ], etc., depending upon dialect. Under secondary stress, as in "gr<u>a</u>dation," the vowel quality is retained, but the vowel loses some of its length and most (or all) of its diphthongal nature. It is an [e], pure and simple. Under weak stress, as in "Can<u>a</u>da," it is completely reduced to schwa, [ə].

3. Note that there are few examples of the diphthongs /ai/, /au/, and /ɔi/ under weak stress. Because of the historical development of these sounds, most are in syllables taking primary or secondary stress. There are a few examples of fully reduced diphthongs, however. The noun "digest" (*Reader's Digest*) has primary stress on the first syllable, but this syllable is reduced in the verb form ('to digest food'), although in many dialects the two are not distinguished. Again because of historical development, diphthongs often alternate with different vowels: for example, "pron<u>ou</u>nce" and "pron<u>u</u>nciation," "den<u>ou</u>nce" and "den<u>u</u>nciation," "impl<u>y</u>" and "impl<u>i</u>cit."

4. Notice that the reduced form of /ju/ is usually /jə/; that is, the /j/ glide is retained under weak stress. Exceptions to this are common, depending upon dialect and the individual word. For example, the word "manufacture" is commonly pronounced [mænəfæktʃɚ] not [mænjəfæktʃɚ].

5. A vowel followed by an r-sound is generally reduced to one single vowel, /ɚ/. For example, note the relationship between "lab<u>o</u>rious" and "lab<u>or</u>."

11.4.4   The transcription of stress

It is normal practice in transcription to differentiate two levels of stress in our representation of vowels – that is, when a vowel has weak stress, it is transcribed with a schwa, but when it has either primary or secondary stress, it is transcribed with its full quality (/e/, /i/, etc.). Thus, while the three levels of stress can be indicated with stress marks, there is no generally accepted way of transcribing the effect of secondary stress on vowel quality.

This lack is usually not a problem. For one thing, the stress marks are available when needed; and for another, it is often satisfactory to ignore the differences in vowel quality under primary and secondary stress for *the purposes of making general transcriptions*, although one *cannot* ignore the phonetic differences for the purposes of providing detailed phonetic description. The real phonetic differences between vowels under primary and secondary stress contribute to natural-sounding speech. Individuals wishing to improve their pronunciation will need to become aware of the subtle differences in vowel quality resulting from stress in order to achieve that improvement.

11.4.4.1   Use of different IPA symbols for the same vowel under different levels of stress

Some confusion is created by the use – recommended by a number of authors – of the symbol /ɪ/ for an /i/ under secondary stress. Certain authors suggest transcribing the word "happy" as [hæpɪ]. However, in most dialects, /i/ under primary stress is different from /i/ under secondary stress, so this usage is confusing. In a broad transcription, transcribe /i/ under primary or secondary stress with the symbol [i] and marking the stress where required.

Within the field of communication disorders in the United States, it has been traditional to distinguish [ɜ] from [ɚ] based on degree of stress. In a word such as *bird* or *first*, the symbol [ɜ] is used; in *father* or *teacher*, [ɚ] is used. There is no particular justification for this distinction. Reviewing the IPA vowel chart, it is apparent that [ə] is a mid central vowel and [ɜ] a lower mid central vowel, so the rhoticized versions of each ([ɜ] and [ɚ]) represent similar, almost identical, articulatory positions, with added rhoticization, so there is no justification for the different symbols. Mark stress with stress marks.

11.4.4.2   Long vowels

Chapter 6, "Vowels," showed that all four long vowels in English are to some extent diphthongs. We discussed the fact that some authors prefer to show that these are diphthongs in the transcription, while other authors feel that, if one is dealing only with English, the simpler system is better. The vowel in the word "boat," for example, can be written /o/, / oː/, /oʊ/, or /oʷ/.

Long vowels tend to be more diphthongized in syllables taking primary stress. In syllables taking secondary stress, they tend to retain their distinct character – long vowels do not become a schwa – but they are less diphthongized. So, in those transcription systems that indicate the diphthongal character of long vowels, sometimes the diphthongal quality is not marked in secondary stress syllables. For example, "tow truck" [toʊ tɹʌk] but "pimento" [pəmɛnto]. The syllable with the /o/ has primary stress in "tow truck" but secondary stress in "pimento."

The important point here is that, phonetically, there is less of a diphthongal character to long English vowels in syllables having secondary stress than those with primary stress; this is true no matter what system is used to transcribe the vowels.

11.4.4.3   Diphthongs

The diphthong phonemes, like /aɪ/ and /aʊ/, retain their diphthongal character in positions of secondary stress. They are a little shorter in duration, and the starting and finishing points of the diphthong may both be a little closer to the neutral rest position of the tongue, than if the diphthong were under primary stress. For example, in the expression *White House* (meaning the US president's residence), "House" has secondary stress. If you have a good ear, you may be able to detect the fact that the diphthong in "House" is a little reduced from its realization in a stressed articulation of "house." However, it is normally not useful to puzzle over those details, but rather to use the generic transcription of the diphthong and to mark stress when that is useful.

The foregoing examples should make it clear that the first two levels of stress are not well distinguished by transcribing different vowels according to degree of stress. When it is important to mark stress, use the stress marks given earlier in this chapter. If the system you are using shows the slight diphthongal quality of long vowels, then the transcription should show the loss of diphthongal quality under secondary stress (if that is indeed accurate for the speech sample being transcribed). The other non-diphthongized vowels should be transcribed the same under primary and secondary stress, and stress should be marked as relevant.

11.5   How languages use stress

As we have seen above, the term *stress* (without modifiers) refers to prominence of differing degrees on different syllables of words having at least two syllables. In English, different patterns of stress can signal meaning differences, as in the pair of words *insight* and *incite*, and an English word stressed on the incorrect syllable will at least sound odd and may be unintelligible.

English is one language among 7,000 or so. How do languages in general use stress? First, we need to note that the term *stress* refers to differential prominence of different syllables of the same word; while monosyllabic languages (languages in which all words or morphemes have only one syllable) are rare, in such languages it is not accurate to speak of stress – there may be prominence, but, grammatically, it cannot be stress.

Another concept to keep in mind is that the following analysis is based on the citation form of words – how speakers would pronounce single words when asked how to say them. Sentence-level prominence phenomena (emphasis) and register of speech can affect stress in context. Prominence at the level of the sentence may affect the prominence of individual syllables beyond what occurs in a citation form.

Finally, while stress *occurs* at the level of words – that is, it can differentiate words – it *functions* at the level of the syllable. That is, it is the *syllable* that carries a particular degree of stress, and that affects the phonetic shape of the *word*.

Here are patterns of stress among the world's languages:

1. Number of levels of stress
    a. Equal stress (1 level only)
    b. 2 or 3 levels of stress
2. Predictability of stress, or information-carrying capacity of stress
    a. Stress entirely predictable
    b. Stress mostly predictable
    c. Stress unpredictable

11.5.1   Nature of this analysis

The purpose of this section is not to perform an analysis in light of current phonological theory. Rather, in order for the reader to gain an understanding of patterns of stress, we will examine the nature of surface stress placement in words of 2 or more syllables. As we noted, if a person simply says the word *incite* alone (not in combination with other words), an English speaker can identify that the word spoken was *incite* and not *insight*. This is because the stress placement is different in the two words. It is in this sense – distinguishing words of at least 2 syllables spoken in isolation – that the following patterns are presented.[6]

11.5.2   One level; equal stress (1a)

If a language stresses all syllables in words equally, it has only one level of stress, and the notion of stress becomes relatively meaningless in any description of the phonetics of that language, though there may still be sentence-level prominence that makes some words more prominent than others.

French is not a perfect example of such a language, but it provides a useful example. For the most part, all syllables but the final syllable of polysyllabic words have equal stress in French. The final syllable typically has slightly more stress, though not a great deal.

In essence, stress is not perceived as an important part of the phonetic shape of words. Non-native speakers of French may put inappropriate stress on various syllables of French words, and this does not greatly affect intelligibility, though it certainly shows a foreign accent.

11.5.3   Two or three levels (1b)

Languages that do have stress typically have 2 or 3 degrees of stress. It is rare for there to be 4 levels of stress that appear in the citation forms of words, though sentence-level phenomena can create 4 levels of prominence in words in context.

---

[6] Some of the world's languages do not have words with more than one syllable, and some others do not normally have words that are spoken in isolation from the rest of the phrase. The discussion in this section does not apply to such languages.

Spanish is a language that has 2 levels of stress. In polysyllabic words, all syllables have secondary stress except the stressed syllable, which carries primary stress.

As we have seen, English is a language with three levels of stress.

11.5.4   Predictability or information-carrying capacity of stress (2)

Languages may have 2 or 3 levels of stress, but whether or not stress carries information depends on whether it is predictable or not. Basic information theory tells us that if a signal (in this case, the "signal" is the stressing of a syllable) is entirely predictable, then it provides (or carries) no information whatever – indeed, it turns out not to be a "signal" at all. If you know which syllable of a word the stress will always fall on, then stress cannot differentiate two otherwise phonetically similar words.

In English, *insight* and *incite* are different words. Simply hearing the word spoken allows you to differentiate them. This is because these 2-syllable words in English have different stress patterns, so the syllable that it does fall on tells the hearer something. In this case, it tells the hearer whether the word spoken was *insight* or *incite*.

11.5.5   Stress entirely predictable (2a)

Old English (spoken up to around 1100 CE) had predictable stress. The first root syllable (i.e., the first syllable that was not part of a prefix) took primary stress, and secondary or weak stress fell on the others. While Modern English has a vast vocabulary borrowed from Latin and Latinate languages, affecting its stress patterns, the Old English pattern can still be seen in words that have been in English since Old English times: *móther, fáther, síster, foregó* (*fore* is a prefix), *forbíd, forgíve,* and *forgét* (*for* is a prefix), and so on. In the word *fórty, for* is not a prefix; it is the root and means 'four' – *ty* is a suffix. (An acute accent marks the primary stress in these example words.)

As such, stress in Old English rarely if ever distinguished between two words spoken in their citation form, the way that *incite* and *insight* can be distinguished in Modern English. Still, the stress had to be correct for a speaker to have a native accent.

Old English is cited as an example of the pattern whereby stress is entirely predictable, but it is not unique. Many modern languages have such a pattern, though details will of course be different from those of Old English.

11.5.6   Stress mostly predictable (2b)

Some languages have stress that is mostly predictable, but have a sufficient number of words with different patterns for stress to carry meaning. A familiar example of such a language is Spanish. Most polysyllabic words in

Spanish have predictable stress: (1) words ending in a vowel or <n> or <s> are stressed on the penultimate (second to last) syllable; no accent-mark is used in the spelling; (2) words ending with a consonant other than <n> or <s> are stressed on the final syllable; no accent-mark is used in the spelling; (3) some words are stressed on a syllable not predicted by rules (1) or (2); in these words, the orthography places an acute accent-mark on the stressed syllable. For example:

termino   'I finish'
terminó   'she, he, it, you (singular formal) finished'
término   'term, terminus'

This analysis is intended to answer the question, "If one of the words *termino, terminó,* or *término* is spoken alone, does a speaker of Spanish know which of the three words was spoken?" At this superficial level of analysis, phonetic stress is shown to distinguish individual words in Spanish; however, most words in Spanish have predictable stress placement.

11.5.7   Stress unpredictable (2c)

When stress is unpredictable, it can be used to carry meaning by differentiating words that would otherwise be the same. It cannot be said that English stress is entirely unpredictable, but it is sufficiently unpredictable for stress to carry meaning in English, as shown by the *insight – incite* example shown above.

In a language where stress is unpredictable, the situation is much like the example of Spanish given in the previous section: *termino, terminó,* and *término* differ only by stress. Spanish is a particularly good example of this phenomenon because it does not have a tertiary or weak level of stress and does not reduce vowels as English does. Therefore, the pronunciation of the 3 words listed above differs only in stress.

Despite words like these fitting the unpredictable pattern well, Spanish stress has been categorized as *mostly predictable* (Section 11.5.6) because the overwhelming majority of the vocabulary has entirely predictable stress.

This brings us to details of English word stress.

11.6   English word stress

As noted, Old English had a stress system in which the placement of primary stress in a word was predictable. This is not true of Modern English; the reason is chiefly that the vocabulary that is borrowed from other languages is frequently borrowed with the foreign stress pattern.

Over 50 percent of the words in Modern English vocabulary have been borrowed from foreign sources, most from the Latinate languages (Latin, French, Spanish, etc.), but from dozens of other languages as well. In most of these words, either the stress pattern of the original language has been retained or an attempt has been made to imitate the original stress pattern when the word has been adapted to English pronunciation. As a result, we have words like *vocábulary*, *pajáma*, and *automátic*, which have stress patterns different from those of original English words like *fáther* and *bérry*. (In this and subsequent paragraphs, the acute accent, ´, is used as a simple way to show primary stress in English words without using IPA.)

For an example of the way foreign words in English are treated, let us look at the example of the English words *personal* and *personnel*. These two words represent English borrowing the same French word twice. In both instances, the original French word was pronounced largely the same, with a small amount of stress falling on the final syllable. *Personal* was borrowed in the late 1300s, and its stress pattern shifted to that of most English words of the time: to the first syllable: *pérsonal*. The word *personnel* was borrowed in 1837, and was distinguished from *personal* by speakers of English. Stress was retained on the final syllable, as in the French original: *personnél*.

The pairs of words *human–humane*, *moral–morale*, and *local–locale* came about in the same way and are contrasted by stress in most varieties of English.

Words in English can be contrasted on the basis of stress alone, without any other phonetic difference to signal the contrast (except, of course, the change in vowel quality that is a direct result of the stress change). Let us look at some examples of this. Noun–verb pairs are often contrasted in English by stress.[7]

Noun	Verb
cónflict	conflíct
cóntrast	contrást
défect	deféct
dígest	digést
éxport	expórt
ímport	impórt
récord	recórd
súbject	subjéct

---

[7] There is great variation among dialects in how these words are pronounced, so some of the examples may not reflect your own pronunciation.

In this list, the unmarked vowel sometimes carries secondary stress and sometimes carries weak stress, varying with the individual word and dialect. There is considerable dialect difference concerning whether all such pairs are contrasted. You may find that in your own speech you have the two pronunciations of "subject" but only one for "digest" or "import." There are some pairs whose form is distinguished by stress in almost all varieties of English. Thus, we can conclude that stress serves a contrastive function. In fact, the effect of stress may be so strong psychologically that we do not even think of the two forms of "defect" as being the same word. (This can be seen in the expressions "a défect in materials" and "the spy will deféct to the other side.") The noun–verb pairs listed demonstrate that words can differ on the basis of stress alone in English (vowel quality, of course, is changed as a result of stress). Other words are similarly distinguished.

But if stress plays a truly distinctive role in English, stress differences should not be limited to pairs of related words, such as the noun–verb pairs and French borrowings provided above – that is, there should be pairs of words that just happen to be stressed differently. And, indeed, such pairs exist – for example, *insight/incite*, *debtor/deter*, *decade/decayed* (in most dialects), *bellow/below*, *demon/demean*, *desert/dessert*, *Concorde/conquered*, *weakened/weekend*, and *coral/corral*.

Even where there is no pair of words that contrast only by stress, it remains true that the stress placement is an essential part of any English word of 2 or more syllables. This is simple to demonstrate by deliberately placing the stress on the wrong syllable; words lose their intelligibility immediately.

In clinical or language-learning contexts, incorrect stress placement may be a serious impediment to understanding of speech.

11.6.1   Contrastive stress

Contrastive stress involves giving an unusually strong stress to a syllable in order to prevent possible ambiguity or confusion. For example, the words "illusion" and "allusion" would normally be pronounced similarly, since the first syllable of each word carries weak stress and its vowel is reduced to schwa, but if it was thought that a listener misunderstood, the speaker might say, "I said állusion, not íllusion," stressing the distinctive syllables. Similarly, "gorilla" and "guerrilla" may be pronounced alike unless contrastive stress is used to differentiate them; the pair "lumbar" and "lumber" would also be subject to such stress for contrastive purposes. Many speakers of English say the word *missile* the same as *missal*. A person trying to make the listener understand that they meant *missal* and not *missile* may make a point of saying each with contrasting stress patterns (and consequent change in the vowels) to make their point.

Of course, context usually supplies the cue; only in unusual circumstances is contrastive stress used. One of the most common instances in everyday speech is numbers: "thirteen" is often confused with "thirty," "fourteen" with "forty," and so on. Here, context is often an inadequate guide to the speaker's intentions, since either number may be possible in the context, so contrastive stress is used.

Even when there is considerable phonetic difference between 2 words, a talker might still want to give a word contrastive stress to be sure the hearer understood. In discussing styles of art, primary stress might be given the first syllable of "impressionism" to be sure to distinguish it from "expressionism."

11.6.2   Stress and spelling

English spelling, for the most part, does not record stress. This lack does not create much of a problem for the native speaker, who has learned the stress pattern and spelling of each word separately, but it does create a problem for two groups in particular, the profoundly hearing-impaired and the non-native speaker or learner of English, since the written word offers few clues to that aspect of the pronunciation.

Stress is reflected in one way in our spelling, however, although for most of us it is simply an additional spelling problem rather than a clear representation of spoken English. When a suffix whose first letter is a vowel is added to a word ending in a consonant letter preceded by a vowel letter, the question arises as to whether to double the final letter of the word. Usually when the final syllable of the root word is stressed, the consonant is doubled. So we have <timber>/<timbered> but <infer>/<inferred>. Double consonant *letters* – remember not to confuse a doubled letter with an actual long consonant – are often, although irregularly, used in English to indicate stress patterns. A doubled letter often indicates that the *preceding* syllable is stressed. Compare "material" and "maternal" on the one hand with "matter" and "mattock" on the other. The latter two are stressed on the first syllable; the former two on the second syllable. But the marking of stress is highly irregular. In the words "catty" and "cater," both stressed on the first syllable, the number of <t>'s relates to the vowel quality and not to stress placement. Different varieties of English may disagree on these conventions as well. The verb *focus* is stressed on the first syllable and the past tense is usually spelled *focused* in the United States, but *focussed* in Great Britain.

11.7   Phrasal stress

Prominence is used within the phrase in English to show the grammatical and semantic relations among the words in the phrase. (A **phrase** is not a random collection of words or a common expression, but a grammatical unit, e.g., noun phrase, verb phrase.)

For example, in an adjective–noun combination, the adjective usually takes secondary stress, while the noun takes primary stress:

It's a white HOUSE.
It's a black BOARD.

This pattern contrasts with compound nouns made up of an adjective plus noun or 2 nouns:

It's the WHITE House.
It's a BLACKboard.

The second element in a 2-part compound may take secondary or tertiary stress. Of course, the situation is complicated if either or both elements have more than 1 syllable. Note that many compound words in English are orthographically 2 words, not 1. They are two words on paper, but in speech they are one compound word. *White House* is a compound noun, as are the italicized words below, like *middle age*, despite the spelling.

Just as word stress provides a means for signaling meaning differences, so too phrasal stress allows a distinction in speech between *blackbird* and *black bird*, between *hot dog* (frankfurter) and *hot dog* (overheated canine), between *English teacher* (teacher of English literature or language) and *English teacher* (a teacher whose nationality is English), and between *German shepherd* (a kind of dog) and *German shepherd* (German sheepherder).

11.8   Emphasis

Prominence at the level of the sentence is called *emphasis*. In emphasis, certain words are given more prominence than others for syntactic and semantic reasons. Emphasis affects the pronunciation of individual words, but it functions grammatically at the level of the sentence or discourse by influencing the meaning or interpretation of the sentence as a whole.

In English generally, content words are given more prominence than function words. Content words are those containing the greatest meaningful information, usually nouns, verbs, adjectives, and adverbs. The function words are those required for grammatical completeness, but generally having a low semantic content. They include prepositions, articles, and so on: this category overlaps with that of words having weak forms, considered in Section 11.10.

Let us examine a sentence to see that this is so:

The man came to the party.

Notice that *man, came,* and *party* have considerable prominence, whereas the two instances of *the* and the word *to* are greatly reduced – i.e., are in their weak forms. The grammatical role of the words governs their degree of prominence. In the foregoing sentence, the word *to* is greatly reduced in a colloquial pronunciation, but the word *to* may have different grammatical roles that change its prominence. For example, in the sentence

The (unconscious) man came to.

the word *to* is not reduced. In this sentence, the word *to* is a particle of the verb – that is, the verb is not *come* but *come to* ('regain consciousness'). The effect is that *to* carries more meaning and is therefore not reduced.

To take another example, examine the word *out* in the following sentences:

He was kicked out of the bar.
He was knocked out in the fifth round.

In the former sentence, "out of" is likely to be much reduced, whereas in the latter sentence, "out" is probably pronounced nearly in its citation form.

It is apparent that stress and emphasis interact in some way. Polysyllabic words, as well as monosyllabic ones, will occur in situations of greater or lesser emphasis. In this case, the degree of prominence of a given syllable will be a combination of the *stress* of that syllable within the word and the *emphasis* of the word as a whole. Generally, the *relative* degree of prominence will be retained. That is, in a polysyllabic word, the weakest syllable stays weakest, and the strongest stays strongest, but the *absolute* level of prominence of the syllables may change as the whole word is given more or less emphasis. For example, the word "pimento" will have three levels of stress internally, whatever its level of emphasis.

For this reason, in analyzing levels of prominence in sentences, we generally distinguish *four* levels, called **primary, secondary, tertiary,** and **weak.** (That is, the terms *tertiary* and *weak* are distinguished in this context, although they are often used interchangeably in regard to word stress.)

11.9   Contrastive emphasis

Just as word stress can be used contrastively (illusion, not állusion), so, too, can emphasis. Very often it serves the purpose of what is called **focus,** or that goes under the name of **new information** versus **old information.** In connected speech (discourse), there is normally a theme or narrative. In any given sentence, some words will serve simply to set the scene by making reference to what the listener already knows, and other words will give *new information* – that is, they will serve as the *focus* of the sentence.

For example, let us imagine a discourse about a parent's wish to talk to her child's teacher. If the listener asked (emphasized word in italics):

You WENT to the school?

the context would be that the listener *knew* that the talker had communicated with the teacher but was confirming (i.e., focusing on, finding out new information) that it was by going there in person, rather than, say, by social media, email, or telephone. But if the listener asked:

You went to the SCHOOL?

the context would be that the listener understood that the talker had traveled somewhere to raise the issue, but wanted to verify that it was at the school, rather than, say, the school board office.

Generally, then, new information is given more emphasis than old information. This is accomplished by increased prominence in the phonetic sense, as well as by syntactic devices that place the words in more prominent locations. This is a pervasive device in English. Let us look at another example. Examine the differences in meaning of the following sentences:

I didn't break it.

> (Yes, I agree that it is broken, but I deny responsibility for breaking it.)

I DIDN'T break it.

> (I strongly deny the accusation in general.)

I didn't BREAK it.

> (Okay, I'll admit I did something to it, but I didn't break it; I only disassembled it: I can put it back together again.)

I didn't break THAT.

(Okay, you caught me breaking some other stuff, but you can't pin this one on me. Notice that IT is replaced by THAT in a position of emphasis.)

Whichever word is emphasized is new information; the others are old. In the third sentence, for example,

I didn't BREAK it.

break is new information. The rest is old information: it is accepted that I did something to it. What is under focus (being disputed in this case, as the sentence is negative) is the question of whether *break* properly describes what happened.

In a similar way, this technique is used to clarify distinctions. One might say

Bill BAKER is bringing the drinks.

if there were another person named "Bill," known to both the talker and hearer, with whom he might be confused.

In the preceding examples, prominence affects whole words, or even groups of words, and also affects the interpretation of the sentence (or phrase) as a whole. Prominence therefore can play a role in the *syntax* of the sentence, whereas *stress* plays a role in the *lexicon* (vocabulary).

11.10   Weak forms

We have mentioned the *citation* form a number of times in this book. The citation form of a word is the pronunciation a person would give if that word were pronounced in isolation. However, as a result of the patterns of prominence in sentences, words (particularly common, short words having little semantic content: prepositions, articles, and the like) are often rendered in a much-reduced form known as the **weak form**.

A few examples of common weak forms follow:

Word	Weak form
the	[ð]
a	[ə]
to	[t] [tə] [ə] (as in "gonna")
and	[ənd] [nd] [n̩]
you	[jə] [j]
he	[i]
-ing	[ən]

Note that the use of weak forms is constrained by the syntax (grammatical structure) of the sentence. For example, the words *going to* are often realized as "gonna" ([gənə] or [gʌnə]). But note the constraint: When *to* is part of a verb infinitive, the weak form is permissible, but when *to* is a preposition, more of it remains. Consider these sentences:

He's *going to* take a trip.
He's *going to* England.

Notice that *going to* may be rendered in its weak form in the first sentence but may be rendered only in its strong form in the second (the vowel may be reduced or elided, but the /t/ will remain).

11.11   Intonation

Intonation is the first of 3 items under heading (2) in the list in Section 11.2 – those suprasegmentals that involve modulation of the *pitch (fundamental frequency)* of the voice.

During the production of speech, talkers adjust the pitch of their voice constantly. When people describe speech as *monotone*, they typically refer to pitch that does not change much.[8] The fact that we use a term with negative connotations, *monotone*, for speech having little pitch variation shows that pitch variation is expected and desired and its absence is undesirable. But there is more than that to our negative reaction to monotone speech: it is harder to understand than speech whose pitch varies. The variations in pitch provide useful information to the hearer; they help the hearer decode the meaning of what they hear. Without these pitch variations, a listener has to work harder to understand what is being said, and listeners find that fact to be annoying.

What information does variation in pitch throughout discourse provide to the hearer? In a language such as English (and an enormous number of others), it helps the hearer understand the relationship among the words that are spoken.

When words are organized together into sentences[9] or utterances, they are organized in such a way as to reveal to the hearer what the relationship is among the words, and therefore what the overall meaning is. Sometimes this is very straightforward:

The cat chased the dog.
The dog chased the cat.

In sentences such as these, the order of the words reveals the meaning.[10] But in a sentence such as

---

[8] Often combined with a rhythm that is more even than is typical of English (Section 11.12.3).

[9] The fact that, in everyday speech, some or even most of the utterances would not be classed as proper or complete sentences if written down is of no consequence for the present purposes. Those utterances make use of many of the same sorts of methods to allow the meaning to be decoded as formal written language, plus some that are unique to the spoken medium.

[10] In many languages, including Old English, these two different sentences could have the same word order, and the meaning would be clarified by having different ways of saying "the cat" and "the dog" that would reveal the actor and the recipient of the action. In many such languages, the different way of saying "cat" and "dog" involve suffixes or other changes to what is basically the same word. Note that such changes are referred to as *inflections*. The word *inflection* can also refer to changes in the pitch of the voice.

Cathy's cat chased the dog.

the relationship between Cathy and the cat is shown by the addition of a [z] at the end of the word *Cathy* (spelled <'s>), and not simply by the order of the words *Cathy* and *cat*. Sometimes the relationship between words is shown by prepositions.

Given the enormous range of meanings that can be communicated, and given that English does not make much use of showing relationships by endings on words, other means must be used to show relationships among the words in sentences.

Consider the following written sentence:

The cotton clothing is usually made of grows in Mississippi.

This is a classic example of what is termed a *garden path sentence*, a sentence that causes the reader to misinterpret the relationships among the words and to discover this only after reading most or all of the sentence.

We typically start out reading the sentence thinking it will continue in this way:

The cotton clothing is usually made overseas.

rather than in this way:

The cotton <u>that</u> clothing is usually made of grows in Mississippi.

For our purposes here, the important observation is that the sentence *The cotton clothing is usually made of grows in Mississippi* can be spoken so as to be understood the first time. It is in reading that the sentence is confusing.

What is present in the spoken sentence that is absent from the written form? Primarily, it is changes in pitch of the voice – that is, **intonation**. Intonation serves to help the hearer understand the structure of the sentence and the relationship among the words, and thereby to extract a clear meaning from the sentence that matches the talker's intent.

Intonation reveals the grammatical structure of the sentence. Patterns of intonation are applied to grammatical units within the sentence – some larger, some smaller in scope – and by doing so they reveal to the hearer what those grammatical units are, how they and the individual words relate to one another, and ultimately the meaning of the utterance.

The two most basic **intonation contours** are **rising** and **falling** – that is, the fundamental frequency of the voice becomes higher or it becomes lower. These patterns are associated with certain types of utterances in a large number of languages.

11.11.1   Falling intonation

This pattern is associated with the following types of utterances (Rogers, 1991, after Crittenden, 1986):

Neutral statement

My dog's name is Digby.
They arrive this afternoon.

Wh-question[11]

When are they coming?
How is that possible?
Where are my keys?
Who did that?
Why did it happen?
What did you see?

Command

Stop shouting.
Please get the chores done.

11.11.2   Rising intonation

This pattern is associated with the following types of utterances (from Rogers, 1991, after Crittenden, 1986):

Tentative statement

They arrive this afternoon?
You're going to the store now?

Yes–No question

Did your car break down?
Has my application been processed?

Request

Would you please finish the job.

More complex sentences, such as "The cotton clothing is usually made of grows in Mississippi," typically contain a number of grammatical units shorter than the overall sentence, and these have their own intonation contours.

---

[11] A wh-question is a question beginning with a question-word, most of which are spelled <wh-> in English: *where, what, why, when, who/whom, how.*

11.12   Timing

The timing of speech involves several factors: the rate of speech, the use of pauses, and the rhythm of the syllables.

11.12.1   Rate

In English, the **rate** of speech of a casual, unexcited nature is about 12 segments per second. It slows down in very formal speech, in speech where there is interference or background noise, and in the speech of a person talking to someone whose hearing or command of the language they expect not to be good. These are examples of *hyperspeech*, as we saw in Section 10.4. On the other hand, it speeds up considerably (to as much as 20 segments per second) when the speaker is excited, speaking informally but hurriedly, or arguing.

In a rough way, the faster speech is, the greater will be the dynamic influences discussed in Chapter 10. Accommodation, particularly coarticulation, will be greater. Similarly, sandhi will increase. The number of segments elided will increase, and in general the articulatory target of the speaker will be less frequently and less completely attained.

All of this stands to reason: the causes of coarticulation, explained in Chapter 10, become all the more compelling as the number of segments per second increases. If nasality spreads onto 2 or 3 other segments at normal speed, it is likely to spread farther at greater speed. One cannot, however, assume that coarticulatory effects will spread twice as far at twice the speed. This is because the articulatory gesture subject to spreading may itself be made more cursorily: lip-rounding, for example, may not extend over twice the number of segments, because the rounding itself is likely to be less; nasality may not extend twice as far, because the velum may not open as far when speech is being produced at higher speed.

11.12.2   Pauses

The title of this section is misleading. **Pauses**, in fact, do not occur very often in speech. We tend to think they are frequent because of orthographic conventions: the space between words on paper; the use of commas, periods, and other punctuation marks that suggest pauses. One place pauses do occur is when the speaker is inhaling.

What is far more common in speech than actual pauses are *prolongations* and *hesitation noises*. Very often what we perceive as a "pause" in speech turns out, upon acoustic examination, to be a prolongation of the preceding sound. That is, the final segment or segments of the word preceding the "pause" are stretched out, such that there is in fact no pause in the sense of a silent period. There is constant vocalization throughout the "pause."

Another way such "pauses" are filled is with hesitation noises, those sounds often written as "um" or "ah" or "er." These are very characteristic of a given language.

11.12.3   Rhythm

The *rhythm* of speech in fact means the rhythm of the syllables. In some languages, the rhythm of syllables is quite regular: each syllable takes approximately the same amount of time to say. In other languages, there is great variability in the duration of each syllable. In the latter case, the variability follows specific rule-governed patterns.

In English, rhythm is tied very closely to the *prominence* of individual syllables. In turn, the prominence of syllables is tied to the *stress* carried by each syllable and to the *emphasis* carried by each word. These two factors combine to create a pattern of strong (prominent) and weak (not prominent) syllables that is unique to each particular utterance spoken.

It is these strong syllables, and not the total number of syllables, that determine the rhythm and duration of an English utterance. For example, consider these sentences:

The *dog barked*.
The *bo*xer *pant*ed.

In each sentence, there are two prominent syllables: "dog" and "barked" in the first; "box-" and "pant-" in the second. The first sentence has 3 syllables, the second has 5: almost twice as many syllables. *But the length of time to say these sentences is very nearly the same*; the length of time between prominent syllables is very nearly constant; the length of time between syllables in general is *not* constant.

The word "boxer" takes more time to say than "dog" in isolation. But in the context of a sentence, the timing is determined not by the number of segments or the number of syllables, but by the *number of prominent syllables*. In this context, then, "dog" and "boxer" are approximately equal in length: "dog" is lengthened; the unstressed syllable of "box-" is much compressed.

Now consider these sentences:

The *dog barked*.
The *bo*xer *pant*ed.
The *dob*erman *pant*ed.

The last sentence now contains 6 syllables, twice as many as the first. Between "dob-" and "pant-" there are now two weak syllables. The last sentence may or may not be longer in duration than the first depending on speaking style, rate, register, and other factors.

In spoken English, the time from one strong syllable to the next strong one is close to being constant. We will call this the *tonic period* (see Sidebar 11.2). During that time period, there may be only the one strong syllable, or there may be the single strong one and 1, 2, or 3 weak syllables.

This type of rhythm, in which timing is essentially constant between prominent syllables, is called **stress-timed rhythm.** It is the rhythm of English and many other languages. It has a particularly uneven pattern, since there is a changing number of syllables between successive prominences.

Many other languages, of which French is a good example, have a type of rhythm based on the total number of syllables. Each syllable is given approximately equal time, so the overall length of a spoken sentence depends on the number of syllables in it. Such a system is called **syllable-timed rhythm.**

It is an oversimplification to say that there are just two types of rhythm patterns. Rather, there is a continuum along which languages fall. English is not a "pure" case of stress timing; a greater number of syllables between prominences will result in a slight increase in time. However, English leans heavily in the direction of stress timing.

If English is spoken with a syllable-timed rhythm, it will sound unnatural, stilted, perhaps pedantic. The learner of English whose native language is syllable-timed can be expected to carry over his native timing when learning English. For teaching purposes, a dramatic demonstration of the appropriate rhythm can be made by speaking in time to a metronome, or to knuckles pounded on the table. An unnatural rhythm is also to be expected in the speech of the profoundly hearing-impaired and in a number of speech disorders.

11.13   Tone

A language such as English, which uses the intonation patterns in the sentence to carry certain aspects of meaning, is often classed as an **intonation language**. By contrast, some languages – such as Chinese, many other Asian languages, many Amerindian languages, and many African languages – use the fundamental frequency (pitch) as a distinctive and inherent part of the *word*, not the sentence. Such languages may be referred to as **tone languages**. In fact, a 2-way distinction such as this is a simplification; for example, Lehiste (1970) makes a 4-way distinction. There are intermediate types, such as pitch accent (Section 11.14), whose tonal properties will be described later. For the purposes of this text, we will make the broad distinction between languages in which pitch functions at sentence level and languages in which pitch functions at word level.

Tone languages are neither exotic nor rare; between a third and a half of the languages of the world are tone languages. Many tone languages, such as Mandarin, have large numbers of speakers, so a large percentage of the world's population speaks tone languages.

The first point to recognize in understanding the principle of tone languages is that the physiological mechanism of adjusting the vocal fold tension and configuration to achieve pitch changes is in principle the same in a tone and in an intonation language. Both types of language use pitch changes to carry meaning. The difference lies in the level of the grammar at which the pitch changes operate. Tone occurs at the level of the word; intonation occurs at the level of the sentence. A comparison could be made with prominence: prominence at the word level is stress, prominence at the sentence level is emphasis. Stress and emphasis play different roles grammatically, but are similar physiologically and articulatorily.

In an intonation language such as English, pitch distinguishes "We're going" from "We're going?" by intonation (patterns of pitch changes).

In a tone language such as Chinese, pitch is not a part of the sentence; it is part of the word. In English, we do not expect "ban" and "pan" to be related in meaning just because there is some phonetic similarity between them. In Chinese, do not expect "ma∨" (falling tone) and "ma∕" (rising tone) to be related in meaning just because there is some phonetic similarity between them. To a speaker of Chinese, the words "ma∨" and "ma∕" sound as different as "pan" and "ban" do to you; they are unrelated words.

To illustrate tone, we will use the example of the Mandarin or Common Tongue dialect of Chinese. Imagine a scale of pitch running from 1 to 5, with 1 as the lowest pitch, 5 as the highest pitch, and 3 being the middle point, close to a person's natural fundamental frequency. The points 1 and 5 are the lowest and highest pitches normally used in speaking without emotion; they do not represent the extremes of a person's musical range. (Speakers of tone languages no more use their full range in normal speech than do speakers of intonation languages.) No absolute musical values can be assigned to these pitch levels, since the levels are relative. There are considerable individual differences in the absolute frequency and range of the voice.

A set of contrasting words is given in Table 11.2. The speed of the pitch change is given as well as the pitches themselves. For example, the two rising tones (tone 2 and tone 3) are different in speed of change, and it is likely that this feature is as important – or more important – in perception than the pitch level differences between tone 1 and tone 2.

Table 11.2 gives the tone patterns of Mandarin applied to the phoneme string /ma/. In a Chinese sentence, the situation is complicated by the fact there is a kind of sandhi between successive tones. The tone for the word *horse* would be different from that given in Table 11.2 in the context of a sentence such as "[The] horse runs." This is similar in principle to the accommodation and sandhi of segments in English that we examined in Chapter 10.

Table 11.2 Tones of the Common Tongue (Mandarin) dialect of Chinese

Tone number	Tone name	Pitch at start and end[a]	Quick or slow change	Example word[b]	English meaning
1	High level	++ → ++	N.A.	ma1	'mama'
2	Mid rising	0 → ++	Quick	ma⌐	'hemp'
3	Low rising	– → – – → + or ++	Slow	ma⌐	'horse'
4	Falling	++ → – –	Quick	ma⌐	'to scold'
–	Neutral	Depends on preceding tone	N.A.	ma	

[a] 0 is the talker's natural pitch. Pitch in 5 steps from lowest to highest: --, -, 0, +, ++.
[b] The tone symbols are explained in Sidebar 11.3.

11.13.1   Intonation in a one-word sentence contrasted with tone

In English, a one-word sentence has the intonation pattern of a longer sentence compressed into one word. So the sentence "No?" has a rising intonation, and the sentence "No!" has a falling intonation. What is the difference between this example and the Chinese word "ma" said with a rising and with a falling tone? There may in fact be no *phonetic* difference. However, there is an enormous difference grammatically. If you asked an English speaker whether "No!" and "No?" were the same word, he would answer that of course they are. The two have the same denotative or dictionary meaning, although the different intonation patterns give a slightly different interpretation to the utterance as a whole. On the other hand, if you asked a Chinese speaker whether "maˉ" and "maˊ" were the same word, he would answer that of course they are not. That would be like asking a speaker of English if there were any difference between "boss" and "bus" or between "tin" and "thin." A pair such as "maˉ" and "maˊ" has nothing common in meaning, unless by coincidence.

Mandarin Chinese has been given only as an example of the principle. Many tone languages exist; each has its own tone system. Few or many tones may be distinguished. There may be a combining of tone with other phonetic features, such as the speed of change noted in the Chinese example.

SIDEBAR 11.3 IPA tone symbols

In the IPA, the symbols for tone are as follows, from lowest tone to highest tone:

˩˨˧˦˥

The 4 Mandarin tones can be written as follows:

1. ma ˥
2. ma ˧˥
3. ma ˨˩˦
4. ma ˥˩

These tone symbols are normally written without spaces between; they are shown here with spaces for clarity. When combined, these symbols create tone contour markers, as shown in Table 11.2 and below:

ma˥
ma˧˥ = ma ˧˥
ma˨˩˦ = ma ˨˩˦
ma˥˩ = ma ˥˩

11.14 Pitch accent

There is a third category of languages in terms of the use of fundamental frequency or pitch to carry meaning. This is the category of languages having *pitch accent*. Some authorities class pitch accent as a type of tone, but most analyses show pitch accent to be a separate category from tone. Varieties of Swedish and Norwegian show a pitch accent phenomenon, as do a wide range of languages including Baltic languages, Basque, Turkish, and Farsi (Persian), among others.

In Swedish, there is a normal ("unmarked") pitch pattern on typical 2-syllable words. A small number of words have a different pitch pattern across the two syllables, typically combined with stress and durational differences. Words that are otherwise pronounced (and usually spelled) alike are distinguished in speech by the different patterns. Pairs such as *anden* ('the duck' with Tone 1, 'the spirit' with Tone 2) and *tanken* ('the tank' with Tone 1, and 'the thought' with Tone 2) exemplify the difference. The tone numbers are specific to Swedish and bear no relation to tone numbers in Mandarin; Tone 1 and Tone 2 are also called *acute* and *grave* accent.

The Swedish word *anden* is shown with Tone 1 and Tone 2 in Figure 11.3.

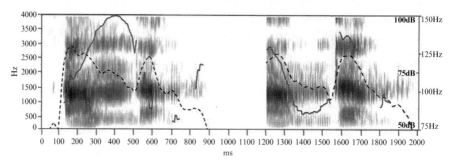

Figure 11.3 Spectrograms of the Swedish word *anden* with Swedish Tone 1 and Tone 2. In the spectrograms, lines can be seen that trace the pitch and intensity of the talker's voice through the pronunciation of the word. The solid line represents the pitch of the voice; the scale at the right runs from 75 Hz to 150 Hz. The broken line represents intensity; the scale at the right runs from 50 decibels (dB) to 100 dB.

It can be seen that in Tone 1, the pitch rises, whereas it falls in Tone 2. Similarly, the second syllable has low pitch in Tone 1, but high pitch in Tone 2.

The concept of a spectrogram is more fully explained in Section 12.8.

These acoustic analyses were performed on sound files found at https://learningswedish.se/courses/1/pages/2-dot-3-word-accent, with permission of the Swedish Institute (si.se).

11.15   Voice quality

Voice quality – the way in which the vocal folds vibrate – can be used to signal meaning distinctions. This topic was addressed in Chapter 8 where voice production was examined, and specifically in Sections 8.6, 8.6.2 ("*Breathy voice, murmur*"), and 8.6.3 ("*Creaky voice*"). It would be useful to review those sections before proceeding.

One of the objectives in the present chapter is to look at the role that suprasegmentals play in carrying information from talker to hearer. We saw in Chapter 8 that breathy voice (or murmur) and creaky voice are used to make phonological contrasts in a number of languages.

It is claimed that, in certain languages, individual segments are produced with murmur, and if this is the case then the term *suprasegmental* is not appropriate because the distinctive voice quality is restricted to a single segment. However, in strictly phonetic (as opposed to phonological) terms, murmur or creaky voice cannot be physically restricted to a single segment in connected, rapid speech. In other languages, voice quality is the property of a syllable or word; we will treat voice quality therefore as a suprasegmental.

Specific examples of voice quality distinctions were presented in Section 8.6, and will not be repeated here. In addition, particular voice qualities may be used to perform *paralinguistic* functions (see Section 1.8 regarding information sources in speech). These often are used to show group membership, and therefore serve a sociolinguistic role. For example, creaky voice appears to be increasingly frequent among young women in the United States and Britain (Yuasa, 2010).

11.16   Articulatory setting

It has often been observed that speakers of different languages seem to hold their speech-producing structures (jaw, lips, larynx) in different positions and with different degrees of tension, and that this can account for some of the difference in pronunciation among languages. This phenomenon has gone under the name **articulatory setting** (also called *articulatory set*), in the sense that each language (or major dialect) has its own characteristic way of holding the articulators: its *setting*. The term *articulatory set* has also been used in the same sense. The term **basis of articulation** has also been used, but Borissoff (2012) claims the two concepts are different, at least in the context of second-language pronunciation teaching. We will use the term **articulatory setting** throughout, without distinction.

Honikman (1964) sums up the issue as follows:

> By articulatory setting is meant the disposition of the parts of the speech mechanism and their composite action, i.e. the just placing of the individual parts, severally and jointly, for articulation according to the phonetic substance of the language concerned. To put this another way, it is the overall arrangement and manoeuvring of the speech organs necessary for the facile accomplishment of natural utterance. Broadly, it is the fundamental groundwork which pervades and, to an extent, determines the phonetic character and specific timbre of a language. It is [inherent] in all that the organs do.

The notion of articulatory setting is intuitively appealing, but it has been resistant to serious scientific investigation, given the many variables inherent in the position of articulators at any given moment; the difficulty of making empirical comparisons of muscle tension between individuals (or even within the same individual); the overall difficulty of measuring speech movements in an extremely fine-grained way while speech is ongoing; and the difficulty of determining whether differences in any measure between individuals is a matter of different articulatory setting or simply differences in anatomy between those individuals.

Wilson and Gick (2014) examined the question in an ingenious way by measuring lip, jaw, and tongue positions *between utterances*. Differences among individuals were controlled for by using fluently bilingual participants. Bilingual talkers' articulations were measured separately while speaking each of their languages.

There appears to be a sound scientific basis for the existence of articulatory setting. Clearly, it has implications for the teaching and learning of a second language, and perhaps for speech learning in profoundly hearing-impaired individuals.

11.16.1   Articulatory setting as a suprasegmental

Articulatory setting, when it is considered at all, is rarely if ever referred to as a suprasegmental. Generally, suprasegmentals are considered to be phonetic adjustments that an individual speaker of a given language can manipulate for the purpose of carrying meaning distinctions. Different syllables can be stressed; different intonation patterns can be applied to a sentence. Setting is unlike those other suprasegmentals in being something that is always and unvaryingly done by talkers.

However, if we look at suprasegmentals as phonetic phenomena that spread across more than a single segment – and that is what *supraseg-mental* fundamentally means – then articulatory setting is the ultimate suprasegmental. Given that using the correct setting is part of pronouncing in a way that other speakers of the same language and dialect would perceive as being "normal" or "natural," it is clear that setting is a fundamentally important element of phonetics.

11.17   Summary table

Type of phenomenon	Name	Affects pronunciation of ...	Affects meaning or interpretation of ...	Section	Comment
Prominence (with effect of juncture in phrasal stress)	Stress	syllable	word	11.4	*incite* or *insight*
	Phrasal stress	syllable (or word in short phrase)	phrase or compound word	11.7	*a white house* or *the White House*
	Emphasis	word	sentence or discourse	11.8	

Type of phenomenon	Name	Affects pronunciation of ...	Affects meaning or interpretation of ...	Section	Comment
Pitch of voice	Intonation	words, phrases, whole sentences, discourse	sentence or discourse	11.11	
	Tone	word or syllable	word	11.13	
	Pitch accent	syllable of word, possibly word	word	11.14	
Timing	Rate	phrases, sentences		11.12.1	approp-riate to language, dialect, register
	Pauses	phrases, sentences		11.12.2	
	Rhythm	phrases, sentences		11.12.3	
Voice quality		individual segment; adjoining segments; entire words or phrases; discourse	word, discourse, or shows group adherence	11.15	
Articulatory setting		everything spoken	does not affect meaning of linguistic units or discourse	11.16	Sounds "natural" in particular language or dialect

11.18   IPA symbols introduced in this chapter

Stress: ['] [ˌ] [ ](no symbol) for primary, secondary, weak stress.
Tone: ˩ ˨ ˧ ˦ ˥ for lowest to highest F_0; ˧ is natural F_0
Tone: contours shown by combining tone symbols. For example, ˩ ˥ = ǎ

11.19   Vocabulary

articulatory setting,
   articulatory set
basis of articulation
breathy voice
citation form

contrastive emphasis
contrastive stress
creaky voice
duration
emphasis

excursion

focus

fundamental frequency (F_0)

(garden path sentence)

hyperspeech

hypospeech

information, new, old

intonation

intonation contour

levels of stress

loudness

murmur

pause

phone

phrasal stress

pitch

pitch accent

primary

prominence

prosody

rate

reduced, reduced vowel

reduction

rhythm

secondary

segment

setting, set

speech prosody

stress

stress-timed

suprasegmental

syllable-timed

tertiary

timing

tone

tone language

tonic period (not a term in general
    use)

voice quality

vowel reduction

weak

weak form

12 Acoustics

12.1 Acoustics – sound

In this chapter, we will turn our attention to the physical aspects of the speech signal. The physical speech signal – the signal that passes from a talker's mouth to a hearer's ear – consists of **sound** or **acoustic energy**. Sound is a physical thing – a form of energy – and, like other physical things, it obeys the "laws" of physics. Sound has a particular form and manifests itself in characteristic physical ways. Given that sound is invisible, usually involves very tiny amounts of energy, and consists of tiny movements so fast that the eye could not see them even if sound were visible, we tend not to have much sense of what sound is and what it is like.

A basic understanding of the nature of sound will lead us to be able to address these three basic questions of interest in phonetics, and which have practical implications for disorders of speech and hearing, and for linguistic matters such as historical sound change in languages:

1. How (by what processes) are the articulatory positions and movements we have studied converted into the sounds of speech?
2. What are the parameters or characteristics of speech sounds? That is, acoustically, what is an /a/, a /p/, etc.; or what are the physical characteristics of those speech sounds?
3. How is speech perceived (a question that we will address in Chapter 13)?

These questions are relevant to an understanding of speech, since the very noises we make are defined by our physical form and by acoustic principles. Fantasy films often show giants, dwarves, animals, or grotesque aliens speaking ordinary English. The very premise breaks basic principles of acoustics, because if a talker had a mouth like that of – for example – a dog or a horse or a giant, the sounds produced *could not* be the same as those produced in the mouth of an average-sized normal human being. Even if a dog were smart enough to talk, it could not make the same kinds of noises you and I do when we talk because of the size and shape of its mouth; acoustic laws would not permit it.

We need to examine basic acoustics in order to proceed to the three questions posed above. Let us start by considering *sound*.

12.1.1   Sound

Sound energy causes the passage of a disturbance through the air (or through another medium such as water, or through the walls of your study room). Sound is energy, specifically *acoustic energy,* and it has the potential to do work[1] – it vibrates the tympanic membrane (eardrum) in the ear, and it can vibrate windows, for example. Sound must have a medium in which to travel; it does not pass through a vacuum. It advances by causing vibratory motion of the molecules of the medium through which it is advancing, which in turn pass the energy by vibrating the next molecules, and so on. Sound travels through the air at a rate of approximately 343 meters per second at sea level and considerably faster through denser materials such as water or steel (see Table 12.1).

Sound travels by a wave motion, in a pulsating or undulatory fashion. The analogy is often made that sounds travel in air as ripples do in a pond. This analogy is a useful one for introducing the behavior of waves, since we have all encountered water waves. There are some important differences between surface waves on the water and sound waves in the air, but these differences will be considered after we have examined some points of commonality.

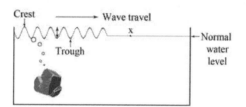

Figure 12.1 A surface wave on water

12.2   Wave motion

If we throw a pebble into a still pond, we see that a series of ripples fans out in all directions from the source of the disturbance. These ripples or waves move onward, while individual water molecules return to their original location after the wave has passed. Let us look at how this works.

In Figure 12.1, a stone has just been thrown into a body of water, and ripples are beginning to move away from the source of the disturbance. Individual molecules of water move up and down as a result of the disturbance. The high points are called **crests**; the low points, **troughs**. Let

---

[1] In physics, *work* is something that occurs when a force acting on a thing causes displacement or movement. When sound moves your TM (eardrum) back and forth, work is being performed.

us look at one particular drop of water on the surface, say the point x in Figure 12.1. It may help to visualize a small object floating on the surface of the water and "riding" the waves. What happens to this object as the wave approaches? As the crest approaches, it rides up to its highest point. As the crest passes, it rides *down* to its original position, and it continues riding down to a low point in the trough of the wave. As the next crest approaches, it rides up past its starting position and back to the peak of the next crest. This continues as long as there are waves passing the spot. Note that this individual drop of water has ridden up and down, up and down, but has *moved forward or backward only by very small amounts or not at all*. The same drop of water is part of each successive wave that passes.

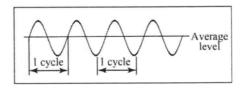

Figure 12.2 The cycle of a wave

It is essential to recognize the fact that, while the wave moves continuously forward, the individual particles of the material through which it travels (in this case, water) do *not* move a great distance; they just oscillate around one average, or rest, position.[2]

12.3 Dimensions of waves

Since waves can vary in a number of ways, it is useful to have a vocabulary to describe their dimensions. First, a term is needed to indicate one single unit of a wave. One **cycle** refers to one complete wave – that is, one complete crest and trough. One cycle can be measured from crest to crest, but it is more usual to indicate one cycle as starting at the baseline, rising above it, falling below it, and rising back up to it again (as marked in the leftmost cycle in Figure 12.2). The word **cycle** does not indicate any measurement; it simply means one complete wave. But the word *cycle* implies something

---

[2] This is a small oversimplification. A molecule of water on the surface (or our small floating object) may move in a somewhat circular pattern, rather than strictly straight up and down. However, it does return to its approximate starting point. The central point here is to understand that the *energy* (the water wave or sound wave) progresses in one direction, while the individual molecules of water or air oscillate but return to their starting point. Energy goes from one place to another, but molecules of the medium stay roughly where they are.

SIDEBAR 12.1 Propagation

Sound, or more specifically sound energy, moves from one place to another through the air. (It can pass through other materials – other media – as well.) The professor talks at the front of the room and you hear them from your seat. It is essential to understand that no *thing* has moved across the room – rather, it is the sound itself, the energy, that has moved.

The manner by which sound energy moves through a medium such as air is called *propagation*: sound *propagates* through the air or through water.

This term emphasizes that the energy is transferred from molecule to molecule, and that every molecule of air along the route interacts with the energy.

Imagine a bucket brigade: a line of people passing buckets of water from one end of the line where the buckets are filled to the other end of the line where someone throws the water onto a fire. *Every person along the line has interacted with each bucket as it passes.* (Of course, a bucket of water is a physical thing, not simply energy, and so the analogy isn't perfect; in sound, it is only energy that passes down the "bucket brigade.")

This is very different from a situation where the buckets of water are loaded into a cannon and fired through the air from the filling station to the fire. In that case, the buckets have *moved* from one

repetitive, and indeed we start our exploration of sound waves with the idea that one cycle will be followed by another that is just like it.

Waves can vary both in their physical dimensions (their size and forcefulness) and in their temporal dimensions (their timing).

12.3.1 Physical dimensions of waves

Waves have physical size. They can be bigger or smaller, longer or shorter. Special terms are used for these dimensions.

One physical dimension of waves is how high the crests are and how deep the troughs are. (This is related to the amount of energy that is behind the wave, what we called *forcefulness* above.) It is called the **amplitude**. The greater the amplitude, the more energy there is, and the higher the crests – and deeper the troughs – of the waves will be.

The second physical dimension is the physical length of one cycle: how far is it from one crest to the next? This dimension is called the **wavelength**, descriptively enough. It can be measured in any unit of length: centimeters, meters, feet, etc. (metric units are most commonly used, as in other scientific domains). Figure 12.3 illustrates amplitude and wavelength.

12.3.2 Temporal dimensions of waves

If we were to decide on a particular constant period of time, say 1 minute, and count the number of cycles (that is, the number of complete waves) that occurred during that period of time, we would have a measure of *how often* or *how frequently* the wave cycle repeats itself. This measure is descriptively called the **frequency** of a wave. The 1-minute time period would probably be useful for counting waves on the ocean, but in dealing with sound, the time period of 1 second is most appropriate. Thus, the standard unit of frequency used to be **cycles per second (cps)**, or the number of complete wave cycles that occur each second. The term *cycles per second* has been replaced by the SI[3] term *hertz (Hz)*, and we shall use the term hertz from here on. So 10 Hz is the same as 10 cps; only the *name* of the unit has been changed, not its meaning,[4] which is that 10 complete cycles are completed in 1 second.

place to the other. By contrast, in the bucket brigade, the buckets have been "propagated" from one end to the other.

Sound energy propagates through a medium, being passed from molecule to molecule. It isn't "shot" from one place to another. Technically, sound does not *move* from one place to another; it *propagates*.

Nonetheless, we may use the words *move*, *advance*, and so on in an informal way, as long as we remember that those words are shorthand for *propagate*.

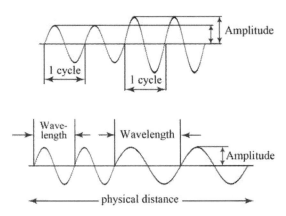

Figure 12.3 Amplitude and wavelength. A. Same wavelength, different amplitudes. Amplitude is a measure of energy and is shown graphically by the displacement from the baseline. B. Same amplitude, different wavelengths. The wavelength is the physical length of one cycle in the air (or other medium) measured in ordinary units of length.

The *period* is the other temporal dimension of waves. As we have seen, *frequency* answers the question, *How many cycles occur in one second? Period* answers the complementary question, *How long does it take to complete one cycle?* There is an inverse relationship between the frequency

---

[3] SI: *Système international* – what is usually called "the metric system" in English.
[4] If you find concepts such as these difficult, it might help to remind yourself each time you see *Hz* or *hertz* that it means simply *cycles per second*.

SIDEBAR 12.2 Frequency

Sometimes we make terms and concepts more difficult for ourselves than they should be. While *frequency* is a technical term, it means the same as its use in ordinary language. What is the frequency of your birthday? *Once a year*. What is the frequency of Sundays? *Once every 7 days*. The answer is always: (a) a certain number of times, in (b) a certain period of time.

The same is true of sound frequency. It answers the question: (a) *how many times does it happen* in (b) *a certain period of time*. The term hertz (Hz) says that the time period is 1 second. So, 300 Hz says that there are 300 cycles in 1 second; 4500 Hz says there are 4,500 cycles in 1 second.

and the period: the more cycles there are per second, the shorter time each cycle must take. Mathematically, one can state the relationship between the two measures as a reciprocal. For example, what is the period in a measured frequency of 10 cycles per second? If there are 10 cycles in 1 second, then each cycle must take one-tenth of a second (0.1 sec). If the frequency is 200 Hz, the period will be 0.005 second (1/200), and so on.

12.3.3 Velocity of waves

The *speed*[5] *of propagation* of a wave refers to the speed at which it **propagates** (advances) through a medium. In the case of ripples on a pond, this speed is visible and easily measurable. A stopwatch will measure the time it takes for the wavefront to cross the pond. Knowing the distance across the pond allows us to calculate the speed. In the case of sound in air, the speed of propagation is approximately 343 meters per second.

The speed of propagation is not related to frequency. This fact is important in any discussion of sound, since high-frequency (high-pitched) sounds travel at the same velocity as low-frequency (low-pitched) sounds. See Table 12.1.

12.3.4 Dimensions of waves – summary

In summary, we have introduced two *physical dimensions* of waves:

- the *amplitude*, and
- the *wavelength*;

and three *temporal* ones:

- the *frequency*
- the *speed of propagation*, and
- the *period*.

---

[5] Technically, there is a difference between *speed* and *velocity*, and it is the latter that is being discussed. However, the standard term is *speed of propagation*, so we will use *speed* throughout this discussion.

Table 12.1 Speed of propagation of sound in air at sea level

A. Speed of propagation changes with temperature. B. Time to propagate 1 km and 1 mile		
A.	Speed of propagation of sound in air at two temperatures	
	Temperature / Units of velocity	0 °C (32 °F)	20 °C (68 °F)
	Meters per second	331.2	343.0
	Kilometers per hour	1192.0	1235.0
	Feet per second	1087.0	1125.0
	Miles per hour	741.0	767.0
B.	How long does it take for sound to propagate these distances at 20 °C (68 °F)?	
	1 kilometer	1 mile
	2.91 seconds	4.69 seconds

One complete wave is a **cycle**.

The rest of this chapter will build on these basic concepts.

12.4 Periodicity

Every statement made so far has implied a wave with a rhythmical type of motion, in which each cycle is exactly like the preceding and following cycle. Such a wave motion is called **periodic**, like the wave shown in Figure 12.4A.

Most types of naturally occurring sound waves are not perfectly periodic; each cycle is unlike the others. Such a wave is termed *aperiodic*[6] (or **nonperiodic**), since it has no regular period. See Figure 12.4B. While some acoustic components of speech are very close to being periodic, many are entirely aperiodic.

In an aperiodic wave, the cycles are not occurring at regular intervals, so one cannot speak of the *frequency* of such a wave motion, and while it might be possible to measure the *wavelength* or *period* of a single cycle, these terms are usually reserved for periodic waves.

While it is true that the terms *frequency* and *period* are not appropriate to describe aperiodic waves, since each cycle is different, it may be that *most* of the cycles in a given aperiodic wave have periods that fall into a

[6] The prefix *a-* (or *an-* before vowels) means 'not' or 'without.'

particular range. As periods correspond to frequencies, and since it is usual to specify sound waves in terms of frequencies, such an aperiodic wave might be said to cover a certain frequency range – say, 4000 to 8000 Hz (or 4 to 8 kilohertz [kHz]). That means that this particular sound wave contains irregular cycles, but that most or all of those cycles have periods corresponding to frequencies between 4 and 8 kHz. We shall see that this is important in describing the acoustic character of fricatives: [s] and [ʃ] are both composed of aperiodic waves. However, if the individual cycles were entirely random, then the two would sound alike. But, of course, they sound different, and that is because they contain different *ranges* of frequencies.

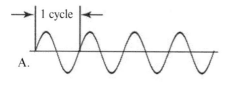

Figure 12.4 A. A periodic wave. Every cycle has the same shape and period – though not necessarily the same amplitude. B. An aperiodic wave. Every cycle has a different period, and typically in aperiodic waves the amplitude and shape of every cycle is different as well.

12.5   Wave motion of sound

We introduced the notion of wave motion through the analogy of waves on water, since they are visible and within everyone's experience. The various terms used to describe waves, such as *wavelength*, *period*, and *speed of propagation*, can be used for both types of waves. However, if we wish to understand the wave motion of sound in air, we must realize that the water wave analogy has its limitations; there are some important differences between the two kinds of waves.

The first difference between the two kinds of waves results from the differences in the media through which they travel. Air is a gas and, like all gases, it completely fills the space that contains it, distributing itself equally throughout, as we saw in Chapter 4. Air can be compressed and rarefied. Water, on the other hand, is a liquid. It will take up the same space whether it is placed in a large container or a small one, and it cannot be compressed.[7]

---

[7] In this section, we are emphasizing the difference between a sound wave and a water surface wave. However, sound can also propagate through water – the sound initiates underwater and propagates through the water to other locations. Similarly, sound can propagate through many solid or liquid mediums, and through other gases besides air. But *sound propagating through water is a sound wave. It is not a water wave* of the type addressed in Section 12.2.

The second way in which sound is different from ripples on a pond is that waves on the water are **surface** waves; they result from a rise and fall in the surface of the water. Sound waves in the air, by contrast, are actually *within* the medium. Sound does not travel along the surface of the air; it propagates *through* the air. (There is no surface of the atmosphere like the surface of a lake; the higher one goes, the thinner the atmosphere. There is no clear dividing line marking the "surface" of atmosphere.)

We can imagine some aspects of sound waves by considering the behavior of the toy called a Slinky. Imagine a long Slinky lying on the top of a table, stretched and held at both ends. If one end is quickly pushed and pulled back to its original position, the shock so generated will travel the length of the Slinky. In fact, if the far end is securely held, the shock may bounce off and travel back to the starting point.[8] The way that the shock travels the length of the Slinky is very much like the way sound travels through the air. Notice that no part of the Slinky moves up and down like the surface of the water.

This brings us to the third difference: in the surface waves on the water, the surface of the water is moving up and down, while the wave front is moving horizontally. These two directions are at right angles to one another. In the Slinky, each individual spot oscillates back and forth about its resting place. This back-and-forth movement is along the same line as the movement of the wave. In this respect, the motion of the Slinky is like that of air molecules disturbed by the passage of sound. Each molecule of air is displaced back and forth on the path the sound travels (see Figure 12.5).

12.5.1   Graphing wave motion

What is happening at a particular point in space that is being bombarded by sound? There is a rise and fall in air pressure as a result of the passage of the disturbance. Suppose some disturbance originates a sound wave. This disturbance compresses nearby air molecules, or forces them more tightly together, creating a place of higher-than-average air pressure. Being elastic, the group of molecules springs back to its normal spacing. This springing brings the air pressure back to normal, but the molecules, in springing apart, continue past their starting point and end up farther apart than they began. This results in a lower-than-normal air pressure. They return to normal spacing, and therefore normal pressure, after the passage of the disturbance. Also, in springing apart so far, the group of molecules disturbs the next group of molecules, compressing them in turn. By this means, the disturbance is passed from molecule to molecule (Figure 12.6). The nature of sound at any one place is

---

[8] This *frequency* demonstration works best on a very slippery surface.

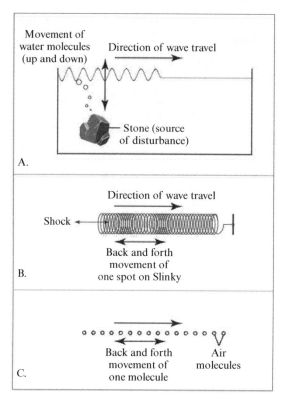

Figure 12.5 Wave motion on water, in a Slinky, and through the air. In each case the wave propagates (travels) in a single direction (although it may reflect back later), whereas a particular molecule or a particular spot moves back and forth around a single place. A. Waves on water, showing that the wave travel is perpendicular to the direction of travel of water molecules. B. A shock wave traveling through a Slinky, showing that wave travel is parallel to the direction of travel of a spot on the Slinky. C. As a sound wave passes through the air, each molecule of air moves back and forth along the same path that the wave travels.

an alternate rise and fall in air pressure. In other words, there is an alternate *compression* and *rarefaction*[9] of the air molecules.

Figure 12.7 shows two periodic sound waves, graphed above a representation of the compression and rarefaction of air molecules. Each undulating wave tracing looks like the earlier diagram of a water wave, but there is an important difference. In the water wave, the rise and fall of the tracing in the graph represented a rise and fall in the surface of the water. In Figure 12.7, the rise and fall of the tracing does *not* represent an up-and-down motion of air particles. Rather, it represents a rise and fall in air *pressure*. (You could say that Figure 12.7 is a *graph*; it is not a *picture*. It conveys scientific data, not an image.)

---

[9] *Compression* is the squeezing together of the air molecules so they are closer together, and *rarefaction* is the spreading apart of the air molecules so they are farther apart. The corresponding verbs are *to compress* and *to rarefy*.

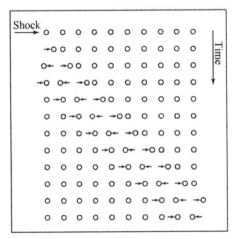

Figure 12.6 Passage of a single cycle of a wave through the air. The circles represent individual air molecules. Each successive row down is a moment later in time. The oscillation of individual air molecules is passed from molecule to molecule. By this means, the single cycle moves along the row, but each individual molecule returns to its original place. If there were a continuous sound rather than a single cycle, the cycle would repeat itself many times per second.

Below the undulating tracing of the wave in each part of Figure 12.7 is a drawing that represents the disturbance created by a continuous wave emitted from a loudspeaker. The vertical lines represent molecular proximity: where the lines are close together, the molecules they represent are close together (i.e., the air is compressed). Notice that the undulating wave is *above* the baseline at the point corresponding to the compression, such as at point *p*. Where the vertical lines are farther apart, the molecules they represent are far apart (i.e., the air is rarefied; pressure is low). This corresponds to the part of the undulating graph *below* the baseline, such as at point *q*.

The undulating graph line in parts A and B of Figure 12.7 is the standard way that a sound wave is represented graphically. But notice that the *x*-axis or baseline in part A is labeled "time" whereas in part B the *x*-axis is labeled "distance." The two look identical but the labeling of the *x*-axis indicates that something very different is represented by the graph line in each part. Much confusion results from a failure to recognize that, while similar visually, the two are different conceptually.

Part A shows air pressure varying over time at one place. Imagine that a microphone (a device sensitive to minute changes in air pressure) were placed near a sound source (the loudspeaker shown below the graph) – *at the point x*, let us say. As the sound wave propagates (travels) through the air past point *x*, the pressure at that point will rise, then fall, then rise, then fall, etc. That is what is graphed: the rise and fall of pressure over time, at

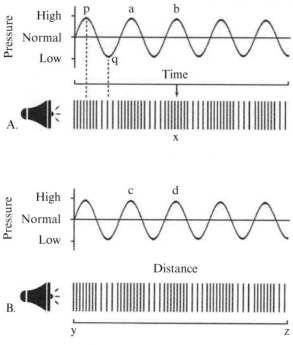

Figure 12.7 **Variations in air pressure** (A and B, upper part) **and molecular displacement** (A and B, lower part) in a sound wave. In both A and B, the graph lines are pressure tracings and the vertical lines beneath represent molecular proximity (see text for a detailed description). A. Air pressure is monitored from the vantage point *x*, a fixed distance away from the sound source. As time passes, the amount of pressure at point *x* is plotted, forming a tracing that shows the variation of pressure over time. Points *a* to *b* indicate the period of the wave. B. Air pressure is measured at different distances away from the sound source. The pressure at all points from *y* to *z* is measured at the same time. The graph shows the changes in air pressure corresponding to the molecular compression and rarefaction depicted beneath. Points *c* to *d* indicate the wavelength of the wave.

one point in space. This would be akin to watching a highway through a tiny observation slit that permitted you to see only a few feet of the road. All you could do is to report whether or not you could see a car at that moment: "Now I see a car, now there is no car, now I see a car," etc. You could even make a graph of your sightings of cars as a function of time, a graph in the style of part A.

What part B shows is very different. Here the point of time is fixed, and the change of pressure is measured at different distances from the sound source. Imagine again that the loudspeaker is producing a continuous sound and, further, that we had some sort of special camera that could take a picture of the density of air (that is, how close together the molecules are). If we took a picture with this camera, we would obtain a photograph like the lower part of Figure 12.7, showing the molecules closer together and farther apart as a function of their distance from the loudspeaker. This imaginary photograph shows different points at the same moment. This would be like an ordinary snapshot of a section of highway; it would show cars at *different places* at the *same moment* (the moment the photograph was taken).

Another way to consider the difference between the concepts shown in parts A and B is to ask yourself what one cycle represents on each graph. In part A, since the x-axis is marked in *time*, one cycle (e.g., from point *a* to point *b*) represents the *time* of a cycle, namely the **period**. In part B, since the baseline is marked in *distance*, one cycle (e.g., from point *c* to point *d*) represents the *distance* of a cycle, namely the **wavelength**.

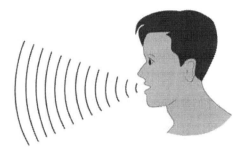

Figure 12.8 Sound waves moving away from a point source. The solid lines represent high pressure, or crests; the midpoints of the spaces between the lines represent points of low pressure, or troughs. Of course, the sound is radiating three-dimensionally, not in one general direction only.

Be sure, whenever you look at a graph of a sound wave, to check what units the *x*-axis is marked in, and thus to understand what the graph is showing.

While surface waves on water are different from sound waves in important ways that have been explained in this section, *sound* propagates through water by essentially the same process as it propagates in air, although at a faster speed.[10]

The movement of sound waves in air is three-dimensional – that is, sound radiates in all directions from a source. This is indicated in Figure 12.8, in which the solid lines represent points of high pressure and the spaces between the lines represent points of low pressure.

---

[10] We noted above that water cannot be compressed the way that air can be. If water were absolutely incompressible, then sound could not propagate in water "by essentially the same process as it propagates in air" because propagation in air depends on the compressibility of air. The solution to this puzzle is that, while water cannot be compressed "the way that air can be," it can be compressed to a very tiny degree. That tiny amount of compressibility is sufficient for sound to propagate through water, and to do so more efficiently and more rapidly than through the air.

12.6   Perceptual dimensions of sound waves

We will see in this section how the various dimensions of sound correspond to what we hear.

12.6.1   Periodic and aperiodic waves

A periodic wave will be perceived as having a tonal quality, as does a single note from a musical instrument. An aperiodic sound will be perceived as being "noisy," like a hiss. A prolonged vowel sound, such as [ɑːːː], is predominantly periodic or *quasiperiodic* (i.e., close to periodic); a voiceless fricative consonant sound such as [s] or [ʃ] is aperiodic.

SIDEBAR 12.3 Frequency range of the human ear

The range of human hearing is often said to be 20 to 20,000 Hz, or 20 Hz to 20 kHz. This range is often cited as a hard and fast fact. At the bottom end of the range, there can be variability among individuals of ±2 Hz (i.e. 18 to 22 Hz as the lower end of the range). At the upper end, few middle-aged adults can hear as high as 20 kHz, and even many children cannot. Of course, a small number of individuals may hear higher than 20 kHz, but, in practical terms, citing the upper limit as 20 kHz is convenient but often too optimistic.

12.6.2   Frequency

The frequency of sounds that we hear is much greater than that of waves on the water. A very good, young human ear can hear sounds between a low of 20 Hz and a high of 16,000 to 18,000 Hz (abbreviated 16 to 18 kHz, where *k* stands for *kilo*, meaning 'thousand'). See Sidebar 12.3. Sounds whose frequency is below 20 Hz may be felt as vibration or heard as a series of individual pulses, and sounds whose frequency is above 18 kHz may not be perceived at all, although many animals (e.g., dogs and bats) can hear sounds of higher frequencies than humans can. It is a universal fact that age reduces our range of hearing, as well as our acuity throughout the range that we do have.

Sounds of a high frequency are perceived as being high-pitched; low-frequency sounds are low-pitched. To get an idea of what particular frequencies sound like, consider the following examples: you can sometimes hear a hum from old fashioned audio systems that are plugged into a power outlet (this is *not* true of battery-powered devices). This hum can be made more audible if the volume is turned up without playing any other sound. The frequency of this sound is 60 Hz, because the amplifier operates from 60-cycle alternating current in North America.[11] Middle C on the musical

---

[11] 50 Hz in much of the rest of the world.

scale, also called C_4, is 256 Hz. The octave scale in music is based on a doubling of frequency: C above middle C (C_5) is 512 Hz, C above that C (C_6) is 1024 Hz, and so on.

12.6.3 Amplitude

The amplitude of sound waves corresponds to the amount of compression and rarefaction that occurs. A bigger original disturbance will cause air molecules to be displaced farther; this causes a greater rise and fall in air pressure. In turn, this causes the eardrums to move a greater distance back and forth. Greater amplitude corresponds to a greater amount of energy in the signal. Greater amplitude is perceived as increased loudness.

Our ears respond to a remarkable variation in amplitude. The minimum amplitude that can be perceived corresponds to the slight pressure needed to displace the eardrums by about the diameter of a hydrogen molecule. The maximum sound amplitude that can be endured without pain corresponds to a sound pressure between *1 million and 10 million times* as great as the minimum amplitude that can be perceived. The range of amplitudes available in a signal is known as its **dynamic range**. The dynamic range of the ear is enormous, much greater than that of the best audio system.

12.6.4 Psychological dimensions of sound

We have noted that a change in frequency corresponds to a change in pitch and that a change in amplitude corresponds to a change in loudness.

Frequency and *amplitude* are concrete, physical dimensions of sound that can be measured accurately and reliably with instruments. On the other hand, *pitch* and *loudness* refer to perceptual or psychological dimensions that can be measured only through subjective reports. That is, pitch can be measured only by asking people what pitch they hear, often in relation to a reference tone. These perceptual dimensions are not as reliably measured as the corresponding physical dimensions, because of the variability of the human machine, extraneous factors such as fatigue, and the interaction between the two dimensions. For example, a certain amplitude may sound loud if its frequency is 1500 Hz, but that same amplitude will seem soft if its frequency is 150 Hz. The ear is simply less sensitive at this lower frequency.

In everyday speech, we use the term *volume* to mean the same as *loudness*. Technically, however, psychoacousticians use the term **volume** to refer to the extent to which a sound is perceived to *fill* a given space; this is different from how *loud* the sound is.

12.6.5   Phase

Imagine two sound waves that are identical in all ways except that their peaks and troughs do not line up, as shown in Figure 12.9B. The difference between these two cannot be described using any of the terms we have met so far. The two waves in Figure 12.9B–D are said to be **out of phase**, whereas the two waves in Figure 12.9A are said to be **in phase**.

The extent to which two waves are out of phase is measured in **degrees**. There are 360 degrees in a circle – and in a cycle – so one quarter of that is 90 degrees, one half is 180 degrees, and so on. Notice how this applies to sound waves in Figure 12.9A–E. In Figure 12.9E, we see two waves whose starting points are 360 degrees out of phase; however, if we consider a point somewhere in the middle of the figure, rather than at the right or left end, we could not tell whether the waves were *in phase* or *360 degrees out of phase*.

12.6.6   Wavelength (λ)

The *wavelength* is the physical length of a single cycle of a wave. It is abbreviated with the Greek letter lambda, λ.[12] Wavelengths for sounds can easily be calculated if we know the speed at which sound propagates and the particular frequency involved. The speed of sound through air is about 340 meters per second at sea level and normal barometric pressure (barometric pressure will affect the speed of sound slightly). Using the values shown in Table 12.1, above, the speed of propagation in 20 °C air is 343 m/s; in 0° C air, it is 331.2 m/s. Wavelengths of several frequencies are shown in Table 12.2.

Table 12.2 Wavelengths in air of some example frequencies

	Frequency	Wavelength (λ) in meters	Wavelength (λ) in feet	Comment
20 °C 68 °F	Middle C (C₄) 256 Hz	1.34 m	4.40 feet	Middle C
	C₅ 512 Hz	0.670 m	2.20 feet	C above middle C
	18 kHz	0.0191 m (1.91 cm)	¾ inch	Highest frequency humans can hear (see Sidebar 12.3)
	20 Hz	17.2 m	56.3 feet	Lowest frequency humans can hear
0 °C 32 °F	20 Hz	16.6 m	54.3 feet	Lowest frequency humans can hear

[12] Lambda is the Greek form of the letter L. So if you think of λ as an L, it makes sense: L stands for *length*.

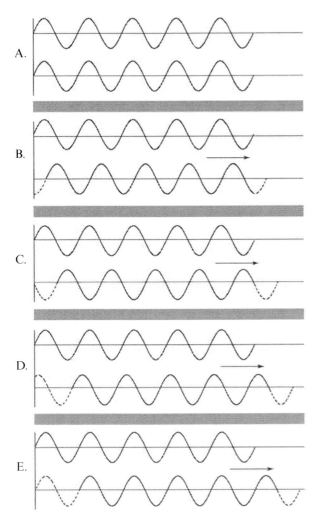

Figure 12.9 Phase. The cycle is considered as if it were a circle of 360 degrees. A. Two waves are in phase. B. The lower wave has moved to the right a quarter-cycle; the two are 90 degrees out of phase. C. The lower wave has moved to the right another quarter-cycle, so that it is now a half-cycle, or 180 degrees, out of phase. D. Another quarter-cycle means that the two waves are 270 degrees out of phase (or 90 degrees out of phase, if considered from the opposite end). E. Another quarter-cycle means one full cycle or 360 degrees out of phase. Since in a periodic wave each cycle is identical, this is really the same as being in phase or 0 degrees out of phase.

The wavelengths in air for a number of example frequencies are shown in Table 12.2. Sidebar 12.4 shows how to make these calculations.

The lowest pitch human beings can hear – 20 Hz – corresponds to the longest wavelength in the examples, 17.2 meters (about 56 feet). The shortest wavelength corresponding to a sound a young human ear can hear – 18,000 Hz[13] – is 0.0191 meters (1.91 cm or about ¾ inch). The wavelength of middle C is 1.34 meters (4.4 feet).

---

[13] For further explanation, see Sidebar 12.4.

Wavelength is dependent upon the speed of propagation of the sound. Compare the two rows in the table for 20 Hz: the wavelength is 0.6 meters, or 60 cm ($\approx$ 2 feet), longer in warmer than in colder air. As another example, sound travels through a steel bar at about 16 times faster than it travels through air; therefore, the wavelengths in steel would be about 16 times longer than they would in air for the same frequency.

SIDEBAR 12.4 Calculating wavelengths

The wavelength of a sound of a given frequency is easy to calculate. Let us take a frequency of 20 Hz as an example. 20 Hz means 20 cycles per second or:

$$\frac{20\ cycles}{1\ second}$$

20 cycles per second can also be seen in the reciprocal: for each 1 second, there will be 20 cycles, or:

$$\frac{1\ second}{20\ cycles}$$

If this latter value is multiplied by the speed of propagation, it can be seen that the seconds cancel out, resulting in a simple division:

$$\frac{1\ \cancel{second}}{20\ cycles} \times \frac{343\ meters}{1\ \cancel{second}}$$

$$= \frac{343\ meters}{20\ cycles}$$

$$= 17.15\ meters$$

Technically, this last value is 17.15 meters per cycle, but "per cycle" is implied, it is not stated.

In this calculation, it is important to keep the time unit constant: seconds in all cases.

12.6.7   Wavelength and phase in localization of sound

It is apparent that, for certain frequency ranges, human beings make use of wavelength in *localizing* sound (that is, in determining from which direction a sound originates); since our ears are a given distance apart, we can perceive whether or not the waves reaching our two ears are in the same phase of their cycle. This mechanism works for a certain range of frequencies: when the wavelength is very long or very short (long or short compared to the width of the head), it is not possible to compare the phase of the wave at the two ears. If you are outdoors and a dog barks, you likely find it easy to turn immediately in the direction of the dog without thinking. But if we hear a bird chirp, we are often left without any idea in which direction to look for the bird because the frequencies in the bird chirp are much higher than the dog bark, and therefore the wavelengths are much shorter.

One of the greatest problems for individuals suffering from a unilateral (one-sided) hearing loss is difficulty in localizing.[14] Fortunately, phase is not the only cue for localizing, so such individuals retain some localizing ability.

---

[14] The focus of this section is localization, but it needs to be said that unilateral hearing loss in school-age and younger children can result in deficits or delays in language acquisition and learning in general. Audiological intervention is essential for such children, for reasons far more important than localization.

12.7   Harmonics

If a sound source is producing a periodic tone of a given frequency, there normally are additional frequencies present that are whole-number multiples of the basic or **fundamental frequency.** Physicists and speech scientists call these additional frequencies *harmonics,* but if you have musical training they may be familiar to you under the name **overtones.**

For example, a fundamental frequency of 100 Hz will typically have harmonics of 200, 300, 400, 500, 600, 700 Hz, and so on. A fundamental frequency of 175 Hz will have harmonics of 350, 525, 700, 875, 1050 Hz, and so on. These are called the *second, third, fourth, fifth* harmonic, and so on. There is no first harmonic; the second harmonic is twice the fundamental, the third harmonic three times the fundamental, and so on.[15]

Because of harmonics, one rarely hears a pure tone; mostly, we hear combinations of tones: the fundamental plus a number of harmonics of different amplitudes. For example, when you hear a note – say, middle C – played on different musical instruments, this "same" note sounds different. In fact, the 256-Hz fundamental will be the same on all these different instruments, but the number of harmonics, and the relative amplitude of each, will be different, accounting for the different sound quality of the same note on each different instrument.

The source of harmonics can be found in the nature of the vibrating object that generates the sound. If that object is rigid, and vibrates as a whole, few or no harmonics will be generated. But if the object is supple (flexible), undulating as it vibrates, it will generate many harmonics. The analogy is often made of a rope. Imagine a rope attached to the wall at one end and held in your hand at the other. Now vibrate the rope up and down – once per second, let us say, in order to have a round number. The *whole* rope will be oscillating at 1 Hz, its fundamental frequency. But each *half* of the rope, if considered on its own or viewed with high-speed photography, is vibrating at 2 Hz, the second harmonic. If you consider the thirds of the rope, each is vibrating at triple the fundamental; the quarters are vibrating at four times the fundamental, and so on. These different frequencies – or *modes of vibration* as they are called – are possible because the rope is flexible.

A "pure" frequency can be created with a tone generator (often a simple app for a tablet or computer). Such a "pure" tone will, by contrast, have almost no harmonics. A "pure" tone is a sound that "feels" very unmusical – even if it represents a precise musical note – owing to its pure (nonharmonic) nature.

---

[15] Some physicists and musical experts use a different numbering system in which what we are calling the *second harmonic* is called the *first harmonic.* Technically, this is more logical and more correct, because the fundamental frequency is not truly a harmonic. However, this more logical system is also more confusing, since the *second* harmonic is then *three* times the fundamental, and so on.

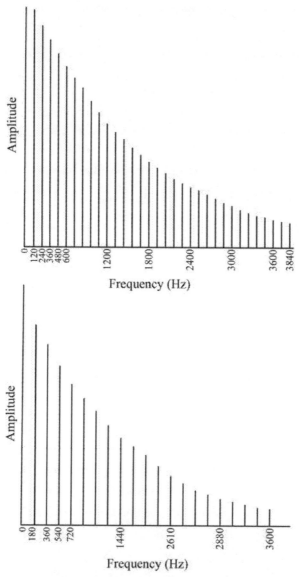

Figure 12.10 Spectra of the glottal source of the voice. Frequency is shown on the *x* axis, amplitude on the *y* axis. A. The graph shows no energy between 0 and 119 Hz, then a lot of energy at 120 Hz, then nothing from 121 to 239 Hz, then a lot of energy at 240 Hz, etc. The F_0 is 120 Hz, a typical adult male F_0. B. The F_0 is 180 Hz, and represents an adult female F_0. Note that there are a larger number of spectral peaks in a voice having a lower F_0.

12.7.1 Harmonics in the voice

We noted in Chapter 8 that vocal fold vibration is not just vibratory (back and forth) but undulatory (wavy) as well. There is an undulatory movement of the vocal folds in the posterior–anterior direction, and in the up–down dimension as well. The undulatory motion means that the vocal fold vibration is much like the motion of the rope in our earlier analogy – but in both horizontal and vertical directions – and, as a consequence, vocal fold vibration is particularly rich in harmonics.

Most adults have fundamental frequencies somewhere in the range between a low of 100 Hz and a high of 300 Hz. But most of us produce audible harmonics up to 4,000 or 5000 Hz, or even beyond. Voices that we perceive as being "rich" or "resonant" have strong harmonics; voices we perceive as "weak" or "thin" or "brittle" are poorer in harmonics. (Falsetto tends to be quite poor in harmonics.) Figure 12.10 shows spectra of the sound produced by the vocal folds of a couple of typical adults: one male, one female.

There are several points to note in Figure 12.10. First, the graph shows what is called the *glottal source* – that is, the sound of the vocal fold vibration *alone*. The pattern of glottal frequencies is modified by the pharyngeal, oral, and nasal cavities, as we shall see later in the chapter. The glottal frequency serves as a source for vocal resonance, but it is *not* the same as the vocal output we hear. Second, this is a different type of graph from what we have seen up to now. It shows a *spectrum* – that is, all of the component frequencies in the signal. It shows the amplitude of each component, and its frequency. The graph consists of a series of lines, because the components are *discrete* – that is, there is (effectively) no sound energy of any frequency between the harmonics. Third, notice that there is a gradual falling off of the amplitude of the harmonics as frequency increases; each harmonic has less amplitude than the next-lowest harmonic. The falloff is about 6 to 12 dB (decibels) per octave for the average voice, typically greater in female than male voices. The graph shows these harmonics abruptly ending below 4000 Hz, while in fact they continue to higher frequencies; however, beyond 4000 or 5000 Hz, they become too low in amplitude to be of much concern in the study of speech and they do not characterize the differences among vowels as lower frequencies do.

12.8   Spectra and spectrograms

We will now make a brief aside to introduce two types of graph with which the reader may not be familiar. These graphs break down a sound into the components that make it up, much in the way that a prism breaks up light so that the individual component colors of light become visible.

The two types of graph, which are related to one another, are the *spectrum* and the *spectrogram*. The plural of *spectrum* is *spectra* or *spectrums*.

It is important to realize that most sounds we hear are not "pure" sounds – that is, they are not made up of just one single pure frequency. Think of the complexity of music that is created by many instruments at once, or think of the sound in a room where many different people are talking. The purpose of both the spectrum and the spectrogram is to break down all the different sounds. In Section 12.9, we will see in greater detail how different sounds combine.

12.8.1 The spectrum

Figure 12.10 shows two *spectra* (or *spectrums*), those of an adult male and an adult female glottal source (that is, the sound of the vibrating vocal folds). In a spectrum of sound, the different component frequencies are shown along the *x*-axis of the graph, the horizontal bottom scale. The amplitude (strength) of the components is shown on the *y*-axis of the graph, the vertical dimension most often labeled on the left. See also Figure 12.11, another spectrum. Note that a spectrum may be made up of lines, as in Figure 12.10, or with a continuous single curve as in Figure 12.11. (In Figure 12.11, the area under the curve has been filled in with shading.) Which style is used depends on the nature of the sound being analyzed and the amount of averaging that occurs during the analysis (i.e., the computational process of making the graph from the original sound). The type of spectrum shown in Figure 12.11 is the more common, but Figure 12.10 is used to show some specific details that would be lost in the other type of spectrum.

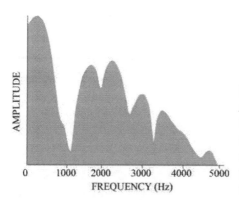

Figure 12.11 A spectrum of sound. The *x*-axis is labeled "Frequency" and the *y*-axis is labeled "Amplitude." This type of graph shows the frequency components of a sound at a single moment in time. This spectrum was made at the approximate center point of the vowel in the spoken word *two*.

12.8.2 The spectrogram

A *spectrogram* shows the same information as a spectrum, *with one important difference*. The *spectrum* shows the components of a sound *at one single moment in time*, but the *spectrogram* shows the components of a sound *over a period of time*, showing whatever changes occur in the sound over time.

The spectrum shows frequency versus amplitude, and the spectrogram shows frequency versus amplitude over time. The spectrogram has a third dimension which must be shown on the flat page or screen. To do this, the spectrum is reoriented as follows:

1. Take a series of spectra, one every few milliseconds in a short phrase.
2. Print these on (virtual) paper, as in Part A of Figure 12.12.
3. Now, stand these up on the edge of the (virtual) paper, with the distance between them proportionate to the time between when each spectrum was made.
   a. Note the orientation of the three dimensions, amplitude, time, and frequency, shown in Part B of Figure 12.12.
4. Think of the graph line of the spectra as showing "mountains" and "valleys" corresponding to high amplitude, low amplitude, and intermediate amplitude.
5. Lay a flat sheet of (virtual) paper on top of the top edges of the spectra, as shown in Part C of Figure 12.12.
6. Color the flat sheet of paper in shades of gray, from white to black. The darkest areas show where the "mountains" on the spectra are the highest. The whitest areas are where the "valleys" on the spectra are deepest. Shades of gray show the intermediate height of the graph lines proportionately.
   a. Add more spectra so that the pattern shows almost continuous change rather than a few large steps, as seen in Part D as opposed to Part C, where there are isolated areas of shading.
7. Part D of Figure 12.12 shows the newly made spectrogram lying flat on the edges of the spectra.

The spectrogram shows time on the x-axis (horizontal), frequency on the y-axis (vertical), and amplitude by darkness of shading. You can think of the darkness of shading as representing how high the "mountains" are rising above the page. That axis, at right angles to the flat page or screen, can be called the z-axis; it is like the shading of land elevation in a topographical map. Figure 12.13 shows a spectrogram.

12.9   Addition of waves

In the previous section, we discussed a situation in which one sound source produces periodic sound waves of several frequencies at once. But the sound waves discussed and illustrated in the early part of this chapter (except for the aperiodic wave) consisted of *one* frequency alone. What happens in a sound wave when several waves are produced simultaneously? How do they combine?

Several simple sound waves can be added together to form a new **complex** sound wave, which is the sum of the component parts, as shown in Figure 12.14. This figure illustrates the sum of a 100-Hz sound wave plus a 200-Hz and a 300-Hz wave.

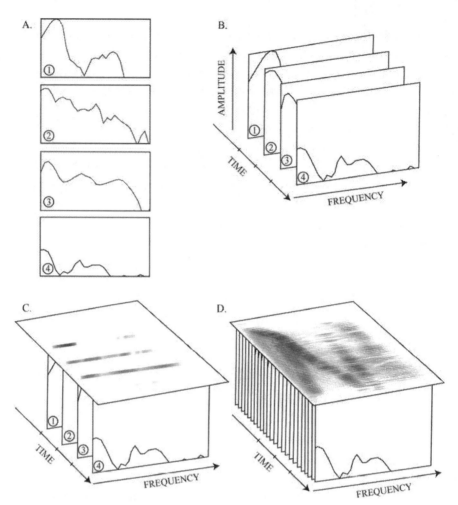

Figure 12.12 Relationship between spectra and a spectrogram.
Part A Four spectra from different points during the author's pronunciation of "why." **Part B** These spectra lined up, spaced according to the points at which the spectra were produced. In the spectra, where the graph line is high, the amplitude is high, and where the line is low, the amplitude is low. **Part C** A flat sheet has been laid on top, and where the graph line on the spectra is high, the sheet is shaded dark, and vice versa. **Part D** If this is done in many, many places, a spectrogram is produced. **A spectrogram** is like thousands of spectra being taken consecutively, and instead of an up-and-down graph line, there is shading to show amplitude.

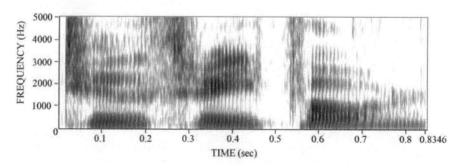

Figure 12.13 A spectrogram of the phrase "two, three, four." Time is shown on the x-axis and frequency on the y-axis. Intensity is show by the darkness of shading.

Remember that the rise and fall of the graph line represents the rise and fall of air pressure at a point in space. If two waves, both in the rising phase of their cycle, arrive at the same point at the same time, the resulting rise in pressure will be doubly fast and doubly great. But if the two waves arrive out of phase – that is, one in the rising phase of its cycle and the other in the falling phase of its cycle – they will cancel each other out (either partially or fully), since, if the pressure is being influenced to rise and fall simultaneously, it will stay balanced in the middle. If there is a large positive pressure and a small negative pressure, then the balance between them will be on the positive side, and vice versa. If the positive pressure and the negative pressure are equal, then they will cancel each other completely.

It can be seen in Figure 12.14 that, when several waves are added together, the amplitude of the resultant wave at any one point is sometimes *increased* by an additive effect of the component waves and sometimes *decreased* by a subtractive effect of the component waves.

Waves A, B, and C in Figure 12.14, like the waves in Figures 12.2, 12.3, and 12.4A, are termed **simple** or **sinusoidal** periodic waves, or simply **sinusoids**.[16] When these are added together, the resultant wave (like wave D in Figure 12.14 and any of the waves in Figure 12.15) is termed **complex**. *The complex wave will be periodic if all of its component waves are.*

Complex periodic waves may have relatively simple or extremely complex shapes (a few are illustrated in Figure 12.15). But no matter how intricate the shape of a complex wave, it is easy to tell whether it is periodic or not. If it has a pattern that is repeated, it is periodic; if it has no repetitive pattern, the wave is aperiodic.

Any complex periodic wave can be divided up into component sinusoidal waves, according to *Fourier's Theorem*, named for the French mathematician who first proposed it. This means that any complex periodic wave, such as any of those shown in Figure 12.15 (and any of an infinite number of others), can be seen as the sum of simple sinusoidal waves of varying frequencies and amplitudes. (Their precise physical properties can be discovered through the application of *Fourier's Theorem*.) The fact that wave D in Figure 12.14 is the combination of sinusoids is easy to accept; it is perhaps harder to see how such wave forms as the square wave in Figure 12.15A can possibly be the sum of sinusoids. It is far beyond the scope of this book to demonstrate the mathematical

---

[16] The term *sinusoid* is derived from the trigonometric function of the same name, whose shape, when graphed, is the same as the shape of a graphic representation of a simple wave. The name is often shortened to *sine*, both in mathematics and in discussion of sound waves.

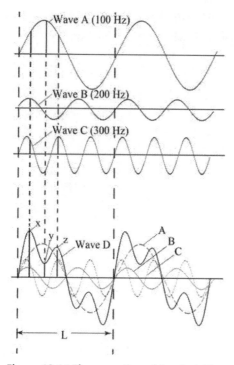

Figure 12.14 The operation of Fourier's Theorem. Three periodic waves, A, B, and C, are shown at the top, and their sum – according to Fourier's Theorem – wave D, is shown below. The three component waves have different frequencies and amplitudes. At each point along wave D, the amplitude can be seen as the sum of the amplitudes of A, B, and C at the same point. Vertical lines are shown at the left to help you to see this addition. When the component wave is below the baseline of the graph, that counts as a negative value when calculating the sum. For example, point x on wave D can be seen as the sum of three positive values from A, B, and C. At point y, wave A contributes a positive value, but waves B and C contribute negative values.

Remember what the wave line represents: pressure at a point in space. The pressure will be the sum of the pressure of all the component waves. It will be a useful exercise to work from left and right through the entire length of wave D to see how it is the sum of the 3 component waves.

L represents the wavelength.

derivation; suffice it to say that *any* periodic wave is the sum of a number of sinusoids.[17]

If the sinusoidal components of a periodic wave are different in frequency by more than a few hertz, then our ears hear the complex wave as having a different quality from a simple wave of the same frequency. (People with a good ear for music can often identify the components.)

---

[17] The Fourier Transform is the division of a complex wave into a series of sinusoids by Fourier's Theorem. It is explained inductively, stopping short of using calculus to prove it mathematically, in Chapter 4 and Section 4.3 of MacKay (2014).

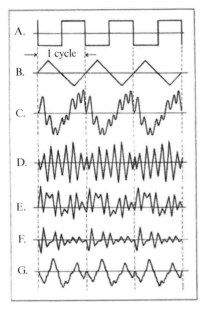

Figure 12.15 Some complex periodic waves. Illustrated are seven of the infinite variety of complex periodic waves. **A.** A "square" wave. **B.** A "triangular" wave. **C.** The sum of a 300 Hz, a 2055 Hz, and a 2350 Hz wave. **D.** The sum of a 400 Hz, a 500 Hz, and a 600 Hz wave. **E.** The sum of a 100 Hz, a 500 Hz, and a 600 Hz wave. **F.** The author pronouncing the vowel /a/ (F0 about 120 Hz). **G.** The author pronouncing the vowel /u/ (F0 about 120 Hz). For ease of comparison, the seven waves have been drawn to different scales to make the length of one cycle the same for all. The fundamental frequency of the wave from which C was drawn is 300 Hz; of E, 100 Hz; and of F and G, about 120 Hz. These different frequencies of course correspond to different wavelengths and periods, so in scale drawings the lengths of the cycles would differ (for example, E would be four times as long as D). They have been made to appear the same length in this drawing so that you can compare the different wave shapes.

As Figure 12.15[18] shows, a complex periodic wave has a cycle that can be identified. As with the simple periodic waves we saw earlier, each cycle is exactly like those that precede and follow.

The frequency of a complex wave is measured the same way as the frequency of simple waves: the number of times the cycle repeats itself each second. Of course, the components of the complex wave each have their own frequencies, most higher than the frequency of the overall complex wave.

A complex periodic wave, like simple periodic waves, will have a somewhat

> **SIDEBAR 12.5 Pressures**
>
> Thinking back to Chapter 4, recall that we are discussing *relative pressures*, not *absolute pressures*. In the present discussion, "positive" pressure is pressure *above normal air pressure*, and "negative" pressure is *pressure below normal air pressure*. When we say that a positive pressure and a negative pressure cancel each other out, the result is *normal air pressure* (not zero air pressure).

melodic quality, as contrasted with an aperiodic wave, which has a harsh or "noisy" quality. *Melodic*, however, does not imply that the sound is necessarily pleasing musically, only that it is not harsh and noisy. For example, if you pronounce a sustained vowel such as "ah," you are producing a complex sound wave that is predominantly periodic.

Here is another example. Online you can find pure tones used for tuning musical instruments. These tones are usually "pure" tones: simple sinusoidal waves. If you play the same note on a musical instrument (or find a

---

[18] Figure 12.15 shows some vowel sounds. Vowels are discussed in a later section.

recording online), the frequency will be the same, but the wave will be complex. That is the nature of the sound waves generated by musical instruments: the same note played on different instruments will have the same fundamental frequency, but the shape of their complex waves (and therefore the frequencies that have been added together) will be unique for each.

The additive nature of sound waves, and the fact that a complex wave can be seen as the sum of a number of simple waves, is basic to speech. The resonant speech sounds, such as vowels, result from the combination of several frequencies or tones into a complex waveform.

12.10   Standing waves

Let us turn our attention to an acoustic phenomenon that plays a fundamental role in resonance, and hence in speech production – namely, the *standing wave.*

SIDEBAR 12.6 Tuning fork

A tuning fork is a steel device shaped like a heavy fork having 2 tines that has traditionally been used to tune musical instruments by providing a reference tone that the tuner can use to match the note produced by the instrument. A separate physical tuning fork is required for each note. Today, tuning forks have almost entirely been replaced by a small electronic tone generator that can be adjusted as required.

A tuning fork is a physical device that vibrates at the specified frequency. A tone generator generates a tone through electronic circuitry. Because the tuning fork is a physical object functioning under the acoustic principles that are being presented in this chapter, the example of the tuning fork is used here, and a tuning fork is illustrated as the sound source in figures such as Figure 12.16 Y.

Recall that, for any given speed of propagation, the wavelength depends on the frequency. The higher the frequency, the shorter the wavelength. Each frequency has a *unique* wavelength, as long as the medium through which it propagates does not change (and the temperature does not change significantly – Table 12.1).

Imagine a sound source that produces a pure tone frequency of 34.3 Hz. By the formula in Section 12.6 (Sidebar 12.4), you could calculate the wavelength in air of that frequency. If you did, you would find that it is 10 meters ($\approx$ 33 ft). Now imagine that the sound source is exactly 20 meters from a wall in a large meeting room.

A continuous sound wave will travel from the sound source to the wall and will rebound off the wall back to the sound source. (In fact, sound waves would go in all directions, but for the moment we are considering only those that follow this direct path.) It is easy to see that 2 complete wavelengths would fit between the sound source and the wall. The reason for the sound source to be double the distance from the wall, allowing 2 full wavelengths to "fit" between sound source and wall, is simply because the illustrations are easier to understand when 2 full cycles are illustrated; there is nothing "magical" about 2 wavelengths.

The fact that there is an exact fit leads to a special situation when the outgoing wave and the returning wave interact. (Naturally, these two waves –

If you wish to hear specific frequencies, you can of course hear them using tone generators from the Internet or as apps on an electronic device. One word of caution, though: the tiny loudspeakers on computers or hand-held devices often poorly reproduce the frequencies demanded.

away from the sound source and back toward the sound source – have the same wavelength, and since very little energy is lost in this hypothetical reflection, we can assume for the purpose of illustration that they have the same amplitude.) In Figure 12.16, we see a portion of the waves from the sound source as they hit the wall and rebound. By the principle we examined in Section 12.6, these two waves *add up to create a wave of double amplitude* (at the particular point in their propagation illustrated in Figure 12.16). But because of the exact fit of the wavelength, the resultant wave has a special property: the points where it crosses the baseline (that is, the points of normal air pressure or *points of zero influence*, as they are called technically) *are always in the same place*. If you consider Figure 12.16, you can see why this is so. Waves A and B will each advance the *same* distance in any given time period, and so the points at which they cancel each other out always land at the same places. In Figure 12.17, one cycle of the wave

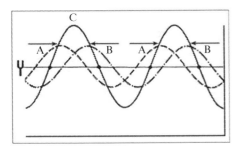

Figure 12.16 A reflected wave. A small tuning fork is used to symbolize the source of the sound wave in this and subsequent figures – see Sidebar 12.6. Wave A (*broken line*) represents sound radiating from the tuning fork. Wave B (*dash-dot-dash*) represents sound being reflected from the wall. Notice that the wavelength fits exactly twice between the tuning fork and the reflecting wall. Wave C (*solid line*) is the sum (by Fourier's Theorem) of waves A and B. Its *points of zero influence* (baseline crossings, also called *nodes*) are always in the same place, if the distance from wall to tuning fork is a whole number of wavelengths.

has been cut into 12 equal parts, so you can follow, step by step, the combination of the 2 waves. By following the illustration frame by frame, you can see why the 3 baseline-crossings (*points of zero influence*) are always in the same place.

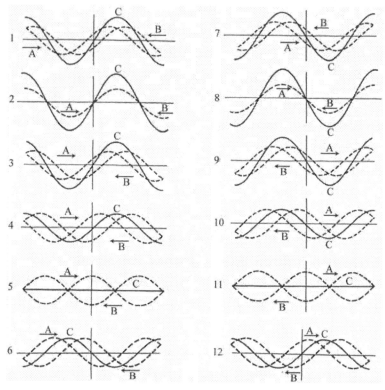

Figure 12.17 A standing wave. The two waves shown in Figure 12.16 are reproduced here, divided into twelve parts. In each successive drawing, waves A and B have been advanced by one-twelfth of a cycle or 30 degrees (remember that both A and B are advancing at the same rate, so each has advanced 60°*relative to the other wave*). Wave C shows the resultant wave. Note the special properties of wave C: its points of zero influence (the points at which it crosses the baseline) *are always the same.* This is different from other sound waves (such as A and B in this drawing or, perhaps more clearly, the waves in Figure 12.9), whose points of zero influence move forward or back.

This type of wave is called a ***standing wave***, because it seems to be standing in one place, not moving forward or back. This is because the points of zero influence (normal air pressure, where the graph of the wave crosses the baseline), called the **nodes**, stay in the same place. The distance between the nodes is *one-half the wavelength* of the wave.

If the waves could be made visible, they would appear as in Figure 12.18. (Remember that the crests and valleys represent air pressure, not the rise and fall of air molecules.) It is hard to illustrate in a fixed image the ongoing wave motion, so it is instructive to find online video of a standing wave in motion.

In the examples given, we considered one original **wave train**[19] and *one* reflected wave train. The same situation would apply if the sound source were in the middle of a room of the correct dimensions. In that case, however, we would have to consider the continuous reflection back and forth. That reflection would mean that the resultant wave would have even greater amplitude.

The standing wave pattern occurs if the distance between source and reflector, or between two reflectors, is any multiple of the distance between nodes. For this reason, it is apparent that the critical factor is not the wavelength, but one half the wavelength.

12.11   Resonance

Resonance is the property of an object to vibrate at a certain "natural" frequency. For example, a guitar string will vibrate at a particular frequency if an external force (a strike or a pluck) supplies the energy to initiate the vibration. Notice that a given guitar string (with no fingering of the frets) has only one natural frequency: pluck it hard or softly, quickly or gently, and it will always vibrate at the same frequency.

That frequency can be changed in a couple of ways.

- Change the physical properties of the string by pressing your finger on the string above one of the frets. Now the string is shorter, and it will have a different frequency of vibration.
- Change the physical properties of the string by replacing it with a string that is much thicker or thinner or made of different material. That will change the mass of the string and it will vibrate at a different frequency.

The resonant vibration can be imparted by an outside oscillation. If you took a sound source and a tuning fork having the same frequency, turned on the sound source, and brought it close to the tuning fork, the tuning fork would begin to vibrate. But this phenomenon of *sympathetic vibration* is selective: if you set your sound source to a *different* frequency (being careful not to choose frequencies that were multiples of one another), the tuning fork would *not* pick up the vibrations, at least not to the same degree. This phenomenon also occurs outside the laboratory;

---

[19] A *wave train* is several or many continuous connected cycles, as in a normal continuous acoustic output (rarely would a sound be produced that was only 1 cycle long, the duration of its period). Figure 12.9 shows a number of wave trains as does Figure 12.15. The bottom two waves in Figure 12.15 come from a human voice, rather than being digitally created, and so they have slight variations between cycles – the cycles are not perfectly identical – but the main point remains.

we see examples often in everyday life. Most of us have been in a car that rattles only when the engine is running at a certain speed. The part that rattles has its own natural frequency and is set in vibration only at a certain engine speed, because at that speed the engine emits a series of pulses whose frequency matches the resonant frequency of the loose part. At other engine speeds, the frequencies do not match, and no sympathetic vibration occurs. Or, to take another everyday example of sympathetic resonance: most of us have had the experience, when playing music loudly, of finding that a certain note makes some object in the room vibrate. Whatever the object is, every time a certain frequency is emitted by the loudspeaker, that object rattles.

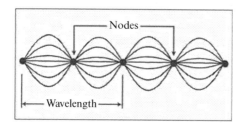

Figure 12.18 A standing wave. Viewed over time, the crests would rise, fall, become troughs, and rise again to crests, as shown in this view at different moments in time, but there would be no apparent movement forward or back. The points of zero influence (baseline crossings), called **nodes** in the case of a standing wave, stay at the same point. There is a node every *half*-wavelength (you can see why by examining Figure 12.17).

It is important to understand that the object is free to vibrate all the time, but that it does not vibrate in sympathy to just *any* sound, *only* to a sound whose frequency matches its own natural resonant frequency. In this way, resonance is *selective*; it acts as a *filter*.

12.11.1 Cavity resonance

So far in this section, we have examined solid objects that vibrate. However, when dealing with speech, we need to look at resonance in air-filled chambers, such as the mouth, pharynx, and nasal cavities. Resonance in an air-filled chamber or cavity is known as **cavity resonance**, and it is of fundamental importance in the production of speech.

Recall from Section 12.10 that when there is a sound wave whose half-wavelength fits exactly any number of times into an enclosed space, a standing wave pattern will be established. Because of the addition of the original and reflected waves, that specific frequency will be emphasized by the enclosed space. The air chamber will *resonate* at that specific frequency.

Other frequencies whose half-wavelength does not divide evenly into the length of the chamber will not be reinforced by the chamber, since the wave and its reflections will not be synchronized to create a standing-wave

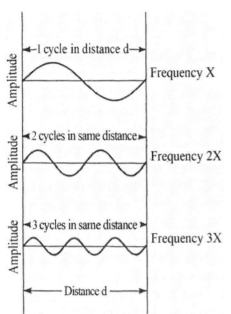

Figure 12.19 Resonance. If a wave of frequency X Hz has a wavelength that fits exactly into a resonator, then other frequencies, such as 2 X, 3 X, etc., will also fit exactly into the resonator. Thus, a resonator tuned to a particular frequency will also be tuned to whole-number multiples of that frequency.

pattern. The air chamber resonator is selective, just like the solid object resonators we saw earlier in this section. If we took a cavity tuned to, say, 256 Hz[20] and introduced a 256-Hz tone into it, that frequency would sound louder. But the sound of, say, a 200-Hz tuning fork would not be reinforced.

Although the cavity resonator is selective, it is not selective for one frequency only. If you double a given frequency, you cut the wavelength in half. Therefore, if the original wavelength fits evenly into a given distance, so will half that wavelength (and other multiples or submultiples of the frequency as well). (See Figure 12.19.)

Now imagine a cavity resonator like that we considered earlier, but different in that its walls are slightly curved (Figure 12.20B). You can see that the distance between the walls is slightly variable. As a result, it is not tuned to a specific frequency; rather, *any* frequency within a small range will set up a standing wave, since a slightly longer wavelength (i.e., a lower frequency) will set up a standing wave where the walls are farther apart, and a slightly shorter wavelength (a higher frequency) will set up a standing wave where the walls are closer together. So this resonator will reinforce a *range* of frequencies, whereas the straight-walled resonator (Figure 12.20A) is tuned to a very specific frequency. The resonator in Figure 12.20A is said to be **sharply tuned**, whereas that in Figure 12.20B is not sharply tuned.

---

[20] Middle C on the scientific scale. On the musicians' scale, the frequency is slightly higher.

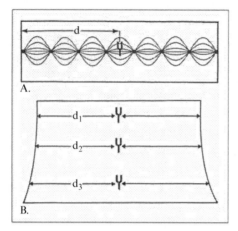

Figure 12.20 Tuning. A. A resonator with straight end walls. Because the distance *(d)* from source to reflection does not vary, this resonator resonates at a precise frequency, X Hz, and its multiples. **B.** In a resonator with curved walls the distance *(d1, d2, d3)* from source to reflection varies, meaning that slightly different wavelengths will set up standing waves, or resonance. Therefore, any of a *range* of frequencies, say 0.9 X to 1.1 X, will set up a standing wave. Resonator A is said to be sharply tuned, resonator B not sharply tuned.

Figure 12.21 shows the output spectrum of a sharply tuned resonator (as in Figure 12.20A) versus one that is less sharply tuned (as in Figure 12.20B). *The speech resonators, having complex organic shapes, tend not to be very sharply tuned.* Note that a resonator acts in a sense as a filter, in that it transfers some frequencies (those that establish standing waves) well, and that it transfers those frequencies that do not match its properties (i.e., no standing wave) poorly.

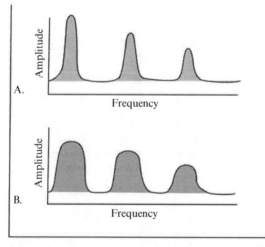

Figure 12.21 Tuning. A. A spectrum of a sharply tuned resonator, as in Figure 12.20A. **B.** A spectrum of a less sharply tuned resonator, as in Figure 12.20B. Both these spectra show the *transfer* through a given resonator. The peaks (technically, *poles*) are at frequencies that set up standing waves; the valleys (technically, *zeros*) are at frequencies where wave patterns cancel each other out. These spectra can be viewed as *filter* functions, in that they map the acoustic filtering of a given resonator.

12.11.2 Open-ended cavity resonator

One more theoretical issue must be examined before we can look at how all of this applies to the vocal tract. The cavity resonators we have looked at so far have had solid walls between which there is reflection. But the vocal tract (like piccolos, flutes, trumpets, etc.) is in effect *an open-ended tube* (the mouth is open at the lips throughout most of speech, and certainly in the production of all vowels). How can there be reflection off the open end of a tube? While it may seem illogical at first, there is reflection from the open end of the tube. The reason is that, within the tube, the standing wave sets up rapid oscillations of pressure. Where these oscillations meet the relatively stable pressures outside the tube, there is such a mismatch of pressure and particle speed that there might as well be a solid wall.

The point of reflection occurs in that part of the cycle where the air pressure is maximally different from normal air pressure (i.e., at a peak or trough in a graphic representation like Figures 12.2 and 12.3), so *in an open-ended resonator it is the one-quarter wavelength or three-quarter wavelength that is critical*, not the half-wavelength as in the completely enclosed resonator. This is shown in Figure 12.22.

An open-ended air space resonates when some external sound source introduces sound waves of the correct frequency or frequencies. This external source is said to **excite** resonance. The resonator resonates at its own natural frequency (or frequencies), which is (are) dependent upon its physical dimensions. In this way, it selects – from any number of external frequencies – the one or ones that match its own properties.

12.11.3 Glass bottle cavity resonator

Here is an everyday example: blow across the neck of a narrow-necked bottle.[21] The bottle emits a loud tone. What is creating this tone? Imagine that the bottle was separated from its neck and that you were blowing

> **SIDEBAR 12.7 Analogy for fast-moving object meeting a still one**
>
> An analogy might help at this point. Water is soft and will not support your weight if you try to stand on it. But if you belly-flop onto the water from a 10-meter diving board, you might as well have landed on solid ground. Similarly, a fast-moving stone will skip on the surface of the water, but a stone that is not moving will sink. In the same way, the fast-moving pressure oscillations within an open-ended tube meet the still air outside the tube and are partially reflected.
>
> With regard to the principle that is under discussion – what happens at the open end of a tube – the "objects" are much smaller. They are molecules of air, not stones or human bodies, but the effect is similar.

---

[21] This works best with a glass bottle. A hard plastic bottle will work less well, and bottles made of flexible plastic may not work at all, as the rigidity of the walls of the bottle affects the reflection of the sound waves.

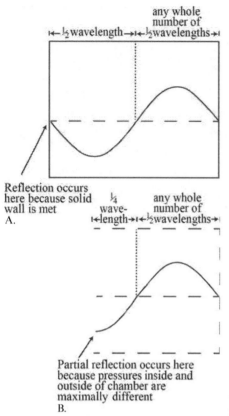

Figure 12.22 Resonance in open and closed resonators. **A.** Resonance within a closed resonator, the type we have examined up to this point. For resonance, there must be a whole number of nodes fitting within the length of the resonator, so the length of the resonator must be a multiple of the half-wavelength. **B.** Resonance within an open-ended resonator, such as the vocal tract. Reflection occurs at the open end at the point of maximum difference from normal air pressure (i.e., at a crest or trough, halfway between nodes). Halfway between nodes is one-half of a half-wavelength, or one-quarter of a wavelength. Thus, the critical length for resonance of an open-ended resonator must be either one-quarter or three-quarters of a wavelength (but not two-quarters or four-quarters, because there are nodes there). In both cases, the neat fit is required – that is to say, some exact multiple of a fraction of the wavelength – because otherwise each successive reflection would put the crests and troughs at a different point. Hence, there would be no standing wave and no reinforcement of that frequency.

across the neck alone. The noise at the neck would be a hushing noise, an *aperiodic* sound (see Figure 12.4B), and that is all you would hear. But with the bottle intact, the neck is attached to a resonator that has its own natural frequencies. It selects from among all the different cycles of the aperiodic sound those that happen to coincide with the bottle's own frequency. Just those few cycles are enough to set up a standing wave, and the bottle emits a loud tone whose frequency corresponds to the wavelength of the standing wave.

Figure 12.23 shows a spectrum of a 330 ml (11 fl. oz) glass drink bottle. A spectrum of this type – known as a **spectrogram** as noted in Section 12.8 – is oriented differently from the spectra shown in Figures 12.10 and 12.21. In Figure 12.23, frequency is shown on the y-axis (the vertical axis), time is shown on the x-axis (the horizontal axis), and amplitude is shown by the darkness of the shading. If you imagined the dark bands to be mountains rising out of the page, and you viewed those mountains from the right edge of the page, the graph would resemble Figure 12.18. However, Figure 12.23 shows changes over time, which Figure 12.21 does not, and that is why the graph has this form: speech is not a constant sound, but one that is changing over time, so the spectral graph must show change over time.

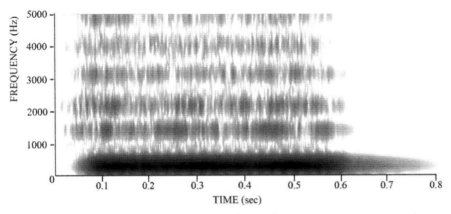

Figure 12.23 Spectrogram of a soft-drink (soda) bottle resonator. Resonances can be seen at approximately 340, 1400, 2170, 3115 Hz, and above.

12.12   Acoustic principles applied to the vocal tract: vowels

We are now in a position to examine the speech production mechanism in light of the acoustic principles we have been examining. In this first part, we will be looking at resonant, voiced speech sounds – that is, the vowels and a few consonants. Later we will look at non-resonant speech sounds such as the fricatives.

As explained in Section 12.7.1, the vibrating vocal folds emit an acoustic signal. This **glottal signal** has its own **fundamental frequency**, and it is accompanied by *harmonics* that are significant up to about 5000 Hz. Figure 12.10 shows the spectrum of this glottal or laryngeal signal. The glottal signal is relatively weak and would sound rather like a party noisemaker if it did not pass through the vocal cavities.

This glottal signal is produced in the larynx, and any sound emitted must pass through the pharynx (throat cavity) and the oral cavity and/or the nasal cavities. These cavities together form an open-ended bent tube. This tube has its own acoustic characteristics, which modify (filter) the signal passing through it.

What distinguishes this tube from, say, the soft drink / soda bottle we examined is that it has a highly complex, irregular shape, and that its size and shape may be changed with tongue, velic, mandibular (jaw), and pharyngeal wall movements.

Each different configuration of the vocal tract has its own resonant frequencies, and the act of speaking involves moving the articulators into the appropriate positions in order to emit the appropriate frequencies.

The vocal tract, having a complex shape, resonates at several frequencies at once. For example, the arching of the tongue in the articulation of most vowels effectively separates the vocal tube into two parts: from the larynx to the arch, and from the arch to the lips. In complex resonators, there tends to be interaction between the standing wave patterns in different parts of the vocal tract, giving rise to multiple resonances.

Resonant speech sounds tend to be characterized by 3 resonant frequencies; these are called **formants**. (Most vowels are recognizable if only the first 2 formants are audible, but sound more natural if the first 3 are heard.) Higher-order formants (a fourth, fifth, sixth) are generally present in the acoustic signal, but they don't affect perception of the vowel in any important way.

The vowel /i/, for example, has formants at the frequencies shown in Table 12.3.

Table 12.3 Formant and fundamental frequencies of the vowel /i/ in American English, based on 48 women, 45 men, and 46 children (Hz) (Hillenbrand et al., 1995)

	Children	Adult females	Adult males
F0	246	227	138
F1	452	437	342
F2	3081	2761	2322
F3	3702	3372	3000

Resonance at each of these frequencies (F1, F2, F3) is excited by the harmonics of the fundamental frequency (F_0). If there is a slight mismatch between the formant frequency and the harmonics, this is not a problem, since the vocal resonators are not sharply tuned. For example, if there is a formant at 2300 Hz and harmonics at 2200 and 2400 Hz (the fundamental being 200 Hz), both the harmonics are emphasized, and the listener hears the prominence in the 2300-Hz range.

The formants are numbered from lowest to highest: 437, 2761, and 3372 Hz are the **first formant**, **second formant**, and **third formant**, respectively, of the vowel /i/ for this group of American females. The three formants are abbreviated *F1*, *F2*, and *F3*. The **fundamental frequency** of the voice is often considered the "zero-th" formant, and this explains the abbreviation F_0 or *F0* for fundamental frequency.

Each vowel has its own characteristic set of formant frequencies. The vowel /u/ has the frequencies in Table 12.4.

These formant values for /u/ are different from those of /i/ and all other vowels.

When two different speakers pronounce the "same" vowel, they will not produce identically the same formant frequencies. Resonance

	Children	Adult females	Adult males
Table 12.4 Formant and fundamental frequencies of the vowel /u/ in American English, based on 48 women, 45 men, and 46 children (Hz) (Hillenbrand et al., 1995)			
F0	249	235	143
F1	494	459	378
F2	1345	1105	997
F3	2988	2735	2343

depends upon the physical dimensions of the resonator, and, after all, the size and shape of the mouth is different in every individual. Male resonating cavities are, on average, larger than female resonating cavities, which are in turn larger than children's resonating cavities. The smaller the cavity, the higher the resonant frequency. The tabled values for adult males, adult females, and children (above) show how different formant frequencies are.

However, the *pattern* of frequencies tends to be constant. Men, women, and children produce the "same" vowel with different formants and different fundamentals, but the similar *pattern* of formants leads us to perceive the vowel as the same.

In some cases, one vowel spoken by a woman may be more like a *different* vowel spoken by a man than the *same* vowel spoken by a man (MacKay, 2014[22]).

You can change the F_0 without affecting the formants. Say /a/ on a low note, a middle note, and a high note. If you keep the articulators fixed, the formants will remain essentially the same. The F_0 will change, and so, of course, will its harmonics, but in normal speech there is always a harmonic near enough to each formant to excite resonance at that formant.[23]

---

[22] For example, a graph of F1 versus F2 values for adult males and females on p. 221 of MacKay (2014) shows that the vowel [ɚ] by a male speaker is closer to the vowels [ʊ] and [o] spoken by a female than to [ɚ] spoken by a female! Note that this graph is based on a different study of formant values than that cited above, and considers only F1 and F2, not F3.

[23] Opera sopranos sometimes hit such high notes – 500 or 600 Hz – that there is a great gap between harmonics. As a result, there is sometimes no harmonic anywhere near a formant, so resonance is not excited at the formant frequency. Since the formants are the essential information needed by the listener, the vowel is unintelligible if they are missing. For this reason, operatic singing is often unintelligible at the higher ranges. See MacKay (2014, p. 226) for an explanation with graphs.

12.12.1   The source–filter theory

Figure 12.10 showed the spectral output of the glottal source. Figure 12.21 showed the resonant characteristics of a couple of resonators with different characteristics. If we made a graph of the resonant characteristics of a particular vocal tract configuration (in the style of Figure 12.21) and superimposed on it the glottal output of Figure 12.10, we would see the spectral characteristics of the given sound (Figure 12.24). The resonant characteristics of a resonator can be conceptualized as a filter, since the resonator lets pass much energy at frequencies corresponding to spectral **poles** (peaks) and does not let much through at the spectral **zeros** (valleys). The result, illustrated in Figure 12.24, is called the **source–filter theory of speech production.**

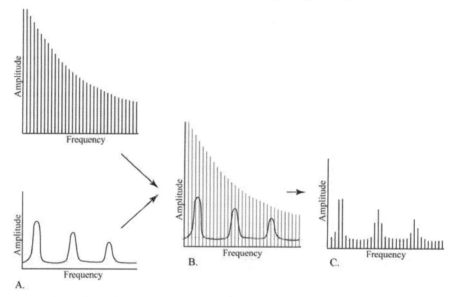

Figure 12.24 The source–filter theory of vowel production. A. *Top,* a spectrum of the *glottal source* as shown in Figure 12.10. This is the *input* or source. *Bottom,* the resonant characteristics at the vocal tract, as in the style of Figure 12.21. The vocal tract resonator can be conceptualized as a **filter,** since it transfers some frequencies better than others. **B.** The **filter** superimposed on the **source.** This is a hypothetical filter, not that of any specific vowel. **C.** The resultant vocalic output, as explained by the **source–filter theory.** Those harmonics that fall at or near the peaks (poles) of resonance shown in part A bottom are transferred with high amplitude and are heard by the listener. Those harmonics that fall in the valleys (zeros) of resonance are transferred with low amplitude and are heard less well.

12.13   Acoustics of vowels

Before looking at the spectra of the various vowels, we should reiterate the effect of the articulatory gestures on acoustic output. The shape and size of the vocal resonators are changed by the various articulatory gestures. In vowels, the arched tongue divides the oral cavity into separate smaller resonators. The back vowels show this most clearly: the *high back* vowel makes a break in the front velar region, the *upper mid back* in the back velar region, the *lower mid back* in the upper pharyngeal region, and the *low back* in the mid-pharyngeal region. In this series, the front tube (lips to arch) has gotten progressively longer, while the back tube (arch to larynx) has gotten progressively shorter, affecting the frequencies of F1 and F2 (Figure 12.25A–C).

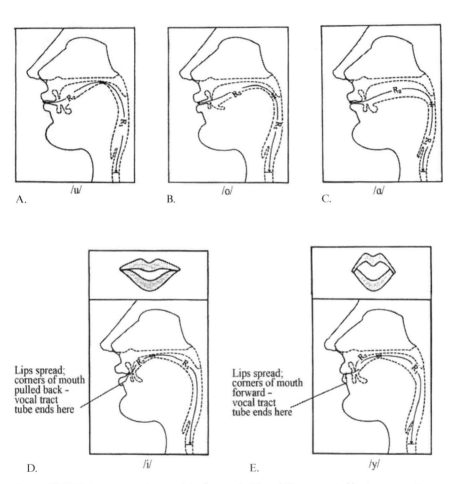

Figure 12.25 A two-resonator model of speech. F1 and F2 are created by two resonators, the back resonator F1 and the front resonator F2. Note that different articulations change the size of the resonators and therefore of the formant frequencies. **A.** /u/. **B.** /o/. **C.** /ɑ/. Notice that, in progressing through this sequence of vowels, the pharyngeal resonator (marked Rl) becomes shorter (therefore resonating at a higher frequency), and the oral resonator (R2) becomes longer. **D.** /i/. **E.** /y/. Notice that the tongue position is the same for /i/ and /y/, although /i/ is lip-spread and /y/ is lip-rounded. Notice how lip-rounding brings the point at which the vocal tract "tube" ends forward – that is, the point at which the inside of the resonator meets the external normal air pressure. Thus the forward resonator (R2) is much longer in rounded than in spread vowels.

The model shown in this figure is simplified. The diameter of the opening between the front and back resonators makes an acoustic difference. The smaller opening in rounded vowels also makes an acoustic difference, in addition to simply lengthening the front resonator.

The shape and size of the opening at the lips can be modified, although to a lesser extent in English than in some languages. In some languages, rounded vowels are articulated with greater rounding and protrusion of the lips than in English, and this has two acoustic effects: the rounding changes the shape of the opening, and the lip protrusion actually lengthens the resonating tube. The vowel /y/, for example, is articulated exactly like /i/, except that the lips are tightly rounded and protruded as for whistling. The two vowels sound very different. The difference in vocal tract length brought about by lip rounding and spreading is illustrated in Figure 12.25D and E.

Let us look now at Figure 12.26, which represents a spectrogram of the vowels /i u ɑ æ/. They show the acoustic components of the vowel sounds of the speech of an adult male.

The salient features to look for in the spectrogram are as follows (cf. Section 12.8): (1) the **frequency scale** is shown along the vertical axis; (2) the **time scale** is shown along the horizontal axis; (3) the **amplitude** is shown by the darkness of the shading: the darker the shading, the greater the amplitude; (4) the **formants** show up as darker bands (a few have been highlighted to aid identification); (5) the **vertical striations** visible in the spectrograms reflect individual cycles of the glottal frequency, each vertical line representing the opening of the vocal folds (the higher the pitch of the voice, the closer together these would be).

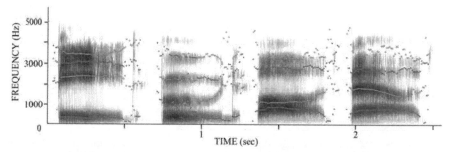

Figure 12.26 Spectrograms of the vowels /i u ɑ æ/ with the formants highlighted. Male American English talker. Vowels are in the context [b__d]: *bead, booed, body, bad*. Formants may not match the frequencies in Tables 12.3 through 12.5 because the spectrograms represent a single talker, whereas the tables are based on more than 40 individuals. Additionally, these vowels are influenced by the following consonant. At the beginning of the vowel, and at the end of the vowel, the articulators are transitioning from the preceding vowel or transitioning to the following vowel. This transition changes the acoustic characteristics of the vocal tract, which in turn modifies the formant frequencies. If a different consonant frame were used for the vowels, those areas of transition would be different. If the vowels were spoken without consonants, there would be no evident transitions. The preceding [b] in this consonant frame does not affect formant frequency much, but the [d] following has a visible effect.

These spectrograms were made from sound files to be found at
www.phonetics.ucla.edu/vowels/chapter3/amengvowels.html. (November 2021).

Table 12.5 shows the values of the formants for adult male, adult female, and children speakers of American English. The values may not correspond exactly to the spectrogram in Figure 12.26 because the spectrogram represents a single talker, while the tabled values are averages of more than 40 talkers.

Table 12.5 Frequencies of F1, F2, and F3 in vowels of American English (hertz)												
	/i/	/ɪ/	/e/	/ɛ/	/æ/	/ɑ/	/ɔ/	/o/	/ʊ/	/u/	/ʌ/	/ɚ/
F1 (Hz)												
M	342	427	476	580	588	768	652	497	469	378	623	474
W	437	483	536	731	669	936	781	555	519	459	753	523
C	452	511	564	749	717	1002	803	597	568	494	749	586
F2 (Hz)												
M	2322	2034	2089	1799	1952	1333	997	910	1122	997	1200	1379
W	2761	2365	2530	2058	2349	1551	1136	1035	1225	1105	1426	1588
C	3081	2552	2656	2267	501	1688	1210	1137	1490	1345	1546	1719
F3 (Hz)												
M	3000	2684	2691	2605	2601	2522	2538	2459	2434	2343	2550	1710
W	3372	3053	3047	2979	2972	2815	2824	2828	2827	2735	2933	1929
C	3702	3403	3323	3310	3289	2950	2982	2987	3072	2988	3145	2143
F0 (Hz)												
M	138	135	129	127	123	123	121	129	133	143	133	130
W	227	224	219	214	215	215	210	217	230	235	218	217
C	246	241	237	230	228	229	225	236	243	249	236	237
Duration (seconds)												
M	243	192	267	189	278	267	283	265	192	237	188	263
W	306	237	320	254	332	323	353	326	249	303	226	321
C	297	248	314	235	322	311	319	310	247	278	234	307

M = men, W = women, C = children. Fundamental frequency (Hz) and duration (seconds) are also shown. Some of these data are a repeat from Tables 12.3 and 12.4. Based on data from 45 men, 48 women, and 46 children. The vowel /ɚ/ is shown as /ɝ/ in the original, designating a stressed / ɚ /, as in *bird*, but not in *butter*. The fact that different vowels have different F_0s is generally attributed to the tongue movements inherent to each vowel. Some movements create a greater pull than others on the hyoid bone and laryngeal structures, and this is believed to modify vocal fold tension, and thus F_0. From Hillenbrand et al. (1995)

12.14   Acoustics of consonants

12.14.1   Plosives

Plosives have an unusual acoustic pattern: during most of the time that the plosive is being articulated (the closure phase), the airway is closed and little or no sound is coming out. During this silent or near-silent phase of the articulation, the spectrogram is primarily blank.

The legend of Figure 12.26 made reference to the change in formant frequency brought about by adjoining vowels. Logically enough, these are called *formant transitions*. Let us look at these in isolation, in stylized drawings. In Figure 12.27, the basic transitional patterns are shown for plosives followed by the vowel /ɑ/. What happens when a different vowel follows the plosive? As can be seen in Figure 12.28, the transitions are different for each combination of plosive and vowel. However, this does not mean that the syllables /di/, /dɛ/, and /dɑ/, for example, have nothing in common. Let us superimpose the stylized formants for these syllables, as shown in Figure 12.29. Notice that the F2 transitions for all the syllables beginning with /d/ point to the same spot; the F1 transitions all point to another, different spot. The other syllables beginning with /d/ would have transitions pointing to the same spots as well. Each of these spots ("x" in Figure 12.29) is called a *locus* (plural, *loci*).

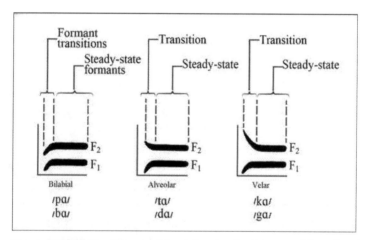

Figure 12.27 Stylized spectrograms showing formant transitions for plosives of each place of articulation followed by the vowel [ɑ]. The formants are determined by the vowel (note that these remain constant for all syllables containing the vowel [ɑ]), but the shape and direction of the transition is determined by the place of articulation of the plosive. Thus, the transitions for [pɑ] and [bɑ] are similar, as are those for [tɑ] and [dɑ], as well as those for [kɑ] and [gɑ]. The members of the pairs are distinguished by factors other than the transitions themselves. The formant transitions (in concert with other acoustic factors) are perceived by the ear as the plosive consonant; the stable period is perceived as the vowel.

Notice that the actual location of the loci on the stylized spectrogram is in the silent portion of the plosive articulation. As can be seen by extrapolating the formants in Figure 12.28, the labials and velars each have distinctive loci, and the locus for F2 is different for each place of articulation. That is, extend the formant transitions backward in the direction they point to, such that they meet, as is done in Figure 12.29. The meeting point for all the extrapolated F2 transitions of syllables beginning with the same plosive indicates the frequency of the locus for that place of articulation. Note that there are two different F2 loci for velars; the division comes between /gɑ/ and /gɔ/ in Figure 12.28.

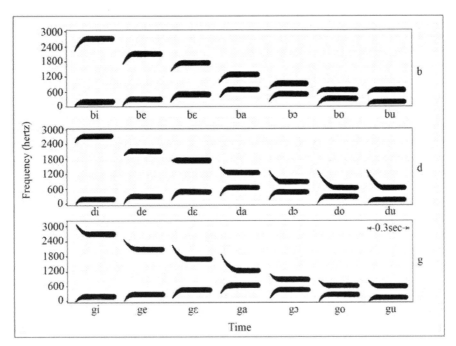

Figure 12.28 Spectrograms of synthetically produced syllables, showing second formant transitions that produce the voiced plosives before various vowels

The formant transitions appear at the *end* of the vowel when the plosive *follows* the vowel (as in Figure 12.26), and if the plosive is situated between two vowels, there are two sets of transitions: those leading into and those leading out of the plosive. For this reason, plosives are likely to be more intelligible when situated intervocalically than at the beginning of a word, preceding a vowel. In this position, two sets of transitions provide information about the place of articulation. Plosives situated at the end of a word are least intelligible.

The acoustic shape of plosive consonants suggests that our perceptual mechanism is quite remarkable. Consider, for example, the fact that, if formant frequencies change slowly, we perceive a diphthong, while rapid

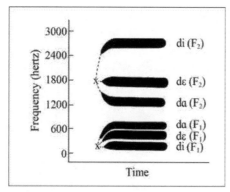

Figure 12.29 The loci of the formant transitions of the alveolar plosives /d/ and /t/.
While the shape of the formant transition changes according to the formant frequency of the
following vowel, the locus remains constant. That is, the formant transitions of the alveolar
plosives always "point" to the same frequency ("x" in the illustration), no matter what vowel
follows. It is thus the frequency of the locus that our ear perceives in identifying the place
of articulation of the plosive consonant. The voiceless plosive /t/ will have very similar, if not
identical, loci to voiced /d/, but there will be a greater delay until voicing starts and formants are
highly audible.

formant transitions are perceived as a sequence of consonant plus vowel.
As another example, a plosive consonant such as /d/ does not have a single
unchanging acoustic quality; rather, the syllables /di/ and /do/ appear to be
less similar acoustically than are /bi/ and /di/. Apparently, our perceptual
mechanism abstracts the loci and identifies them, even though they are just
hypothetical dots on a graph in a period of relative silence.

In summary, several acoustic cues lead to our perception of different plosives: (1) voiced and voiceless plosives having the *same* place of articulation are distinguished by aspiration and voice onset time; and (2) different
places of articulation are distinguished by patterns of formant transitions,
as well as by the noise burst of aspiration, when this is present.

12.14.2   Fricatives

Fricatives are produced with audible air turbulence. This turbulence creates
noise – that is, sound that is aperiodic in nature. Aperiodic sound shows up
on the spectrogram as an uneven shading across a wide frequency range.
(Aperiodic sounds have no regular period, but contain individual cycles
having many different periods. So, when they are analyzed acoustically,
they show their various components, which appear on the spectrogram as
a shaded area extending over a range of frequencies corresponding to the
component cycles of the aperiodic wave.) Acoustically, aspiration is like a
fricative. In order to produce the frictional sound of a fricative, a certain
minimum airflow must pass through a minimum constriction. Figure 12.30
shows a spectrogram of several voiceless fricatives.

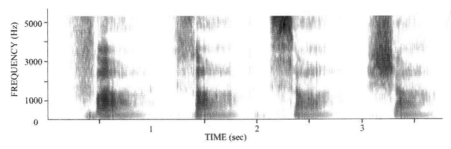

Figure 12.30 Spectrograms of voiceless fricatives

12.14.3 Approximants

Figure 12.31 gives spectrograms of several approximants. Glides in particular resemble vowels, with a strong formant pattern, but one that changes through time, given that glides are characterized by movement of the articulators.

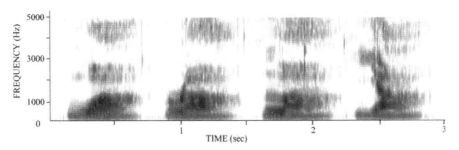

Figure 12.31 Spectrograms of several approximants

12.14.4 Nasals

Figure 12.32 shows spectrograms of several nasals. The spectrograms reveal a formant structure like vowels and approximants. Less sound energy is radiated from the nostrils than through an open mouth, and it can be seen that there is reduced amplitude in the spectrograms of the vowels.

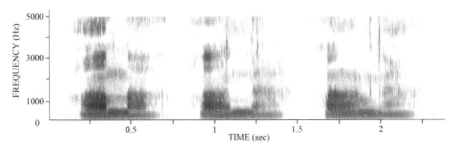

Figure 12.32 Spectrograms of several nasal consonants

12.15   Vocabulary

acoustic energy
amplitude
aperiodic
cavity resonance
complex
compression
crest
cycle
cycles per second cps
degree (of phase)
dynamic range
F_0
formant, F1, F2, F3
Fourier's Theorem
frequency
fundamental frequency
glottal signal
glottal source
harmonic
hertz, Hz
in phase
lambda, λ
localization
locus, loci
loudness
mode of vibration
node
nonperiodic
out of phase
overtone

period
periodic
periodicity
phase
pitch
pole
propagate
propagation
quasiperiodic
rarefaction
rarefy
resonance
simple
sine
sinusoid, sinusoidal
sound
source–filter theory
spectra
spectrogram
spectrum
speed of propagation
standing wave
trough
tuning
vertical striation
volume
wave train
wavelength, λ
zero

13 | Interlocutors: Talkers and Hearers

13.1   Interlocutors, talkers, and hearers

An *interlocutor* is a person taking part in a conversation, and therefore that person is engaged in both talking and hearing. The majority of this book concerns the first of these, talking, but we need to address the individual who hears the speech of others, and the interactions between the two. Phonetics is about the sounds of speech, and speech, as a human activity, is normally about the interaction between two or more people.

The hearing system interacts with the speech production system of the talker to monitor speech as it is produced, as shown by the small degree of deterioration in speech production of individuals who become profoundly hearing-impaired after language acquisition is complete.

A couple of notes on terminology: The word *interlocutors* is perhaps a bit old-fashioned, but the word is used to emphasize the involvement of at least *two* individuals who are alternating roles as talker and hearer. The terms *talker* and *hearer* are used very deliberately (they are standard terminology in the field) to be neutral as to intentionality or social role. The word *speaker* can mean someone giving a public address, and it has a number of other senses that we don't want to evoke here, so *talker* is used.[1] The word *listener* implies a deliberate act, the intention of hearing, but not all the speech we hear is something we are deliberately listening to. So we say *hearer*.

The term *utterance* is used to mean 'the thing said' without getting into determining whether what was said was a complete sentence or a phrase or an expression or an expletive. Every utterance has phonetic content that is of potential interest to us; the grammatical form of the utterance does not change that.

There is an interaction between talker and hearer; in live speech, it is possible to ask for clarification (except in certain social situations). Additionally,

---

[1] There is one exception. Throughout the book, we have used the word *speaker* in the sense of 'talker' when referring to a specific language. That is, we have written *a speaker of English* or *an English speaker* rather than *a talker of English* or *an English talker* because the specific use of the term *speak* or *speaker* is so fixed in English when the meaning reflects the *competence* to speak a given language.

in speech, the content can be clarified by tone of voice, pauses, and even gestures to clarify meaning that would be ambiguous if the text were printed – that is, speech contains *suprasegmentals* (Chapter 11) that serve to disambiguate in a way that punctuation barely starts to do in writing.

13.1.1   The talker

As stated by Jakobson, Fant, and Halle in *Preliminaries to Speech Analysis* (1952), "we speak in order to be heard, in order to be understood." While a talker may talk to themself or to no one in particular, or otherwise talk without seeming purpose, talking is usually done with the intent that someone else hears what we say. Therefore, the talker pays some attention, conscious or unconscious, to the effectiveness of their speech.

13.1.2   The hearer

The hearer may be a listener – that is, someone who is actively trying to hear and decode speech – or may be someone who is overhearing speech that is within earshot. While a hearer may fail to understand, for a range of reasons, more often the hearer does decode the incoming speech. This is the topic of Section 13.4, "Speech perception."

13.2   Speech versus written text

The notion that written language is not much different from spoken language of which a written record has been made is quite common, but the reality is very different. Speech and writing are very dissimilar, serve quite different purposes, and face different constraints.

13.2.1   Types of written and spoken language

Written language can be intended for long-term use, and considerable care is taken to create a written text that is error-free and clear. Textbooks, instruction manuals, nonfiction writing in general fall into this category. Fiction writing (essentially story-telling) may have a slightly different form, avoiding some formalities of other types of written language, but still carefully created and checked, at least in works published by reputable publishing houses.

Other written language may be designed for very temporary use (a shopping list, for example) and may not consist of sentences or even phrases, and may be produced with little attention to detail or correctness.

Some kinds of written language, such as texting, maximize input efficiency by reducing the number of written letters or characters to a minimum; in order to decode such messages, it may be necessary to be familiar specifically with this kind of writing and, in particular, with the shortened forms of words or phrases that it uses – and these are particular to specific communities.

Similarly, spoken language is of many types, ranging from very formal to very casual. We can further distinguish between planned speech (perhaps, but not necessarily, using a written text) and spontaneous speech. Spontaneous speech demands all steps in the production of spoken language at once: ideation,[2] vocabulary choice, syntactic planning, and the planning and execution of the movements of speech. Reading aloud, reading from a semi-memorized text, or reciting memorized lines removes some of these demands (but may replace them with others when reading aloud from an unfamiliar text). Indeed, the difference has clinical implications: persons who stutter in spontaneous speech may be able to recite memorized text (including songs, poetry, and text such as might be produced by an actor in a play) without stuttering or hesitation – a clear indication that recitation is different from spontaneous speech production, which is again different from reading aloud.

13.2.1.1   False primacy of the written form

Given how much emphasis there is on writing and written communication in our society (and despite the claim that we are becoming a post-literate society), there is a tendency to judge what speech is through the rose-colored lens of written language.

One of the places in which this is very obvious is in the way that languages are taught to non-native speakers – it is almost always through the medium of the written language. In a couple of ways, this is not, at first glance, a bad thing. Many individuals learn faster or better if they can see the written form at the same time as hearing words. And many individuals want to be able to read in a second language, but are less interested in conversing in that language. However, this often has the undesirable effect of leading to common spoken usages being ignored in the second language class. For instance, in English, the written form of "Would you do it?" is at great variance with the way such an utterance would be pronounced in colloquial speech. If the second language student is taught only the formal pronunciation, closely reflected in the spelling, they may not understand this simple question if it is spoken naturally by a native speaker. This is not a desirable result, and is the source of considerable frustration on the part of language learners.[3]

---

[2] Formulating what one wants to say, and how to say it.

[3] This topic has been addressed in Section 10.12 under the heading "Sandhi."

13.2.2   Characteristics of speech and written language

Let us briefly examine some of the differences between speech and written language.

- Speech is as old as the human species, and while there is some controversy about this, it is most probable that some precursor of speech dates from before the existence of *Homo sapiens*. Writing was invented only about 5,200 years ago.[4]
- All humans who are not affected by certain neurological or physical anomalies speak. This has been true since there have been human beings. It is only for a relatively short time in the history of our species that humans have written, and for the great majority of the time since writing was first developed, very few people have been literate. Even in today's world, large numbers of people are non-literate.
- Writing provides a semi-permanent or permanent record unless explicitly destroyed, whereas speech is ephemeral – it disappears immediately upon production. A practical means of recording the sound of speech has been available for only a little more than a century, and the current fact that speech recording devices are in the hands of most people most of the time (in the form of note-taking apps and video recorders in smart phones and tablets) is a very recent phenomenon. Speech has been ephemeral for almost the entire time it has existed.
- Any time there are more than a few speakers of a language, there will be dialect differences based on geographical and social factors. In writing, by contrast, there is pressure to have a single system of writing that transcends dialect barriers. For instance, there would probably be some misunderstanding in conversation between individuals from Glasgow, Scotland, and those from San Francisco, California, and that is a normal and not very important fact. However, there could be very tragic consequences if the written repair or operational manuals for a commercial airliner were understood differently by maintenance technicians or pilots from these two different places. The written form of the language is deliberately more standard than speech.[5]
- Much of the time, written language is perceived to be more formal than speech. There are of course exceptions, such as formal speeches or casual scribbled notes, but the act of writing is more effortful than talking, and

---

[4] Parts of the first 4 items in this list are adapted from an article by William Bright on the Linguistic Society of America (LSA) website, though they include information from other sources: www.linguisticsociety.org/resource/whats-difference-between-speech-and-writing.

[5] While it goes beyond our purpose here, Martin Joos' *The Five Clocks* (1967) provides interesting perspective on styles of usage.

once a person has made the effort of writing, they usually devote at least a bit more effort to "getting it right."

- In many circumstances, spoken language is subject to interruption for clarification (or for correction or through impatience), whereas in writing one tries to anticipate confusion on the part of the reader and take the steps necessary to make the written text clear and unambiguous. Besides, the reader cannot question the writer in any immediate way – or, more often, at all.
- Speech is spontaneously learned by any child (in the absence of neurological or physical anomalies); indeed, the only way to prevent such learning is to isolate the child from spoken language input. Learning to speak a language from hearing speech input is a kind of biological imperative. By contrast, individuals typically learn to write only with explicit direct instruction; reading and writing are not a biological imperative, though humans are very capable of mastering these skills.
  - It is believed that writing was invented 3 times in human history. Phonetically or phonologically based writing was likely invented only once. It is clear that the concept and practice of writing did not come easily to our ancestors, whereas speech is as natural as breathing.
- To greater or lesser degrees, written language is, in a sense, a different language from spoken language. That is, the vernacular (the way that ordinary people really talk) is vastly different in many aspects of the grammar in comparison to the written form. This is truer of some languages than others, and some social strata than others.
  - A case in point: Swiss German. Swiss German is a *very* different language from German. Speakers of standard German largely cannot understand Swiss German (though some words would be familiar and recognizable). However, Germans and Swiss Germans *write* the same language, and that written language is formal High German.[6] So speakers of Swiss German, if they want to write, can write only in a language that they do not normally speak (and many cannot speak).
  - Written Arabic is very different in most cases from the spoken language used by those who write it. Arabic varies quite a bit regionally, but the written form varies much less.

---

[6] The term *High German* refers to a formal dialect that is regionally based but has taken on the role of standard dialect. It is called "high" because of the elevation above sea level of the region in which it is spoken, and in contrast to "low" German, spoken in areas of low elevation.

- Many utterances in speech would be unclear or ambiguous if written; in speech, there are many ways of modulating the phonetic output, as we have seen under the heading of "suprasegmentals" (Chapter 11). Subtleties of inflection that help a hearer decode an utterance are severely impoverished when speech is converted to writing.

The nature of the language used in spontaneous speech, as opposed to writing, is very different in other ways from those mentioned above. Speech is far more **repetitive** than writing. Hearers cannot go back and re-hear what has been said, as they can re-read parts of a written text, so speech demands repetition that writing does not. Speech is **highly inflected** in ways that writing is not. That is, speech makes use of all available *suprasegmentals* to ensure that meaning is fully decoded. Speech is **expansive**, requiring many more words to say what could be said in writing in many fewer words.

By contrast, written text is **compact** and **efficient**. That is, many fewer words are used to express the same idea. The structure of the sentences is selected in order to communicate the meaning without circumlocution. Many expressions used in speech are not used at all in writing (except where details of a conversation are written down). In writing intended for long-term use by many readers (for instance, technical manuals), the text is extensively revised with a view to making it clearer, less ambiguous, and direct.

Written language may make use of grammatical structures that are rarely used in speech, either because they sound "stiff" or too formal in speech, or because they place demands on processing (perception) that would be too much in speech because the material passes too quickly, whereas the reader of a text can go back to previous lines for clarification.

Let me give a couple of examples of the difference between writing and speech from personal experience.

13.2.2.1   Example 1: written language spoken

As an academic, I have often attended congresses where other academics present papers they have written as a contribution to scientific knowledge in the field. A certain percentage of presenters, for reasons ranging from inexperience to shyness to being uncertain of their spoken English, simply read a paper that they have written, verbatim, in a monotone voice. Quite often, the written paper that they are reading would be clear and easy to read silently to oneself, and its expression would be straightforward and compact in that situation. However, such a style does not work well when spoken. I have often sat in the audience, understanding almost every individual word the presenter spoke, but having very little idea what their paper was trying to communicate.

Compact written language does not work well when spoken, especially not when presented rapidly and with little inflection.

13.2.2.2   Example 2: spoken language written

As an expert witness in court and in quasi-legal proceedings,[7] I have read court testimony by other experts in my own field. These are court records of the exact words of another expert witness who was speaking spontaneously in response to an oral question from counsel in open session. When spoken words are written down, they are necessarily stripped of all pauses, intonations, gestures, stress, emphasis, and so on. Just the words are written, along with sentence punctuation created by the transcriber. My experience is that these documents are extremely hard to read for meaning, while I am certain that, had I been present when the testimony was given, I would have understood not simply the main meaning, but the subtle implications, and that without any particular effort. An exact transcription of speech can be very confusing to read.

13.2.2.3   The lesson of these examples: writing and speech are very different

These examples show just how vastly different spontaneous speech is from carefully written text. Good written text cannot be spoken aloud, nor spontaneous speech written down, if easy comprehensibility is to be maintained.

One example is the writing of a good speechwriter – that is, someone who writes out a text with the intention that it be spoken publicly by an individual such as a politician. In this instance, the trick is to make the writing reasonably compact and sophisticated without crossing the line to where its intelligibility would be low if read aloud – it is written language meant to be heard aloud, not read.

13.3   Rate of information transfer

Languages encode meaning or information in complex ways, and the details of how this is done vary tremendously among languages (despite languages having great similarities at a deeper level). Individual languages have greater or lesser complexity at different levels of the grammar. For example, in the phonetic domain, languages vary in the number of phonemes they have, from a low of 11 to a high of 112 (Rotokas and !Xóõ, respectively[8]).

---

[7] Such as tribunals regarding the registration of trademarks.
[8] Source: www.vistawide.com/languages/language_statistics.htm.

Overall, languages must have sufficient complexity to allow for the full range of meanings that languages are capable of expressing. One way that a language could add to the complexity of information transfer would be to allow words and sentences to be much longer, or to allow many more words to be necessary to express ideas.

In terms of human evolution, however, it would seem that communicative efficiency – the ability to transmit more information in less time – would be the best way of doing things. To take the cartoon staple of cavemen fighting a sabre-tooth tiger – assuming that the cavemen have a full-fledged human language – it is essential that the message from one to another be passed quickly and accurately for injury to be averted and hunting to be successful.

An important study (Pelligrino et al., 2011) demonstrated that different languages – including unrelated languages from different language families – arrive at a very similar rate of information transfer from talker to hearer. In this study, English, French, German, Italian, Japanese, Mandarin, Spanish, and Vietnamese[9] were shown to have very similar rates of information transfer. These languages vary in a wide range of factors: Mandarin has almost no grammatical inflections while German is a highly inflected language; words in Mandarin are generally monosyllabic, where many German words are quite long. Some of these languages have grammatical gender where others do not. The nature of the syntax of utterances varies greatly among languages. As we saw above, the number of phonemes in one language is approximately 10 times (one order of magnitude) greater than the number in another language.[10]

In essence, languages "solve" the problem of information transfer in vastly different ways – with remarkable variation in all aspects of their grammars – but appear to arrive at solutions having very similar efficacy. It is hard to ignore the implication that, through evolution, languages have come close to the maximum rate of information transfer possible using speech as the medium of transfer, given the limitations of our production and perception mechanisms.

One of the means of information transfer efficiency occurs at the phonetic/phonological level. A language with very few phonemes requires (on average, and all other things being equal) longer words than one with a large number of phonemes. But this "disadvantage" may be compensated for at other levels of the grammar.

---

[9] Vietnamese was chosen as the comparison language and assigned an information transfer rate value of 1. The other languages in the study showed information transfer rates from 0.74 to 1.08.

[10] Of course, neither of these languages was included in the study referred to in this section.

13.4 Speech perception

Speech perception is the process of comprehending speech that one hears. In this short section in a book about phonetics, we cannot cover this topic in detail, but it would be useful to examine some of the basic issues.

13.4.1 The telephone model ...

All of us have used a telephone; we have entered the individual digits of the phone number on the keypad (or clicked on an individual's name in an address book and let the electronic device enter the digits). Each of the digits entered generates a specific tone[11] and that tone is sent along the telephone lines (whether copper wires or fiber-optic cables), or through the air on cellular radio frequencies, continuing on until it reaches a switching unit that interprets the number and sends a ring signal to the appropriate telephone. That switching unit "perceives" the desired phone number.

It is natural for us to think that speech works in a similar way. A word is composed of phonemes and, in pronouncing a word, the talker produces the sound of each phoneme, like the tones of the individual digits in a phone number. When the sound of the word reaches the brain, interpretation centers extract the string of phonemes, the way that the telephone exchange equipment extracts the string of numbers. So there really isn't that much difference between entering a phone number such as 555-1234 – and having it decoded – and saying the word *yellowing*, with its 6 phonemes, /j-ɛ-l-oʷ-ɪ-ŋ/, and having the brain of our interlocutor decode it.

It seems, through this analogy, that the perception of speech would be a trivial process. After all, technology of the early 1960s could cope, automatically and economically, with "Touch-Tone" telephone dialing, correctly "interpreting" and connecting billions of telephone calls.

13.4.2 ... isn't a good analogy

The purpose of the rest of this section is to demonstrate how poorly the telephone dialing analogy matches up with the reality of perceiving words that have been spoken, and the many ways in which the reality of speech perception is infinitely more complex than automated decoding of the sound of telephone numbers.

Most of the issues to be addressed arise from the fact that phonemes are highly variable and the boundaries between them are ill defined and varying. This is very different from the nature of the tones associated with phone numbers – these latter have very little variability and have clear

---

[11] Actually, a pair of specific tones played simultaneously.

boundaries. The telephone exchange receives unambiguous, clear data from the telephone from which the call is being made; by contrast, the speech signal contains a great deal of ambiguity, and thus spoken words, when they reach our ears and then our brain, require not simply *decoding*, but the much more involved process of *perception*.

13.4.3   Bottom-up, top-down

The decoding of a telephone number by the telephone exchange system has traditionally been an entirely **bottom-up** or **data-driven** function.[12] That is to say, the determination – by the telephone exchange system – of which individual phone the caller wants to connect to is determined by the sound of the tones coming down the line, and nothing else.

It is in this sense that such function is called *data-driven*: the data (i.e., the sound of the individual number tones) are *the only information* that is used by the telephone exchange to determine which particular telephone to put the call through to.

If we think of the telephone exchange as having a "higher" function than an individual telephone (because the telephone exchange has to interpret the incoming information) – if we think of the exchange as having some sort of executive function – then it makes sense to call this process *bottom-up*: the "lower"-level device, the individual telephone, provides all of the information needed by the exchange to make the identification of the desired phone number.

As we will see, the perception of speech requires a considerable amount of **top-down processing**, in which the higher device (in this instance, the brain) applies a great deal of intelligence (processing power) to decipher and disambiguate the incoming signal. Marslen-Wilson and Welsh (1978) propose a model "in which top-down processing constraints interact directly with bottom-up information to produce the primary lexical interpretation of the acoustic–phonetic input."

13.4.4   Segmentation

The decoding of telephone numbers, as described above, makes use of a particular characteristic of the signal coming from a dialed phone number – namely, the incoming signal is composed of discrete units: 7 digits, or 10 with area code, in the type of phone number used in North America. That is, the incoming signal can be easily segmented and the individual units distinguished.

---

[12] While, in more recent years, some level of artificial intelligence has been injected into these systems, the point remains that, for many, many decades, these systems worked error-free without modern information technology and artificial intelligence.

By contrast, the way that individual speech sounds are produced leads to gradual transitions and overlap between sounds, as we saw in Chapter 10. This is different from the sharp, abrupt changes between the digits in a phone number. This creates a serious problem for the speech perception centers of the brain: determining where one phoneme ends and another begins. This is the problem of *segmentation.*

Figure 13.1 shows the nature of the problem visually, in a comparison between the sound of a dialed phone number and a spoken word.

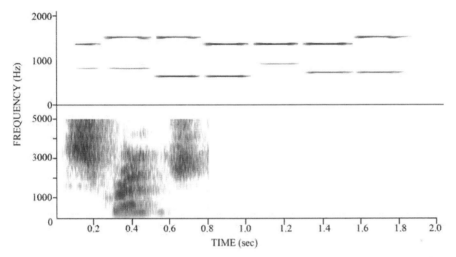

Figure 13.1 Segmentation of speech. Spectrogram of the tones of a phone number and of a single word with a similar number of segments as there are tones. The phone number is 893-2056, and the word is *scrunched* [skɹʌntʃt]. Notice how much easier it is to visually segment the phone number than the word. The final [t] of *scrunched* is unreleased, and therefore we are counting 7 segments in the word, same as the number of tones in the phone number.

13.4.5   Invariance (context, individual, speech conditions, encoding)

The success of telephone switching equipment in directing calls without error is dependent in part upon the *invariance* of the signal. That is to say, the sound of the "3" button on a telephone makes the same sound, always. While there might be some tiny frequency differences among different individual telephones, any such variance remains extremely small. Importantly, the sound of the "3" button will never ever come close to the sounds of the "2" or the "4" buttons.

Speech, however, is very different. There is a great deal of **variance** in the sound of a given phoneme, so much so that the sounds of some pairs of different phonemes sometimes overlap so that one sounds like the other. This is particularly true of vowels in a language such as English – English has a large number of different vowel phonemes, and so they are closer in sound to one another than vowels in a language that has, for example, 5 vowel sounds.[13]

For instance, English distinguishes the phonemes /i/ and /ɪ/, as in *Pete* and *pit*. When recordings are made of individuals talking in normal conversation, and the sounds of these vowels are analyzed, it is found that some instances of each vowel phoneme overlap acoustically with the other. In other words, sometimes they sound the same!

By the same token, the same phoneme may sound very different on different occasions, said by different speakers, and in different phonetic contexts.

13.4.5.1 Context causes variance

As we saw in Chapter 10, the sounds preceding and following the phoneme in question will affect the details of its articulation, and thus the details of the sound produced. A vowel sounds different if followed by a voiced or by a voiceless plosive, for example.

These effects do not simply apply within words, but across word boundaries as well, a phenomenon known as **sandhi**, as we also saw in Chapter 10. For example, the sound of the final sound of "could" and the first sound of "you" combine in the phrase "Could you go?"

13.4.5.2 Individual talkers cause variance

Each talker has their individual way of pronouncing sounds, though there remains variability within each individual. There is also systematic variance based on the age and sex of the talker – ultimately related to the length of the individual's vocal tract and loss of tissue elasticity with age. Additionally, in some cultures there are gender-based ways of talking that introduce other variance across the population.

So much does the size of the vocal tract influence the acoustics of individual phonemes that a given female talker's phoneme may more resemble a *different* phoneme produced by a male than the *same* phoneme produced by a male (MacKay, 2014, p. 221).

Imagine how the telephone switching system might function if each individual telephone sent out different sounds than other telephones for a given numeral! The task the human brain faces in decoding speech far exceeds any problems faced by telephone switching equipment.

---

[13] English is unusual in having such a high number of vowel phonemes. It is much more common for languages to have 3 to 7 vowel sounds.

13.4.5.3   Speech conditions cause variance

The conditions under which speech is produced will affect the sounds of individual phonemes. For instance, it is possible to produce intelligible speech with a mouth full of food. However, the specifics of the sounds of the phonemes are changed. Similarly, if the individual has certain types of illnesses (such as ones that greatly reduce the pressure of exhaled air or interfere with vocal fold vibration), it may affect the individual speech sounds, though they may remain entirely intelligible to others.

If a person talks over a loud background noise, it is likely that their articulation of sounds will change from their normal speech production.

Overall, many factors cause the sound of a given phoneme to vary greatly due to a number of considerations. What is extraordinary is that, within limits, our speech perception centers overcome this obstacle and allow us to comprehend what is said despite these variances.

13.4.6   Speaker normalization

As noted, different talkers produce different sounds when they say the same thing. Some of this difference in sound is due to systematic differences in the talkers – most importantly, the overall length of the vocal tract. This, in turn, correlates strongly with the overall size of the talker's physical frame. Some of the difference among talkers is idiosyncratic, having to do with individual speech habits and small variations in the shape of the vocal tract.

In order to perceive speech produced by different talkers, the hearer must "compensate" for differences in sounds generated by longer or shorter vocal tracts. This subconscious mental process in the hearer is known as *speaker normalization. Normalization* means changing in accordance with some standard (or "normal") value, and speaker normalization is a kind of mental process of modifying the incoming speech signal so that it conforms to a standard.[14]

Here is an anecdote from personal experience in which this normally unconscious process can come to conscious awareness; it is an experience shared by many people. Sometimes, when I telephone a company or other enterprise, the person or recording answering the phone may make a statement, such as a company slogan, that was not expected. Sometimes, I initially do not understand what is said, but by the end of the sentence I understand and can mentally reconstruct the initial parts of the sentence

---

[14] This statement is intended as a metaphor to help the reader understand what must be accomplished; it is not intended as a description of how the process functions.

that I did not understand when they were spoken. What is happening is that it takes hearing several words to be able to normalize for this particular talker, then that normalization factor can be applied to the rest of what the same talker says, and – to a small extent – retroactively.

There are a number of factors that contribute to the ability to normalize talkers' speech successfully. One of these is the ratio of Formant 1 and Formant 2 (F1 and F2),[15] a ratio that remains relatively (not absolutely) constant among talkers despite differences in vocal tract length. Context is another factor – in a given context, particular vocabulary items may be expected. It is said that standard greetings, especially between strangers, help to permit quick normalization due to the predictability of the words of greeting.

The fundamental frequency of the voice (F_0) may help as well. If the F_0 falls in the typical female range, then the hearer can expect the formant values to be more typical of female than of male talkers. Visual information can help when talking face to face since formant values tend to correlate to gender and body size.

13.4.7   Perceptual constancy, categorical perception

A general principle of perception that is not restricted to speech is *perceptual constancy*. For example, if you see a dog, you recognize it as a dog whether you see it from the front or the side or above. The enormous variation in size, color, and shape among dogs does not prevent you from recognizing them all as dogs. That is, the perception of a dog is constant despite the huge variation in how they look.

The phonetic possibilities of the human vocal tract are enormous. A great range of different sounds is possible. Each individual language (and each dialect of the language) makes use of a limited range of these sounds, and allows a range of slightly different variants of the sound. We can call this list of sounds or phonemes a list of *categories*. A talker's production of a particular sound (in a word) induces a hearer (who is a speaker of the same language) to perceive the sounds to be in one or another of these categories, and not to perceive any of them as "between this sound and that sound" even if in reality the sound in question fell between the categories. Perceiving speech sounds, despite variations in them, as being representatives of different categories is called *categorical perception.*[16]

For example, many experiments and demonstrations have been performed based on the fact that it is possible to construct a range of recordings that

---

[15] See the section on formants in the acoustics chapter: Section 12.12.
[16] The term *categorial perception* is sometimes used in order to emphasize that the process does not involve what we would call *categories* in other areas – that this is a very specific perceptual function.

form a continuum of steps between an English /p/ and an English /b/, normally with a vowel making syllables such as /pɑ/ and /bɑ/, and the steps between. All of the recordings, except the ones at either end of the continuum, represent sounds that are truly between /p/ and /b/. If these are played one at a time to individuals who are asked to identify what they have heard, they will identify the syllables as /pɑ/ or /bɑ/, never something partway between. Note, however, that the speaker of a different language may make different responses because the categories in that language are different from in English.

To reiterate: when a range of syllables are played that are partway between English /pɑ/ and English /bɑ/, native speakers of English hear them as one of /pɑ/ or /bɑ/. They do not hear them as partway between. That is, their perception of the sounds is **categorical**: the syllable falls in one or the other category, and is not seen as something representative of a non-category.

Assignment of an incoming sound to one or another category (i.e. hearing it as one or another phoneme) is something that is done automatically and very rapidly, without conscious input.

13.4.8 Hearing impairment, dialect, L2 accent, noisy environment

We noted in Subsection 13.4.3 that a telephone switching system functions in an entirely **bottom-up** or **data-driven** fashion, using the clear and unambiguous sound of the telephone number. As we have been explaining throughout Section 13.4, the sound of the speech signal is not as clear as telephone tones and is ambiguous in many ways.

Several factors can decrease the clarity of the incoming speech signal. Among them is hearing impairment on the part of the hearer, or the talker speaking a dialect that is less familiar to the hearer than their own. Additionally, the talker might have a second language (L2) accent or the environment may be noisy.

13.4.9 Top-down processing

Given the well-known ambiguities in the speech signal, it becomes clear that, in addition to the bottom-up processing of speech, perception of spoken language involves a good deal of top-down processing as well. We have alluded to the existence of such mechanisms under the headings of segmentation, invariance, and categorical perception.

Since the incoming speech signal is highly variable and often does not have unambiguous boundaries between phonemes, the central processor in the brain must impose some order and make sense of that signal – it is not the simple task of "reading" the incoming beeps that the traditional telephone exchange has to do.

Before proceeding to a discussion of top-down processing, it must be said that everything starts in a bottom-up fashion. A talker says something and the hearer takes in the available data from the speech stream. There is typically some ambiguity in the speech signal, something that needs to be clarified, and the characteristics of the particular talker's speech must be adjusted for. What the hearer finally perceives, after top-down processing, must conform to the data that were heard in the original speech signal. In that sense, all speech perception starts with bottom-up processing. (Sometimes we are surprised by the misunderstandings of speech that occur in real life, and might be inclined to believe that what was perceived is not at all consistent with the data in the speech signal. However, what is perceived will be consistent with *the aspects of the incoming signal that were captured by the hearer* and sent to their brain.)

The following are among the factors that have a top-down influence on the perception of speech.

13.4.9.1 Topic

The subject that two interlocutors are discussing may influence how a particular word or words are interpreted. There is not much difference (in some dialects, at least) between the sound of the words *will* and *well*. The same phonetic signal might be interpreted as one or the other depending on whether the topic of conversation was inheritance or finding water under the earth. Knowledge of the topic leads the speech processor to favor one interpretation over the other.

13.4.9.2 Word

Let us say that a word is spoken and its sound signal is not absolutely clear. It might be [tif] or it might be [tiθ]. Since only the second word exists in standard American English, the hearer is likely to perceive the second, namely *teeth*.[17] There is a bias toward hearing real words, and a bias toward hearing more common words. "Common" words may depend on the topic of conversation – if two colleagues in a particular specialized field are talking, then a word that would be rare to the general population may be a common word in that context.

13.4.9.3 Phonemic restoration

Numerous studies have shown that, if a single phoneme is replaced or masked by an extraneous sound such as white noise, a beep, or other sound,

---

[17] At the time of writing, both *teef* and *teaf* exist as nonstandard words, either dialectally or as subculture slang, so speakers of these will have different constraints on their perception, as compared to people from the general population.

hearers will believe that they have heard the missing phoneme. If asked about the intrusive sound, they will typically state that the sound occurred at a different point in the utterance than where it truly occurred; they will not realize that they have not heard a particular phoneme.

Since the phoneme in question was not present in the recording – it simply was not there – the only explanation for its presence in hearers' minds is that their brains put the sound there. This is perhaps the clearest type of top-down processing, since the phoneme in question could not have been processed bottom-up: it was not there to be processed.

13.4.9.4 Context and grammar (in its broad sense)

The context and grammatical structure of an utterance will help the hearer decode in the case of ambiguity of the incoming speech.

These two sentences do not sound different when spoken without special emphasis:[18]

- The teacher showed the video.
- The teachers showed the video.

In the context of a narrative about a single teacher debating whether or not to show a particular video to their class, this sentence would be heard with a singular word *teacher*. In the context of a narrative about two or several teachers debating whether or not to show a particular video to their classes, this sentence would be heard with the plural word *teachers*.

Even if we recorded one of the two sentences (again, spoken normally, without special emphasis that would reveal whether the word is *teacher* or *teachers*) and played the exact same recorded sentence in one or the other of the contexts, hearers would be certain that they heard either the absence of the *-s* or the presence of the *-s*.

Imagine the following sentence spoken without the context of a preceding narrative:

- Both the teachers showed the video they were discussing yesterday.

Again, in ordinary General American speech, this would sound the same if the talker imagined the word *teacher* to be singular (again, no special emphasis). Yet any speaker of General American would be certain of having heard the *-s* at the end of *teachers*, even if the plural ending was entirely assimilated into the initial sound of *showed*.

The point here is that the grammatical structure of the sentence requires that *teachers* be plural; the word *both* demands the plural. That grammatical

---

[18] It is possible to say these sentences so that the two phones sound different, but the point is that in ordinary General American casual speech, these would sound the same.

necessity ensures that a speaker of this variety would be certain of hearing a [s] sound even if it was not present. This is a clear example of top-down processing. Grammatical knowledge modifies the perception of the incoming speech signal.

It would be useful here to emphasize a point about these top-down influences. Top-down influences will be in accord with the hearer's knowledge and dialect. If the hearer speaks a dialect other than one corresponding to formal written English (and we all do in one way or another), they will be influenced by the grammar and vocabulary of their own dialect, not necessarily the one of the talker, or the writer, or the one used in formal situations.

13.4.9.5 McGurk effect

This effect, named after one of a pair of researchers who first reported it, demonstrates that visual input can affect what one hears in a very particular way. In the classic example, a sound recording is made of a person saying "ba-ba" [ba ba]. The sound is carefully synchronized to a video of the same individual saying "ga-ga" [gɑ gɑ]; the original sound track is eliminated so only the "ba-ba" plays with the video. People watching and listening to the video most commonly hear "da-da" [dɑ dɑ], a sound that does not occur visually or auditorily! If the same listener closes their eyes, then they "correctly" hear [ba-ba].

This is a demonstration of top-down processing, because information that arrives through the visual channel affects what a person hears (perceives). The data that cause the person not to perceive the [ba ba] signal correctly is not in the acoustic signal; it must have been present in the brain (through the visual route), leading to the anomalous interpretation of the syllables.

13.4.10 In sum

The hearer of spoken language is presented with a complex, rapidly varying acoustic signal. This signal lacks explicit markers for the division between phonemes or between words. Worse, the signal does not contain clear, unvarying sounds corresponding to each phoneme: different sounds correspond to the same phoneme, and sometimes the same sound corresponds to different phonemes.

Despite this fact, the hearer recognizes words and other meaningful units in speech and does so with a very high level of accuracy, then determines the underlying grammatical relationships among the words, permitting the hearer to extract meaning from the overall utterance.

So the central issue in speech perception is how hearers resolve the phonological units within the variable incoming phonetic stream, and integrate those into a determination of the content and meaning of what the talker is saying.

13.5 The ear

While, in popular speech, "the ear" often refers to just the external part on the side of the head (called the *pinna* in anatomical terminology), the ear is a complex organ consisting of several basic parts that are hidden from view inside the bones of the skull. These various parts perform a number of remarkable tasks. First, the ear captures the tiny amount of energy in *sound waves* passing through the air (Chapter 12) and transfers the airborne vibratory energy to a liquid medium in the inner ear. Then those vibrations are analyzed in terms of their *amplitude* and *frequency* characteristics – some of this analysis occurs locally in the ear (in technical terms, *peripherally*) and the rest of the analysis is performed in the brain (*centrally*).

It is important to understand just how minuscule the amount of energy is in the weakest (lowest-amplitude) sounds that we can hear, and how remarkable it is that such sounds are heard at all.

For purposes of understanding the anatomy and functioning of the ear, it is divided into three parts: the *outer ear*, the *middle ear*, and the *inner ear*. We will consider each in the following sections. See Figure 13.2.

13.5.1 Outer ear

The *outer ear* collects sound energy and channels it toward the middle ear. The external part that is visible is the *pinna*, as noted above. This gives way to the *auditory canal* leading inward toward the middle ear. The auditory canal is also called the *external auditory meatus*, the *ear canal*, and various other combinations of terms. The ear canal and pinna combine to increase the sensitivity of human hearing.

Ear wax, known as *cerumen*, is secreted into the ear canal and is normally slowly moved toward the outside of the body. It is possible for cerumen to form lumps and to dry out, causing blockages in the ear canal. These will reduce hearing acuity (i.e. raise hearing thresholds) and/or cause pain or discomfort.

The pinna has a characteristic shape, and various parts of the pinna have specialized names. The shape of the pinna not only captures sound energy, but it aids in permitting the hearer to determine the direction from which sound comes, at least within certain frequency ranges.

The outer ear ends at the *tympanic membrane*, which is the anatomical terminology for what is informally called the *eardrum*.

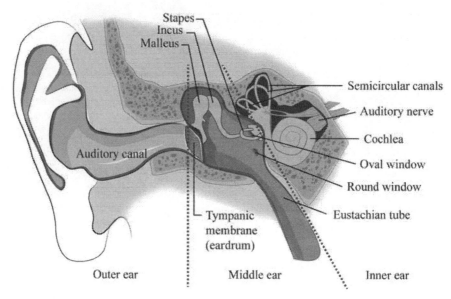

Figure 13.2 The ear

13.5.2   Middle ear

13.5.2.1   Tympanic membrane

The *tympanic membrane* (*TM*) or *eardrum* is a thin membrane that creates an airtight seal between the *outer* and *middle ear*. It is about a square centimeter (1 cm², or about 0.16 square inches) in area.

   Under normal circumstances, the pressure in the air surrounding a person and the air pressure within their middle ear are the same, a necessary state for the best hearing. One would think that this would mean that the TM would be flat, but, in fact, it is bowed inward (forming a slight cone shape) where it adheres to one of the *ossicles* (small bones) of the middle ear (specifically, the *malleus* or *hammer*).

13.5.2.2   Middle ear cavity

The *middle ear space* or *middle ear cavity* is an air-filled cavity within the temporal bone of the skull. It is lined with epithelial tissue. Normally, it does not connect in any way to the atmosphere surrounding the individual, though the air pressure within it should be the same as the surrounding atmosphere. However, the two pressures can come to differ from one another for any of a number of reasons: oxygen is absorbed into the tissues surrounding the middle ear, reducing pressure inside; changes in weather cause the air pressure surrounding the individual to change – either to increase or decrease; the individual can change altitude by walking up or down hill, driving, or taking a plane.

   To maintain equal pressure inside the middle ear cavity and the atmosphere surrounding the individual, it is necessary to connect the two bodies of air temporarily. This is accomplished through the *Eustachian tube.* The Eustachian tube is a tubular duct running from the middle ear to the *nasopharynx.* Because of where its entrance is located, you cannot see the entrance in the mirror or by looking into the mouth of another person; it is above the velum.

During swallowing and yawning, the entrance to the Eustachian tube may open temporarily, permitting air pressure to equalize between the middle ear space and the surrounding atmosphere.

If the air pressure on the two sides of the TM is unequal, the TM will be stretched and distorted. This will reduce hearing acuity, it can be quite painful, and if the difference is too great, it could cause the TM to rupture.[19] This is why babies cry when airplanes take off or land: there is typically a large, rapid change in air pressure inside the aircraft cabin at these times.

13.5.2.3 Ossicular chain

Within the middle ear is a "chain" of three small bones called the *ossicles* (meaning 'small bones'). These ossicles are *articulated* one to another, meaning that there are bendable joints between them – not permitting as much movement as the elbow or the knee, but joints nonetheless.

In common parlance, the three bones (starting at the TM and working toward the inner ear) are called the *hammer,* the *anvil,* and the *stirrup,* based loosely on the shapes of the bones. The anatomical terms are *malleus, incus,* and *stapes.*[20] The malleus adheres to the TM, and the "*footplate*" of the stapes presses against the *oval window* of the *inner ear.*

There are also small muscles in the middle ear. These are involved in a reflex loop such that when unusually loud noises are heard, the muscles contract, disarticulating the ossicular chain, and thus reducing the amplitude of the sound that arrives in the inner ear. This helps to protect the delicate structures in the inner ear from the assault of very loud noises.

13.5.3 Function of the middle ear

It is often said in short introductions to the structure and function of the ear that the middle ear "transmits" vibrations from the outer ear / TM to the inner ear. What any such statement fails to address is this: why is such a complex structure, with so many moving parts (as well as susceptibility to infection and damage), required for this seemingly simple job of "transmitting" vibration?

---

[19] Often, in video of the scene of an explosion, one sees individuals bleeding from the ears. What has happened is that the tremendous wave of air pressure thrown out by the blast ruptures the eardrum and may damage other tissue in the ears, so bleeding occurs.

[20] ... which mean *hammer, anvil,* and *stirrup,* but in Latin, like many anatomical terms used in English.

Indeed, the ears of reptiles are simpler than those of mammals, having (among other differences) only 1 ossicle. The mammalian ear, resulting from the evolutionary migration of two bones associated with the jaw to the inner ear, has 3 ossicles and is more sensitive than the reptilian ear.

What purpose does this complex mechanism of three little bones perform?

13.5.3.1   Impedance mismatch

The inner ear, which we discuss below, is filled with a viscous liquid and the sensory cells (those that convert sound into a sensation in the nerves that the brain interprets as sound) are immersed in this liquid. This liquid is responsible for transmitting the vibratory energy of sound to the sensory cells that the liquid surrounds. This means that the vibrations – rapid changes in air pressure – must be transmitted from the medium of air into the medium of liquid. Such transmission is very difficult because the properties of air and liquid are very different. In technical terminology, there is an *impedance mismatch* between the two substances that transmit sound to the end-organ of hearing, and sound energy does not transfer well from one medium to the other where a large impedance mismatch is present.

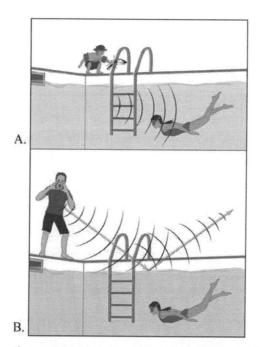

Figure 13.3 Underwater swimmer hears the metal ladder vibrating underwater, but does not hear a voice generated above the water.

Imagine a friend swimming below the surface of the water in a swimming pool. Bang on the railing of the ladder with a metal object. The vibrations in the railing will send sound waves into the water and your friend will hear the sound clearly. See Figure 13.3A.

Now, with your friend's head below water again, shout at her. Will she hear you? Not a chance (Figure 13.3B).

The first part of this little experiment shows that sound waves propagate through water without difficulty. (Water is a different liquid than that in the inner ear, but the principle is the same: they are both liquids.) However, the second part of the experiment shows that sound waves in the air do not enter water very well. Indeed, as you shout at the surface of the water, almost all of the sound energy of your voice simply reflects off the surface of the water, with only very small amounts of sound energy penetrating the surface (see Figure 13.4). The *impedance mismatch* at the air–water interface prevents transmission of sound energy (it provokes the reflection of most of the energy, as shown in the figure).

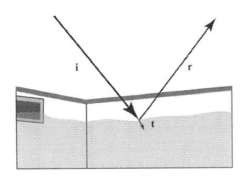

Figure 13.4 Impedance mismatch. A sound wave moving through air strikes the surface of the water. This is the incident wave (i). Very little of the sound energy is transmitted (t) into the water. Most of the energy is reflected (r) off the surface of the water, due to the impedance mismatch of the two media through which the sound is propagating.

The liquid in the inner ear is more viscous (thicker) than the water shown in Figures 13.3 and 13.4, so the impedance mismatch is even greater than between air and water. The upshot of this is that airborne sound waves would be mostly reflected – never reaching the organ of hearing – if not for the special properties of the middle ear.

13.5.3.2 Impedance matching device
The middle ear doesn't simply *transmit* sound energy from outer to inner ear; it acts to match the impedances of the two mediums (air in the ear canal and fluid in the inner ear) so that sound *can* be transmitted. In technical terms, the middle ear is an *impedance matching device*.

The middle ear makes use of two principles in order to accomplish this feat: it *concentrates energy*, and it uses the *principle of the lever*.

13.5.3.3 Concentrating energy
Most of us have used a magnifying glass to concentrate the rays of the sun and make some plant material catch fire. The direct rays of the sun are not

sufficient to set the material on fire. But if you take all of the sun's energy over an area the size, let us say, of half the palm of your hand, and concentrate all that energy on one small spot with the magnifying glass, then that greater amount of energy is sufficient to set the material on fire or to burn its surface.

The ear captures energy over the surface of the TM, which is approximately 1 cm² in surface area. All of that energy (what is not lost in transmission) enters the inner ear through the oval window, which has a tiny surface area. The sound energy has been concentrated – collected from a large area and concentrated on a small area – so that it is strong enough to move the liquid in the inner ear, which is much denser and more resistant to movement than the molecules of air through which the sound arrived at the outer ear. See Figure 13.5.

Figure 13.5 A magnifying glass captures the sun's energy over the entire glass surface, and concentrates it on one small spot

13.5.3.4   Principle of the lever

The *principle of the lever* is one that is used by all kinds of machines, including simple ones such as a shovel or a wheelbarrow. Basically, it permits trading force for distance. See Figure 13.6.

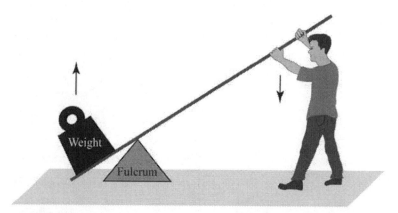

Figure 13.6 The lever permits the trading of force for distance. The man can pull down with less force than the weight, but he must move his end of the lever farther than the weight will move. The oval window moves less distance than the TM, but does so with greater force.

In the figure, the lever (basically a board) runs from the weight to the man's hands. In between is a support called a fulcrum. In this instance, the fulcrum is much closer to the weight than to the man. Let us say that the distance from weight to fulcrum is 1 unit, and from fulcrum to the man's hand is 6 units. This means that if the man pushes down with 1 kilogram of force,[21] the other end of the pole pushes up with 6 kilograms of force. The man has multiplied the force he can exert with the lever, and is thus able to lift a weight that would otherwise be too heavy for him. But there is a cost: the man must push the lever 6 centimeters of distance for every 1 centimeter that the weight is raised. So: distance moved is traded for force.

A lever effect is provided by the configuration of the ossicles in the middle ear.

13.5.3.5   Combining principles

The middle ear combines these two principles in order to change the energy in a sound wave propagating in air to create a wave propagating in the liquid in the middle ear. That's why we have a middle ear. It greatly multiplies the sensitivity of our hearing compared to sound waves in air directly striking the oval window. In effect, by combining these principles, the middle ear acts as an amplifier of the incoming sound.

13.5.4   Inner ear

In the drawing of the anatomy of the ear, Figure 13.2, you will see that there are two major parts of the inner ear: the *cochlea* and the *semicircular canals*.[22] The semicircular canals make up the principal part of the *vestibular system*, a sensory organ responsible for balance and orientation in three-dimensional space. Because of the close connection between the cochlea and the semicircular canals, it is possible for disease processes to affect both systems; for example, Menière's disease can result in problems of balance and orientation, as well as hearing loss (temporary or permanent). However, we will have nothing more to say about the vestibular system beyond the fact that both it and the hearing mechanism share the same cranial nerve. This nerve is called the *auditory nerve* or *cranial nerve VIII* (eighth cranial nerve), but other names are sometimes used that reflect the dual function of the nerve.

---

[21] Readers may know that the kilogram ($\approx$ 2.2 lbs) is not truly a unit of force. However, it is sometimes informally used as one when making a simple point such as has been done here.

[22] ... and, between them, the *vestibule*, which is not labeled in the drawing and which will not be mentioned again.

As shown in Figure 13.2, the other major component to the inner ear is the *cochlea*. This is where the end-organ of hearing is located – it is where vibration is transformed into electrical signals that the brain can then interpret as sound.

13.5.5   The cochlea

13.5.5.1   General structure of the cochlea

The cochlea is shaped like a snail – indeed, its name comes from the Greek word for snail. The shape is that of a spiral tube that becomes smaller in diameter as one goes farther from the large end. The cochlea turns through 360° 2.75 times – that is, it makes 2¾ circles. The cochlea is filled with fluid and is subdivided into parallel channels that will be outlined below. The end of the cochlea nearest the middle ear is its *base* or *basal* end. The end of the cochlea farthest from the middle ear (at the center of the spiral) is its *apex* or its *apical* end. See Figures 13.2 and 13.7.

Think of the cochlea as a tube that becomes progressively smaller, with both ends blocked off. Now, mentally curl that tube into a tight spiral, and you have the general form of the cochlea.

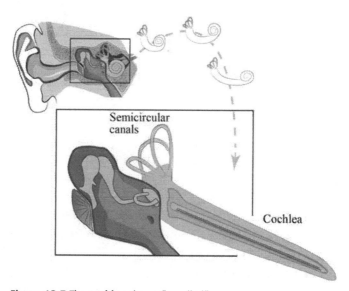

Semicircular canals

Cochlea

Figure 13.7 The **cochlea** shown "unrolled"

The large end of the cochlea forms part of the "walls" of the middle ear cavity. The membrane separating the cochlea from the middle ear cavity has two points of particular interest. The first of these is the *oval window*, where the *footplate* of the *stapes* ("stirrup") rests. The second of these is the *round window*,[23] which is a small area of the membrane that can bulge outward in response to pressure on the fluid (Figure 13.7).

As you will recall, vibration is transmitted through the ossicular chain to the footplate of the stapes. This means that, when sound is present, there is a pulsating pressure on the oval window from tiny movements of its footplate. As the oval window presses inward, it displaces fluid within the cochlea. Fluid cannot be compressed the way air can, so the displaced fluid has to move somewhere. The cochlea cannot bulge outward because it is encased in bone. The pressure is relieved by the *round window* bulging outward.

13.5.5.2   Scalas or scalae

We have stated that the cochlea is filled with fluid, but the situation is more complex than that. Along the length of the cochlea, there are two membranes that cross the cochlea, from side to side. They divide the interior of the cochlea into three channels or passageways. Each of these channels is called a *scala*,[24] plural *scalas* or *scalae*. See Figure 13.8, which shows the cochlea partially "unrolled" for clarity.

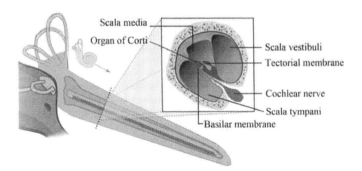

Figure 13.8 The **cochlea** shown with the scalas visible

On the cochlear side of the *oval window* is the *scala vestibuli*. On the cochlear side of the *round window* is the *scala tympani*. The channel between these two scalae is the *scala media*; as will be explained shortly, this is where sound is processed into neural signals. Because of the positioning

---

[23] The word *window* should not be interpreted as an opening; there is no opening between the cochlea and the middle ear in normal circumstances. The "windows," oval and round, are flexible areas in the membrane that can bulge inwards or outwards, in response to movements of the stapes and pressure in the fluid of the cochlea.

[24] From the Latin word for 'ladder,' but it is more intuitive to think of the scalas as *channels* or *passageways*.

of the two membranes, the cross-section of the scala media is roughly tri-angular (Figure 13.8).

The apical end of the scala media is closed off and therefore its fluid cannot mix with that of the other scalas. The fluid in the scala media is different from the fluid in the other two scalas. The fluid in the *scala media* is called *endolymph.*

The closed apical end of the scala media stops just short of the apical end of the cochlea, so there is a small crescent-shaped passageway around the end of the scala media, called the *helicotrema.* Because the scala vestibuli and scala tympani are connected in this way, the fluid is the same in these two scalas. This fluid is called *perilymph.*[25]

13.5.5.2.1 Route of the vibratory energy. The vibrations caused by sound waves contacting the tympanic membrane cause vibrations in the ossicles, which in turn are conducted to the footplate of the stapes, as we have seen. The footplate of the stapes vibrates the oval window, transferring the vibrations to the fluid within the cochlea, initially to the perilymph in the scala vestibuli.

Vibrations propagating through the perilymph in the scala vestibuli will necessarily create movement in the membrane separating it from the scala media, and thus transfer vibrational energy into the endolymph. This, in turn, will cause movement in any structure within the scala media. Movement of the scala media will cause movement of the perilymph in the scala tympani as well.

13.5.5.3   Membranes and the organ of Corti

The membrane that separates the scala media from the scala vestibuli is called *Reissner's membrane.* (See Figure 13.9.) It is a simple membrane that is flexible enough to permit the transmission of pressure waves in the perilymph into the endolymph of the scala media. Vibrations caused by sound are converted into electrical signals within complex structures located inside the scala media.

The *basilar membrane* is situated on the separation between the scala media and the scala tympani. Situated along the basilar membrane is the *organ of Corti.* It is at the organ of Corti that sound detection occurs – that is, it is where the movements of the endolymph are converted to signals in the nerve pathways. Remember that Figure 13.9 is a cross-section of the cochlea at one point. Therefore, the organ of Corti is a long strip, following the full length of the scala media.

---

[25] Here's a way to remember. *Endo* means 'in' or 'inside', as in *endoscope. Peri* refers to the outside of something, as in *perimeter* ('outside measure') or *peripheral.* Endolymph is in the *inside* channel (scala media) and perilymph is in the *outside* channels.

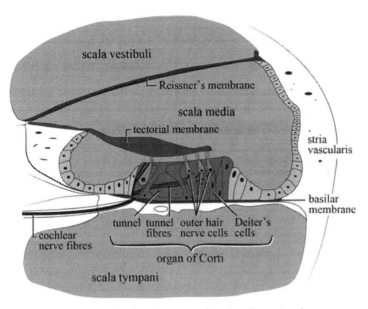

Figure 13.9 Scala media, showing organ of Corti and associated structures

As can be seen in Figure 13.9, situated within the organ of Corti are cells called **hair cells.** Since this figure shows a cross-section, keep in mind that for each of the 4 hair cells that are shown, there is a row of such cells along the organ of Corti, coming forward out of the image, and back into the image, making a total of about 15,000 hair cells in each ear. The hair cells that are closer to the center of the spiral are called **inner hair cells,** and those closer to the outer edge of the cochlea are called **outer hair cells.**

The term **hair cell** can be misleading. Indeed, these are cells that have tiny hair-like structures, but the word *hair* refers only to the shape and proportions of these structures; they do not resemble hair in any other sense. These structures are correctly called **stereocilia** (singular *stereocilium*), and some groups of hair cells include one **kinocilium.**

The stereocilia (plus kinocilia where they are present) protruding from a single hair cell form what is called a **hair bundle.** Figure 13.10[26] shows a closer view of the organ of Corti. It can be seen in this image that the stereocilia are attached to – they are part of – the hair cells. They may touch, *but are not part of,* the **tectorial membrane** that is above them.[27]

---

[26] www.researchgate.net/figure/Schematic-representation-of-the-organ-of-Corti-The-figure-shows-the-different-cell-types_fig1_224899283 (redrawn).

[27] The tectorial membrane is "above" the hair cells in Figures 13.9 and 13.10; the structures are illustrated in this fashion for clarity. In the real ear, the cochlea spirals around so that the membrane is below the hair cells in certain places.

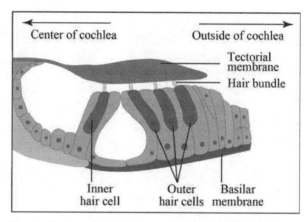

Figure 13.10 Basilar membrane, organ of Corti, and the tectorial membrane.

Schematic representation of the organ of Corti. The figure shows the different cell types and extracellular structures in the organ of Corti.

When the fluids of the cochlea are agitated by the presence of sound, the tectorial membrane and the hair cells do not move in unison, given the flexibility of the structures. Relative to the hair cells, the tectorial membrane moves side-to-side and gets closer or farther away from the stereocilia, in a back-and-forth motion.

As a result, the stereocilia may be touched by the tectorial membrane, and may be pushed in one direction or another. As the drawing shows, the stereocilia in a single hair bundle are of different lengths. As a result, smaller relative movement of the tectorial membrane may touch only the longest stereocilia, whereas a greater movement may cause contact with the shorter ones. This forms part of the mechanism by which the loudness of sound can be perceived.

13.5.6   Pitch perception

Humans can hear a wide range of frequencies, from a low of 20 Hz to a high, in a healthy young ear, of 20,000 Hz. Additionally, frequencies that are close to one another can be distinguished with remarkable precision. How is the cochlea able to distinguish the frequencies of sound? This ability is known as **pitch perception.** As we saw in Chapter 12, **frequency** is the measure of a physical phenomenon in the material world: the number of times per second that a pulsation repeats. **Pitch** is how we perceive different frequencies – how "high" or "low" a sound *seems*.

We have seen in the previous section that movement of the basilar membrane causes the stereocilia to be stimulated by the tectonic membrane. This results in a sensation of sound. But how is pitch perceived? How does the organ of Corti send information to our brain that distinguishes different pitches? Our current understanding is that three mechanisms are involved in pitch encoding within the cochlea, though one of these three is predominant.

13.5.6.1 Temporal theory

The *temporal theory* says, essentially, that individual pulsations or cycles within a sound are "counted," in the sense that neurons respond to each cycle. Therefore, on the input of a 30 Hz sound, 30 impulses per second will be carried on nerve pathways. A primary limitation of this theory is that even moderate frequencies (for example, 625 Hz, close to the musical note A_1) involves a number of cycles per second that far outpace the ability of neurons to respond that fast. This mechanism could only account for the pitch perception of very low-frequency sounds.

13.5.6.2 Volley principle

The *volley principle* explains how a variant of the temporal theory can account for the encoding of frequencies that are somewhat above those that could conceivably be encoded through the temporal theory. The temporal theory cannot explain the encoding of frequencies that are higher than the maximum times per second that a neuron can fire, but the volley principle explains how this may occur.

An idealized example will show the volley principle. Imagine a frequency that is 4 times greater than a single neuron can fire. But now, instead of giving the job of sending a pulse for every cycle in the sound to a single neuron, the job is given to 4 neurons. Each of the neurons fires *once for every 4th cycle*. Neuron #1 fires every 4th cycle, *starting with the 1st cycle*; neuron #2 fires every

CLINICAL NOTE 13.1 Bone conduction

Hearing occurs when the hair cells of the cochlea are stimulated. Most of the time we hear because sound has propagated through the air, through the outer and middle ear, to the cochlea.

However, vibration within the cochlea creates the sensation of hearing, no matter how it is caused. If sound is propagated through the bones of the skull, this will result in perceiving sound – remember that the cochlea is encased in bone. For example, some of the sounds of our own chewing, particularly hard or crunchy foods, are conducted through the teeth, which in turn conduct vibrations to the bones of the skull, which in their turn vibrate the cochlea.

In cases where the outer and/or middle ears are non-functional, the person can still hear if another route is found for the sound waves to reach the cochlea. This is the realm of *bone conduction hearing aids*. These devices do not send amplified sound down the ear canal like conventional hearing aids – rather, they vibrate skull bones.

Bone conduction is used in other situations as well. When a person must hear speech or other complex signals in an extremely noisy environment, air conduction into the ear canal may be blocked (to prevent interference from loud ambient noise) and an electromechanical device is used to vibrate skull bones.

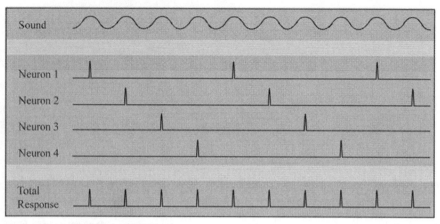

Figure 13.11 The volley principle

4th cycle, *starting with the 2nd cycle*; neuron #3 fires every 4th cycle, *starting with the 3rd cycle*; and similarly with neuron #4. This way, each of the neurons fires less than its maximum ability, but the total signal from all 4 neurons, when added together, provides accurate information of the number of cycles in the original sound. See Figure 13.11.

In fact, this principle can only increase sensitivity to higher frequencies to a limited extent. Most of the frequencies to which the human ear can respond are still too high for the temporal theory to account for their perception, even when extended by the volley principle.

13.5.6.3   Place theory – tonotopicity

In Section 12.11, we discussed the concept of **resonance**. While in that section our focus was on cavity resonance, resonance is a more general phenomenon. Given the physical properties of the cochlea, its length and its gradually diminishing diameter, different sound frequencies will resonate at different physical locations along the cochlea. The effect is that different frequencies will cause a maximum displacement of the basilar membrane at different points along the length of the cochlea. Figure 13.12 shows a map of frequency encoding at these various points along the length of the cochlea.

The place theory accounts for the greatest range of frequencies to which human hearing is sensitive. This is particularly true for the mid and high frequencies. It is believed that the temporal theory, supplemented by the volley principle, accounts for pitch perception in the very low frequencies.

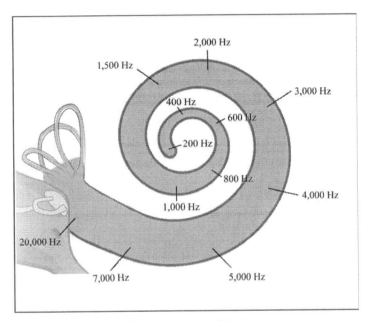

Figure 13.12 Place encoding on the organ of Corti

The term *tonotopicity* is used to designate the distribution of sensitivity within the cochlea. The element "tono" refers to tones or pitches in sound. The element "top" refers to place (as in *topography*). The term *tonotopicity* refers to the distribution, along the length of the cochlea, of sensitivity to different frequencies.

13.5.6.4 Peripheral processing – inhibition and feedback loops

The purpose of this short section is to point out that details of the encoding of sound by the inner ear are extremely complex, and the above description provides a general outline but only scratches the surface.

Peripheral processing occurs in the cochlea, the organ of hearing, not in the brain. Processing in the brain would be *central*, not *peripheral*, processing.

While the *place theory* broadly accounts for pitch perception for all but the lowest of frequencies, it fails to account for the *precision* with which frequencies can be perceived. The place theory states that physical resonance along the cochlea creates maximal displacement at different points, as noted above. However, resonance will result in the displacement of wide sections of the cochlea. If the incoming sound signal contains one specific frequency, or perhaps a small range of frequencies, the part of the organ of Corti that is displaced will correspond to a much wider range of frequencies than the incoming signal. Yet we will perceive a specific signal; our perception will not reflect the entire area of displacement.

That is, our ability to discriminate[28] among frequencies that are very close to one another is not fully explained by physical resonance and the place theory.

So how are we able to detect a very small difference between two tones? Tonotopicity is supplemented by 2 types of peripheral processing within the cochlea. These are *inhibition* and *feedback loops.*

Inhibition Since a broad area of the cochlea will have strong displacement through resonance, some hair cells will be stimulated even though they are some distance from the hair cells that precisely correspond to the frequency of the signal. Yet these more distant hair cells do not send a signal telling the brain that there is sound energy at that frequency. The mechanism that accounts for this is called *inhibition.* The (wrongly) stimulated hair cells must be *inhibited from firing,* even though they are stimulated. If they fired, they would send false information, so firing must be suppressed.

Feedback loops How does inhibition take place? There are a number of important *feedback loops* within the organ of Corti. This means, among other things, that the stimulation of certain hair cells results in a signal being sent to other hair cells, inhibiting them from firing. In this way, the perception of pitch can be refined and made more precise.

Both mechanisms – feedback loops that permit inhibition, and inhibition itself – are extraordinarily complex.

13.5.7   In summary

The ear functions to capture sound waves in the air and to convert those sound waves to neural signals that encode important characteristics of the sound – most notably, loudness and pitch.

The outer ear captures the sound waves and directs them toward the tympanic membrane (eardrum). The middle ear does the difficult job of transforming the sound waves into vibration that has greater force so that the vibration can be transmitted to the fluids of the inner ear.

The inner ear receives those vibrations in the cochlea, a snail-like structure. The vibrations transfer through the fluids of the cochlea. This, in turn, causes movement of the organ of Corti. Those movements cause the

---

[28] *To discriminate* is to detect the difference between stimuli. At 4000 Hz, humans can distinguish among tones 0.3 percent apart (Lopez-Poveda, 2014). In real terms, that would mean distinguishing 3988 Hz from 4000 Hz.

hair cells to be stimulated through contact with the tectorial membrane. Feedback loops and inhibition help to create highly focused perception of pitch – more than can be explained by the physical resonances within the cochlea itself.

13.6 Hearing

13.6.1 Thresholds

13.6.1.1 The meaning of thresholds

A *threshold* is the point at which a major change occurs. If you cross the threshold of a room as you enter through the doorway, the threshold marks the point at which being *outside* the room changes to being *inside* the room. With hearing, the absolute threshold is the point at which not hearing a sound (because it is too soft) becomes hearing the sound (because it has been turned up to where it is just loud enough).

The **threshold of hearing**, or **absolute threshold**, is the amount of sound energy required to just be able to hear the sound – actually, it is the amount of sound energy required so that the individual hears the sound one of every two times the sound is presented (i.e., 50 percent of the time).

A higher threshold means that more sound energy is required before the person can hear the sound – in other words, that person has poorer hearing than a person whose hearing threshold is lower. A lower threshold means more acute hearing.

13.6.1.2 Pure-tone thresholds

A basic hearing test examines a number of factors, among them the individual's thresholds at specific sound frequencies. By **pure-tone thresholds**, we mean the thresholds of detection of tones having a single frequency, not more complex sounds. Typically, these frequencies are tested: 500, 1000, 2000, (3000), 4000, (6000), and 8000 Hz, separately in each ear. The values 3000 and 6000 are in parentheses because they are intermediate values, not octave values, and are not always tested. In Figure 13.13, those intermediate values have been tested and results reported.

13.6.2 The audiogram

The **audiogram** (Figure 13.13) is the standard format for representing the state of an individual's pure-tone hearing thresholds. The thresholds that are shown on the audiogram are determined by presenting sounds of the given frequencies to the patient at different loudness levels and allowing the patient to signal that s/he has heard the sound in question. Presentation is through headphones that are precisely calibrated.

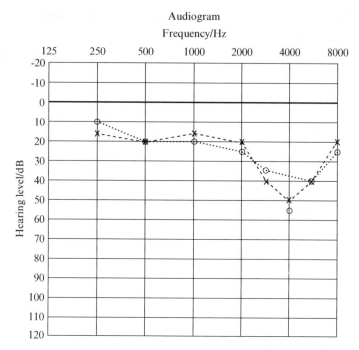

Figure 13.13 Audiogram. The "O" symbols represent the right ear, and the "X" symbols, the left ear. In a color image, they would be red and blue, respectively. The individual whose audiogram is shown has a pattern of loss centering on 4000 Hz, typical of noise-induced hearing loss caused by machinery.

Threshold values for the left ear are marked with blue X's; values for the right ear with red O's. A line of the same color is drawn to connect the values for each ear. In Figure 13.13, the different colors are represented by different types of dotted line; these are typically solid colored lines in practice.

The *x*-axis of the audiogram (that is, the horizontal scale along the top) represents the different frequencies. A frequency of 125 Hz is often shown on this scale, but is rarely tested in practice. Higher-pitched sounds are to the right, and lower-pitched sounds to the left.

The *y*-axis of the audiogram (the vertical axis shown on the left side) represents the thresholds, and is demarcated in dB HL: ***dB HL*** means ***decibels Hearing Level***. There are a number of different dB scales used for different purposes; the HL decibel scale is adapted specifically to human hearing. On this scale, "normal" hearing at each frequency is represented by 0 dB. While the number 0 (zero) might suggest 'nothing,' the decibel scale is a scale that compares two values, rather than simply representing a single value. Therefore, you can think of 0 dB as meaning 'zero difference from something.' The "something" is "normal" hearing, so 0 dB means 'zero difference from normal hearing.'

It may seem odd that the numbers on the vertical axis get larger toward the bottom. These are the amplitudes of the sounds that are presented to the patient. If you have to present a louder sound before the individual can hear it, that means that the individual has poorer hearing. So X's and O's that are higher on the audiogram represent better hearing (lower thresholds) and those lower down represent poorer hearing acuity (and therefore higher thresholds).

13.7 Effects of hearing impairment on speech production

This book is chiefly about phonetics and the *production* of speech, though we've taken a short journey into the reception and perception of speech. We will take a short look now at the role that hearing speech plays in learning to talk and learning the sound system of speech.

We will look in the next sections at *prelingual hearing loss* – that is, hearing loss prior to learning language – and *postlingual hearing loss* – that is, hearing loss after the individual has learned to speak.

13.7.1 Prelingual hearing loss

Prelingual hearing loss can be *congenital* or *acquired*. *Congenital* hearing loss appears at birth. *Acquired* prelingual hearing loss is defined as that occurring before the first birthday.

Language acquisition (learning of one's language) occurs typically through a natural process whereby the infant hears language spoken and gradually, over time, identifies patterns and picks out words, structures, and other features of language. Phonetically, acquisition involves narrowing in on the phonetic categories (phonemes) in the language spoken around the infant and being able to produce those sounds, as well as producing variant sounds resulting from accommodation and suprasegmentals.

CLINICAL NOTE 13.3 Middle ear infections

Infections within the middle ear are common in children. These infections typically cause fluid to infuse the middle ear cavity. This causes the functioning of the middle ear to be seriously compromised, and therefore sound reaching the cochlea is much reduced in amplitude. The effect is hearing impairment (usually temporary, but middle ear infections in some cases permanently affect middle ear functioning).

Usually, the brief time that such infections persist does not create lasting problems in language and skills acquisition. However, when these infections are long lasting or when they recur very frequently, the cumulative effect may have deleterious consequences.

CLINICAL NOTE 13.4 Cochlear implants 2

In cases of profound hearing loss, cochlear implants may be chosen as the means to restore a level of hearing.

Cochlear implants can only function if the nerve pathways within the cochlea are normal, so that the electrodes will stimulate nerves corresponding to the appropriate frequencies (according to the place theory).

At any age, hearing loss can range in degrees from mild to profound, and the effect upon language acquisition will depend to some extent upon the severity of the loss. However, hearing loss described as *mild* is truly mild only in the case of an adult who has long since acquired language. For them, "mild" hearing loss may be a slight inconvenience, or may not even come to the conscious awareness of the adult. However, *any* hearing loss, no matter how "mild," is always significant prelingually, and is always significant throughout childhood and adolescence in terms of its negative effect upon language acquisition and upon acquisition of knowledge and skills in general, including, in many cases, social skills.

Clinical intervention can help with language acquisition, and so it is imperative that hearing screenings be undertaken with infants as young as it is practicable, in order to know if special intervention is required.

13.7.2   Postlingual hearing loss

As we all know, older adults often tend toward mild to moderate hearing loss, a problem primarily due to noise in industrialized societies. Typically, satisfactory remediation can be achieved with amplification devices.

Disease processes, genetic predisposition, and injury can lead to profound hearing loss in adults, and indeed hearing loss across the lifespan can reach a profound level in some individuals.

There may be some deterioration over time in phonetic precision of speech in individuals with severe or profound hearing loss postlingually. This is an indication that the feedback loop of hearing oneself talk plays a role in maintaining phonetic competence.

The consequences of severe to profound hearing loss in older adults demonstrate the social role that speech plays. Older individuals with severe to profound hearing loss tend to have less and less social interaction of a verbal nature, due to the increasing difficulty of communication through speech. The deteriorating social interaction and reduced input from other sources of sound result in increasing isolation, which has a negative effect upon well-being and health.

13.8   Vocabulary

absolute threshold
amplitude
apex, apical end
audiogram
auditory canal
auditory nerve, cranial nerve VIII
basal end, base
basilar membrane
bone conduction
bottom-up, top-down
categorical (categorial) perception
central
cerumen
cochlea
cochlear implant
data-driven
dB HL
decibel, dB
ear; outer, middle, inner
endolymph
equal loudness contour
Eustachian tube
external auditory meatus, ear canal
feedback loop
footplate (stapes)
frequency
hair bundle
hair cells, inner, outer
hearer
hearing loss; postlingual,
    prelingual
hearing threshold
helicotrema
impedance
impedance matching device
impedance mismatch
incus
inhibition

inner ear
interlocutor
invariance
kinocilium
lever, principle of
malleus
McGurk effect
middle ear
middle ear infection
middle ear space, cavity
nasopharynx
normalization
organ of Corti
ossicle
ossicular chain
outer ear
oval window
perceptual constancy
perilymph
peripheral, central
phonemic restoration
pinna
pitch
pitch perception
place theory, tonotopicity
pure-tone threshold
Reissner's membrane
resonance
restoration, phonemic
round window
sandhi
scala media
scala tympani
scala vestibuli
segmentation
semicircular canals
sound wave
speaker normalization

speech perception
stapes
stereocilia
suprasegmentals
talker
tectorial membrane
temporal theory
threshold, pure tone, hearing

tonotopicity, place theory
top-down
tympanic membrane, eardrum
utterance
variance
vestibular membrane
vestibular system
volley principle

Glossary

Notes on definitions and vocabulary

- Definitions are provided specifically within the context of the field of phonetics and speech science. Many of these words have broader definitions in general use and/or other technical senses in other fields.
- Many terms are ordinary, everyday words but with a very specific meaning within this field.
- A word shown in *italics* in the definition has its own entry in this glossary. (In some instances, italics may be used for emphasis.)
  - If a plural word is shown in italics, the glossary entry is likely to be found under the singular form of the word.
  - If two words in sequence are shown in italics, they may be listed in the glossary as a single phrase or as two separate, individual entries.
  - A word in italics shown in one form may have an entry under a different form of the word – e.g., the words *contrasting* or *contrasted* in italics may refer to the entry *contrast*.
- In the definitions, directions such as up and down, forward or back, relate to the anatomical position used generally in phonetics: erect, standing position, with head held erect facing left, and directed forward relative to the body.

Nouns in this lexicon having irregular plural forms

Singular	Plural
bronchus	bronchi
locus	loci
nucleus	nuclei
spectrum	spectra

abdominal	having to do with the abdomen or belly
abdominal cavity	lower division of the trunk of the body, below the thoracic cavity
abduction, to abduct	of the *vocal folds*, bring together by muscular force
absolute pressure	pressure measured on a scale in which zero equates to the absence of pressure, contrasted with *relative pressure*
accommodation	changing individual *phones* to be more similar to surrounding phones
	In the following, *sc is the sound causing the change* and *su is the sound undergoing the change (the sound that has been changed)*
• anticipatory	• su precedes sc
• contact	• su and sc are in contact
• contiguous	• su and sc are in contact
• diachronic	• accommodation occurred historically and is now unchanging
• distant	• there is at least one phone between su and sc
• double	• su is preceded and followed immediately by an sc
• left-to-right	• sc precedes su
• noncontiguous	• there is at least one phone between su and sc
• partial	• su acquires a feature of sc, but does not become the same as sc
• progressive	• sc precedes su
• regressive	• sc follows su
• right-to-left	• sc follows su
• total	• su becomes identical to sc
• synchronic	• phenomenon occurs in the contemporary spoken language
acoustic energy	sound as a form of energy
adduction, to adduct	of the *vocal folds*, separate by muscular force
aerodynamic	having to do with the movement of air (or other fluid)
affricate	*consonant* made up of a *plosive* followed by a *homorganic fricative*
air pressure	*pressure* exerted by the air upon all objects, in all directions
airflow	movement of air
airstream mechanism	*mechanism* or system used to generate *airflow* for production of *speech* sounds
alveolar, alveolar ridge	referring to the usually convex ridge of bone directly behind the upper incisors, designating a *place of articulation*

alveopalatal	referring to the region of the roof of the mouth on the border between the *alveolar* and (hard) *palatal* areas, designating a *place of articulation*; also, *postalveolar*
amplitude	strength or degree of energy of a wave signal
anatomy	physical structure of the body
aperiodic	of a wave motion, not *periodic*
apex (tongue)	tip of the *tongue* as a *place of articulation*
apico-postalveolar	*articulation* in which the *apex* of the tongue contacts or *approximates* the *alveopalatal* or *postalveolar* region; a *retroflex* articulation
approximant	*speech* sound with some characteristics of *vowels* and some of *consonants*; including *glides* and sounds for which the term *liquid* is traditionally used
approximate	bring into close physical proximity; get close to
approximation	bringing into close physical proximity as in the *approximation* of 2 *articulators*
articulate	make the movements required to produce *speech* or individual *phones*
articulation	act of making gestures required to produce a *phone* or produce continuous *speech*
articulation: primary, secondary	primary *articulation* of a *consonant* is what is normally described as its *place* and *manner of articulation*; secondary articulation is an additional gesture that narrows a different place of articulation through the *approximation* of the *articulators*
articulator	anatomical structure involved in the production of a *phone*
articulator, active, passive	see previous; the active articulator (such as the *tongue*) moves; the passive articulator is immovable and is approached by the active articulator
articulatory setting, articulatory set	"default" or normal position of *articulators* in producing *speech*, said to be different between languages or even *dialects*, accounting for some of the difference between similar sounds in the two speech varieties
arytenoid cartilages	2 highly movable cartilages to which the posterior end of the *vocal folds* is attached
ascender	part of a written letter that rises above the height of *vowel* letters
aspiration	small blast or "puff" of air accompanying the release of some *plosives*; in English, accompanying the release of *voiceless* plosives that are the initial sound in a stressed *syllable*

assimilation	as used in this book, a form of *accommodation* in which a sound changes in a major way; in some authors' work, what we are calling *accommodation* in general
atmosphere (unit) (atm)	unit of *pressure* equivalent to normal air pressure at sea level
ATR	advanced *tongue root*; the root of the tongue brought forward to widen the *pharynx*
back (tongue)	posterior half of the *tongue dorsum*
back (verb)	to change the *place of articulation* to a more posterior place of articulation
backness	position of an *articulation* or *tongue* position on the back-to-front dimension
ballistic	of an articulatory gesture, an abrupt movement propelled by a brief rapid muscle contraction, but that continues by *inertia* after the contraction is relaxed
basilar lamina	anatomical layer in the structure of the *vocal folds*
basis of articulation	*articulatory setting* or *articulatory set*
Bernoulli principle	principle of fluid (air) flow by which *pressure* is lowered as the fluid's speed increases to pass through a narrowing or *constriction*
bilabial	of, or using, both lips
blade (tongue)	section of the surface of the *tongue* that lies below the *alveolar ridge* at rest; posterior to the *tip* and anterior to the the *dorsum*
blending	*speech error* in which parts of two words are merged into a single erroneous non-word
body planes	3 planes that cut the body, each at right angles to the other, allowing designation of body parts and orientation
breathy voice	*vocal fold* vibration in which the *glottis* is never entirely closed, allowing considerable air to flow during *voicing*
bronchus, bronchi	the *trachea* divides into two bronchi, each of which leads to one of the *lungs*. Singular: bronchus
buccal speech	*speech* in which the airstream is generated within the mouth, suitable only for anterior sounds as posterior oral structures are used to generate the airflow
buccinator muscle	*muscle of facial expression* in the cheek that pulls back on the corners of the mouth
cardinal vowel	one of a set of 8 idealized *primary vowels* that define the outlines of the vowel *quadrangle*. Sometimes a second set of 8 *secondary* vowels are also referred to as cardinal vowels

cavity resonance	*resonance* of or in an air-filled space involving reflected sound waves
central	midway position of the *tongue* or *vowel articulation* on the back–front dimension
citation form	slow, careful pronunciation of a given word as opposed to the way the word is pronounced in non-self-conscious, rapid *speech*
cleft palate	a *palate* that is "cleft" (split) due to incomplete fusion of parts of the *primary* and/or *secondary* palate during gestation
click	*speech* sound produced with the *ingressive velaric* airstream *mechanism* (plus one attested sound produced with the *egressive* velaric airstream mechanism)
close	in official *IPA* terminology, *high*, said of a *vowel*
close mid	in official *IPA* terminology, *upper mid*, said of a *vowel*
closing phase	first phase of *plosive articulation* in which the
closure phase	*articulators* are moving toward a position that will block all *airflow*; unrelated to the *acoustic* use of the term *phase*
	the phase of *plosive* production in which the air passageway is blocked for a short period of time
coarticulation	as used in this book, a form of *accommodation* in which a sound changes in a minor way
complex	a complex *periodic* wave is one that is composed of 2 or more *sinusoidal* waves
compress, compression	reduce the amount of space a given quantity of air is contained within, or increase the amount of air contained in that space; the act of doing this
consonant	speech sound that involves blocking the airstream, forcing it through a narrowing greater than for the *vowel* [i], or diverting it through the *nasal cavity*
constriction	narrowing in the passageway through which the breath-stream flows
context	another term for phonetic *environment*
contrast	in languages' sound systems, sounds are said to contrast when the change from one to the other (forming a *minimal pair*) has the potential to change the meaning of the word
contrastive emphasis	*emphasis* on a particular word or words in order to distinguish different possible meanings of an *utterance*; for example, *I didn't break it* as opposed to *I didn't break it*

contrastive stress	greater than usual *stress* on a *syllable* in order to clarify what might otherwise be misunderstood: *allusion, not illusion*
conus elasticus	structure in the *larynx*
coronal	phonological, not phonetic, term for the arched *tongue dorsum* in *articulation*
coronal plane	*body plane* that transects the erect, standing body vertically, parallel to the side-to-side plane of the body, through the center line or anterior or posterior to that point
cover	in modeling the *vocal folds*, the surface layer or layers, as opposed to deeper tissue layers
cover–body model	model of *vocal fold vibration* taking into account the constraints the *cover* places on the movement of the deeper tissue, and vice versa
creaky voice	*voicing* produced with considerable tension of *laryngeal* muscles, producing a *tone* with irregular periods and a gravelly sound; *phoneme* in some languages, and a marker of social group in others
crest	in a surface wave such as a water wave, the high point of the wave; in graphic representations of sound waves, the equivalent point is typically called the *peak*
cricoid cartilage	cartilage of the *larynx*, effectively the highest *tracheal ring*, on which the *arytenoid cartilages* are situated
cycle	single complete wave; any portion of a *wave train* longer than one cycle will include repetition; any less than a cycle will be incomplete
cycles per second, cps	measure of *frequency* equivalent to *hertz*
degree (of phase)	specification of a point along the length of a *cycle* by use of a scale from 0° to 360°
degree of voicing	refers to *voice onset time* of *plosives*
dental	having to do with the teeth; as a *place of articulation*, specifically the upper incisors
descender	vertical stroke of a written letter that goes below the line on which most letters rest
diacritic, diacritical mark	mark written above, below, or through a letter that modifies what sound the letter represents, also called an accent
dialect	form of a spoken language defined by geographical, social, religious, etc., speech community
diaphragm	band of muscle in the shape of an inverted bowl separating the thoracic from the abdominal cavity, which contracts on inhalation in abdominal breathing

digastric muscle	muscle that runs from the interior of the chin through a tendon loop on the *hyoid bone* to the *styloid process*
diglossia	situation of a person who knows two varieties of his own language – one often being a written form that is quite different from the spoken form
diphthong	*vowel* sound whose *timbre* changes significantly from start to finish, paralleling movement of the *articulators* during its production
diphthongized	a *vowel* is said to be diphthongized if the vowel is a *diphthong*, but with a minor degree of movement or change in *timbre*; English [i e u o] are often described as diphthongized. Term also used to describe a vowel that has undergone a change from *monophthong* to diphthong.
dissimilation	process opposite of *accommodation*, by which, historically, similar or identical *phones* close to one another become less similar through a change in one or the other, or both
distant accommodation	*accommodation* that occurs where the *phone* causing the change and the sound undergoing the change have at least one phone between them
dorsal	of an *articulation*, having to do with the *dorsum* of the *tongue*
dorsum (tongue)	region of the surface of the tongue between the *blade* and the *root*, consisting of the *front* and the *back*, that lie below the (hard) *palate* and the *velum*, respectively, at rest
dynamic, dynamics	having movement
egressive	of the breath stream, outgoing, moving from *lungs* to the outside of the body
egressive pulmonic airstream	*airstream mechanism* used by all languages in the world
ejective	also called *glottalized consonant*; consonant (almost all *plosives*) produced with the *egressive glottalic airstream mechanism*
elision, elide	deletion of a *phone* in a word; to delete such a phone
emphasis	greater *prominence* given to a word or words within an *utterance*; a *suprasegmental*
environment (phonetic environment)	in respect to a particular *phone*, several phones preceding and several phones following the particular phone, as well as *suprasegmental* features affecting the particular phone and those close to it
epenthesis, epenthetic	change in the pronunciation of a word in which a new sound is inserted into it, often separating adjacent *consonants*

epiglottis	a a cartilage in the *larynx* that covers the *laryngeal vestibule* in swallowing, and that plays little direct role in speech
esophageal	having to do with the *esophagus*
esophagus	the tube extending from the back of the throat (*pharynx*) to the stomach, to which it carries swallowed food and liquid
excursion	movement of the *tongue* from, or extent of movement from, the tongue's rest position
expiration; expiratory	breathing out, exhaling; having to do with exhaling
extrinsic	see *tongue muscles, extrinsic*
F0, F$_0$	"F-zero"; *fundamental frequency*; frequency of *vibration* of the *vocal folds*
false vocal folds	see *ventricular folds*
fiber-optic	optical fibers are used in fiber-optic *laryngoscopy* to allow light to be shone on the *vocal folds* and video images to be captured
fistula	an opening connecting two anatomical cavities or passages that are not normally connected
flap	a *laminal* speech sound made with a *ballistic tongue* movement, having a very brief period of closure
focus	word or topic representing the central target of an *utterance*, that affects the *suprasegmentals* of the utterance
formant, F1 F2 F3	name of a *pole* in the *resonance spectrum* of a *vowel* or *approximant*; typically 3 are identified, although vowels may be distinguished by 2 and more than 3 are present
fortis	of a *consonant*, strong, or typical of *voiceless* consonant; opposite: *lenis*
Fourier's Theorem	statement of mathematical truth (not a theory) that a *complex* wave can be "decomposed" into simple, *sinusoidal* waves
frequency	number of repetitions of an event per unit of time, in sound waves measured in *cycles per second* using the unit *hertz*
fricative	a *manner of articulation* in which air is forced through a narrowing or *constriction* such that the *turbulent airflow* generates an *aperiodic* sound
front	to change the *place of articulation* to a more anterior one
front (tongue)	the anterior portion of the tongue *tdorsum* lying at rest under the (hard) *palate*

frontal (coronal) plane	see *coronal plane*
fronting	changing the *place of articulation* to a more anterior one
frontness	location of a specific *articulation* on the front-to-back scale
functional residual capacity	volume of air left in the *lungs* after passive exhalation or complete relaxation of respiratory muscles
fundamental frequency (F$_0$)	*frequency* of *vibration* of the *vocal folds*
genioglossus muscle	fan-shaped muscle originating at the inside of the chin and inserting into the midline of the *tongue*
glide	type of *phone* – an *approximant* – characterized by movement toward or away from a *vwel*
glottal	having to do with the *glottis*, and, by extension, having to do with the *vocal folds*
glottal cycle	single *cycle* of *vibration* of the *vocal folds*
glottal signal	*tone* produced by the vibrating *vocal v folds*
glottal source	in the *source–filter theory*, the *tone* produced by the vibrating *vocal folds*
glottal stop	a stop or *plosive consonant* in which the blockage is created by closing the *glottis* with the *vocal folds*
glottalic	referring to the (closed) *glottis* specifically in the context of *airstream mechanisms*
glottalization, glottalized	changed from non-glottal to glottal *articulation*; having a secondary glottal articulation; produced with the *egressive glottalic airstream mechanism*
glottalized consonant	another term for *ejective*
glottis	space between the *vocal folds*; disappears when vocal folds pressed together
glyph	symbol used to write language in any writing system, defined by its shape, such that two different forms of what are considered to be the "same" single letter, such as *a* and *a*, or *e* and *ε*, are different glyphs
H&H theory	*hyperspeech* and *hypospeech* theory, an explanation of the range of articulatory precision and rate, attributed to the functional communicative needs
half-long	describes a *phone* that is longer than normal but not double-long (the latter would be called *long*)
haplology	sound change whereby one of two identical, or very similar, *syllables* is deleted; for example, the word *probably* is not *probable-ly*

harmonic	*tone* that is a whole-number multiple of a basic *frequency*
harmonic series	a series of *tones*, each of which has a *frequency* that is a whole-number multiple of a basic frequency
hearer	person who hears speech, whether or not they intend to listen
height	in the classification of *vowels*, the placement on a 4-step gradation of the space between the surface of the *tongue* and the *palate*
hertz, Hz	unit of *frequency* equivalent to *cycles per second*
high	in the classification of *vowels*, a vowel that has the minimum distance between *tongue* surface and *palate* (without becoming a *consonant*) is said to be *a high vowel*
homorganic	produced at the same (or very similar) *place of articulation*
hyoglossus muscle	muscle attached to the *hyoid bone* that inserts into the soft tissue of the *tongue*
hyoid bone	horseshoe-shaped bone attached to the top of the *larynx*, and to which some *tongue* and some laryngeal muscles are attached
hypernasality	excess of *nasal timbre* in the voice; *nasalization* of *phones* that should not be nasalized
hyperspeech	on a continuum of degree of precision, effort, and time put into *articulation*, speech that has a high degree of these 3 traits
hypospeech	on a continuum of degree of precision, effort, and time put into *articulation*, speech that has a low degree of these 3 traits
implosive	*plosive* sound made wherein the *air pressure* behind the blockage is lower than surrounding air pressure so that the rush of air upon release moves from outside the body to inside
impound	to impound is to capture within a space; in phonetics it refers to the capture of higher-pressure air before release in *plosive* production
in phase	see *phase*
inches of mercury (inHg)	a measure of *air pressure*
inertia	property of *mass*, resisting acceleration or deceleration. If stopped, it resists moving; if moving, it resists stopping.

inferior horn (thyroid cartilage)	one of two long *processes* descending from the main body of the *thyroid cartilage* to the point where they articulate with the *cricoid cartilage*
inferior longitudinal tongue muscle	lower of 2 layers of muscle running lengthwise in the *tongue*
inferior pharyngeal constrictor muscle	lowest of 3 constrictor muscles of the *pharynx* whose effect is to reduce the size of the pharynx by pulling its walls closer together
information, new, old	in language, data that is first introduced to the reader or *hearer* is new information; reference to data that has previously been introduced – or which is general knowledge possessed by all – is old information. *Suprasegmentals* and/or language form may reveal the distinction.
ingressive	of the *airstream*, moving from outside the body into the body through the mouth or nose
initiator, initiating mechanism	of *airstream mechanisms*, the structure or complex of structures that generates the *airflow* or *air pressure*
insertion	insertion of a muscle is the end of the muscle attached to a bone or cartilage or soft tissue and which moves more than the other end of muscle when it is contracted. The other end is the *origin*.
inspiration, inspiratory	breathing in, drawing air into the *lungs*
intercostal muscles, internal, external	muscles of *respiration* located between the ribs; internal layer situated on the *lung* side of the *ribs*, and external situated on the side of the ribs closest to the skin
interdental	between teeth; *articulation* with the *tongue blade* touching both upper and lower incisors
International Phonetic Alphabet (IPA)	the official alphabet of the International Phonetic Association, used to write the sounds of any spoken language unambiguously; others have supplemented it to include means to write disordered speech
International System of Units	called the metric system in English, an international standard system of measures
intonation	patterns of changes in *fundamental frequency* during an *utterance* that relate to the grammatical structure of the utterance, and help reveal that structure to the *hearer*
intrinsic	see *tongue muscle, intrinsic*
invariance	lack of *variance*; speech contains great variance due to *context*, *talker*, and other factors

inversion	the reversal of the position of two *phones*, normally in sequence
IPA	see *International Phonetic Alphabet*
italic style	style of typeface in which vertical strokes in letters slant toward the right, as opposed to roman style
iteration	*speech error* involving the unwarranted repetition of a *phone*
jitter	variation in *frequency* in a sound signal, specifically fluctuation in the *fundamental frequency*
key word	word used in print to exemplify a sound; the problem with key words is that the writer and the reader may pronounce the key word differently
kilogram (kg)	unit of *mass* in the *SI* (metric system). Not a unit of force or pressure, but sometimes used informally in this sense
kilopascal (kPa)	unit of pressure in the *SI* (metric system) equal to 1,000 *pascals*
labialized, labialization	produced with a *secondary articulation* involving *rounding* of the lips; change from a nonlabial to a labial articulation
labiodental	(lower) lip in contact with upper incisor teeth; a *place of articulation*
lag, voicing lag	*voicing* starts after a *plosive* is released; may be long or short
lamina propria, deep, intermediate, superficial	layers in the physical structure of the *vocal folds* that influence the nature of the movement of the vocal folds in *vibration*
laminal	of speech *articulation*, made with the *blade* of the *tongue*
laminar	of *airflow*, smooth, without eddies; opposite of *turbulent*
laryngeal	having to do with the *larynx*, designating a sound made with the *vocal folds*
laryngeal vestibule	"entrance" to the *larynx*, as seen from the *pharynx*
laryngectomee	a person who has undergone a *laryngectomy*
laryngectomy	the surgical removal of the *larynx*, normally to treat a malignant condition; results in a situation where a person breathes through a *stoma* in the neck and requires *pseudovoice* to speak
laryngopharynx	the inferior portion of the *pharynx*
laryngoscopy	viewing the *larynx*, in particular the *vocal folds*; performed with a mirror or a *fiber-optic* device
larynx	complex structure in the neck permitting food and liquid to be swallowed without entering the *lungs*; contains the *vocal folds*, which produce *voicing*

lateral approximant	an *approximant* made with blockage by the *tongue* in the center of the *oral cavity*, with openings between the sides of the tongue and the inside of the cheeks
lateral fricative	a *fricative* produced with the noisy *constriction* between the edge(s) of the *tongue* and the inside of the cheek(s)
lateral release, lateral plosion	*release* of a *plosive* by narrowing the *tongue* such that release occurs over the side(s) of the tongue
latin alphabet	the ordinary alphabet used for English, European, and many other languages; also called the *roman alphabet*, a term avoided in this book
lax	type of *vowel* distinguished from *tense*
lead, voicing lead	*voicing* starts before a *plosive* is released; may be long or short
length	duration of a speech sound, not its *timbre*
lenis	of a *consonant*, soft or weak or typical of *voiced* consonant; opposite: *fortis*
levator palati (levator veli palatini) muscle	a pair of muscles that serve to raise the *velum* during closing of the *VPP*
levels of stress	in a language using stress, degrees of stress recognized within that language; English has 3, Spanish has 2
lexicon	mental "dictionary" or list of vocabulary items in the head of a speaker of a given language
ligature, tie bar	a stroke written above or below a pair of *IPA* symbols, tying them together. Sometimes used for *diphthongs* or *affricates*
lingual	of, or having to do with, the *tongue*
lingual airstream mechanism	a less common name for the *velaric airstream mechanism*
liquid	traditional term for the group of *consonants* including /l/ and / ɹ/ in English. Term not recognized in official *IPA* terminology, but commonly used; IPA classifies these sounds as *approximants*.
localization	identification of the source of a sound or of the direction from which the sound is coming
locus, loci	hypothetical point on a *spectrogram* representing the *frequency* at which *formant transitions* between a *plosive* and a *vowel* are "pointed"
Lombard effect	the effect whereby *talkers* increase the *amplitude* of their voice in response to background noise or other competing sound
long	having a considerable duration; a reference to temporal *duration*, not to *timbre*

long lag	see *lag*
long lead	see *lead*
loudness	perception of how loud a sound is; not an objective measure of its energy level, which is called *amplitude*
low	of *heights* of *vowel* production, made with the *tongue* in the lowest position; called *open* in official *IPA* terminology
lower case	of alphabetic letters, non-capital, small, or "little" letters, as used in text other than at the beginnings of sentences or with proper nouns; as contrasted with *upper case*
lower mid (open-mid)	of *heights* of *vowel* production, the second lowest of 4; *lower mid* is the term usually used in North America; *open-mid* is official *IPA* terminology
lungs	two large structures in the *thorax*, made up of multiple lobes, in which the body exchanges gases with the atmosphere; source of the *airstream* used for most – not all – speech sounds
mandible	the lower jaw; it is movable, hinged at the temporomandibular joint
manner of articulation	of *consonants*, the way in which the *airstream* is modified; each manner of articulation defines a class of *phones*
mass	in physics, the amount of physical material in an object, related to its *inertia*; mass is pertinent to the *vibration* of the *vocal folds*
masseter muscle	powerful muscle in the cheek that closes (elevates) the lower jaw (mandible)
maxilla	upper jaw
mechanism	process by which an action occurs; e.g. mechanism of *respiration*
metalanguage	language used to discuss language
metaphony	*noncontiguous accommodation* in *vowels*
metathesis	*inversion* or exchange of two *phones* in a word, as either a historical change or contemporary process, such as the metathesis of [k] and [s] from old English *axian* to modern English *ask*
mid central	a place of *vowel articulation* that is midway on the vertical dimension (mid) and midway on the horizontal dimension (central)
middle pharyngeal constrictor muscle	middle of 3 constrictor muscles of the *pharynx* whose effect is to reduce the size of the pharynx by pulling its walls closer together; the middle constrictor is at the height of the *tongue root* and *oropharynx*

midsagittal	*sagittal body plane* made on the midline of the body; see *sagittal plane*
millibar (mbar)	one-thousandth of a bar, a unit of *air pressure*
millisecond, ms, msec	one-thousandth of a second; 0.001 seconds; common unit for measuring speech events
minimal pair	pair of words that differ by only 1 *phone*; existence of such a pair in a language demonstrates the *contrastive* or *phonemic* nature of the difference between the phones
modal voice, modal frequency	modal voice is the most natural type of voice and is most efficient in using the *airstream* to create the sound of *voicing*
mode of vibration/ voicing	*voice quality*
monophthong ("pure" vowel)	*vowel* whose *timbre* does not change from start to finish; contrasted with a *diphthong* or *diphthongized vowel*
morpheme	a minimal unit of meaning which might be a word or part of a word. *Cats* contains two morphemes: *cat* and *-s*, the latter denoting plural.
morphophonological, morphophonemic alternation	alternation in the form of a meaningful unit of language (a morpheme), a difference that elsewhere would be phonemic, such as the plural morpheme in English, pronounced [s] or [z] or [əz]
murmur	*breathy voice* used distinctively
muscle fiber	individual long slender cell in a muscle
muscles of facial expression	muscles in the facial area that attach and insert in superficial tissue layers (as opposed to bones or cartilages), responsible for certain speech gestures as well as facial expression
mylohyoid muscle	a muscle attaching to the *hyoid bone* and the lower borders of the *mandible*; roughly triangular in shape
myoelastic aerodynamic theory	a theory of *vocal fold vibration* taking into account muscle force, tissue elasticity, *airflow*, and *Bernoulli's principle*
nasal	referring to the nose, the *nasal cavities*, and to *phones* made with the *velopharyngeal port* open
nasal cavities	cavities between the *velopharyngeal port* and the opening of the nostrils through which air flows in *nasal* breathing, and which provide a characteristic *timbre* to speech sounds made with the velopharyngeal port open. The two cavities are situated on opposite sides of the body's center line, bilaterally symmetrical.

nasal release, nasal plosion	*release* of a *plosive* where the release does not permit *airflow* to exit the *oral cavity*, but rather directs it through the *nasal cavities*
nasal vowel	*vowel* produced with *nasality* when the nasality is *phonemic* in the particular language
nasality	characteristic *timbre* of *phones* produced with the *velopharyngeal port* open and the sound modified by the *nasal cavities*
nasalization	process of, or fact of, adding *nasality* to speech sounds
nasalized vowel	*vowel* produced with *nasality*. Where the terminology is precise, a nasalized vowel is produced with phonetic nasality, but the term does not specify whether the nasality is distinctive (*phonemic*) or not. Compare *nasal vowel*.
nasopharynx	upper part of the *pharynx* hidden from direct view by the *velum*
natural human language	human language that is the native language of a speech community and used for ordinary discourse
neutral (rounding)	of lip position in *vowel articulation*, neither *rounded* nor *spread*
node	in a *standing wave*, points at which the curve remains at a single point on the baseline, also called <u>point of zero influence</u>
non-syllabic	not *syllabic*, not forming the *nucleus* of a *syllable*
noncontiguous vowel accommodation	*metaphony*
nonperiodic	not *periodic*, *aperiodic*
nucleus, nuclei	the most sonorous [*sonority*] element in a *syllable*, the sound that is essential to there being a syllable
off-glide	a *glide* that makes the transition from a *phone* (usu. a *vowel*) to the following phone (usu. a *consonant*)
on-glide	a *glide* that makes the transition to a *phone* (usu. a *vowel*) from the preceding phone (often a *consonant*)
open	in official *IPA* terminology, the *low vowel height*, as in a low vowel
open mid	in official *IPA* terminology, the second lowest *vowel height*, as in a lower mid vowel
oral airstream mechanism	a less common name for the *velaric airstream mechanism*
oral cavity	mouth cavity
orbicularis oris muscle	muscle making up much of the body of the lips and capable of pursing the lips into a circular shape in *vowel rounding*

order of acquisition	order in which small children learn the sounds of the language(s) spoken in their presence
origin	origin of a muscle is the end of the muscle usually attached to a bone or cartilage and which moves less than the other end of the muscle when it is contracted. The other end is the *insertion.*
oropharynx	middle part of the *pharynx*, including the part visible through the open mouth
out of phase	not in *phase*
overlaid function	notion that, in evolutionary terms, old structures with another biological function are adapted to a new function; in this instance, speech is overlaid on structures required for processing of food, swallowing, and exchanging gases
overtone	musicians' term for *harmonic*
palatal	having to do with the (hard) *palate*; as a *place of articulation*, describing the proximity of the *tongue* to the region of the *palate*
palatalization, palatalized	having a *secondary articulation* in the region of the (hard) palate; change from a non-palatal to a palatal *primary articulation*
palate	in phonetic terminology, the hard palate, the part of the roof of the mouth with underlying bone between the *alveolar ridge* and the *velum*. In medical and anatomical terminology, the hard palate as well as the velum.
palate, primary, secondary	primary and secondary palate refer to structures during fetal development that fuse to become the palate; relevant to speech because the failure to fuse can prevent normal speech production
palate, soft	the *velum*
palatopharyngeal constrictor muscle	*superior pharyngeal constrictor muscle*
parietal pleura	the *pleura* attached to the inner surface of the *thoracic cage*
pascal (Pa)	a unit of pressure in the *SI* (metric system)
peak	highest point on the graphical representation of a sound wave
period	the temporal duration of a single *cycle* of a wave
periodic	of wave motion, having a series of *cycles* that have the same *period*
periodicity	characteristic of being *periodic*
perseveration	*speech error* involving the prolongation of a *phone*

pharyngeal	having to do with the *pharynx*
pharyngeal speech	rare form of *airstream mechanism* originating in the *pharynx*
pharyngealization, pharyngealized	having a *secondary articulation* in the region of the *pharynx*; change from a non-pharyngeal to a pharyngeal *primary articulation*
pharyngoesophageal junction	where the *pharynx* meets the superior end of the *esophagus*
pharynx	the cavity behind the *oral cavity* extending from the top of the *larynx* to the part of the *nasal cavity* behind the *velum*
phase (1)	each of a series of steps in the production of *plosive consonants*
phase (2), in phase	*phase* refers to a particular point along the length of a *cycle*, identified by degrees (0° to 360°); *in phase* means that two waves are in synchrony
phonation	production of a speech sound in the *larynx*; often used as a synonym for *voicing*
phone	individual speech sound; a *segment*
phoneme	*phone* or group of phones that, taken together, form a contrastive, distinctive sound within a given language
phonetic environment	see *environment*
phrasal stress	*stress* within a short phrase, generally distinguishing different potential meanings
physiology	functioning of anatomical structures and systems
pitch	perception of the *frequency* of a sound; with respect to *voicing*, can be used to mean *frequency*
pitch accent	change of *fundamental frequency*, usually associated with a change in timing and/or *stress*, that is used distinctively in a language
place of articulation (PoA)	location where the *primary articulation* of a *phone* takes place, term usually used in reference to *consonants*
platysma muscle	superficial muscle under the chin; may play a role in opening the jaw
pleura, pleurae: visceral, parietal	See *visceral pleura* and *parietal pleura*
pleural cavity	space between the two pleurae, normally very narrow and filled with fluid
plosive	*consonant* in which the *airstream* is fully blocked and then released
pole	in a *spectrum* of *resonance*, a high point in the graph representing strong resonance

postalveolar	*articulation* just posterior to the *alveolar ridge*; in the *alveopalatal* region
postvocalic	after a *vowel*, following a vowel
pounds per square inch (psi)	unit of *air pressure*
pressure: absolute, relative	pressure is the force outward in all directions from a body of air that is confined. The atmosphere of the earth, thus the air all around us, is under pressure due to the force of gravity.
pressure differential	difference in *air pressure* between two areas, significant because, if given a chance, air will flow rapidly from the higher to the lower pressure region, possibly creating a speech sound
primary	primary *vowels* are *front unrounded* and *back rounded* vowels, as opposed to *secondary* vowels, which have the opposite *rounding*
process (on bone or cartilage)	a convex "bump" or protrusion, which can be long and thin, on a bone or cartilage; commonly a point of attachment of a muscle or muscles
prominence	standing out from the background, highlight. Prominence in speech is given by increased *loudness* and increased precision of *articulation*. A *suprasegmental*
propagate	sound waves propagate, meaning that their energy moves through space by interacting with the material (air or other) through which it moves
propagation	the act of energy moving through space by means of interaction with the material through which the energy moves
prosody	specifically, *suprasegmentals* as a whole
pseudovoice	voicing substitute that is created by a mechanical device or body system other than the *vocal folds*, such as belch-talking
pterygoid muscle (lateral, medial)	muscles within the *temporomandibular joint* that aid in lowering the jaw
pulmonic	having to do with the *lung*; a pulmonic airstream is an airstream propelled by the lungs
quadrangle, vowel quadrangle	four-sided figure representing the limits of possible vowel articulation
quality	characteristic sound of a *vowel* or other resonant speech sound, distinct from the duration of the sound, also called *timbre*

quality: phonetic, affective, personal, transmittal	in Traunmüller's terminology, these "qualities" are aspects of the speech signal that provide information on these different domains
quasi-periodic	of a sound wave, almost *periodic*, having slight variations between *cycles* that prevent it from being perfectly periodic, but almost so
rarefy, rarefaction	to reduce *air pressure*; a reduction in air pressure
rate	of speech, pace at which it proceeds, measured in *syllables* per second or per minute, for instance
recoil (elastic recoil)	tendency to rebound to original dimensions after stretching or compressing; such a rebounding
reduced, reduced vowel	of a *vowel*, having a shorter duration and less distinct *timbre*, being articulated closer to the *mid-central* position
reduction	fact of a *vowel* being *reduced*
register	forms of speech appropriate in different social settings
Reinke's space	a layer near the surface of the *vocal folds*, also called the *lamina propria*
relative pressure	pressure measured not in absolute units of pressure, but measured relative to another pressure; many actions in speech depend on relative or comparative pressure rather than *absolute* pressure
release	the moment in *plosive* production when the vocal tract closure is opened
residual capacity	see *functional residual capacity*
resonance	oscillation of a physical object or *cavity resonator* at its "natural" *frequency*
respiration	breathing, flow of air into and out of the *lungs*
retraction	of the *tongue* or other structure, moving in a backward direction
retroflex	a type of speech sound made with the *tongue* curled so that the *tip* is pointing upwards in the *postalveolar* region
rib	one of the bones encasing the *thorax*, typically curved running from the *sternum* to the vertebral column, half encircling the thorax; some ribs run only part of this distance and are attached only at the posterior end
rib cage	the bony structure, consisting of *sternum*, *ribs*, and vertebral column, that encloses the *thorax*
risorius muscle	facial muscle attached at the corner of the mouth running posteriorly and inserting into superficial tissue in the cheek

roman alphabet	the ordinary alphabet used in English, European languages, and many other languages; called the *latin alphabet* in this book
roman style	style of type in which letters are oriented vertically, as opposed to *italic style*
root (tongue)	of *places of articulation*, the part of the surface of the *tongue* that faces the *pharynx* and which cannot be seen through the oral opening
rounded	of *phones* (especially *vowels*), produced with the lips formed into a circular shape, with or without additional protrusion of the lips
rounding, lip rounding	moving the lips into a circular configuration with or without additional protrusion of the lips
RTR	retracted tongue root; the tongue root moved backward into the *pharynx*, making the passageway narrower
sagittal plane	*body plane* that transects the erect, standing body vertically, at right angles to the side-to-side plane of the body, through the center line (bisecting the vertebral column) or to the left or right of the center line.
SAMPA	Speech Assessment Methods Phonetic Alphabet, a phonetic alphabet made up of ASCII characters, a restricted set of characters from the early days of computer text
sandhi	*accommodation* and other combinatory effects that occur across word boundaries
sans, sans serif	sans serif denotes a typeface that does not have small additions at the ends of the strokes. Times New Roman is a serif font, and Arial is a sans serif font. "Sans" is often used as a short form of "sans serif."
schwa	*mid-central vowel*; in English, found in unstressed *syllables*
schwar	*mid-central* rhotic *vowel*
secondary	of *vowels, front rounded* and *back unrounded*, in contrast to *primary vowels*
secondary articulation	see *articulation: primary, secondary*
segment	individual speech sound or *phone*; as a verb, to divide the continuous sound stream or speech movements into individual speech sounds
serif	in typefaces, a decoration consisting of a short line at right angles to the ends of strokes

setting, set	see *articulatory setting, set*
shimmer	a variation of *amplitude* or *loudness* in a sound signal, specifically in the voice
short, short vowel	of a *vowel*, having a brief duration; unrelated to the *timbre* of the vowel; everyday language uses this term to identify vowel timbre
short lag	see *lag*
short lead	see *lead*
SI (Système international)	the international system of measures, usually called the "metric system" in English
simple	describes a *vowel* of unchanging *timbre*; a *monophthong*, as opposed to a *diphthong*
sine	short form of *sinusoid* or *sinusoidal*
sinusoid, sinusoidal	of sound waves, a shape that corresponds to the mathematical function of the same name, corresponding to a pure *tone*
sonority	the greater the sonority of a class of speech sounds, the greater the component of *periodic* sound, the less the component of *aperiodic* sound, and more commonly the class of sounds is used as a *syllable nucleus*
source–filter theory	explanation for the production of resonant speech sounds in which the source (periodic sound produced by the *vocal folds*) is filtered through the *pharynx* and *oral cavity*, and sometimes the *nasal cavities*
speaker	as the term is used in this book, a *talker* when the term refers not only to the act of talking, but to the ability to speak in a particular language
spectrogram	visual graph of *acoustic* properties of an *utterance*, showing time on the x-axis, *frequency* on the y-axis and *amplitude* on the z-axis
spectrum, spectra	*acoustic* composition of a sound; a graphic representation of the acoustic composition of a sound
speech	audible production of the sounds of language
speech community	a group of people who share the same language and interact with one another using spoken language
speech error	"slip of the tongue"; misarticulation or incorrect word or *phone* selection
speech prosody	another term for *suprasegmentals*
speech sound	individual *phone* or *segment*, represented by a distinct symbol of the *IPA*
speed of propagation	velocity of sound energy through a medium

spread	of *vowel articulation*, produced with the corners of the mouth pulled back as in the vowel [i]
squamous epithelium	a layer in the anatomical structure of the *vocal folds*
standing wave	wave resulting from the combination of two identical waves propagating in opposite directions, giving the illusion of a wave that is stationary
sternohyoid muscle	muscle attached to the *sternum* and inserting into the *hyoid bone*
sternum	breastbone
stoma	opening in an anatomical structure created through surgery
stress	a *suprasegmental* that gives *prominence* to *syllables* within words and carries meaning in some languages, such as English
stress-timed	speech is stress-timed if the period between stressed *syllables* is approximately equal, rather than depending on the number of syllables spoken, called *syllable-timed*
stroboscopic effect	the visual effect whereby seeing a series of still images of a moving object makes the object appear to move more slowly, to move backwards, or not to move at all. Used in the visualization of the *vocal folds*
stylohyoid muscle	muscle originating at the *styloid process* and inserting into the *hyoid bone*
styloid process	sharply pointed *process* of the temporal bone of the skull, pointing downward from a point below the ear canal
subglottal pressure	the *air pressure* below the *glottis*, below the *vocal folds*
suction	supposed ability of an area of low pressure to "pull" air and objects toward it; in reality, the high pressure <u>pushes</u> toward the area of low pressure
superior horn (thyroid cartilage)	one of two long *processes* rising from the main body of the *thyroid cartilage* as far as the *hyoid bone*
superior longitudinal tongue muscle	upper of 2 layers of muscle running lengthwise in the *tongue*
superior pharyngeal constrictor muscle	upper of 3 constrictor muscles of the *pharynx* whose effect is to reduce the size of the pharynx by pulling its walls closer together
supraglottal	above the *glottis*; above the *vocal folds*; above the *larynx*
suprasegmental	any of a number of prosodic features of speech that extend to multiple adjacent *phones*
syllabic	of a speech sound, permitting a *syllable* to exist by providing a syllable *nucleus*; by definition, *vowels* are all syllabic

syllabicity	character of being *syllabic*
syllable	unit of speech composed of a *nucleus*, which is a *vocalic* sound, with optional sounds preceding and/or following the nucleus. Preceding and following sounds are usually *consonants*, but must be of lower *sonority* than the nucleus. The nucleus is normally a *vowel* (*monophthong* or *diphthong*), but may be a syllabic consonant; more rarely, the nucleus is a sound with lower sonority than a syllabic consonant.
syllable: open, closed	an open syllable is one whose final sound is a *vowel*; a closed syllable is one whose final sound is a *consonant*
syllable-timed	speech is syllable-timed if the duration of all *syllables* is approximately equal, rather than depending on stressed syllables; the latter is called *stress-timed*
target	ideal articulatory position of a *phone*, seen as an objective in the production of connected speech, but which is often not entirely attained because of the demands of preceding and following phones
temporalis muscle	powerful muscle that elevates the mandible (jaw)
temporomandibular joint (TMJ)	the joint between the lower jaw (mandible) and the skull (at the temporal bone)
tense	a descriptive term for *vowels* that correlates to the position of the *tongue root* (advanced or retracted). Additional physiological changes may be involved in a vowel being classed as tense or *lax*
tenseness	the degree to which a *vowel* is *tense* or *lax*; the quality of being tense (of a vowel)
tensor palati (tensor veli palatini) muscle	paired muscle of the *velum* that widens the velum, helping to ensure a complete seal of the *velopharyngeal port*
tertiary	weakest of 3 levels of phonetic *stress*
thorax, thoracic, thoracic cage	the upper part of the trunk of the body, containing *lungs* and heart; separated from the lower trunk (the *abdomen*) by the *diaphragm*
thyrohyoid membrane	membrane between the *thyroid cartilage* and the *hyoid bone*
thyroid cartilage	cartilage at the front of the *larynx* whose protrusion is called the Adam's apple in men; the *vocal folds* attach to the back of this cartilage
tie bar	mark, also called a *ligature*, written above or below a pair of letters, showing them to have status as a single distinctive sound of changing quality

timbre	of a *vowel* or resonant speech sound, also called *quality*; the characteristic sound of the vowel due to the unique *acoustic* spectrum of that vowel
tip (tongue)	the point or *apex* of the *tongue*
tone	as a *suprasegmental*, a specific *frequency* or change of frequency that signals the meaning of a word; the specific frequency depends upon the usual *fundamental frequency* of the individual *talker*
tongue	extremely flexible and mobile structure in the mouth that plays a fundamental function in articulating the sounds of speech; also involved in chewing, swallowing, and tasting
tongue (tip, blade, front, back, dorsum, root)	most agile organ of speech *articulation* situated in the mouth; for the purpose of classification of speech sounds (esp. *consonants*), its surface is divided into regions – from anterior to posterior: the *tip*, the *blade*, the *dorsum* (further divided into front and back), the *root*
tongue muscles: intrinsic, extrinsic	intrinsic tongue muscles change the shape of the *tongue*; extrinsic tongue muscles move the body of the tongue up, down, forwards, and back within the *oral cavity*
tonic period	term not in general use; as used in this book, the period of time that includes one strongly stressed *syllable* plus unstressed syllables that are not included in another tonic period
trachea	the "air pipe" descending from the *larynx*, which then bifurcates (splits in two) into two *bronchi*, leading to the *lungs*
tracheal cartilages/ rings	the cartilages that give form to the *trachea*; more in the shape of the letter C, rather than true rings
transcription: phonemic, broad, phonetic, narrow	in phonetics, the writing of a sound or *utterance* using the *International Phonetic Alphabet*. Phonemic or broad transcription uses the same symbol for every instance of the same phoneme, despite variations. Phonetic or narrow transcription attempts to record all phonetic differences, whether or not the difference is phonemic in a given language.
transition	movement or change from one *phone* to the next; the rapid shift in *formant frequency* between a *plosive* and a preceding or following *vowel*
transitional	having to do with movement or change from one *phone* to the next

transitional glide	*glide* that serves to permit movement from one *phone* to the next, at least one of which is normally a *vowel*
transverse (horizontal) plane	*body plane* that transects the erect, standing body horizontally
transverse tongue muscle	muscle whose fibers run horizontally from one side of the *tongue* to the other
trill	a *phone* characterized by *aerodynamic vibration* of an *articulator* (*uvula, tongue tip,* lips)
trough	low point between peaks of surface waves (such as water waves); in descriptions of the graph of a sound wave, called "valleys"
turbinates	scroll-like structures in the *nasal cavities,* relevant to phonetics because they muffle sounds as they pass through the nasal cavities
turbulent	of the flow of air, not smooth, but rather composed of eddies and multi-directional flow
two-mass model	a model of *vocal fold vibration* that divides the *mass* of the folds into an upper mass and a lower mass, in an effort to account for their vibratory motion
typeface	style of lettering; same as *font* as the term is used to describe lettering used by computers
umlaut	a process active in Germanic languages, and vestigial in English, by which *back vowels* are *fronted* in certain forms of words. Also, name of a *diacritic* used in the orthography of Germanic and other languages showing *vowel quality*; similar in form to a *dieresis*, but different in what it represents
Unicode	standard by which every *glyph* used in writing language has a unique coding in computer systems; contemporary computer text is usually Unicode, but earlier forms of computer text were not
unrounded	not *rounded*; term may be used, ambiguously, for both *neutral* and *spread* lip posture
upper case	of alphabetic letters, capital or "big" letters as used at the beginnings of sentences or with proper nouns; as contrasted with *lower case*
upper mid (close mid)	of *heights* of *vowel* production, the second highest of 4; upper mid is the term usually used in North America; *open-mid* is official *IPA* terminology
utterance	something said, without regard to it being a word, a sentence, or other particular structure

uvula, uvular	structure attached to the posterior end of the *velum*, located centrally, and hanging down
vacuum	region with nothing, not even air, within it; in casual parlance, a region of *rarefaction*, having greatly reduced *air pressure*
variance	normal state of speech; *phones* vary greatly in their *acoustic* form
velar	having to do with the *velum* or *soft palate*; usually used to describe the position of the *tongue articulation* in relation to the velum
velaric	referring to the *velum* specifically in the context of *tongue* contact with the velum as an airstream *initiator*; the *velaric airstream mechanism* used in the production of *clicks*
velarization	addition of a *secondary articulation* in the region of the *velum*; a change from non-velar to velar articulation
velic	having to do with a movement of the *velum* itself in the opening or closing of the *VPP*
velopharyngeal port (VPP)	passageway – that can be opened or closed – connecting the *oropharynx* with the *nasal cavities*
velum	also called the *soft palate* and the velum palati, the soft, movable, muscular posterior part of the roof of the mouth, itself involved in distinguishing *nasal* from non-nasal sounds, as well as being used to identify the location of an *articulation* by the *tongue*
ventricles of Morgagni	spaces between the (true) *vocal folds* and the *ventricular folds*
ventricular folds	two folds of tissue in the *larynx* superior to the (true) *vocal folds*, separated from them by the *ventricles of Morgagni*, also called the *false vocal folds*
vertical striation	pattern on a wideband *spectrogram*, one of a series of vertical lines that together represent *voicing* – each striation being an opening of the *vocal folds*
vertical tongue muscle	a muscle within the body of the *tongue* whose fibers run vertically, allowing the tongue to be made flatter and wider
virgule	formal name for a slash mark: /
visceral pleura	the *pleura* encasing each *lung*
vocal folds (vf)	muscular folds of tissue within the *larynx* that vibrate to produce *voice*

vocal ligament	layer of the anatomical structure of the *vocal folds*, which in turn is made up of the intermediate and deep layers of the *lamina propria*
vocalic	of or having to do with a *vowel*; the aadjective of "vowel" is "vocalic"
vocalis muscle	muscle making up a significant portion of the body of the *vocal folds*, acts in configuring the *glottis* and position of the *arytenoid cartilages*
vocoid	*vowels* plus *consonants* that can be *syllabic*
voice	*voicing*; presence of, or production of, a *tone* generated through the *vibration* of the *vocal folds*
voice onset time (VOT)	time period from *release* of a *plosive* until start of *voicing*; a negative value if voicing precedes release
voice quality	mode of *voicing*; different qualities of voice, such as *breathy* or *creaky voice*
voiced	of a speech sound, produced with *voicing*
voiceless	of a speech sound, produced without *voicing*
voicing	presence of, or production of, a *tone* generated through the *vibration* of the *vocal folds*
volume	technically, characteristic of sound by which it seems to fill a space, as distinct from *loudness*, which is how loud it sounds to the *hearer*. Informally, *loudness* is called *volume* in everyday language.
VOT	*voice onset time*
vowel	speech sound, almost always *voiced*, produced with *resonance* and with no more *constriction* of the vocal tract than required to produce the vowel [i]
vowel harmony	feature of the sound systems of some languages by which all the *vowels* within a particular grammatical unit (defined by the particular language) share a particular articulatory feature, such as *front* or *high* or *lax*
vowel length	duration of a *vowel*; do not confuse with the everyday usage in which "long" and " short" vowels refers to the *timbre* or *quality* of the vowel, not duration
vowel reduction	see *reduction*
VPD, VPI	velopharyngeal dysfunction; velopharyngeal insufficiency or incompetence
VPP (velopharyngeal port)	passageway – that can be opened or closed – connecting the *oropharynx* with the *nasal cavities*
wave train	the same *cycle* (same *frequency* and same *amplitude*) repeated continuously

wavelength	physical dimension of a single *cycle* of a wave
weak form	form of a common, short word, when spoken in normal, rapid speech; for example, *to* being pronounced [t], or *is* pronounced [z]
whisper, whispering	production of entirely *voiceless* speech while creating a *fricative*-like sound at the *glottis* or between the *arytenoid cartilages*
whispery voice	alternate name for *for murmur* used by some authors
X-SAMPA	Extended Speech Assessment Methods Phonetic Alphabet. Extended version of the SAMPA alphabet developed by John C. Wells for clinical purposes
zero	in the *spectrum* of a resonant sound, a range of *frequencies* that have very low *amplitude*, usually due to anti-resonance

References

Baken, R. J. 1987. *Clinical Measurement of Speech and Voice.* London: Taylor and Francis Ltd.

Boë, Louis-Jean, Jean Granat, Jean-Louis Heim, et al. 2013. "Reconstructed Fossil Vocal Tracts and the Production of Speech: Phylogenetic and Ontogenetic Considerations." In Claire Lefebvre, Bernard Comrie, and Henri Cohen (eds.), *New Perspectives on the Origins of Language,* 75–128. Amsterdam: John Benjamins.

Borissoff, Constantine L. 2012. "Basis of Articulation or Articulatory Setting?" *IATEFL Pronunciation Special Interest Group Newsletter,* 46, Feb. (International Association of Teachers of English as a Foreign Language).

Burnett-Deas, Andrea. 2009. "VOT of Ejectives, Implosives, and Plain Stops in Yukateko, Mopan, and Itzaj Maya." MA thesis, Southern Illinois University. Abstract available at: https://opensiuc.lib.siu.edu/theses/78.

Butcher, Andrew. 2016. "The Sounds Humans Make When Speaking." In Keith Allan (ed.), *The Routledge Handbook of Linguistics,* 62–82. London: Taylor and Francis.

Campbell, Lyle. 2013. *Historical Linguistics: An Introduction.* Edinburgh University Press.

Cruttenden, Alan. 1997. *Intonation.* Cambridge University Press.

Cummings, Louise. 2013.*The Cambridge Handbook of Communication Disorders.* Cambridge University Press.

Delattre, Pierre C., Alvin M. Liberman, and Franklin S. Cooper. 1955. "Acoustic Loci and Transitional Cues for Consonants." *Journal of the Acoustical Society of America,* 27, July.

Diez, Friedrich. [1853] 2011. *Etymologisches Wörterbuch der romanischen Sprachen,* Vol. I. Charleston, SC: Nabu Press.

Fry, Dennis. 1977. *Homo Loquens: Man as a Talking Animal.* Cambridge University Press.

Hillenbrand, James, L. A. Getty, M. J. Clark, and K. Wheeler. 1995. "Acoustic Characteristics of American English Vowels." *Journal of the Acoustical Society of America* 97 (5), May: 3099–111.

Honikman, Beatrice. 1964. "Articulatory Settings." In D. Abercrombie, D. B. Fry, P. A. D. MacCarthy, N. C. Scott, and J. L. M. Trim (eds.), *In Honour of Daniel Jones,* 73–84. London: Longman.

Jakobson, Roman, Gunnar Fant, and Morris Halle. 1952. *Preliminaries to Speech Analysis: The Distinctive Features and Their Correlates.*

Cambridge, MA: MIT Acoustics
Laboratory.

Jones, Daniel. 1972. *An Outline of English Phonetics*. Cambridge: Heffer.

Joos, Martin. 1967. *The Five Clocks*. Boston: Houghton Mifflin Harcourt.

Ladefoged, Peter. 2005. *Vowels and Consonants: An Introduction to the Sounds of Languages*. Oxford: Wiley-Blackwell.

Lane, H., and B. Tranel. 1971. "The Lombard Sign and the Role of Hearing in Speech." *Journal of Speech, Language and Hearing Research* 14 (4): 677–709. https:// doi.org:10.1044/jshr.1404.677.

Lehiste, Ilse. 1970. *Suprasegmentals*. Cambridge, MA: MIT Press.

Lieberman, Philip. 1963. "Some Effects of Semantic and Grammatical Context on the Production and Perception of Speech." *Language and Speech*, 6: 172–87.

Lieberman, Philip. 2006. *Towards an Evolutionary Biology of Language*. Cambridge, MA: Harvard University Press.

Lindblom, B. 1990. "Explaining Phonetic Variation: A Sketch of the H&H Theory." In W. J. Hardcastle and A. Marchal (eds.), *Speech Production and Speech Modelling*, 403–39. Dordrecht: Kluwer Academic Publishers.

Lopez-Poveda, Enrique A. 2014. "Development of Fundamental Aspects of Human Auditory Perception." In Raymond Romand and Isabel Varela-Nieto (eds.), *Development of Auditory and Vestibular Systems*, 287–314.

Amsterdam: Elsevier/Academic Press.

Lustig, Anton. 2010. *A Grammar and Dictionary of Zaiwa*. Amsterdam: Brill.

MacKay, Ian R. A. 2014. *Acoustics in Hearing, Speech and Language Sciences: An Introduction*. Boston: Pearson (Allyn & Bacon).

MacNeilage, Peter. 2010. *The Origin of Speech* (Oxford Studies in the Evolution of Language). Oxford University Press.

Maddieson, Ian. 2008. "Glottalized Consonants." In Martin Haspelmath, Matthew S. Dryer, David Gil, and Bernard Comrie (eds.), *The World Atlas of Language Structures Online*. Munich: Max Planck Digital Library, chapter 7. Available at http://wals.info/feature/7.

Marslen-Wilson, W. D., and A. Welsh. 1978. "Processing Interactions and Lexical Access during Word Recognition in Continuous Speech." *Cognitive Psychology*, 10 (1): 29–63: https://doi.org/10.1016/0010-0285(78)90018-X.

Mueller 1848 (cited by Titze)

Nolan, F. (1999). "Speaker Recognition and Forensic Phonetics." In William J. Hardcastle and J. Laver (eds.), *The Handbook of Phonetic Sciences*. Oxford: Blackwell.

Pellegrino, François, Christophe Coupé, and Egidio Marsico. 2011. "A Cross-Language Perspective on Speech Information Rate." *Language*, 87 (3): 539–58.

Pulgram, Ernest. 1970. "Homo Loquens: An Ethological View." *Lingua*, 24: 309–42.

Riad, T. 2003. "The Origin of Danish stød." In Aditi Lahiri (ed.), *Analogy, Levelling, Markedness: Principles of Change in Phonology and Morphology*, 261–300. Berlin: Walter de Gruyter.

Rogers, Henry. 1991. *Theoretical and Practical Phonetics*. Toronto: Copp Clark Pitman.

Story, Brad H. 2002."An Overview of the Physiology, Physics and Modeling of the Sound Source for Vowels." *Acoustical Science and Technology*, 23 (4), July.

Titze, I. R. 1980. "Comments on the Myoelastic–Aerodynamic Theory of Phonation." *Journal of Speech, Language, and Hearing Research*, 23 (3), Sept.: 495–510.

Titze, Inigo R., and Daniel W. Martin 1998. "Principles of Voice Production." *Journal of the Acoustical Society of America*, 104 (1148).

Trager, George L., and Henry Lee Smith. 1951. *An Outline of English Structure*. Battenburg Press.

Traunmüller, Hartmut. 1994. "Conventional, Biological and Environmental Factors in Speech Communication: A Modulation Theory." *Phonetica*, 51: 170–83.

van den Berg, Janwillem. 1958. "Myoelastic Aerodynamic Theory of Voice Production." *Journal of Speech, Language, and Hearing Research*, 1, Sept.: 227–44: https://doi.org:10.1044/jshr.0103.227.

Wilcox, Sherman. 1992. *The Phonetics of Fingerspelling*. Amsterdam: John Benjamins.

Wilson, J., and B. Gick. 2014. "Bilinguals Use Language-Specific Articulatory Settings." *Journal of Speech, Language, and Hearing Research*, 57(2), Apr. 1: 1–13.

Yuasa, I. P. 2010. "Creaky Voice: A New Feminine Voice Quality for Young Urban-Oriented Upwardly Mobile American Women?" *American Speech*, 85 (3): 315–37. https://doi.org:10.1215/00031283-2010-018.

WEBSITES

http://clas.mq.edu.au/speech/acoustics/frequency/vocal_tract_resonance.html

https://en.wikipedia.org/wiki/Extensions_to_the_International_Phonetic_Alphabet (November 2018)

www.ncbi.nlm.nih.gov/pmc/articles/PMC3706038

Learning Swedish. https://learningswedish.se/courses/1/pages/2-dot-3-word-accent (November, 2018)

www.phonetik.uni-muenchen.de/~hoole/kurse/artikul/multi_voice.pdf from Sounds of the World's Languages

Index

Introductory Note: References such as '178-79' indicate (not necessarily continuous) discussion of a topic across a range of pages. Wherever possible in the case of topics with many references, these have either been divided into sub-topics or only the most significant discussions of the topic are listed. Because the entire work is about 'phonetics' and 'speech science', the use of these terms (and certain others which occur constantly throughout the book) as an entry point has been restricted. Information will be found under the corresponding detailed topics.

Made in the USA
Middletown, DE
09 April 2024

52766569R00283